CONTEMPORARY TERRORISM:
SELECTED READINGS

Contemporary Terrorism

SELECTED READINGS

Edited by John D. Elliott &
Leslie K. Gibson • Bureau of
Operations and Research •
International
Association of
Chiefs of Police

ELEVEN FIRSTFIELD ROAD • GAITHERSBURG, MARYLAND

Library of Congress Cataloging in Publication Data

Main entry under title:

Contemporary terrorism.

  Bibliography: p.
  1. Terrorism--Addresses, essays, lectures.
I. Elliott, John D. II. Gibson, Leslie K.
HV6431.C65   301.6'33   78-19053
ISBN 0-88269-]25-2

ISBN-0-88269-125-2

Printed in the United States of America

TABLE OF CONTENTS

FOREWORD

The threat of terrorism has developed to the extent that not only governments are challenged, but there is a potential impact on every private citizen. Key political figures are taken hostage, business executives are murdered, and mass hostage situations are becoming more common. Terrorist incidents which previously appeared to be isolated and transitory have now taken on more serious proportions. We are continuously alerted to the development of new radical philosophies and tactics. Violent acts are perpetrated on a random basis and there is no safe haven. Society is alarmed and appropriate action is required of those who protect our civil liberties.

The International Association of Chiefs of Police is the world's leading Association of police executives and represents approximately eleven thousand members. Every member is acutely aware of the all-encompassing threat that terrorism presents to peaceful existence, and the concern for the rights of individuals is utmost in the minds of law enforcement throughout the world.

Since 1893 the IACP has represented and promoted the sharing of expertise among an increasing number of police chief executives. During the last two decades, the IACP has increased the emphasis on development of terrorist-related programs. An obvious need for information and for the development of a comprehensive approach to a very serious problem has spurred these efforts. We have attempted to establish a flow of information on the subject through various means—workshops, seminars, and the production of numerous publications.

The scope and complexity of the enigma of terrorism make it difficult for any single organization to provide a total service. For this reason, the

x IACP has encouraged the development of professional efforts in every possible area to complement our own work in this field. Currently, we are working closely with the United States National Advisory Committee's Task Force on Disorders and Terrorism and with the United Nations' Economic and Social Council and Crime Prevention Branch.

This text is offered as a supplement to our previous endeavors. It is designed to be used as a reference for those concerned with the terrorist threat. We believe that it is a valuable aid which will lead to a greater understanding of the actions of terrorists and to methods of coping effectively.

Norman Darwick
Director
Bureau of Operations and Research
International Association of
Chiefs of Police

PREFACE

There are numerous books on terrorism which attempt to deal with various aspects of the current threat, but none which encompasses all ramifications of the problem today. IACP developed this textbook in response to the need for a thought provoking source of information which would contain the broad scope of thinking by many eminent authorities on terrorism. We hope it will function as a useful reference for the practitioner, serve the needs of the student, and pique the interest of the layman.

Basic to the editors' scheme in selecting articles is the assumption that the threat of terrorism will not subside without positive intervention. Quite the contrary, it must be driven out of modern society by employing both proven and emerging law enforcement techniques. Implicit here is the positive belief that terrorism can be defeated without compromising democratic values or overreacting to terrorist confrontations. Success in this struggle will require an enlightened public as well as knowledgeable practitioners combating this criminal menace.

In keeping with this objective, this book of readings supports these efforts by bringing together a wide range of articles from a variety of publications which may not be readily available to the reader. The editors have sorted through the hodgepodge of literature on terrorism that has grown without an organizing framework and have brought the best together in a single source commentary. The book provides a fundamental reference that will contribute to a better understanding of this threat to society with a view towards successfully coping with its present and future variations. It provides a focal point for current action, thinking, and teaching on terrorism in addition to being a baseline from which to measure subsequent progress.

Frank D. Roberson
Assistant Director
Bureau of Operations and Research
International Association of
Chiefs of Police

INTRODUCTION

Contemporary terrorism involves modern variations on old techniques which are far more dangerous than ever before because of their tremendous potential destructive power. Current indications are that it will become more serious over the coming decade as terrorists capitalize on the advantages of improved weapons technology and growing international support from radical governments. Terrorists have maintained the offensive role and governments have had to react to their innovations. During this action-reaction cycle, terrorists have been forced to cross new thresholds of violence to retain their momentum. This has resulted in a greater need to understand contemporary terrorism by those who must protect society if they are to cope successfully with present and future variations.

Contemporary Terrorism *is designed specifically to meet this need by bringing together the best informed research on the subject in a single source. A focus was required to select the best material and to organize it in a manner which supports quick, thorough understanding and comprehension. Articles were chosen which provide background and perspective on contemporary terrorism in general, not just the specific activities of a single group or geographical region, nor a weighty treatise which deals with contemporary terrorism either as an abstract phenomenon or attempts to develop a general theory of terrorism (or even political revolution). The organizational focus used here is based on an examination of the trends and transitions of contemporary terrorism. This provides an informational inventory with which to evaluate terrorism's overall threat potential. Only after developing an understanding of the threat can one begin to consider the response of threatened societies within the rule of law.*

Contemporary terrorism has spared neither the developing states of the Third World nor the modern industrialized states. Its degree of permeation into society's fabric is indicated by the continuing commentaries on "living with terrorism." Actually, several European societies are already living with it. Countermeasures and responses have been employed successfully in some cases, as evidenced by the dramatic decline of skyjacking in the United States. Notable successes of the Israelis, the Dutch, and the West Germans demonstrate that determined governments can cope with the terrorist threat.

Governments must announce their general policies of dealing with terrorists in very clear terms and then adhere to them. The well known United States policy of not bargaining with terrorists provides the best model. Those nations which have succumbed to terrorist demands have suffered repeat attacks, whereas attacks against the United States have actually declined since 1976. There is no doubt that terrorism can be resisted successfully and the international community is well advised to close ranks and follow the American example. Neither the United Nations nor other international organizations such as the Council of Europe have as yet gone far enough in this direction.

There are significant indications of growing cooperation in the operational aspects of response. This involves far more than information exchanges. More importantly, it is the exchange of *direct assistance* such as that provided by several governments during the West German police rescue of hostages at Mogadishu. Crucial roles were played by the United States, the United Kingdom, and several important middle eastern and African nations, particularly Somalia. It is now obvious that antiterrorists are becoming as well organized and internationally supported as the terrorists themselves. This situation, and the reduction of major terrorist incidents during 1977, has tantalized some analysts into believing that the terrorist threat is beginning to dissipate. In the view of these analysts, terrorism is a cyclical phenomenon that is being defeated by its own futility of purpose. This is a dangerous, erroneous point of view. The terrorist threat has not diminished; rather, it has increased. Some terrorists may now even contemplate ascending another rung on the escalation ladder involving nuclear blackmail, toxic chemical substances, or mass hostage situations.

The simplest way to convey the significance of this threat is to review briefly the three transitions contemporary terrorism has made while migrating to the industrialized societies. First, the transition to *urban guerrilla warfare* in the sixties, in which guerrillas moved their tactics from their traditional battleground to ambush the government in the cities. Second, a consideration of *transnational terrorism* in the early seventies, during which political violence migrated via skyjacked jumbo jets to the industrialized societies. And, finally, the emerging transition to *international* terrorism in which terrorism will be controlled by sovereign states.

Urban guerrilla warfare provides a means of challenging legitimate governments as it demonstrates those governments' inability to protect their citizens. It is not significantly different in its application from rural guerrilla warfare. The same requirements hold true for popular support, recruitment, security, and other aspects of their strategies. In the long history of guerrilla struggles, cities have frequently been the scene of clandestine underground activities. Some of these have had tragic results for the participants, such as those involved in the Warsaw ghetto uprisings. Other struggles have been more successful, such as that of the Maquis in Paris at the end of World War II. In the post-World War II revolutions, cities did not play a dominant role—as illustrated by the China experience, in which Mao surrounded the cities with a hostile countryside and choked them off. In the fifties, the Cubans were more successful in their direct application of guerrilla techniques in urban areas. Many of these techniques have since been refined as guerrillas have convincingly shifted their attacks to the cities.

The Guevara's failure provided a major reason for this shift to the cities. Bolivia was selected as a testing ground for the *foco* theory developed by Che and Regis Debray, a French intellectual who joined him there. Essentially, this concept made operational Che's three fundamental views on the conduct of revolutionary movements in Latin America: popular forces can win, it is not necessary to wait until all conditions of revolution exist because the insurrection can create them, and the countryside is the basic area for armed fighting. Debray had elaborated on this foundation by arguing that revolutionary leadership alone could cause the symptoms of crisis and understanding which would create popular support for a revolutionary movement. Che's death in 1967, and Debray's subsequent imprisonment, demonstrate how seriously the *foco* theory failed its first operational test. But the elitist idea of revolutionary leadership provoking crisis without mass popular support has since thrived in an urban environment.

Other reasons for the shift to Latin American cities during the sixties and seventies may be accounted for by those factors which reduced the effectiveness of rural guerrillas. Foremost among these is the increasing technological sophistication of armed forces and security forces, with the result that modern weaponry, communications, mobility, and tactics routed guerrillas from their traditional strongholds. This situation limited guerrillas access to their most important resource—the people. Rural guerrillas responded by arming themselves with the *foco* theory and by moving to urban areas where they could be assured of support by groups unhappy with governments in power.

Thus far the *foco* theory has not produced an identifiable revolution. Those applying it have ignored the role of popular support and continued to build a vanguard movement of elitists who have relied on terrorism to broadcast their message. Slowly the transition was made from urban guerrilla warfare to transnational terrorism because of its demonstrated success as a means by which a small group could attack the government and its institutions without having overwhelming popular support. By the late sixties it became apparent to other revolutionary groups that the tactics and methods by which urban guerrilla warfare was being pursued could be expanded to a regional context. Many thought that terrorism could provide a catalyst for extending guerrilla warfare to encompass all parts of the globe.

TRANSNATIONAL TERRORISM

The transition to transnational terrorism is particularly significant because it carried terrorists onto a new stage where they could perform before the mass media, and where they could allow their ingenuity and ability to innovate full reach in their new surroundings. Media impact and the success of the activities of urban guerrillas caused their techniques to spread from the developing countries to the more industrialized societies of Western Europe and North America.

In the early stages much of this transfer resulted in nothing more than the adoption of urban guerrilla techniques by domestic dissidents. Terrorism was involved, but initially it was manageable terrorism, associated with hostage cases involving skyjackings and bombings. This changed dramatically as guerrillas became terrorists and began to disregard the traditional conventions of warfare. As parts of the world went to war with terrorism, the problem became increasingly complicated by of two factors: (1) "One man's terrorist is another man's freedom fighter" and (2) Chalmers Johnson's "three T's"—targets, technology, and toleration. A current example of the first factor is readily provided by the PLO's Yasser Arafat. The components of the second factor illustrate some of the major reasons behind the rapid expansion of the terrorist threat to industrialized societies.

Building on the friendly relations established between Latin American urban querrillas, transnational terrorism began to widen its scope in the early seventies. This development significantly increased the threat of terrorism. Transnational terrorism quickly attained far wider range than urban guerrilla warfare, which remained essentially national in scope. Its ability to conduct extensive regional and limited global thrusts was quickly demonstrated by the Japanese Red Army, the Popular Front for the Liberation of Palestine, and the Baader-Meinhof gang. Moreover, the success of transnational terrorism, as perceived by the terrorists, is accelerating the transition to *international terrorism*.

Transnational terrorism, like other forms of terrorism, is politically motivated. It becomes *trans*-national by virtue of its mobility; it transcends national boundaries. Its ideological foundations, operational techniques, and support infrastructure have demonstrated the ability to cross continents with amazing ease. There is nothing particularly novel about this explanation today. We can now positively identify three stages of development within the growth or maturation of transnational terrorism as a threat to legitimate governments.

In the first stage, logistics support was provided, based on ideological compatibility. Logistics support included weapons, explosives, safe houses, transport, funding, and communications. Training was soon introduced in a different manner than was common in rural and urban guerrilla warfare situations. Rather than sending a team to train terrorists operating in a national setting, terrorists were sent abroad to established terrorist training camps. The Baader-Meinhof gang, for example, trained in Jordan with the Fedayeen before returning to West Germany and launching their terror offensive in 1972. The intensity of the training led them easily to cooperate in the next stage of transnational terrorism.

In the second stage, various terrorist organizations of different nationalities and different ethnic groups cemented their ideological and communal relationships by conducting terrorist operations in support of each other. Some of these operations were of short duration and consisted of the detonation of a single bomb. Others, like the Japanese Red Army's attack on the Lod airport on May 30, 1972, were far more serious. From the perspective of the terrorists, they were also far more effective. To a certain extent this development caught the general public and many internal security forces by surprise.

Much of the time innovative ability has kept the terrorists ahead of those seeking to neutralize or limit their destructiveness. This failure is also displayed in the third stage, which is characterized by greater *coordination* of terrorist attacks and actual *participation* by third country nations in the planning, support, and conduct of transnational terrorism. Examples of this multinational cooperation and apparent coordination by terrorists were present in the OPEC raid, at Entebbe, and at Mogadishu.

Early in 1977 this type of terrorist cooperation was discussed by several journalists and according to the Associated Press, a NATO report was published stating that "an international terrorist network is operating globally with help from radical governments." The AP press report listed the governments supporting terrorists as: Iraq, Syria, South Yemen, and Cuba. Much of this activity, like the Entebbe hostage situation, was tied to the support of the PLO by other terrorists movements and we now know that several governments are actively cooperating with terrorists.

Today we continue to see this highly developed cooperation among multinational terrorist teams. It is well known and well documented. Some difficulty is being experienced in establishing the limits of *coordination* effected by the Palestinian Liberation Organization and the PFLP; however, the difficulty is mostly a question of magnitude. Certainly the PLO is well organized for such planning and coordination of terrorist attacks. Moreover, it has a well-integrated logistics network extending throughout the Middle East, North Africa, and Western Europe.

Since transnational terrorism is now operating in its third stage of development, we can see positive signs of the next transition, in which terrorism will become a greater threat. Countermeasures are becoming more effective against domestic terrorists and this will have a favorable impact on the security community. However, terrorism is easily transported to the designated target area and international cooperation against the threat of transnational terrorism is not yet as effective as it ultimately must be. This vulnerability—particularly of industrialized societies, where the targets are—and the ability of terrorists to exploit new technology, will provide the impetus for the third transition of terrorism.

INTERNATIONAL TERRORISM

The transition to international terrorism represents its most advanced stage. More damage is done by fewer people with a smaller audience and it is difficult to determine who is actually responsible for a destructive incident until an organization takes credit for the operation. International terrorism embraces the same techniques, perspectives, and objectives as other forms of terrorism; the salient difference is that a sovereign state (as compared to a "non-state actor" such as the PLO) now exercises the command and control function. This relationship makes it possible to designate targets which may result in mass casualties. Unlike its antecedents, normative inhibitions will not pose a constraint for international terrorism. Extensive operations near the threshold of conventional war will be accompanied by intelligence exploitation and very sophisticated denial measures within international organizations.

When a nation such as Libya, for example, "controls" a PLO operation it probably has only a tenuous command of the operation. However, the move to control (such as target designation and attack techniques) is only a short step from providing logistics, intelligence, and ideological support. Other nation states have demonstrated this same ability to launch international terrorism. As international terrorism begins to pay larger dividends, it will continue to expand its operational area. This expansion will include both the usual criminal expansion, radical governments bent on assisting various revolutionary movements, medium and large powers bent on improving their regional positions vis-a-vis their neighbors, and surreptitious involvement of the super powers. It is conceivable that the type of surrogate operations described by Brian Jenkins of the Rand Corporation could take place. Such operations are made to order for the large and powerful as well as for the small and weak nations and can be made non-attributable to the sponsoring nation.

Today, terrorists continue to rely on the same weapons they have traditionally used: the bomb and the gun. There are a variety of modern bombs, fuzes, and guns that are small and, like Uzi, fire fast and are easily concealed. Terrorists may begin to employ advances in science and technology to gain their objectives. Greater use will be made of man-portable weaponry with a high first-round kill probability, ancillary communications equipment, more destructive demolitions, and highly refined intelligence and countersurveillance techniques to avoid detection and compromise.

Possible employment of mass destructive weapons represents a threat of staggering magnitude for many industrialized societies and an increasing number of those in the Third World. With the proliferation of nuclear power plants and other sources of dangerous nuclear material, it will become easier for terrorists to obtain or construct a nuclear device. The current debate over the possibility of the use of a nuclear device continues. Many analysts consider such a possibility unlikely because it contradicts the basic objectives of the terrorists. The Nuclear Regulatory Commission also considers the threat unlikely, but they agree that it cannot be completely discounted.

Less attention has been directed towards the use of toxic substances, even though they are easier to develop and disseminate than a nuclear device. In fact, a poison gas factory in Vienna which reportedly produced a type of nerve gas used for criminal purposes has already been put out of action by police. Implications of the threat of international terrorism will expand as this transition progresses and industrialized societies become more popular targets.

Regardless of whether surrogates are employed by intelligence organizations or terrorists are controlled by a political power, numerous possibilities exist for expanding this emerging transition. It is a safe wager that acts of international terrorism will increase.

Threatened societies can best arm themselves by developing countermeasures and responses based on a thorough understanding of the causes and components of contemporary terrorism.

I PERSPECTIVES ON CONTEMPORARY TERRORISM

The objective of this section is to build a perspective based on factual understanding. The articles by Fromkin, Smart, and Pierre consider the most important components of contemporary terrorism—its strategy, power, and politics. Each of the authors emphasizes the political objectives of terrorism and offers thought-provoking commentaries useful for shaping a response within the rule of law.

Flexibility and unpredictability have been key characteristics of contemporary terrorism. These features have been evident throughout the transition to transnational and international terrorism and are given new perspective by Milbank's report for the U. S. Central Intelligence Agency. Milbank provides not only essential statistical information and sound working definitions, but a prognosis for future terrorist acts.

Complete comprehension of contemporary terrorism would be aided significantly by an understanding of the motivation and psychological make-up of the terrorists themselves. Unfortunately, there is little information of this nature, but one of the best articles available is a complete profile by Russell and Miller which emphasizes emerging trends in terrorist organizations. This leads to Section III, the discussion of threat potential.

Fromkin considers political terrorism a disorder of our modern world and warns that we have not yet witnessed its complete application as a political strategy. Building his commentary on several well known historical and contemporary examples, he provides a background against which to distinguish trends over the years. This article highlights the indirect approach of terrorists, aiming at psychological results, to force governments to over-react and set the stage for revolution. Accordingly, terrorism wins or loses only in terms of how societies respond to it.

The following article is reprinted by permission from *Foreign Affairs*, July 1975. Copyright © 1975, by Council on Foreign Relations, Inc.

The Strategy Of Terrorism

by DAVID FROMKIN

The grim events at the Athens airport on August 5, 1973, were in a sense symbolic. Dreadfully real to those who were involved, the occurrences of that day also transcended their own reality, somewhat as myths do, epitomizing an entire aspect of contemporary existence in one specific drama.

When the hand grenades were hurled into the departure lounge and the machine gunners simultaneously mowed down the passengers waiting to embark for New York City, it seemed incomprehensible that so harmless a group should be attacked. The merest glance at their hand-luggage, filled with snorkels and cameras, would have shown that they had spent their time in such peaceful pursuits as swimming, sunbathing, and snapping photos of the Parthenon.

The raid had been undertaken on behalf of an Arab Palestine. Yet the airport passengers had done the Arabs no harm. Their journey had only been to Greece. Palestine had nothing to do with them; it was another country, across the sea, and its problems were not of their making. Moreover, Athens was a capital friendly to the Arab cause—as was Paris, the scene of more recent airline attacks.

Similar incidents have occurred with terrible frequency throughout the 1960s and 1970s. The generations that have come to maturity in Europe and America since the end of the Second World War have asked only to bask in the sunshine of a summertime world; but increasingly they have been forced instead to live in the fearful shadow of other people's deadly quarrels. Gangs of politically motivated gunmen have disrupted everyday life, intruding and forcing their parochial feuds upon the unwilling attention of everybody else.

True, other ages have suffered from crime and outrage, but what we are experiencing today goes beyond such things. Too small to impose their will by military force, terrorist bands nonetheless are capable nowadays of causing enough damage to intimidate and blackmail the governments of the world. Only modern technology makes this possible—the bazooka, the plastic bomb, the submachine gun, and perhaps, over the horizon, the nuclear mini-bomb. The transformation has enabled terrorism to enter the political arena on a new scale, and to express ideological goals of an organized sort rather than mere crime, madness, or emotional derangement as in the past.

Political terrorism is a distinctive disorder of the modern world. It originated as a term, and, arguably, as a practice, less than two centuries ago and has come into the spotlight of global conflict in our lifetime. Whereas both organized and irregular (or guerrilla) warfare began with the human race, political terrorism emerged as a concept only in 1793. As a political strategy, it is both new and original; and if I am correct, its nature has not yet fully been appreciated.

Of course nobody can remain unaware of the upsurge of global terrorism that has occurred in recent years. But the novelty of it has not been perceived. Force usually generates fear, and the fear is usually an additional weapon. But terrorism employs the weapon of fear in a special and complicated sort of way.

The disassociation of fear from force in the context of organized politics emerged first in the Reign of Terror, the episode (1793-1794) during the history of revolutionary France from which the English and French words for terrorism derive. The terrorists in question were, of course, Robespierre and his satellites, St. Just and Couthon. Sitting as a faction in the Committee of Public Safety, their accusations of treason sent victims to the guillotine in droves. By the mere threat of accusation against their fellow Committee members, they used the entire Committee, thus united, in order to dominate the National Convention and the other public bodies of the French Republic.

Robespierre was overthrown when his system was used against him. His mistake was in letting Joseph Fouché know that he was the next intended victim; and Fouché, the wily intriguer who later became Napoleon's minister of police, made the best possible use of his few remaining days. He persuaded the feuding, rival politicians of his day that they had to unite against the triumvirs or else face execution one by one; fear of the regime should cause them not to serve it, but to overthrow it.

On 8 Thermidor (July 26, 1794) Robespierre made another mistake when he told the Convention that he had prepared a new list of traitors in their midst—and then refused to tell them whose names were on the list. Fouché's warnings were confirmed, and his counsel was heeded. When Robespierre entered the National Convention late in the stormy summer morning of 9 Thermidor, he found a mob of delegates united by the determination to murder him before he could murder them; and that was the end of him.

Robespierre had coerced a nation of 27 million people into accepting his dictatorship. His followers sent many thousands either to jail or to their deaths; one scholar's estimate is 40,000 deaths and 300,000 arrests. Yet when retribution came and Robespierre and his group of supporters were executed, it turned out that in all there were only 22 of them.

Of course it is not meant to suggest that this is the whole story of the French Terror. Yet what emerges most strongly from any account of these events is the dramatic disparity between the objective weakness of the Robespierre faction, whose numbers were few and whose military resources were limited, and their immense subjective power, which allowed them to kill, imprison, or control so many. There was no need to fear the triumvirs other than the fact that other people feared them and therefore would execute their orders. Their power was unreal; it was an illusionist's trick. No citadels had to be stormed, no armies had to be crushed, in order to overthrow them. If the public ignored what they said, then the terrorists went back to being political nobodies. Their dictatorship vanished in an instant when Robespierre and his colleagues were prevented from reaching the speakers' platform on 9 Thermidor.

In the end, the terrorists overreached themselves, and men saw through them and stood up to them. Then—and only then—it became clear that France had never had anything to fear from them other than fear itself.

Perhaps the closest parallel to Robespierre's method was that followed by the late Senator Joseph McCarthy in 1950-54. Like Robespierre, McCarthy claimed to have lists of traitors whose names he would not immediately reveal, and many did his will in order to avoid being accused by him of treason or of lack of patriotism. And, like Robespierre's, his power stopped when he went too far and Joseph Welch, his Fouché, stood up to him on television. But McCarthy never seized supreme power in the country, nor did his accusations send people to the guillotine. In that sense it can be said that Robespierre has had no successors.

Since his time, in fact, political terrorism has become especially notorious in a different cause from that in which Robespierre used it. It has been used to destroy governments rather than to sustain them. This changed the way in which many people thought of it as a political strategy and how they viewed its adherents. As revolutionaries, terrorists have come to seem romantic figures to many. Their life of dangers and disguises, risks and betrayals, conspiracies and secret societies, exerted a powerful fascination. As torn and tormented characters, they provided authors with the stuff of which complex and interesting novels can be made.

Though the terrorists seemed romantic, until recently they also seemed ineffective. Until the Irish Treaty of 1921, they scored no significant political successes. The most famous of the terrorist groups up to that time was the Terrorist Brigade of the Russian Socialists-Revolutionists; and not merely did they fail to change the Tsarist government in the ways in which they desired, they also failed to pick up the pieces when it was overthrown by others. Plekhanov, Lenin, Trotsky and the other Russian disciples of Marx had seen more clearly in placing their emphasis on mass organization rather than on individual terrorism. The Bolsheviks came to power by winning the metropolitan workmen, the sailors of the Baltic fleet, and the soldiers to their side. Organization proved to be the key to victory. It was not individual gunmen but armed masses who seized power in Russia. Revolution, like war, is the strategy of the strong; terrorism is the strategy of the weak.

It is an uncertain and indirect strategy that employs the weapon of fear in a special sort of way in which to make governments react. Is fear an effective method? Is fright any kind of weapon at all? What can terrorists hope to accomplish by sowing fear? How can it help their side to vanquish its opponents? Clearly it can do so in many ways. Fright can paralyze the will, befuddle the mind, and exhaust the strength of an adversary. Moreover, it can persuade an opponent that a particular political point of view is taken with such deadly seriousness by its few adherents that is should be accommodated, rather than suffering casualties year after year in a campaign to suppress it.

All of these elements came together, for example, in the struggle that led to the independence of southern Ireland. It is difficult to disentangle the role of terrorism in this achievement from the other elements that were involved, for the Irish also had put in motion what was, in effect, a guerrilla warfare campaign. Moreover, the Liberal members of the coalition that then governed the United Kingdom had a political commitment that went back more than a quarter of a century to the cause of Irish Home Rule. Yet there can be little doubt that terrorism played a major role in causing Britain to tire of the struggle.

Terrorism can also make heroes out of gunmen, and thereby rally popular support to their cause. The problem this creates for them is that when the time comes to make the compromises necessary in order to negotiate the terms of their victory, the glamour wanes, and with it, the political support. Michael Collins was a romantic figure who captured the imagination of all Ireland as long as he was an outlaw; but when he sat down to make peace, he was seen by many in a much different light. As he signed the Irish Treaty of 1921 on Britain's behalf, Lord Birkenhead remarked to Collins, "I may have signed my political death-warrant tonight"; to which Collins replied, "I may have signed my actual death-warrant." Eight months later Michael Collins lay dead on an Irish roadway with a bullet through his head.

Just as it can make gangsters into heroes, terrorist provocations can also make policemen into villains. The Black-and-Tans who fought the Irish revoluntionists were, in an objective sense, so successful at repression that Michael Collins told an English official afterwards, in regard to the July 1921 peace negotiations: "You had us dead beat. We could not have lasted another three weeks." Yet Black-and-Tan methods made the cause of repression so odious that Britain was induced to choose another course of action.

Brutality is an induced govermental response that can boomerang. It is this ability to use the strength of repression against itself, in many different ways, that has enabled terrorist strategies to succeed in many situations that have, rightly or wrongly, been described as colonialist in the modern world.

Sophisticated approaches have been developed along these lines. One of these was explained to me and to others at a meeting in New York City sometime in 1945 by one of the founders of the Irgun Zvai Leumi, a tiny group of Jewish militants in what was then the British-mandated territory of Palestine. His organization had no more than 1,000 or 1,500 members, and it was at odds with the Palestinian Jewish community almost as much as it was with the mandatory regime. Yet he proposed to combat Great Britain, then a global power whose armed forces in the Second World War numbered in the millions, and to expel Great Britain from Palestine.

How could such a thousand-to-one struggle be won? To do so, as he explained it, his organization would attack property interests. After giving advance warning to evacuate them, his small band of followers would blow up buildings. This, he said, would lead the British to overreact by garrisoning the country with an immense army drawn from stations in other parts of the world. But postwar Britain could not afford financially to maintain so great an army either there or anywhere else for any extended period of time. Britain urgently needed to demobilize its armed forces. The strain would tell; and eventually economic pressure would drive the Attlee-Bevin government either to withdraw from Palestine or else to try some reckless and possibly losing gamble in an effort to retrieve the situation.

It can be argued that such is in fact what happened. Of course Britain might have withdrawn anyway, at some other time or for some other reason. But that is really beside the point, for the Irgun wanted independence then and there, in order to open up the country to refugees from Hitler's Europe. They got what they wanted when they wanted it by doing it in their own way.

There were two flaws in the Irgun strategy. It would have failed had the British not reacted to the destruction of buildings as they were expected to do. If instead they had done nothing at all, maintained only a modest military garrison, and sent for no reinforcements, all that would have happened would have been that a few more buildings would have been blown up and the owners would have collected the insurance money and would have rebuilt them; and the Irgun would have proved a failure.

In the second place, the plan of attacking property without hurting people proved to be unrealistic. Accidents inevitably occur when violence is unleashed. Almost a hundred persons were killed when the Irgun blew up the King David Hotel in Jerusalem. According to the plan, they should have been evacuated before the blast, but in actual life people misunderstand, or their telephone line is busy, or somebody forgets to give them the message in time. Moreover, terrorism generates its own momentum, and before long the killing becomes deliberate. The bloodshed caused by the Irgun isolated it politically and alienated the rest of the Palestinian Jewish community. The British failed to perceive or exploit this situation. But Ben-Gurion did; in 1948 he made use of it to crush the Irgun, for the Israeli army might have been unwilling to carry out orders to attack those unloading the Irgun ship the *Altalena,* if the Irgun had not used up its political credit before then by the taking of too many lives.

Yet despite its flaws, the strategy was sufficiently ingenious so that the Irgun played a big part in getting the British to withdraw. Its ingenuity lay in using an opponent's own strength against him. It was a sort of jujitsu. First the adversary was made to be afraid, and then, predictably, he would react to his fear by increasing the bulk of his strength, and then the sheer weight of that bulk would drag him down. Another way of saying this is that the Irgun, seeing that it was too small to defeat Great Britain, decided, as an alternative approach, that Britain was big enough to defeat itself.

In the 1950s, the nationalist rebel group in Algeria developed yet another method of using the strength of an occupying power against itself. Their method was to induce that strength to be used as a form of persuasion.

For, in Algeria, the whole question was one of persuasion. The problem initially faced by the miniscule band of Algerian nationalists that called itself the National Liberation Front (or, in its French initials, FLN) was that Algeria at that time had little sense of national identity. Its population was not homogeneous; and the Berbers, the Arabs, and the settlers of European descent were peoples quite different from one another. The name and separate existence of Algeria were only of recent origin. For most of recorded history, Algeria had been no more than the middle part of North Africa, with no distinct history of its own. Legally it was merely the southern part of France. The French had treated Morocco and Tunisi as protectorates, with separate identities, but not Algeria, which was absorbed into France herself. With sarcasm, Frenchmen used to reply to Americans who urged independence for Algeria by saying that, on the same basis, the United States should set Wisconsin free or give back independence to South Carolina.

It was a jibe that went to the heart of the matter. Colonial empires were coming to an end in the 1950s and 1960s. If Algeria was a nation, then inevitably it would set free to govern itself. Only if it were genuinely a part of France could it continue to be ruled from Paris. All depended, therefore, on whether the indigenous population could be convinced by the French government that Algeria was not a separate country, or upon whether they could be persuaded by the FLN to change their minds so as to think of themselves as a nation.

The FLN strategy of terrorism addressed itself to this central and decisive issue. By itself, as has been said, terror can accomplish nothing in terms of political goals; it can only aim at obtaining a response that will achieve those goals for it. What the FLN did was to goad the French into reacting in such a way as to demonstrate the unreality of the claim that there was no distinct Algerian nation. Unlike the Irgun, the FLN did not set out to campaign merely against property; it attacked people. It used random violence, planting bombs in market places and in other crowded locations. The instinctive French reaction was to treat all persons of non-European origin as suspects; but, as Raymond Aron was to write, "As suspects, all the Muslims felt excluded from the existing community." Their feeling was confirmed when, in the middle 1950s, the authorities further reacted by transferring the French army units composed of Muslim Algerian troops out of Algeria and into mainland France, and replacing them in Algeria by European troops. By such actions they showed in the most unmistakable way that they regarded no Algerians as Frenchmen except for the European settlers. They spoke of we and us, and of they and them, and did not realize that their doing so meant the end of Algérie Française.

Thus the French conceded the issue of the war at its very outset. They threw away the potential support of Muslim Algeria because they were skeptical of the possibility that it could be obtained. From that moment the conclusion of the conflict was foregone. Once the sympathies of the population had shifted to its side, the FLN was able to outgrow mere terrorism and to organize a campaign of guerrilla warfare. It also was enabled to appeal to world sympathies on behalf of a people fighting for its freedom. From the French point of view all had become hopeless; for no amount of force can keep an unwilling population indefinitely in subjection. Even though the FLN had written the script, the French, with suicidal logic, went ahead to play the role for which they had been cast.

The FLN success was therefore a special case. It required a particular kind of opponent. It could not be duplicated in other circumstances and conditions.

Revolutionist-terrorists of the last decade have failed to perceive the special characteristics of the colonialist situation that facilitated success for Irish, Irgun, and Algerian terrorists. They have tried to apply the strategy of terrorism in situations that are essentially different. This has been true, for example, of extremist groups seeking to overthrow liberal-pluralistic regimes during the 1960s. Their theory has been that their terrorist attacks would force hitherto liberal regimes to become repressive, a change which in turn would alienate the masses, thus setting the stage for revolution. But it has not worked out that way in practice. In the United States, for example, terrorist bomb attacks have not led to any change at all in the form of government, much less to a transformation of America into a police state. On the other hand, in Uruguay, once the model democracy of Latin America, the terror of the Tupamaro bands has led to a military dictatorship that brutally destroyed the Tupamaros, but that does not seem, at least as yet, to have led to the predicted reaction by the masses in favor of revolutionary action.

Other revolutionary groups have taken a somewhat different approach. They have argued that liberal democracies are already police states. Thus, the object of revolutionary terrorist action should be to reveal this hidden reality to the population at large. Unthinking reaction by the authorities to terrorist provocation would accomplish the desired result. Thus the aim of terrorism would be to trick the government into taking off its mask.

In open societies such as Great Britain and the United States, the liberal democratic features have proved to be a face and not a mask: there is nothing to take off, and the strategy failed because its factual premise proved to be untrue.

In closed societies, the strategy has been to show that authoritarian regimes are actually impotent despite their outward show of virility. In such circumstances, supposedly, by demonstrating that the public authorities are powerless to enforce law and order, a campaign of terror can cause a government to collapse; but the flaw in the theory is that the terrorists usually are not strong enough to take its place. Either some more broadly based group will seize power, or else, as in Argentina, private groups will take the law into their own hands and retaliate in kind against murder and extortion, so that society relapses into a semi-anarchic state of reprisals and blood feuds, where terrorists are buried with their victims.

It is against this background that Arab Palestinian terrorism has seized the attention of the contemporary world. It is aimed at Israel; it is aimed at the Arabs who live within Israel; and it is aimed at the world outside. It is, in other words, a mixed strategy. Each of its mixed aspects has to be considered separately. All that Arab terrorism can accomplish in the land that has been promised to so many is to frighten and to threaten the Arab inhabitants of Israel in order to keep them from cooperating with the Israeli authorities. Israel itself, however, cannot be terrorized into disappearing of its own accord; yet removing Israel from the map has long been the proclaimed goal of the Arab terrorist movement.

Terrorism can be employed more successfully in colonialist situations than in Palestine because a colonial power suffers the disadvantage of fighting the battle away from its own base, and also because a colonial power, having a country of its own to which it can withdraw, is under no compulsion to fight to the bitter end. The Israelis, though termed colonialist by the Arabs, are fighting on home territory, and they have no other country to which they can withdraw; they fight with their backs to the sea. They can be goaded into a self-defeating reaction, but unless they permit that to happen, nothing can be done to their domestic public opinion that is likely to destroy them. The Arab terrorists therefore have turned elsewhere, and have attacked the arteries of world transportation in hopes that a world indifferent to the merits of the Arab-Israeli dispute will turn against the Israelis in order to end the annoyance of a disrupted airline service.

In doing so they have strayed across a frontier and into the eerie world of Mr. McLuhan, and they have transformed terrorism into a form of mass communication—but communication aimed at the whole world and not, as in the case of Algeria, mostly at the indigenous population. Theirs is a campaign that needs publicity in order to succeed, and therefore they have come to operate within the ambit of contemporary public relations and communications arts: the world of cinema, camp fashion, and pop art, in which deadlines and prime time are the chief realities and in which shock value is the chief virtue. If audiences throughout the world react with horror, and turn against the political cause in whose name so many innocent people have been harmed and killed, the strategy will have backfired. So far they have not done so and it has not done so.

It is a corruption of the human spirit for which all political sides are responsible. The left-wing journalist Paul Johnson wrote an article some months back arguing that left-wing movements are as much at fault as anybody else for accepting the murder of the innocent as a legitimate means for the pursuit of political ends. He quoted the sixteenth-century humanist Castellio, "who was lucky to escape burning by both Catholics and Protestants, and who pointed out in his tract for toleration, *Whether Heretics Are To Be Persecuted?*, that no certitude of righteousness justifies violence: 'To kill a man is not to defend a doctrine, it is to kill a man'." Appalled at the welcome accorded by the United Nations to the leader of the Arab terrorists, Johnson wrote that, "Step by step, almost imperceptibly, without anyone being aware that a fatal watershed has been crossed, mankind has descended into the age of terror."

If this is an age of terror, then it has become all the more important for us to understand exactly what it is that terrorism means. Terrorism, as has been seen, is the weapon of those who are prepared to use violence but who believe that they would lose any contest of sheer strength. All too little understood, the uniqueness of the strategy lies in this: that it achieves its goal not through its acts but through the response to its acts. In any other such strategy, the violence is the beginning and its consequences are the end of it. For terrorism, however, the consequences of the violence are themselves merely a first step and form a stepping stone toward objectives that are more remote. Whereas military and revolutionary actions aim at a physical result, terrorist actions aim at a psychological result.

But even that psychological result is not the final goal. Terrorism is violence used in order to create fear; but it is aimed at creating fear in order that the fear, in turn, will lead somebody else—not the terrorist—to embark on some quite different program of action that will accomplish whatever it is that the terrorist really desires. Unlike the soldier, the guerrilla fighter, or the revolutionist, the terrorist therefore is always in the paradoxical position of undertaking actions the immediate physical consequences of which are not particularly desired by him. An ordinary murderer will kill somebody because he wants the person to be dead, but a terrorist will shoot somebody even though it is a matter of complete indifference to him whether that person lives or dies. He would do so, for example, in order to provoke a brutal police repression that he believes will lead to political conditions propitious to revolutionary agitation and organization aimed at overthrowing the government. The act of murder is the same in both cases, but its purpose is different, and each act plays a different role in the strategies of violence.

Only an understanding of the purpose for which such an act is undertaken can enable us to know the nature of the act. When Julius Caesar was murdered in the Roman Senate, it was an assassination of the traditional sort, intended to eliminate a specific figure from the political scene; but had he been killed there by the representative of a subversive sect, intent on plunging his dagger into the first Roman leader he encountered in order to provoke a certain political response from the Senate, it would instead have been an act of political terrorism.

It is because an action of the same sort may be undertaken by two different groups with two quite different ends in view that terrorism is so often confused with guerrilla warfare, for terrorists and guerrillas often seem to be doing the same sorts of things. Both of them, for example, often sabotage transportation facilities. When T. E. Lawrence led his classic guerrilla warfare campaign against Turkish rule in Arabia, he systematically dynamited railway tracks and bridges. Lawrence's strategy was later explained by Winston Churchill as follows: "The Turkish armies operating against Egypt depended upon the desert railway. This slender steel track ran through hundreds of miles of blistering desert. If it were permanently cut the Turkish armies must perish." And Lawrence therefore rode on camel back across the sands to destroy the enemy army by blowing up its transportation facilities. In recent years those who say that they wish to destroy the state of Israel have also blown up transportation facilities in the Arab desert; in this case, jet airplanes belonging to civil aviation companies. Yet if thereby they were to permanently cut the airline networks of TWA or BOAC they would not cause the Israeli army to perish. Indeed the fate of such civil aviation companies is a matter of indifference to the terrorists. Lawrence the guerrilla leader attacked a railway because he wanted to destroy it, whereas Arab terrorists attack an airline even though they do not want to destroy it.

The distinction is of more than academic importance. The French lost their empire over Algeria when they mistook terrorism for guerrilla warfare. They thought that when the FLN planted a bomb in a public bus, it was in order to blow up the bus; whereas the real FLN purpose in planting the bomb was not to blow up the bus, but to lure authorities into reacting by arresting all the non-Europeans in the area as suspects.

The terrorist is like a magician who tricks you into watching his right hand while his left hand, unnoticed, makes the switch. It is understandable that the French authorities in Algeria became totally obsessed by the need to stamp out criminal attacks, but it was fatal to their policy to do so, for the violent attacks were merely a subsidiary issue. The tiny FLN band of outlaws could have blown up every bus in all of Algeria and never won a convert to their cause of independence. Failing to understand the strategy of terrorism, the French did not see that it was not the FLN's move, but rather the French countermove, that would determine whether the FLN succeeded or failed.

It may be the case that the current Israeli policy of attacking Arab terrorist bases in southern Lebanon is another example of concentrating too much attention on preventing terrorist actions and too little attention on foiling terrorist purposes. The Israeli policy is certainly understandable on many grounds, and valid arguments can be adduced in its support; but the weakening of an essentially benevolent Lebanese government, as well as the further estrangement of world opinion, are results of the Israeli raids into Lebanon that may outweigh the value of using that particular approach to the problem of combating terrorism.

For the Israelis, threatened by enemies outside of their society, the problem is an enormously difficult one. For societies threatened only by enemies from within, it is considerably less so. The very wickedness of terrorism makes it a vulnerable strategy in such a society. Other strategies sometimes kill the innocent by mistake. Terrorism kills the innocent deliberately; for not even the terrorist necessarily believes that the particular person who happens to become his victim deserves to be killed or injured. It is horrifying not merely because of the deed that that is done but also because at first the deed seems pointless. If you want to make war on the United States on behalf of Puerto Rican independence, why blow up a historic tavern in New York's financial district? What has Fraunces Tavern got to do with Puerto Rico? Why not attack the alleged forces of occupation in Puerto Rico instead? If you opposed by force and violence the continuation of U.S. aid to South Vietnam, why threaten to destroy the Smithsonian Institution? What had its plant collections and its ichthyological specimens to do with American policy in Southeast Asia? The destruction seems so purposeless that it is a natural reaction to turn on those who perpetrate it in hatred and in anger.

The tragedies that befall great public figures can sometimes seem to have been deserved; but when a man on the street is killed at random on behalf of a cause with which he had nothing to do, it is a different matter and provokes a different reaction. In a homogeneous society, at any rate, it leads to a reaction against the terrorism, and it renders it vulnerable to a campaign that politically isolates it in order to physically destroy it, for the nature of the attacks tends to demonstrate that terrorists are enemies of the people rather than merely of the government. It is for this reason that Che Guevara, as a theoretician and practitioner of guerrilla warfare, warned against the strategy of terrorism, arguing that it hinders "contact with the masses and makes impossible unification for actions that will be necessary at a critical moment."

Even in the international arena, terrorist movements are vulnerable when their actions alienate support. This was tacitly recognized by the Palestine Liberation Organization (PLO) when on January 29, 1975, it announced that henceforth it had decided to treat hijacking of airplanes, ships, or trains as crimes and would impose death penalties on hijackers if their actions led to the loss of life. Whether the PLO will indeed abandon its campaign of terror against international transportation remains to be seen. Yet the declaration of its intention to do so is in itself significant, for its suggests a realization that a point has arrived when a public identification with terrorist activity will harm rather than help. This is because terrorism is so much more evil than other strategies of violence that public opinion sometimes can be rallied against it.

Indeed, in view of its inherent weakness, it is remarkable how many political successes have been scored by the strategy of terrorism in the last few decades. Its success seems to be due in large part to a miscomprehension of the strategy by its opponents. They have neglected the more important of the two levels on which terrorism operates. They have failed to focus on the crucial issue of how the manner in which they, as opponents, respond affects the political goals of the terrorists. Discussion instead has centered on the criminal justice aspects of the question: prevention and punishment.

Much has been written, for example, about the technological defenses that have been developed or could be developed against terrorism in order to prevent it from occurring. This can be a highly useful line of approach, as the successful use of electronic surveillance devices at airports seems to have demonstrated. It may even be advisable to require that any new technologies that are developed from time to time should incorporate some sort of internal defense against attack, much as environmentalists argue that pollution control devices should be incorporated in equipment and its cost charged to the manufacturers. Yet no technology is perfect, and there will always be somebody who will manage to slip by any defenses that can be created.

Prevention of terrorism in non-technological ways scarcely merits discussion. Perhaps one day the social sciences will teach us how to drain the swamps of misery in which hatred and fanaticism breed, but at the moment that day seems far distant. The hollow formalism of the law offers, if anything, even less help. Ingenious schemes for new international tribunals and procedures have been proposed, and they completely miss the point. The manifest unwillingness of many governments to use existing legal remedies against terrorism shows that the real problem is the lack of a will and not the lack of a way. For example, it was only when an attack was staged at the Paris airport that the French Minister of the Interior, in January of 1975, proposed to negotiate an international convention to provide for the punishment of terrorist acts. It is not any kind of genuine solution, in any event, but it will be interesting to see if Michel Poniatowski perseveres in even so ritualistic a response as this after the fleeting memory of injured national pride fades from view. There are all too many who object to terrorism only when they are its victims.

Far more effective than the reaction of M. Poniatowski was that of the French press. There were suggestions in the newspapers that the pro-Arab policy of the French government should be reversed because it had failed to prevent the attack at Orly airport. Within days the Palestine Liberation Organization strongly condemned the attack. It also announced that it had taken measures to punish persons who engaged in the hijacking of airplanes, boats or trains. What the French journalists had correctly intuited was that the locus of the struggle was not at the Orly airport: it was at the Elysée Palace and at the Quai d' Orsay.

The overriding questions are not legal or technological; they are philosophical and political. Terrorism is the indirect strategy that wins or loses only in terms of how you respond to it. The decision as to how accommodating or how uncompromising you should be in your response to it involves questions that fall primarily within the domain of political philosophy.

Those who are the targets of terrorism—and who are prepared to defend themselves by doing whatever is necessary in order to beat it—start with a major advantage. The advantage is that success or failure depends upon them alone. Terrorism wins only if you respond to it in the way that the terrorists want you to; which means that its fate is in your hands and not in theirs. If you choose not to respond at all, or else to respond in a way different from that which they desire, they will fail to achieve their objectives.

The important point is that the choice is yours, That is the ultimate weakness of terrorism as a strategy. It means that, though terrorism cannot always be prevented, it can always be defeated. You can always refuse to do what they want you to do.

Whether to pay the price of defeating terrorism is increasingly going to be a major question in our time. The answer is relatively easy in most kidnapping and ransom situations: experience has shown that blackmailers and extortionists usually are encouraged to try it again if you give in to their demands the first time. So, if you can do so, you should accept the consequences, however terrible, of standing firm in order to avoid an infinite sequence of painful events.

But the price of doing so is constantly rising, as technology increases the range and magnitude of horrible possibilities. Terrorist outrages, when they occur, are bound to become more deadly. Increasingly, we will be under pressure to abridge our laws and liberties in order to suppress the terrorists. It is a pressure that should be resisted.

In our personal lives we sometimes have to choose between these alternatives: whether to live a good life or whether to live a long life. Political society in the years to come is likely to face a similar choice. An open society such as ours is especially vulnerable to terrorist violence, which seems to threaten us with ever more dreadful and drastic fates. Have we the stoicism to endure nonetheless? Will we be tempted to abandon our political and moral values? Will we be willing to go on paying an ever higher price in order to defeat the terrorists by refusing to respond in the way they want us to?

Of course it would make things easier if terrorism simply would go away. It seems unlikely to do so. The weapons are at hand, and they probably will be used, for terrorism will never cease until the day when the Old Man of the Mountain loses his last disciple. The old man was grand master of the sect called the Assassins (hashish-ins) because of the hashish which he gave them. The old man, according to Marco Polo, used to drug his young disciples and transport them while they were asleep to his secret pleasure garden, persuading them when they awoke in it that it was paradise itself. Drugging them again, he would transport them back to the everyday world while they slept. Never afterward did they doubt that their Master could and would reward them with eternal paradise after death if they did his killing for him while they were alive. And so they did do his killing for him.

If anything, the modern world seems to breed more and more votaries of this peculiar sect. They seem to thrive and multiply everywhere in the world, bomb or machine gun in hand, motivated by political fantasies and hallucinations, fully convinced that their slaughter of the innocent will somehow usher in a political millennium for mankind. *"Voici Le Temps Des Assassins,"* as Rimbaud wrote in the dawn of the industrial age; and we do indeed live in the time of the Assassins.

Smart emphasizes the capacity of terrorists to exert power by creating fear. Many governments have responded to terrorist power by granting their demands. This has resulted in an increase in demands accompanied by increasing vulnerabilities of industrialized societies. Smart concludes that terrorist power is not invincible, however, and can be defeated by any society with sufficient political will.

This article is reprinted by permission from *International Journal*, Volume XXX, Number 2 Spring 1975, Toronto, Canada.

The Power of Terror

by I. M. H. SMART

Some would hold the subject to be meaningless. 'Terror,' says Hannah Arendt, 'is not the same as violence; it is, rather, the form of government that comes into being when violence, having destroyed all power, does not abdicate but, on the contrary, remains in full control . . . Violence can destroy power; it is utterly incapable of creating it.'[1] It becomes increasingly difficult to have much respect for such a view as occasions multiply on which international as well as national politics are clearly affected by the threats and actions of men whose power depends not on their numbers but only on the fear aroused by their demonstrated willingness and ability to use violence. Power, if it means anything, must be a transitive concept, reflecting the application of some faculty for constraining the thoughts or motions of its objects: 'the capacity to induce others to behave according to patterns in one's own mind.'[2] To pretend that the violent criminal, lunatic, or political terrorist is incapable of constraining the actions of others—incapable of power—is to be ignorant of both violence and politics. As to 'terror,' the emotion is, after all, no more than an extreme of the fear which lies, in one form or another, at the root of all political relationships whether it be fear of punishment, of deprivation, or of exclusion from the relationship itself. Here, however, we are concerned only with one conventional use of the word: the 'terror' of the 'terrorist,' the fear evoked by the individuals or the small groups of individuals whose capacity to constrain the behaviour of others resides not in reason, in numerical preponderance, or in any legitimate exercise of authority, but only in the perception that they are able and willing to use violence unless their demands are satisfied.

That terrorists are powerful, if not generally then in specific contexts, is apparent. Convicted criminals are released, ransoms paid, budgets increased, policies modified—all for fear of what violent terrorists might otherwise do. The question is not whether the terrorist is powerful, but why. There is widespread inclination to regard political terrorism as a rising tide. If it is, why should that be so? What is it that enables small numbers of men and women, acting in present circumstances, to convert their demonstrated willingness to use violence into such effective power?

Whatever our current impressions, there is nothing new about terrorism or its power. Some in western Europe and North America may, perhaps, have been all the more astonished by the actions of Black September, the Irish Republican Army (IRA), or the Front de Libération du Québec (FLQ) because their own countries, in the years since 1914, had been afflicted by international wars more than by the terrorist violence characteristic of that earlier period which ended with the terrorist murder of an archduke at Sarajevo. The fact is that the history both of terrorism and of its direction towards political power is a long one. Nor has the essential character of terrorism changed since its inception. What has, perhaps, changed is an emphasis. Albeit with many exceptions, the form in which political terrorism most frequently manifested itself in the past was that of assassination. The power of subversion, if not compulsion, was sought through the killing of an individual enemy or, in many cases, through the disruption occasioned by his death. The alternative of seizing hostages and threatening, rather than using, lethal violence was more typical of the criminal terrorist—the kidnapper or the bandit—seeking financial rather than political gain. The alternative technique has been taken over in the last few years, however, by political terrorists. Assassination has not become less frequent, as Northern Ireland so fully demonstrates, but it has increasingly been joined, as a political method, by the seizure of hostages, whose survival is made dependent upon the concession of a political reward.

The power of the political terrorist has thus come to be based in part upon the classic techniques of extortion, rather than only upon the techniques of violent disruption. The distinction was never clear cut in the past, and the change recently apparent represents no more than a shift of emphasis. The shift is nevertheless suggestive. At least some of the political terrorism now familiar seeks its rewards not in the chaos or irrational behaviour provoked by its actions but in what are taken to be the rational responses of governments or others to its extortionate demands. One of the questions to be asked is whether this means that some of the political structures towards which terrorism is directed have become more susceptible to extortion and more willing, therefore, to concede some measure of power as a reward for the restraint of terrorist violence.

Today's political terrorists may be more powerful and more dangerous than most of their predecessors in part because they have found ways to exploit exactly those qualities of political rationality and social responsibility on which some of today's governments base their titles to legitimacy.

Not all of today's governments seem to be more vulnerable than yesterday's to terrorist extortion. Political terrorists have had almost no success in extorting political ransoms from governments in developing countries or from authoritarian régimes of either the right or the left. In those states, such political terrorism as we have seen since 1945—in the Middle East, India, southern and central Africa, southeastern Asia, Spain, Portugal, Greece, Latin America, or the Soviet Union itself—has been of the disruptive, rather than extortionist, kind. Violence has not been threatened but used, and has commonly met with a violent response. The result has sometimes been a species of chaos from which the authors of terrorism have extracted political advantage. It has hardly ever been a voluntary concession of such advantage by governments faced with actual terrorist violence, still less by those merely threatened with its potential use. Only in the case of governments in the social democracies of the industrialized 'Western' world have terrorists persistently found a ready audience for political blackmail based upon the credible threat of force alone. What are sometimes called the post-industrial stages of economic development, when they occur within a democratic framework, impose a range of social and political costs which we are only beginning to perceive. I have argued elsewhere, for example, that it is the post-industrial democracies which are vulnerable to what I have called 'devolution' or secession *in situ*'—the wilful rejection of governmental authority by non-revolutionary but alienated and potentially violent groups within the state.[3] We now find that it is also those democracies which are particularly vulnerable to the threat of terrorist violence.

Some of the reasons for this phenomenon are obvious. Democracy, with its emphasis on consent and its distaste for forcible compulsion, tends to project norms of legitimate behaviour which involve the deprecation of violence. Non-violence becomes, as it were, an index of a democratic government's ability to govern democractically. In such circumstances, there is a strong inhibition on the use of violence even against those who threaten violence thmselves. Stronger still is the inhibition on any violence by government the effects of which cannot clearly be limited to those directly responsible for terrorist threats or actions, even when that violence is no more than the implicit sanction which sustains counter-terrorist precautions. The expectation is that democratic governments will not resort to violence within their own domains. Indeed, it is expected of them that, while preserving their own citizens from the implementation of violent threats, they will not only avoid any restriction on the liberty of the citizens but also behave with the utmost restraint towards those who utter the threats. One result is that a British home secretary, reacting to a rising wave of actual as well as potential terrorist violence, must describe as 'draconian' and as 'unprecedented in peacetime' a set of responses which

28   not only are studiedly non-violent but would also, in the majority of countries beyond the 'Western' democracies, be regarded as puny.[4] We would not have it otherwise, but we must recognize that a greater susceptibility to violent terrorism and to the political effects of its threatened use thus constitutes one of the prices which we are willing to pay for our own insistence on the anti-violent norms of democratic legitimacy.

The cost of democracy extends beyond that obvious consideration. It is commonplace, for example, that the international connections of certain terrorist movements impose a further constraint upon governments within whose territory they operate. Effective action to eradicate such agencies of terrorism may have to include action against their bases in other states, but such action may well entail an unacceptable risk of provoking and licensing a wider international conflict. What is less obvious is that the potential ramifications of responses to terrorism *inside* a democratic country may impose a comparable restraint. Because democracy cannot, in the final analysis, tolerate authority derived from any immutable hierarchy, but can only accept authority derived from consent in the light of efficient performance, it follows that the government of a democratic society cannot, in the end, claim a prescriptive and exclusive right to forms of domestic action generally denied to other sections of the community. Government in a democracy is expected to conform, in its behaviour, to the general norms of the society. If it behaves otherwise, it cannot claim to do so as of right—as could its authoritarian counterparts and predecessors—but must be prepared instead to licence as well as to encourage the modification of the general norm concerned. Thus, a democractic government which persistently adopts violent means of responding to terrorism, despite the generally non-violent norms of democratic societies, may achieve local success in the short term, but at the longer term expense of providing other groups within the society with a basis for claiming to use violence legitimately in their own interest.

If terrorism can profit from the constraints placed upon governmental action in a democratic system, it can also exploit the general characteristics of the system itself, especially when its aim is to extract political concessions by threatening violence, rather than to achieve political advantage by using it. In particular, terrorists can and do exploit the egalitarian and individualist values characteristic of the 'Western' democracies but uncommon or weaker elsewhere. On numerous occasions, political as well as financial concessions have been extracted from democratic governments by a credible threat to kill a handful of hostages or even a single individual. In other places, or at other times, such a threat would have had no comparable effect; if it had not merely been ignored, it would have provoked a violent reaction in which the death of a few hostages would have been seen as a small price to pay for the destruction of their captors. In the democracies, however, the deliberate sacrifice of a few innocent lives is seen to be socially unacceptable, even when it may be apparent that it would permit government to act to the longer term advantage of the society as a whole. The immediate value of the individual life outweighs the ulterior interest of the group. Again, that is a characteristic norm of the 'Western' democratic system, and again government cannot claim any prescriptive right to act against it. Meanwhile, the terrorist commonly acts in accordance with a directly contravening norm: that the ulterior interest of the 'cause' outweighs the value of any individual life, including his own. He is thus encouraged to accept risks and to threaten or engage in lethal violence to an extent which democratic government is peculiarly incapable of imitating. Once more, we would not have it otherwise. Once more, we must be aware of the price which we pay for our values. We no longer see it to be expedient that one man— still less one woman or child—should die for the sake of the people. The terrorist looks at it differently. In that difference resides much of the reason why our own societies must now be so vulnerable to the power of terrorist extortion.

It is important, of course, that terrorists themselves are not entirely immune to the normative constraints of the societies within which they operate. To the extent that they depend upon the connivance, or at least complacency, of some part of the local population, they must be cautious about acting in ways which might so offend that population as to alienate them from all support. In ideal circumstances, any terrorist threat or action would automatically alienate its author from all members of a democratic society. The practice, as we know, is different. However, even terrorists operating in the name of a disaffected ethnic or religious minority within a democratic state have been known to alienate most members of that same minority by their actions and to suffer betrayal and defeat as a consequence. Perhaps only the terrorist operating exclusively on behalf of a 'foreign' cause outside the borders of the state concerned, and thus isolated, by definition, from local sympathy, is immune to that danger. In that sense, the Palestinian terrorist operating in, say, Scandinavia is inevitably less constrained by local conventions than the IRA gunman in Ulster. Being associated with no domestic group, he is necessarily less sensitive to domestic norms. At the same time, like all terrorists, he can exploit not only the general inhibitions on the use of violence by a democratic government but also the particularly strong inhibitions on the use of such violence within the government's own jurisdiction. If the representatives of a 'foreign' cause were to launch a violent attack on the frontiers of a democratic state, they would be met with force. When they launch such an attack from within that state, they initiate an internal conflict to which the application of anything more than minimal force by government is seen to be undesirable or even illegitimate.

The stress so far laid on the vulnerability of democratic societies to terrorism is not enough to explain all that we currently sense as the power of terror. There *is*, it seems, a vulnerability inherent in the democratic system. Normative inhibitions on the use of force hamper governmental reactions to terrorist violence, actual or potential. The value placed on individual lives opens the way to terrorist extortion. But not all democratic societies appear to be equally susceptible to terror. The level of their susceptibility is ostensibly related not only to their relative allegiance to democracy but also to their relative economic development. Nor are the cruder quantitative criteria of economic development an obviously sufficient guide on their own. Something also seems to depend upon the qualitative character of development. In particular, it is the highly industrialized democratic countries with high levels of urbanization—or, at least, industrialized urban areas within such countries—which offer apparently ready, as well as attractive, targets for terrorist extortion as well as terrorist violence. Commercial units—warehouses, docks, airports, and even department stores—represent concentrated foci of high economic value. Services and public utilities—transport, communications, energy and water supplies, sewers—constitute nodes of vulnerability. Industry itself, in its manufacturing, distributing, and marketing activities, seems to conspire to present the terrorist with targets of great value and low security. The city also offers human targets: not only the mass of ordinary citizens, whose density ensures that a terrorist bomb can cause a high number of casualties, but also a large number of men and women who, because of their own prominence and their wide identifiability, may serve as particularly valuable hostages. Yet it is the vulnerability of its commerce, its services, and its industry which seems, above all, to make it the terrorist's shooting gallery. In all these circumstances, it is, perhaps, surprising that, with the obvious exception of attacks on aircraft and airports, terrorists have not made more frequent or more determined efforts to strike at the most sensitive nerve centres of the post-industrial city: at its communications or energy systems, its basic services, or its water supplies. The reason may lie, in part, in the fact already noted that many terrorist groups are themselves vulnerable to active rejection by particular sections of the local population. To destroy the essential services upon which their own sympathizers, and even their own families, depend may be the shortest route to the rejection and denunciation which they fear. By the same token, it is again the 'foreign' terrorist, unconnected with any local group, who is likely to be least inhibited by such a fear. And so, indeed, it seems. In the Middle East and in western Europe, those terrorist attacks which have been made upon the nerve centres of an urban society have most frequently been traceable to terrorists acting on behalf of a 'foreign' cause.

Whether or not terrorism has fully exploited the opportunities offered by the number of nodal points within a technically sophisticated urban environment, there is no doubt that technological progress has continued to multiply the potentially attractive targets for terrorist action. Even if it is 'foreign' terrorists who have hitherto taken advantage of that phenomenon, 'domestic' terrorists must be expected to follow suit on some occasions, especially when they are desperate or isolated enough to have no concern for any local political constituency. In this connection, technically is potentially, if not actually, on the side of the terrorist. But there is at least one other connection in which the tendency of technological progress to serve the terrorist interest is already actual, especially within the democracies. The connection is that of communications.

The relationship between the mass media and civil violence is a vexed and difficult question. The relationship between the media and terrorism is more obvious and less controversial. The terrorist, unlike the rioter, is unlikely to be stimulated by the chance of performing in front of a television camera or a microphone. The fact that he can rely upon television, radio, and the press to broadcast so widely and so quickly the news of his actions or his threats is, however, important. Unless the media are controlled to an extent generally incompatible with democratic norms he can be sure that his actions will be reported to the whole of the society within which he wishes to exert power. The result may be revulsion and hostility, but it will also be to substantiate threats of further action and thus to support his future extortion of political concessions. Moreover, he can be sure that his extortionist threats will themselves be carried by the media to the widest possible audience, rather than be confined to the knowledge of the government alone. Indeed, the media, operating freely within a democracy, assist him at every step. They inform him of his potential targets. They ensure that the sensitivity of a whole society is exposed to his threats. They report his actions, thus according him some apparent status, giving credibility to his subsequent menaces and communicating his achievements to his own constituency, inside or outside the country in which he acts. Once more, this complex and irreplaceable service is one which he can expect to receive nowhere more readily than within the 'Western' democracies. Once more, the liberties which we value exact a price.

Communications technology, in its widest sense, gives terrorist groups more than the services of the mass media. It gives them also the ability to move information, materials, and people at essentially the same speed as the governments which they confront. That capacity did not exist even a century ago. Before the full development of the steamship and the railway and the advent of the telegraph, telephone, radio, and aeroplane, governments had enjoyed enormous advantages over their citizens through their control of the most rapid and efficient means of comunication. Today, the terrorist, smuggling men and weapons by jet aircraft and exchanging information and instructions by radio, can compete on equal technical terms with the communications resources of governments. That, indeed, has been one general tendency of technological progress in the twentieth century: to erode the technical monopolies of governments and to act as the equalizer between legitimate authority and the terrorist. When the equalizing effect of mass education is also taken into account, it seems that social as well as technical progress has inevitably had the side-effect of ensuring that those with a motive for terrorism will now have the knowledge, the skills, and the equipment to operate effectively against the abundant targets which the same progress has itself provided.

It has sometimes been argued that the one area in which technological advance has preserved, if not increased, the advantage of government over the terrorist is that of weapons. The fact is that the gap between state-owned means of violence and what people can muster by themselves . . . has always been so enormous that technical improvements make hardly any difference.[5] The argument is somewhat naïve. In the first place, the sophistication of the weapons readily available to the modern terrorist is impressive: surface-to-air missiles, anti-tank rockets, advanced explosives, automatic rifles, helicopters, and the rest. In the second place, the crucial relationship of the terrorist's weapons, especially in a developed urban environment, is not to the arsenals of the national armed forces but to the far more limited means available to a local police force or to the essentially unarmed civilian population which constitutes or contains his primary targets. In the third place, the nature of modern weapons and means of destruction, like the nature of modern communications systems, tends to offer the terrorist either parity or local superiority. The range and accuracy of modern small arms enable one man to strike from a distant and protected position. Automatic weapons enable him to reach many victims in a short time. Above all, modern explosives and modern fuses and remote control devices make it possible for a single terrorist to threaten or cause extensive damage and appalling casualties with only a minimum risk to himself. In other words, within the environment which concerns him, the technology of armament has provided the terrorist with an increasingly favourable 'exchange ratio' of lethal force. One horrifying possibility now to be considered is that he may be able to increase that exchange ratio to an almost unimaginable extent by exploiting nuclear materials and technology to make either a crude nuclear weapon or, at least, a device for dispersing lethally toxic plutonium within an urban area. The possibility is, in a sense, remote; neither the security efforts of governments nor the difficulties of making a nuclear device are trivial. There should be no doubt, however, that the possibility exists. At least one (unsuccessful) extortionist demand has already been based upon a (fictitious) claim to have constructed a nuclear weapon.[6] If other and better-founded terrorist threats of nuclear destruction are not to follow, this is one area in which democratic societies will have to look very hard at the historical tendency of technological progress to tip the balance of relevant force in the terrorist's favour.

When all is said and done, the basis for the strength of contemporary terrorists is obvious enough: the powerful weapons and the highly efficient communications and logistic systems of modern technology directed with the skill and knowledge imparted by modern education against the wide range of extremely valuable and very vulnerable targets characteristic of modern industrial society. All of this the processes of development have themselves thrust into the terrorist's hands. The strength of the terrorist is not, however, the power of terror; the latter, even if founded upon strength, exists in the mind of the society with which the terrorist is at war. Finally, therefore, we come back, as we should, to sociology and politics. In the 'Western' democracies, we have chosen, freely and consciously, to construct a system which is both particularly vulnerable to terrorism and peculiarly handicapped in responding to it. We have rejected hierarchical authority based on innate rights in favour of authority based upon efficient performance and upon conformity to a set of general norms which deprecate violence. We attach an extremely high value to individual life and to the unimpaired possession of general liberty in a variety of forms, including liberty of movement and information. We have striven to diffuse knowledge, skill, and political power as widely as possible within our societies. At the same time, in our desire for economic progress, we have tended to create societies in which social and technical change have outpaced institutional evolution, and the pressures of political alienation on disaffected individuals are consequently high. We have so far been prepared to pay that price and other prices for maintaining the system of social democracy which we have chosen. We should not close our eyes to the fact that one such price is that, in our willing vulnerability to its threats and actions, it is we who give terror its undoubted power. If we ignored that, we might inadvertently derogate from our fundamental values in seeking to become less susceptible to terrorism. That, however, would be to concede far more power to terror than it deserves or can otherwise obtain.

NOTES & REFERENCES

[1] Hannah Arendt, *On Violence* (New York, Harvest Books, 1970), pp. 55-6. The mutually exclusive relationship between 'power' and 'terror' asserted in this extraordinary statement can only, to be fair, be derived from Dr. Arendt's idiosyncratic attempt (pp 44-6) to define 'power,' 'strength,' 'force,' 'authority,' and 'violence' in ways which serve her own thesis, even at the expense of dissociating words from their conceptual foundations and converting them into mere algebraic symbols to be deployed at will.
[2] Arleigh Burke, 'Power and Peace,' reprinted from *Orbis* in F.R. Barnett *et al.,eds,* *Peace and War in the Modern Age: Promises, Myths and Realities* (Garden City NY, Anchor Books, 1965), p 19.
[3] The Advanced Societies: Revolution or Devolution?' *International Journal*, XXVIII (summer 1973), 403-17.
[4] The Rt Hon Roy Jenkins, MP, speaking in the British House of Commons, 25 November 1974.
[5] Arendt, *On Violence*, p 48.
[6] In Orlando, Florida, on 27 October 1970; see Mason Willrich and Theodore B. Taylor, *Nuclear Theft: Risks and Safeguards* (Cambridge, Mass, 1974), p 80.

Pierre does not consider international terrorism a transitory phenomenon and is concerned with methods of coping. After reviewing terrorists' motivations, he examines the governmental response to actual cases, early progress at the United Nations, and specific applications of international law to skyjacking and kidnapping. Particularly interesting are his policy suggestions for proper political response.

Reprinted by permission from *Orbis,* a journal of world affairs, published by the Foreign Policy Research Institute, Volume XIX, Winter 1976, #4.

The Politics of International Terrorism

by ANDREW J. PIERRE   III.

International terrorism is a new, growing and increasingly important phenomenon in present-day world politics. Hardly a week now goes by without the hijacking of an airplane across national boundaries, or the kidnaping of a diplomat or foreign businessman, or some other violent incident in the name of a political cause.

Lydda Airport, outside Tel Aviv, May 30, 1972: A group of Japanese terrorists belonging to the Rengo Sekigun, or Red Army, stepped off a plane and indiscriminately killed twenty-seven people, most of whom were Puerto Ricans commencing a Holy Land pilgrimage. First contacted by the Popular Front for the Liberation of Palestine in North Korea, the Japanese had been flown from Tokyo to Lebanon for several months' training in guerrilla camps, and were then sent to Paris, Frankfurt and Rome to await their mission. They were equipped with Czechoslovakian automatic weapons acquired in Italy but financed with Libyan money.

Munich, the Olympic games, September 5, 1972: Members of the Black September organization attacked the quarters of Israeli athletes, resulting in the death of eleven, some as they were to be flown out as hostages.

Campana, Argentina, December 6, 1973: A Marxist guerrilla group known as the People's Revolutionary Army kidnaped the American manager of an Exxon refinery, releasing him four months later for a ransom of $14.2 million in cash purportedly to be distributed to the poor for food, clothing and medicine.

Amsterdam, July 24, 1974: A Japanese jumbo jet en route to Tokyo was hijacked by Palestinian terrorists and blown up in Tripoli, Libya.

Dubai, November 21, 1974: A British Airways VC-10, on a stopover between Brunei and London, was hijacked by the Matyr Abou Mahmoud squad, a Palestinian splinter group opposed to Yasir Arafat. After asking for the release of jailed terrorists in the Netherlands and Egypt, and killing one German passenger, the hijackers and some released terrorists surrendered to authorities in Tunis and were subsequently turned over to the PLO.

Cordoba, Argentina, February 28, 1975: The U.S. consular agent, John Patrick Egan, was shot to death by leftist Montoneros guerrillas in an abortive plot to force the release of imprisoned colleagues.

Kuala Lumpur, August 4, 1975: Five Japanese Red Army terrorists shot their way into the American Embassy and seized fifty-three hostages. The incident was terminated three days later after another five terrorists were released from jail in Japan and all made their way by air to asylum in Libya.

These examples are only some of the better known among hundreds of such incidents. To give an approximate idea of the growth of international terrorism, in the twenty years before 1969 there was an average of five hijackings per year; in the early 1970s the average was over sixty annually. The past six years have witnessed more than 500 major acts of international terrorism including over sixty-five kidnapings with international ramifications.

There is nothing new about terrorism per se. The term first came into modern usage during the Reign of Terror in revolutionary France. It commonly refers to the threat of violence and the use of fear to coerce, persuade or gain public attention. Terror has been used by ideologies of both the Right and the Left, by the former to repress a population and by the latter to win self-determination and independence. Terror has been used by governments as an instrument of state as well as by guerrillas or insurgents as an instrument of subversion.[1]

The concept of *international* terrorism is more difficult to endow with a universally accepted definition. In this analysis it will refer to acts of violence across national boundaries, or with clear international repercussions, often within the territory or involving the citizens of a third party to a dispute. Thus it is to be distinguished from *domestic* terrorism of the sort that has taken place in Ulster, the Soviet Union or South Africa, Admittedly, the line is often thin between terror which is essentially domestic and that possessing a clear international character.

International terrorism is usually, though not exclusively, political in intent and carried out by nongovernmental groups, although they may receive financial and moral support from nation-states. Many of the Palestinian Liberation Organization (PLO) terrorist activities have taken place outside the boundaries of Israel, have been financed or abetted by some Arab states, and have affected nationals of third countries. Most of the victims have been innocent bystanders, such as the American tourists machine-gunned in the waiting room of Athens airport. (The terrorists thought the tourists were bound for Israel, although in fact they were about to board a plane to New York.) Targets are often selected because of their connection to a foreign state, i.e., diplomats and foreign businessmen, or because they have become symbols of international interdependence, such airlines with overseas routes or multinational corporations.

Due to its international character, this form of terrorism is of particular concern to the world community. Repressive or violent activities totally within national boundaries may be of real and valid concern, but they are obviously less amenable to pressure and change through international action by means of diplomacy or law. Moreover, the motivations of international terrorists are often related to the world community and public opinion abroad. The attacks upon Maalot and other towns in northern Israel in 1974 were designed, by the admission of the Al Fatah, to gain the Palestinians a place at any forthcoming Geneva negotiations on the Middle East.

It is unlikely that international terrorism is a passing and transitory phenomenon. The trend toward the weakening of central authority in governments, the rise in ethnic and subnational sentiments, and the increasing fractionalization of the global political process point toward its growth as a form of political protest and persuasion. Classic balance of power diplomacy is of little utility in dealing with it, for violent acts of small groups of people, or individuals, are difficult for governments to control. International terrorism is likely to continue and to expand because in the minds of many of its perpetrators it has proven to be "successful."

Technological change and growth account for much of the new strength and disruptive capacity of terrorist groups. Television gives the terrorist instant access to the world's living rooms, thereby enabling him to draw global attention to his cause. The mobility offered by the modern jet aircrafts allows him to strike at will almost anywhere in the world and then move on to safe asylum. Hence, advances in technology have made it possible for a large society to be directly affected by a small band of terrorists.

Yet the increasing frequency of international terrorism is only beginning to be understood and has thus far received relatively little sustained, analytic attention. We are at the rudimentary stages of learning to cope with it. In this article we will examine the response to international terrorism as it has evolved in the practie of governments, at the United Nations where it has been identified as a major item of international concern, and through the processes of international law. Policy suggestions will be made for the future. But first, in order to understand him better, we must look at what it is that moves and motivates the terrorist.

There is no simple explanation for the causes of international terrorism, nor is there common agreement on its purposes and ends. Perceptions about the legitimacy of the means vary dramatically. What to one man is an outrageous act of lawlessness and immorality—e.g., the shooting of innocent passengers on a hijacked Pan American plane in Rome, the assassination of the German ambassador in Guatemala, or the murder of apartment dwellers at Qiryat Shemona—appears to another as an unfortunate but necessary step toward achieving a political goal rooted in existing or perceived injustice and deprivation. As we will see later, these differing perceptions have been transformed into the diverging attitudes of governments at the United Nations and elsewhere.

Motivations for international terrorism vary from case to case and are often complex, but their roots can be discerned in one or more of the following profiles:

(1) The terrorist is dedicated to a political goal which he sees as one of transcendent merit. The aim of the *fedayeen* (Arabic for "self-sacrificers") has been to gain political salience for the Palestinian cause. By making their goal appear viable to the Arab world, they have received financial and political assistance from Moslem states that support, or feel compelled to support, their cause. The Tupamaros in Uruguay and the People's Revolutionary Army (ERP) in Argentina have sought popular support through th widespread use of terrorist tactics that induce the government to react harshly and therefore appear oppressive in its response.[2]

(2) The terrorist seeks attention and publicity for his cause. The world becomes his stage as contemporary media enable him to dramatize his goals effectively and attempt to win over public opinion. A display of determination and devotion to the cause focus world attention upon it and may induce sympathy. In an age seemingly lacking in heroics, a cause for which an individual is prepared to sacrifice his life appears to some as worthy of support. Without the flamboyant terrorist acts of recent years the Palestinian issue would probably have remained relatively neglected and would be ranked lower on the international agenda than it is today. In this sense the PLO has achieved considerable success.

(3) The terrorist aims to erode support for the established political leadership or to undermine the authority of the state by destroying normality, creating uncertainty, polarizing a country, fostering economic discord and generally weakening the fabric of society. Attacks on foreign business firms, such as multinational corporations and their executives in Latin America, have forced them to reduce or close down their operations, as in the case of IBM and the Ford Motor Company, thereby creating unemployment and fanning discontent among the population that can be channeled into activities against the government. Attacks on civil aircraft and in the lounges of airports have sought to reduce air travel and tourism to Israel through psychological disruption and the spread of fear. Sometimes the intent is to provoke a government to ill-judged meas-

ures of repression that will alienate public opinion.

(4) The terrorist's actions can be a measure of deep frustration when there is no legitimate way to redress grievances. It may be an act of desperation when a political impasse has been reached. As such, terrorism can be a sign of fundamental weakness as well as of momentary strength. Zeal and determination often compensate for an inherent position of weakness, for not having full backing for one's political aims. At the same time terrorism can be perceived as a patriotic deed. Palestinian perpetrators of terrorism—those who survive—return home as heroes to their people.

(5) The terrorist may seek to liberate his colleagues in foreign jails. Aircraft hijacking appears to be an especially popular way of securing the release of prisoners. In September 1972 three members of the Ustashi, a Croatian terrorist organization, by hijacking an SAS airliner forced the Swedish government to release from prison six Croats who had been convicted in the murder of the Yugoslav ambassador in Stockholm. The next month, a Lufthansa flight from Beirut to Ankara was hijacked to Zagreb and the plane released only after Arab terrorists in West German prisons had been set free.

(6) Finally, the terrorist may desire money so as to buy arms and finance his organization. Some claim that they want to distribute food and shelter to the poor and needy. The kidnaping of foreign executives for ransom has become endemic in Latin America in recent times. Because corporations are willing, if forced, to pay substantial amounts to secure the release of their executives or avoid the sabotage of their plants, terrorism can be lucrative. Such companies as Amoco, Peugeot and Pepsico are reported to have paid large ransoms to terrorists in Argentina. Some demands are for perceived just causes, while some, as in Mexico, can take on the form of banditry. Sometimes appearance is deceptive: at the Bank of America in Beirut a representative of Douglas Aircraft was shot by ordinary bank robbers posing as *fedayeen*.[3]

Modern society has become highly vulnerable to the terrorist deed. The crowded environment of the urban metropolis presents a "soft" target. Mass disruption of ordinary activities could be readily achieved through tampering with the electrical grid system, or by poisoning or polluting a city's water supply. In case of a more limited aim, the new sealed-window office building is subject to chemical and biological contamination through the air ventilation system. Poisonous powder on subway tracks can spread noxious germs throughout parts of a city. Such activities could be highly successful in generating mass fear and social disintegration.

Technology is making efficient tools available to terrorists. Ingenious timing and detonating devices are increasing the capacity for selective violence. Particularly worrisome is the prospect of civilian airliners being shot at by portable hand-held surface-to-air missiles as they land at or take off from airports. In January 1975, Arab terrorists with bazookas attempted to destroy El-Al airliners while on the runway at Orly field in

Paris. Heathrow Airport in London was twice surrounded last year by tanks and troops following reports that Arab terrorists planned to use Soviet-made SAM-7 missiles to bring down an aircraft. These missiles, which are only fifty-four inches long and can be dismantled and packed in a small suitcase, had reportedly been smuggled into Brussels from Libya; some were also found in an Arab apartment just three miles from Rome's Leonardo da Vinci Airport. Another danger is terror by mail—on one occasion the secretary of the defense attaché at the British Embassy in Washington was maimed by a letter-bomb.

The risk of nuclear materials being stolen and used by terrorist groups is also to be taken seriously. The growth in use of nuclear reactors to generate electrical power will yield large amounts of fissionable materials in the form of plutonium that can be used to manufacture nuclear explosives or weapons with relative ease. Should terrorists succeed in diverting such materials to their purposes, not to speak of the real possibility of stealing nuclear weapons, they would acquire fearsome means with which to threaten communities and governments.[4]

Clearly, the vulnerability and fragility of contemporary society, in combination with the availability of sophisticated technology, increases the potential for disruptive activities. Moreover, modern communication aids the terrorist in his search for publicity by making possible detailed, on-the-spot coverage of his acts even when they occur in remote parts of the world. His ability to count on the media to dramatize and instantaneously inform the world of his activities—and thereby his cause—should not be underrated as a stimulus and an incentive.

COPING WITH INTERNATIONAL TERRORISM

Dealing with terrorism has become a problem of some magnitude and urgency, and is increasingly recognized as a challenge to the community of nations. Yet the political dynamics of international terrorism make coping with it an extremely difficult and subtle task. The need will not be limited to responding to terrorism or deterring it with the threat of punishment. Of equal importance—some would argue, far greater—is the need to prevent it by treating its underlying root causes.

This is the clear lesson of the debate on terrorism in the United Nations. Following the tragedy at the Munich Olympics, Secretary-General Kurt Waldheim asked the Twenty-seventh General Assembly to consider "measures to prevent international terrorism and other forms of violence which endanger or take innocent human lives or jeopardize fundamental freedoms." The Assembly agreed to his request, but amended it to include "the study of the underlying causes of those forms of terrorism and acts of violence which lie in misery, frustration, grievance and despair and which cause some people to sacrifice human lives, including their own, in an attempt to effect radical changes."

Debate in the Sixth Committee of the General Assembly and in a specially appointed thirty-five-state Ad Hoc Committee on International

Terrorism brought out wide divergencies in perceptions of the problem. The principal interest of many of the developing countries was to avoid anything that could be used to suppress, or deny the legitimacy of, national liberation movements. Because many member-states had themselves been born out of rebellion and revolution, it was argued that condemnation of others who might be following similar courses, e.g., Palestinians, would be wrong and incongruous. This view was widely shared by African and Arab as well as many Asian countries. Some insisted that any consideration of international terrorism must begin with the condemnation of "state terrorism" as practiced by governments. Thus the Syrian Arab Republic said it was convinced "that the main cause of violence is the colonialist and imperialist policies and practices, as well as the crimes, of racist regimes against peoples.[5]

The principal proposal placed before the United Nations has been an American draft of a "Convention for the Prevention and Punishment of Certain Acts of International Terrorism." Wisely, the convention is narrowly drawn and does not attempt to deal with all acts of terrorism. In no way does it cover domestic terrorism designed to alter the political order within a single country. Rather, it focuses on the "export" of violence to third countries and innocent parties, undertaken by persons who kill, seriously assault or kidnap other persons in such a manner as to commit an offense of "international significance." According to Article I, it would be limited to acts in which each of four separate conditions apply: The act is committed or takes effect outside the territory of a state of which the alleged offender is a national; is committed or takes effect outside the territory of the state against which the act is directed; is committed neither by nor against a member of the armed forces of a state in the course of military activities; and is intended to damage the interest of or obtain concessions from a state or an international organization.[6] It would therefore not apply to acts of terrorism committed by a "freedom fighter" struggling within his country in a war of national liberation, but would be pertinent to most of the major international terrorist incidents of recent times.

Despite its limited approach, the convention failed to receive general support at the United Nations. The more radical view, most often espoused by African and Arab governments, held that terrorism was part of the struggle for national liberation and the right of self-determination, and therefore should not be considered an international offense. This argument was also made by Yasir Arafat in his speech at the UN when he equated his struggle with that of George Washington against the British colonialists. Moderate countries acknowledged the need to address the problem but emphasized the necessity to deal with long-term solutions and the grievances that lead to terrorism. Even West European governments were reluctant to take action. Debate within the United Nations has thus far led to no productive results. Experience suggests that while the majority of countries in the world body acknowledge the danger spreading terrorism poses for international order, the politics of international terrorism are such that many countries are still more willing to condone than to condemn it.

SKYJACKING

It may be that progress can be more readily in coping with specific types of international terrorism, such as aerial piracy or the kidnaping of diplomats. The case of aircraft hijacking is instructive, for within the past year incidents have decreased considerably as a result of security measures taken unilaterally by a number of countries, as well as a bilateral agreement between Cuba and the United States. Progress achieved in this way, however, has been outside of efforts to deal with terrorism on a worldwide level.

The rash of skyjacking that began in 1968 produced two conventions on this aspect of terrorism: the Hague convention of 1970 for the Suppression of Unlawful Seizure of Aircraft[7] and the Montreal convention of 1971 for the Suppression of Unlawful Acts Against the Safety of Civil Aviation.[8] Both are concerned with aerial piracy, the former requiring that countries either extradite or prosecute hijackers; the latter requiring that any kind of sabotage of aircraft, such as blowing up planes on the ground, also be dealt with by prosecution or extradition. An earlier accord, the Tokyo convention of 1963,[9] requires countries to return a plane and its passengers after it has been hijacked.

These conventions have proven to be weak legal instruments, and a considerable number of states have not signed them. Some of the nonsignatories provide safe haven for hijackers. The existence of sanctuaries, or "hijack havens," primarily in the Middle East, encourages political terrorists to assume—usually correctly—that they can escape punishment.[10]

Accordingly, Canada and the United States have urged the 128-country International Civil Aviation Organization (ICAO) to adopt sanctions against states that grant asylum to hijackers or fail to penalize them. At a meeting of the ICAO held in Rome late in 1973 for the purpose of protecting international civil aviation and strengthening existing conventions, special attention was given to hijacking; yet, while various proposals were made to curb aerial terrorism, the conference terminated in stalemate. As in the case of the UN deliberations on international terrorism, hijacking was seen as more of a political than a criminal act. The Arab-Israeli dispute unfortunately overshadowed the conference, which convened shortly after Israel intercepted a Lebanese commercial airliner outside Beirut and forced it to land in Israel; the Israeli action was condemned by the ICAO. In its dismay at the failure of the ICAO conference, the International Association of Airline Pilots threatened a pilot boycott of its own on nations tolerating hijackers. At its annual conference in March 1975 in Vienna it called for the adoption of a "no sanctuary" policy so that hijackers would know that they would be arrested, tried in court, and punished wherever they went.

A large proportion of the American aircraft that have been successfully hijacked since the mid-1960s have been taken to Havana. This recourse has now been effectively eliminated by an agreement reached between Cuba and the United States through the good offices of Switzerland. The reception a hijacker can now expect will be less hospitable, the Castro Government having agreed that such persons will be either extradited or prosecuted. Presumably Fidel Castro became tired of serving as host to ordinary criminals and psychopaths acting without political commitment. A little noticed exception, however, provides for "persons . . . being sought for strictly political reasons . . . in real or imminent danger of death without a viable alternative for leaving the country."[11] Another set of measures that has reduced hijacking in the United States and some other countries has been the screening of passengers and luggage for hand weapons, and additional airport security programs.

KIDNAPING

Another form of international terrorism that has grown dramatically has been the kidnaping of diplomats. Officials representing their governments abroad become elite targets. Host governments feel a special obligation toward their well-being, an obligation firmly rooted in diplomatic custom and international law. Terrorist groups are therefore effectively able to use diplomats as hostages in seeking the release of jailed colleagues, or in publicizing their domestic political struggle around the world. A kidnaping may give a small group leverage with a government out of all proportion to its true significance.

The first important diplomatic kidnaping in the present era was that of C. Burke Elbrick, the U.S. ambassador to Brazil, in 1969. He was released in exchange for fifteen political prisoners who were flown to Mexico and subsequently made their way to Cuba. Since then there have been several dozen diplomatic kidnapings, usually of West European (Germans and Britons are particularly in demand) or American officials, almost all in Latin America, and especially in Brazil, Argentina, Uruguay and Guatemala; some have ended in assassination. In the past decade thirteen American diplomats have been assassinated; twelve have been wounded; twenty others have been kidnaped and later released. Particularly striking was the kidnaping and death in 1973 of the American ambassador to the Sudan, his deputy and a Belgian diplomat at the hands of Black September terrorists following their demand for the release of Arab guerrillas held in Jordan and Israel, the freeing of Robert Kennedy's assassin, Sirhan Sirhan, and the liberation of members of the Baader-Meinhof gang in jail in West Germany.

As it became evident that Latin America was specially susceptible to this type of international terrorism, the Organization of American States in 1971 drafted a convention for the protection of diplomats. The desire to give it universal application subsequently led the United Nations International Law Commission to suggest a similar convention, which was adopted in amended form by the General Assembly in December 1973.

Under its provision, the kiddnaping, murder or attack of diplomats and other "internationally protected persons" is to result in either extradition or prosecution of the offender.[12]. This convention is now open for signature and is without doubt a forward step. The limits of its usefulness in helping to resolve the entire problem of terrorist kidnaping and assault are evident, however, when one considers that the majority of such incidents occur not to diplomats but to businessmen. Beyond common-sense precautionary measures, no effective way has been found to prevent the kidnaping of businessmen.

WHAT IS TO BE DONE?

The remedies for international terrorism sought at the United Nations and through international legal conventions, though commendable, are of only limited utility. The problem is not so much one of law as one of politics. The evidence suggests that there are a substantial number of states, or groups within them, that view terrorism as an acceptable answer to perceived oppression—or feel politically restrained from saying otherwise—and are therefore prepared to condone it. Because international terrorism is a form of political violence and ultimately requires political solutions, an effective response must come to terms with its political dimensions. Steps for coping with terrorism will therefore need to include both *measures of prevention* and *measures of deterrence*. Only through a combination of the two, consciously pursued in parallel, can we hope to reduce and eventually eliminate this spreading epidemic.

Prevention would require giving more attention than we now do to economic, social and political grievances and sources of frustration. Individuals are more likely to turn to violence if they lose hope, if life seems not worth living, and if the "system" appears to be unresponsive to legitimate protest. Prevention would attempt to eradicate the conditions that spawn terrorism by looking for long-term solutions. It would seek to find and strengthen common interests, and constructively channel remaining discontent. At a minimum, it would seek to offer alternative, nonviolent forms of protest.

This, quite obviously, has implications for the whole spectrum of U.S. foreign policy, ranging from our relatively modest level of foreign aid to our seemingly close relations, on occasion, with unattractive political regimes. With specific respect to alleviating international terrorism, we should in certain cases encourage our embassies abroad to know of, and where possible give a fair hearing to, dissident groups which are not outside the law, for example in Latin America. This would involve showing proper regard for such groups without necessarily giving them official endorsement. We should be specially sympathetic in countries where dissident groups are seeking social justice and other ideals with which we can associate. This would be a way of rewarding dissidents who have a just cause and who do *not* resort to terrorist activities. At the same time, we should bear in mind that terrorism may also be used by governments. Measures to curb international terrorism would be given wider acceptability and be considerably enhanced if they were coupled with concern for "state terrorism" by nondemocratic regimes that use such tactics to remain in power or to repress dissidence.

It may be instructive to ponder the case of the Palestinians, the most conspicuous producers of international terrorism. Until recently they were, or felt that they were, forgotten men. After Israel's victory in the 1967 war, the world seemed to have lost interest in their cause. At the same time, many Palestinians remained year after year in crowded, squalid refugee camps. Little attention was paid to their economic and political grievances. The Arab states did little to further their interests; Israel in effect refused to admit of their existence. To this day, the United States has not opened a real dialogue with Palestinian leaders. Although there may have been valid overriding reasons, the Palestinians are only too aware that neither Dr. Kissinger nor his top aides met with them during their repeated swings through the Middle East while conducting step-by-step negotiations in the aftermath of the Yom Kippur war.

Spectacular acts of terrorism, reprehensible and tragic as they have been, have now helped in focusing the world's attention on a solution to their problem. For the first time, there is serious attention being given to the creation of some type of Palestinian state encompassing the West Bank of the Jordan River and the Gaza Strip. The need to preserve the "national rights" of the Palestinians in a peace settlement is now acknowledged by the Arab states. Acting out of frustration and with relatively little to lose, the Palestinians have effectively used terrorism to their advantage. Meanwhile, unfortunately, the habit has developed. On the one hand, terrorism has been used to support the demand that the Palestinian Liberation Organization be invited to any Geneva talks. On the other, the radical Palestinians, who reject an Arab-Israeli settlement except on their own terms, have used terrorism to disrupt an accommodation. This was the avowed purpose of the Al Fatah extremists who landed on the beach and seized a Tel Aviv hotel in March 1975. Following the second Sinai disengagement agreement, PLO extremists displayed their displeasure with Anwar Sadat by seizing Egypt's envoy in Madrid.

Looking back, one can justifiably ask whether farsighted meaures of preventive diplomacy might not have succeedd in keeping the terrorist genie in the bottle in the Middle East. To the extent that concern over terrorism is a component of our Middle East policy, it would seem desirable at some stage to open channels of communication with Palestinian leaders—in particular, the more moderate ones—with the hope that this might create pressures among the Palestinians either to isolate extremists or keep them under control.

Prevention, however, is a long-term process that must be continuously pursued. In the short run, measures of *deterrence* are more likely to be effective in coping with international terrorism. There are a number of specific measures that should now be undertaken by nations acting in concert.

First, and most important, acts of terrorism, especially those involving random killing, should not continue to go unpunished. Although hard data are not available, it is quite clear that Arab terrorists have been repeatedly set free by governments in Western Europe and the Middle East. Of the more than 150 Palestinian terrorist who have been arrested in Western Europe in the past five years, all but nine, according to one estimate, have been quietly released with or without trial. Terrorists who make their way back to the Middle East, either on hijacked aircraft or by transfer to authorities in Kuwait, Libya or South Yemen, have been repeatedly released, sometimes with a vague but unconvincing promise of a trial by the PLO, which at present has no legal basis to set up a court.

There are perfectly understandable reasons for this pattern of non-punishment. Government fear acts of reprisal. They are aware that imprisoning terrorists invites new acts of terrorism, including the seizure of hostages designed to secure the release of colleagues in jail. This has already occurred. Moreover, given the present oil situation and the risk of a selective boycott, countries dependent upon Middle East sources of supply are likely to wish to avoid offending Arab sensibilities and will give priority to such types of considerations. Within the Arab world, where there is admiration for the courage and determination of "freedom-fighters" even among those who disapprove of their tactics, governments tend to back away from the difficult political decision imprisonment would involve. Accordingly Sudan, after giving repeated assurances that the eight Black September terrorists who murdered the American ambassador and his deputy in Khartoum would be punished, eventually bowed to Arab pressure and released them in spite of a court sentence to life imprisonment.

Washington was right, in my view, to make a vigorous protest in this case and recall its new ambassador. We should seek to convince governments in Western Europe, the Middle East and elsewhere that terrorism is a threat to the safety of international society and must be dealt with through due process of law, judiciously but firmly. If terrorists are detained, others may be discouraged from following the same course. Once terrorists see that their activities will be costly, they might be persuaded to seek less violent means of venting their grievances.

Second, deterrence would be enhanced if specific sanctions were imposed against countries that shelter hijackers and saboteurs of planes by granting safe asylum. These could include a suspension of commercial air traffic to countries that let hijackers off scot free, or a boycott of their airliners by withholding permission to land. Since the ICAO has failed to take effective action, this could be accomplished by a series of bilateral accords providing for extradition or prosecution, using the Cuban-American agreement as a model. If a consensus could be reached that countries protecting hijackers will be boycotted by civil aviation, and that hijackers will be punished, a major step would be taken toward deterring this form of terrorism.

Related to this is the question of the availability of aircraft in response to terrorist demands for transportation out of a country and the granting of landing rights for refueling purposes. It has become the custom of terrorists to expect that they can flee by demanding a plane and a crew. This should now be reversed, with governments agreeing among themselves, and publicly declaring beforehad, that they will not provide aircraft for the use of terrorists or even temporary landing rights. The Japanese government has recently moved in this direction, following its embarrassment in having made available a Japanese Air Lines plane to transport five Red Army terrorists and five colleagues, who had been imprisoned, from Malaysia to Libya.

Third, countries that believe in the need to control international terrorism should cooperate on practical precautionary steps that might be undertaken together. Chief among these is the sharing of intelligence data and other information about terrorist organizations, their membership, structure, leaders, motivations, and so on. The United States has established a cabinet-level committee and appointed a Special Assistant to the Secretary of State for Combating Terrorism. His activities involve both contingency planning and coordinating action once a terrorist incident develops; a few other countries, including West Germany, have now established similar offices. Like-minded governments should be encouraged to set up bureaus for this purpose and develop cooperation among them. Technological aids, such as devices for improving airport security throughout the world, should also be shared. Nations possessing atomic reactors should tighten existing precautions to safeguard against the theft or diversion of nuclear materials. Some international cooperation along this line is already in progress, but it should be broadened and deepened. Most important, the states that share a common perception of the dangers of international terrorism should act now to concert their efforts, without waiting for the agreement of all member-states of the United Nations.

This intergovernmental cooperation is especially important in light of increasing evidence of transnational linkages between terrorist groups with varied purposes, even located in different continents. Such collaboration often exists to facilitate the flow of arms and information. The Japanese Red Army, for instance, has established ties with the PLO, and in Europe it has had contacts with a number of terrorist groups, including the Baader-Meinhof group in West Germany, while operating for a time out of a perfume shop in the center of Paris. There have also been reports of close contacts between the Irish Republican Army and the ETA, a Basque separatist group in Spain. International linkages of this type can be of considerable practical significance to terrorist organizations in increasing their outreach and effectiveness. Although one cannot yet speak of a "brotherhood" of terrorists, in the past two years a number of "networks" have been uncovered. They should be combated through international cooperation among as many countries as possible. In this manner the very internationalism of terrorist movements might contribute to their undoing.

Fourth, the communication media have a special responsibility in taking care not to encourage acts of terrorism and violence by giving them

H.1-6

undue publicity. Such acts often possess a particular aspect of sensationalism designed to attract public attention out of proportion to the real importance of the event. Terrorism is usually directed at the watching audience, rather than the real victims. Although, obviously, newsworthy incidents of terrorism cannot and should not be suppressed, television and the press must avoid being manipulated by terrorists for their own advantage. This suggests a need for restraint and prudence by the Fourth Estate in its reportage of terrorism.

Fifth, in regard to American policy, we might re-examine our present blanket "no ransom" policy in dealing with international terrorism. After the Khartoum incident President Nixon firmly stated that the United States would not pay ransom, reasoning that "the nation that compromises with the terrorist today could well be destroyed by terrorism tomorrow." But the evidence is hardly available or clear that this would be the case, and the analogy between political terrorism and ordinary criminal blackmail ("extortion breeds extortion") may be somewhat misleading. If a Boeing 747 filled with 350 American citizens was about to be blown up, would Washington still refuse to buy their safety? If the chairman of the Senate Foreign Relations Committee was kidnaped by Tupamaros, would the U.S. government not be willing to release a few foreign terrorists, or urge another government to give in to such terrorist demands?

Many countries have shown greater flexibility in the face of a grave situation, as France did in ransoming her ambassador to Somalia for $100,000 [in 1976]. Even Israel, which also has a "no ransom" policy, was prepared to set it aside in order to save the lives of eighty-five children at Maalot, Premier Golda Meir explaining that she would not resist "on the backs of our children." We might therefore be more flexible than our declared policy would indicate, judging each case on its own merits and negotiating when the situation seems to call for it. The former U.S. Ambassador to Tanzania, W. Beverly Carter, was penalized after he assisted in the release of four American students in August 1975 by helping a private rescue team make contact with the kidnapers. Surely some latitude should be accorded the ambassador on the scene so that he can draw a sensible balance between the requirements of general policy and the need for humane action. It should be noted, moreover, that American corporations have concluded that they will pay ransom, if necessary, in order to save the lives of their executives overseas. Large sums have indeed been paid in recent years—sometimes, it has regrettably turned out, to extortionists masking their aim in political rhetoric.

Finally, the community of states should seek as broad a consensus as possible establishing that acts of international terrorism—especially indiscriminate violence when the victims are innocent third parties sitting in planes, walking the streets or resting at home—are, regardless of motive, beyond acceptable norms of behavior. It should be made clear that when the terrorist deliberately inflicts death and destruction on the innocent, rather than on the enemy, he is crossing an ethical threshold and com mitting a crime against humanity as a whole. Even if political reasons dim the prospects for a UN convention on the "export" of terrorism, or early ICAO action on hijacking is unlikely, it should be possible to create a moral climate that will help to deter random violence. In this connection, it might be usful to re-examine a proposal first made in 1937 after the assassination of King Alexander I of Yugoslavia and French Prime Minister Louis Barthou at Marseilles, for the establishment of an International Criminal Court to be granted jurisdiction over terrorist crimes of international character in lieu of national judicial process.[13] Such a court might, in some circumstances, be an appropriate and less political means of handling modern terrorist crimes.

Responding successfully to international terrorism will require both the balm of prevention and the sting of deterrence. It will involve piecemeal coping rather than comprehensive solution. The enduring difficulty will be to reconcile the imperatives of international order and safety with the legitimate grievances that give rise to despair and violence. Moral dilemmas will abound.

We must be prepared to accept the fact that terrorism could become a new form of warfare. With the increasing availability of relatively small and inexpensive means of destruction, a handful of men could have an enormous impact upon states and societies anywhere. Some countries might even prefer to arm and use terrorists to pursue their foreign policy objectives, rather than accept the stigma of direct and visible involvement in a conflict with another state. They might view terrorist activities as a continuation of warfare by other and more effective means, in which the constraints applying to conventional warfare under accepted standards of international behavior and law could be conveniently disregarded. Thus terrorism could be intentionally used to instigate an international incident, to provoke an enemy, to carry out acts of sabotage, or to incite a repressive reaction against a group in a country.

Terrorism is a relatively inexpensive and efficient way of doing a great deal of harm, and doing it without the political embarrassment that can be attached to many overt state actions. In some ways, therefore, it could become an alternative to conventional wars—not necessarily an undesirable step. It is not too early to think creatively about arms control—in the political sense—for international terrorism. Should terrorism continue to grow, as appears likely, it will enter the mainstream of world politics. Then, even more than today, it will present a major political, legal, arms-control and, perhaps above all, moral challenge to us all.

NOTES & REFERENCES

[1] The best theoretical work on terrorism remains E. V. Walter, *Terror and Resistance; A Study of Political Violence* (New York: Oxford University Press, 1969). Most other studies only touch on terrorism in the context of internal conflict or querrilla war. See, for example, J. Bowyer Bell, *The Myth of the Guerrilla* (New York: Alfred Knopf, 1971); Robert Moss, *The War for the Cities* (New York: Coward, McCann and Geoghegan, 1972); Harry Eckstein, *Internal War* (New York: Free Press, 1964). "State terrorism"

50

is discussed in Barrington Moore, Jr., *Terror and Progress in the U.S.S.R.* (Cambridge, Mass.: Harvard University Press, 1954). For two recent studies, see Richard Clutterbuck, *Living with Terrorism* (London: Faber and Faber, 1975) and Brian Jenkins, *International Terrorism: A New Mode of Conflict* (Los Angeles, Calif.: California Seminar on Arms Control and Foreign Policy, Research Paper No. 48, 1975).

[2] See Maria Esther Gilio, *The Tupamaro Guerrillas* (New York: Saturday Review Press, 1972); Jack Davis, *Political Violence in Latin America* (London: International Institute for Strategic Studies, Adelphi Paper No. 85, 1972); Robert Moss, *Urban Guerrilla Warfare* (London: International Institute for Strategic Studies, Adelphi Paper No. 79, 1971).

[3] Fascinating insights into the terrorist's frame of mind are to be found in a "minimanual" written by Carlos Marighella, a Brazilian terrorist, five months before he was killed in an ambush. For extracts see *Survival*, March 1971, pp. 95-100.

[4] For the best exposition of this problem, see Mason Willrich and Theodore B. Taylor, *Nuclear Theft: Risks and Safeguards* (Cambridge, Mass.: Ballinger Press, 1974).

[5] United Nations General Assembly, 27th Session, Ad Hoc Committee on International Terrorism, A/AC. 160/2, p. 16.

[6] United Nations General Assembly, 27th Session, Sixth Committee, A/C.6/L., p. 850.

[7] U.S. Department of State, *United States Treaties and Other International Agreements,* Vol. 22, Part 2, 1971, pp. 1641-1684.

[8] *Ibid.,* Vol. 24, Part 1, 1973, pp. 565-602.

[9] *Ibid.,* Vol. 20, Part 3, 1969, pp. 2941-2958.

[10] Interestingly, the Soviet Union, which has its own hijacking problem, has signed the above conventions and generally endorses Western attempts to tighten international laws dealing with aerial piracy. See Y. Kolosov, "Legal Questions of the Security of Civil Aviation," *International Affairs* (Moscow), April 1974, pp. 42-46.

[11] *Department of State Bulletin,* March 5, 1973, pp. 260-262.

[12] Convention on the Prevention and Punishment of Crimes Against Internationally Protected Persons, Including Diplomatic Agents, *ibid.,* January 28, 1974, pp. 91-5.

[13] Manley O. Hudson, *International Legislation,* Vol. VII (Dobbs Ferry, N.Y.: Oceana Publications, 1941), pp. 878-893.

Milbank provides working definitions of international and transnational terrorism before reviewing terrorism's trends and directions over the past decade. Particular attention is devoted to statistical examination of terrorist operations in order to develop a data bank for further analysis and forecasting.

Reprinted by permission. Originally published through the Library of Congress as a Research Study of the Central Intelligence Agency, in April 1976. The study does not represent a CIA position.

International and Transnational Terrorism: Diagnosis and Prognosis

by DAVID L. MILBANK

I. THE OBJECTIVES AND BOUNDARIES OF INQUIRY

Political violence predates recorded history. As a distinctive form of political violence sporadically employed by rulers and ruled alike, terrorism is probably not much younger—albeit it owes its name and subsequent conceptual flowering to the French Reign of Terror (1793-1794). Nor is the spill-over of terrorist activity onto the international stage a particularly recent development: witness the stir caused by various anarchist groups operating in Europe and North America in the late 19th and early 20th centuries as well as by the behavior of a few of their more self-interested political contemporaries. Some 70 years ago, for example, a renegade Moroccan chieftain foreshadowed a tactic favored by a number of terrorist groups today by kidnapping two foreign businessmen (one English, the other of dubious American citizenship) in a successful effort to get England and the US to pressure France into forcing the Sultan to accede to a long list of demands—including a substantial ransom, the release of a large number of prisoners, the cession of two territorial districts, and the arrest of a few key enemies.

But despite historical precedents and parallels, modern-day terrorism is very much a function of our times. Advances in technology and growing world interdependence have afforded terrorists new mobility, new targets, new weaponry, and the near certain prospect that their more dramatic acts will receive prompt and world-wide publicity. Moreover, recent changes in the overall political and economic climate have provided terrorists with a somewhat more hospitable environment in which to operate.

Indeed, there has been such an upsurge of terrorist activity in recent years that some observers have warned that we may be entering a veritable age of terrorism. Among other things, there has been a marked increase in the number of active terrorist groups as well as in the number of countries in which they are operating. Internal and international cooperation among terrorist groups has also risen notably. There has been a trend toward bolder and more dramatic actions, with an accompanying escalation of casualties, damage, and demands. And most importantly, perhaps, there has been a quantum jump in terrorist incidents affecting the interests of more than one state.

Not surprisingly, these developments have generated unprecedented interest in terrorism as a subject for serious research and analysis. In sharp contrast with the situation which prevailed only a decade or so ago, existing literature—both open and classified—now offers a wide range of useful insights into the root causes, logic, and characteristic attributes of political terrorism as well as a substantial number of detailed case studies.

The trouble is that the picture which emerges is still confused and incomplete. For one thing, there is as yet no generally accepted definition of terrorism *per se,* much less of its international or transnational variants. For another, much of the work that has been done on terrorism suffers from the limiting effects of narrowly focused tactical concerns or of particularistic institutional and personal biases. And, largely because of these differing perspectives and priorities, little progress has been made toward development of a comprehensive and readily accessible data base. In short, we are still hard put to explain the current state of affairs or to venture firm predictions about the future.

Of necessity, therefore, this study is an exercise in both synthesis and innovation. It is confined to an examination of international and transnational terrorism as defined in Section II below (with primary emphasis on transnational terrorism as, in the short term at least, potentially the more injurious to US interests). Its principal underlying assumptions are three. The first is that the basic societal problems and tensions that can give rise to political violence—and thus to terrorism—are likely to prove particularly intractable in this era of rapid change, growing nationalism and ethnicity, and world-wide economic strains. Such irritants may, in fact, be treated as "givens" in the global environment for many years to come. The reader is forewarned that because of this, and because they have already received considerable scholarly attention, these factors will not be subjected to extensive analysis here.[1]

Corollary to the above, it is assumed that the potential for domestic, international, and transnational terrorism will remain high in the decade ahead and that the scope of the problem will therefore depend primarily on factors affecting the opportunities, alternatives, and behavioral constraints faced by the group actors involved.

Finally, it is postulated that man's *subjective* perception of "reality" serves as the primary determinant of his political behavior. Hence, without neglecting the many factors that have affected—or that may affect—the objective capabilities and options of terrorist groups, this paper repeatedly draws attention to those variables (e.g., cultural heritage, credo, and changes in the overall political environment) that can shape or alter the prisms through which the terrorists concerned view the world around them.

Broadly stated, the objectives of the study are to gain a better understanding of the dynamics and consequences of international and transnational terrorism since 1965, to identify those factors likely to promote or inhibit such activity in the years ahead, and to assess the implications of these findings with respect to U.S. policies and interests. Such goals preclude any effort to gauge the extent of the threat posed to U.S. interests and world order by any particular terrorist group or consortium. Given the host of variables that would have to be considered, that task must remain the province of traditional and painstaking case-by-case analysis. It is hoped, however, that the substantive generalizations and methodological techniques that are set forth below will provide a valuable frame of reference for more definitive treatments of specific aspects of the terrorism problem.

II. ESTABLISHING AN ANALYTICAL FRAMEWORK

Definitions As a first step, it is necessary to cut through some of the semantic and value-generated fog which currently surrounds the concept of terrorism and to spell out precisely what sort of behavior falls within the purview of this study. In part, the existing confusion is attributable to journalistic license and a popular tendency to label terrorist a host of acts in which the element of terror is clearly incidental to other and more pressing objectives. But, as amply illustrated by the tortured and fruitless efforts of a 35-member *ad hoc* UN committee to define (and thereby, in effect, to outlaw) international terrorism not long ago, the heart of the problem lies in differing moral perspectives and priorities.[2] Simply stated, one man's terrorist is another man's freedom fighter.

Since terrorism always involves the deliberate breach of generally accepted bounds for individual or collective violence, it is difficult to define in totally value-free terms. Nevertheless, it can be set in a relatively rigorous and objective perspective. A good way to begin is by quoting a perceptive description of the characteristic attributes of terrorism by one of the leading specialists on the subject.

The threat of violence, individual acts of violence, or a campaign of violence designed primarily to instill fear—to terrorize—may be called terrorism. Terrorism is violence for effect: not only, and sometimes not at all, for the effect on the actual victims of the terrorists. In fact, the victim may be totally unrelated to the terrorists' cause. Terrorism is violence aimed at the people watching. Fear is the intended effect, not the byproduct, of terrorism. That, at least, distinguishes terrorist tactics from mugging and other forms of violent crime that may terrify but are not terrorism.[3]

Political terrorism is, then, the above sort of violence employed in pursuit of political objectives. It is, as claimed by its practitioners, "propaganda of the deed." It is calculated violence aimed at influencing the attitude and behavior of one or more target audiences. Its proximate objectives may include publicity, coercion, extortion, disorientation and despair, provocation of unpopular countermeasures, and (with regard to the terrorists themselves) morale-building. Its ultimate goals can be either concrete (e.g., the seizure or consolidation of political power or the attainment of ethnic self-rule) or nebulous (e.g., the fomenting of worldwide revolution).[4]

The foregoing observations and generalizations form the basis for the definitions of international and transnational terrorism that are employed in this study. These are as follows:

> *Common Characteristics:* The threat or use of violence for political purposes when (1) such action is intended to influence the attitudes and behavior of a target group wider than its immediate victims, and (2) its ramifications transcend national boundaries (as a result, for example, of the nationality or foreign ties of its perpetrators, its locale, the identity of its institutional or human victims, its declared objectives, or the mechanics of its resolution).
>
> *International Terrorism:* Such action when carried out by individuals or groups controlled by a sovereign state.
>
> *Transnational Terrorism:* Such action when carried out by basically autonomous non-state actors, whether or not they enjoy some degree of support from sympathetic states.[5]

Just how meaningful the posited distinction between international and transnational terrorism is likely to be in the longer run is, of course, open to question. But for the time being, at least, the two phenomena do pose questions and problems of a qualitatively different order. For one thing, since it involves the behavior of state actors, international terrorism can in theory be handled and contained within the framework of the existing international system with only minor adjustments. Moreover, its practitioners seem to be somewhat fewer—or, with a few notable exceptions, at least more restrained—than at some other points of time in the recent past. Transnational terrorism, on the other hand, has been growing in both geographic scope and intensity. And the international system is still ill equipped to deal with autonomous non-state actors.

Method At best, discussions of methodology carry the risk of blurring and diluting the analytical thrust of a research paper. But the subject at hand presents something of a special case—one in which a few words about the analytical techniques employed are needed to lay the groundwork for subsequent discussion. For one thing the myriad of factors which bear on terrorist activity dictated adoption of a multi-disciplinary approach. For another, the fuzzy boundaries that separate terrorism from other forms of violence—and the previously cited lack of any generally accepted analytical approach or comprehensive and logically organized data base—required the construction of a relatively detailed framework for screening and ordering the available information.

Briefly, a number of working hypotheses derived from a survey of the existing literature on both terrorism and political violence *per se* were used to generate a list of (1) key group and environmental variables that appear to have affected the scope, nature, and intensity of international and transnational terrorism in recent years, and (2) analytically useful event characteristics. (Those initial hypotheses that survived subsequent testing appear, together with later additions, as judgments and conclusions at various points in this study.)

III. THE PHENOMENA IN RETROSPECT

What, Where, and When? As previously indicated, international and transnational terrorism were not yet matters of much official or academic concern in 1965. In contrast to other forms of political violence, there simply had not been very much of either since the close of World War II—at least not of the sort that made headlines. Moreover, much of what there was had been associated with—and overshadowed by the more important consequences of—clear-cut adversary relationships stemming from either the Cold War or the anti-colonial struggle. For the most part, noncombatant third parties had been left unmolested.

It is true, of course, that two brief flurries of skyjacking had already drawn attention to a potential new problem area. But for the most part, neither had involved more than a few actions that would be classified as terrorism under the definition employed here. The first, in the early 50s, had been comprised almost entirely of Eastern European aircraft commandeered for the sole purpose of escape to the West. And while the second, which extended from the late 50s to the early 60s, had been climaxed by the first postwar hijackings of American airliners (thereby prompting the U.S. to press for a comprehensive international convention covering crimes committed on civilian aircraft engaged in international aviation), it too had been attributable primarily to individuals seeking personal advantage—e.g., expedient transport to or from Cuba or outright extortion—rather than political leverage or impact.

In any event, skyjackings tapered off again in 1963. The overall level of international and transnational terrorist activity remained relatively low through 1966, then turned upward against the backdrop of intensi-

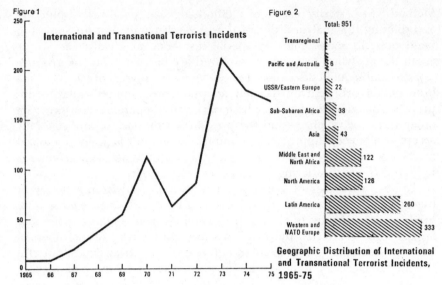

Figure 1

International and Transnational Terrorist Incidents

Figure 2

Total: 951

Transregional	1
Pacific and Australia	6
USSR/Eastern Europe	22
Sub-Saharan Africa	38
Asia	43
Middle East and North Africa	122
North America	126
Latin America	260
Western and NATO Europe	333

Geographic Distribution of International and Transnational Terrorist Incidents, 1965-75

fied Palestinian guerrilla activity that preceded the 1967 Arab-Israeli war. Admittedly, the record up to that point is sketchy. For one thing, the mass media still lacked either the incentive or the technical means for systematic and comprehensive coverage of terrorist incidents-and many undoubtedly went unreported. But even if Figure 1 below substantially understates the number of international and transnational terrorist incidents that occurred in the 1965-1967 period, the international impact of such activity was negligible. Indeed, when the qualitative dimension is added in, 1968 emerges as a watershed year. At that juncture, a combination of Palestinian initiatives and the cumulative impact of the broader environmental trends discussed below seems to have finally sensitized dissident groups throughout the world to their latent and growing potential for effective transnational terrorist activity.

From 1 January 1968 through 31 December 1975, there were at least 913 recorded international and transnational terrorist incidents.[6] Of these, 123 were kidnappings; 31 were barricade and hostage episodes; 375 entailed the use of explosive devices of one type or another; 95 were armed assaults or ambushes; 137 involved the hijacking of an aircraft or other means of transportation; 59 fell under the category of incendiary attack or arson; 48 constituted assassination or murder; and 45 were characterized by other forms of violence. All told, more than 140 terrorist organizations—including a number of fictional entities created to shield the identity of the perpetrators of some particularly shocking or politically sensitive acts—from nearly 50 different countries or disputed territories (e.g., Palestine) have thus far been linked to this activity, and there may have been more.[7] Figure 2 portrays the overall geographic distribution of international and transnational terrorist incidents for the 1965-1975 period.

Despite the widespread and continuing popularity of certain "tradi- tional" forms of violence (e.g., assassinations and highly discriminate bombings), the picture which emerges from the statistics underscores a number of marked regional and time-related variations in the frequency and nature of *transnational* terrorist incidents.[8] Sub-Saharan Africa and large parts of Asia have, for example, been relatively free of such activity. So too has the Soviet/East European region. Latin Americans have demonstrated a particular affinity for kidnapping foreign diplomats and businessmen. On the other hand, except for skyjackings, seemingly indiscriminate and potentially bloody spectaculars—e.g., mass hostage episodes, large bombs in public places, Lod Airport type massacres of innocent bystanders, and the destruction (or attempted destruction) without warning of passenger-carrying aircraft—have most frequently been the province of extremist formations from the Middle East, Europe, and Japan.

For its part, skyjacking reached near epidemic proportions in 1970 only to taper off sharply thereafter. There were, in fact, fewer recorded terrorist skyjackings in all of 1975 than there were in an average month just five years earlier. The dramatic decline in popularity of this particular form of terrorist violence has, however, been partially offset by a rise in equally unsettling barricade and hostage episodes.

Another point brought home by the data examined is that although transnational terrorists have, until recently at least, rarely sought to wring concessions from Washington, American targets—whether human or physical, official or private—have consistently been among the most popular for attack. For example, between mid-1969 and early 1973 (when tightened security and the implications of the U.S.-Cuba agreement made American planes seem less attractive), U.S. aircraft figured in about 30 percent of all skyjackings. Moreover, this ratio is relatively modest in comparison to U.S. experience with some other forms of terrorist activity, especially kidnapping. *Indeed, the available data suggests that over the past eight years, U.S. citizens or U.S. facilities have been victimized in at least one-third of all transnational terrorist incidents.*

The hard fact is that substantial pockets of popular opinion in many parts of the world are prone to identify the U.S. with reaction, intervention, and "neocolonial" exploitation. Hence, American targets have a high symbolic value for "anti-imperialists" of both nationalistic and ideological persuasion. Moreover, such targets also tend to have a high "embarrassment quotient" in relation to the governments of the countries in which the attacks occur and, if different, the governments against which the terrorists levy their demands.

The next-mentioned trend—that toward bolder actions—has been uneven. Moreover, its precise contours defy precise definition for they depend on unavoidably subjective judgments concerning the relative difficulty, risk, and shock value associated with often quite dissimilar incidents. Nevertheless, the inherent dynamics and logic of a campaign of terrorist violence are such that it has a natural propensity to escalate over time. Globally, this has found reflection in the adoption and spread of aggressive new tactics. Locally, it has been manifested in the tendency of certain groups to probe the effective limits of any such innovation that they elect to employ before scaling back on its use or on their associated demands. Thus we have witnessed:

—the multiple skyjacking operation staged by the Popular Front for the Liberation of Palestine in September 1970 which capped the wave of aircraft sezures that had begun two years earlier;[9]

—the all time record for multiple and cumulative diplomatic kidnappings established by the Tupamaros between mid-1970 and early 1971 in their effort to secure the release of about 150 imprisoned collaborators;

—the escalation of the amount of ransom demanded by Argentine terrorists for the release of kidnapped multinational corporation executives from $62,500 in 1971 to a reported figure of over $60 million in 1975.[10]

Because of the complexity of the relationships involved, the sensitive nature of much of the available information, and the questions which are raised with respect to the past and present role of various state actors, the third trend that toward more extensive international cooperation among terrorist groups—deserves detailed examination in a separate research study.

So far, at least, the efforts of various terrorist groups to promote broad regional and inter-regional coordination through the holding of periodic conferences and the formation of such umbrella organizations as Latin America's Revolutionary Coordination Junta (JCR) seem to have generated more smoke than fire.[11] But at a lower level, a growing network of overlapping *ad hoc* alliances and mutal assistance arrangements have added on ominous new dimension to the terrorist threat.

Although terrorist groups in the Western Hemisphere seem to have been entering the picture more often of late, this phenomenon has been most evident in Europe and the Middle East where the advantages that can be derived from transnational cooperation have brought together some strange bedfellows indeed. For example, support rendered by individuals associated with the anarchist Baader-Meinhof Gang facilitated preparations for the attack on the Israeli Olympic team which was staged by the extremist but relatively non-revolutionary Palestinian Black September Organization in the fall of 1972. Not only have the Popular Front for the Liberation of Palestine (PFLP) and the Japanese Red Army (JRA) teamed up in a number of dramatic ventures, but—as suggested by the fact that the three Japanese gunmen who executed the Lod Airport massacre in May 1972 carried papers forged in Germany and weapons that they had picked up in Italy—both organizations have received assistance from a number of other terrorist groups in various parts of the world. The Turkish People's Liberation Army has used Palestinian training camp facilities in Syria and has reciprocated by attacking Israeli targets in Turkey. The Irish Republican Army (IRA) has developed links with a number of terrorist organizations outside the UK and Northern Ireland, including separatist groups in France and Spain as well as some

Overall, more and more groups throughout the area have begun providing each other with arms, safe housing, and other forms of support. In fact, there is evidence that a European-based terrorist "service industry" has emerged in the form of organizations devoted primarily or exclusively to providing training, documentation, and other specialized assistance to revolutionary and national liberation movements in all corners of the world. Just how complicated this web of interrelationships has become is well illustrated by France's celebrated—but still murky—"Carlos Affair" and its recent dramatic sequel in Vienna.

Why? The commonalities, differences, or changes in patterns of behavior that have been described thus far are, of course, attributable to the interplay of a host of variables. Only a few of these, i.e., the ones that seem to have had the greatest direct bearing on the timing, scope, and nature of the *internationalization* of terror, are addressed at any length below. No attempt is made to develope some sort of model or overreaching theory with respect to this phenomenon. Far more modest, the objective here is simply to ascertain to what extent the current rash of transnational (and, to a lesser degree, international) terrorist activity is attributable to broad regional and global trends and developments as opposed to unique and possibly transitory local problems and circumstances.

A few general observations—some of them, perhaps self-evident—are needed to set the problem in perspective and to lay the groundwork for further analysis. First of all, *transnational terrorism* is by nature more congenial to urban than to rural-based groups and is thus characteristically spawned by societies at a mid to advanced stage of socio-economic development. Resort to *international terrorism,* on the other hand, is just as likely to result from calculations concerning the relative efficacy of alternative methods for bringing national power to bear in a given situation as from an outright dearth of national resources. Hence, such behavior is not the special province of any particular category of state.

Modern-day practitioners of transnational terrorism have benefited from a generally permissive international environment—a point which will be elaborated below. For the most part therefore, the *constraints* on their behavior have either been a function of local environmental factors affecting their objective capabilities, opportunities, and alternatives or have been self-imposed for tactical or philosophical reasons.

These latter restraints are, of course, uncertain, for personal predilections can be overshadowed by frustration or desperation. Nevertheless, *cultural heritage* has been a key factor affecting individual terrorist groups' perceptions of the limits beyond which the level or intensity of violence is likely to become counterproductive. Moreover, although generalization is difficult because the ideological mix is different in almost every case, so has what is here termed the group's *credo* or *ethos.* The sharp differences in behavior between the two wings of the IRA and among the various Palestinian terrorist groups are evidence enough of this. But far more research is needed before confident judgments will be possible with respect to just what combinations of beliefs are most likely to foster repeated resort to extreme and indiscriminate forms of violence.

Since the extent and efficacy of internal security controls bear heavily on the frequency, form, and domestic impact of transnational terrorist incidents in any given country, *the proliferation of this form of political violence has both contributed to and fed upon the recent trend toward more widespread resort to various forms of authoritarian rule.* On one hand, open societies and weak or permissive authoritarian regimes are particularly vulnerable to such activity—and to its domestic ramifications. On the other, rigid and forceful authoritarian rule can foster transnational terrorism by forcing dissidents to operate abroad.

Together with earlier references to the basic societal problems that can give rise to various forms of political violence, the foregoing observations focus on the human and local environmental factors affecting the extent, nature, and domestic impact of transnational or international terrorist activity in different parts of the world. The question remains, however, as to just why there has been such a marked and enduring upsurge in transnational terrorism over the past eight years. In part, this phenomenon is attributable to a war-punctuated regional conflict affecting the interests of a large number of nations and attended by particularly deep-seated feelings of bitterness and frustration. But it would not have grown to its present dimensions were it not for the concurrent convergence and acceleration of a number of changes in the global environment that had been taking shape much earlier.

These trends are difficult to disaggregate. Technological advance, growing global interdependence, and the increasing urgency attached to forced draft modernization in many parts of the world are, for example, closely interrelated. But each bears brief comment.

The impact of *new technology* on terrorist capabilities with respect to weapons, mobility, and tactical communications has already been cited. As evidenced by the development of ever more sophisticated letter bombs, the occasional employment of missiles, and the staging of coordinated actions in widely separated locations, it has been significant. But whatever the nature of a terrorist act or the means of its execution, it must be remembered that the role of the media is critical to the spreading and intensification of its psychological impact. Hence, among all the technological advances in recent years, the development of *satellite communications,* and in particular, their upgrading in 1968 to include a television capability have unquestionably been among the most important in making transnational activity seem attractive to terrorist groups. The advent of satellite communications has also fed and underscored the thickening network of political, economic, and technological dependencies and obligations now commonly subsumed under the rubric of *interdependence.* Whether or not this term has been abused of late, the growth in both the numbers and importance of international, transnational, and (as a consequence of the centralizing imperatives of local modernization efforts) subnational linkages over the past decade has had at least a two-fold impact on the world-wide potential for terrorism. On the one hand, it has created a host of new, vulnerable, and potentially highly disruptive targets for terrorist attack (e.g., commercial and communications centers, transportation hubs, international power grids and pipelines, super tankers, and jumbo aircraft). On the other, it has generated a sort of identity crisis that has been reflected in a troublesome countervailing upsurge of nationalism and ethnicity.

For their part, the many other strains and dislocations associated with *the process of modernizing change* have swelled the ranks of the alienated in many parts of the world. They have also added millions of emigre workers to the international pool of political exiles and refugees which terrorists can exploit for cover, recruits, and various forms of operational support.

The upsurge in transnational terrorism has also been aided and abetted by a *"revolutionary" turn in the overall political environment* somewhat reminiscent of that experienced about 200 years ago. The postwar order has, in fact, come under challenge from all sides: from the developing nations of the Third World; from "maverick" Communist regimes; from dissatisfied second rank powers; and from a broad array of social forces fired, with differing degrees of responsibility, by a new sense of "social conscience."

By late 1967, the potential for a general escalation of political violence was clear. Viewed in this context, the Palestinians' dramatic entry into the air piracy business in 1968 becomes something of a logical if unexpected extension of a chain of developments that had included the emergence of the unruly New Left, a further proliferation of violence-prone splinter groups, and the first indications of the general post-Guevara shift in emphasis from rural to urban guerrilla warfare in Latin America.[12]

The characteristics and contours of this "revolutionary atmosphere" have undergone some change in the intervening years. The salience of some of the original contributory issues, e.g., Vietnam, has faded. But, as amply illustrated by the increasingly sympathetic treatment accorded to the Palestine Liberation Organization (PLO) in the United Nations General Assembly (UNGA) and other international forums over the past 18 months, that of the new moral, political, and economic standards championed by the Third World has not.[13] On the contrary, now backed by the new political clout of the Arab oil states, these values appear to be gaining in force. In short, the established postwar international political system has been cast into something of a state of flux—with all that that implies with respect to its effective order-keeping capabilities.

Terrorists have benefited from this overall state of affairs in many ways. Among other things, it has:

—Accorded an aura of legitimacy to the acts of any terrorist group claiming leftist revolutionary or national liberation movement status;
—Frustrated efforts to develop more effective international countermeasures;
—Facilitated transnational contact and cooperation among terrorist groups;
—Fostered a significant increase in the number of national, transnational, and international organizations providing national liberation move-

ments and other "progressive" dissident formations with various forms of direct and indirect support.

The attitudes and behavior of supportive states—ranging from those willing to provide little more than kind words and occasional safe haven to those that regularly furnish practicing or potential terrorists with funds, arms, training, documentation, and other operational support—have constituted another key global environmental *factor* affecting the scope and nature of transnational terrorist activity during the period under review. *Variable* might be a better term, however, for the extent of such assistance has fluctuated with changing appreciations of broader interests on the part of the state actors involved. For example, 1975 witnessed a distinct downward trend in such support.

In any event, if one excludes the simply indulgent or indifferent (including those liberal Western European states like France and Switzerland that, because of their strategic location and the extensive protection they accord to democratic rights and freedoms, have become involuntary hosts to all manner of foreign dissident groups) the list of nations in question dwindles to less than a score. Counting a few states that have recently retired—or partially retired—from the business, these "activists" include (but are not limited to) Libya, Cuba, the U.S.S.R., China, North Korea, Algeria, the People's Democratic Republic of Yemen, Tanzania, Congo, Zaire, Egypt, Syria, Iraq, and, however reluctant it has been to engage in such activity, Lebanon.

In some of these states, most of the support rendered to foreign revolutionary or guerrilla formations has been directed toward influencing the course of developments in one or two neighboring states or territories. And for many, perhaps most, the actual promotion of terrorist violence has been no more than a largely unintended byproduct of their activities. Nevertheless, in one way or another, all of them have directly contributed to the recent upsurge of transnational terrorism.

Two or three bear special mention. Take Libya, for example. The oil-rich Qaddafi regime has for some years been the world's most unabashed governmental proponent of revolutionary violence. And from the number of times that Libya has been linked to specific terrorist groups and incidents—including Carlos' raid on the OPEC meeting in Vienna—it would appear that Colonel Qaddafi has also been one of the world's least inhibited practitioners of international terrorism

Tripoli's focus has been on nationalist formations, whatever their ideological coloration or religious leanings. Thus, the recipients of its favors (in the form of various combinations of financial, logistical, and technical support) have been numerous and varied. In addition to some of the more militant Palestinian splinter groups, they have included the Irish Republican Army and a number of less widely known guerrilla movements based in the Philippines, Ethiopia, Somalia, the People's Democratic Republic of Yemen, Chad, Morocco, Tunisia, Thailand, and Panama.

This list is not exhaustive. Moreover, it bodes well to grow since, despite Tripoli's professions of reluctance to grant safe haven to the JRA terrorists who seized the American Consulate General in Kuala Lumpur in August 1975, there have as yet been no convincing indications that Colonel Qaddafi has undergone a change of heart.

Moscow's posture has been more ambiguous. Basically, the Soviets have had serious misgivings about the utility of transnational terrorist activity. They have repeatedly warned that excessive violence can tarnish the reputation of those involved and have stressed their belief that such tactics are not only generally unproductive but can lead to unforeseen and possibly uncontrollable adverse consequences. At the same time, however, the Kremlin's broader interests—including, importantly, those stemming from its continuing adversary relationship with Peking—have denied it the option of a straightforward hands-off policy. Thus, after a period of hesitancy, the Soviets began channelling funds, weapons, and other assistance to fedayeen groups through a number of intermediaries in 1969. All indications are that they continue to do so today.[14] Similarly, they have continued their long-standing program (the more innocuous aspects of which are publicly associated with Moscow's Patrice Lumumba University) of bringing young revolutionaries from all parts of the Third World to the Soviet Union for training and indoctrination. And like Carlos, some of these individuals have subsequently cropped up on the transnational terrorist scene.

There is also a considerable body of *circumstantial* evidence linking Moscow to various terrorist formations in Western Europe. That some linkages exist may, in fact, be taken for granted, for the broad considerations cited above give the Soviets ample reason for selectively attempting to monitor, penetrate, and gain some influence over such groups. But for obvious reasons, they have had to be very circumspect. They seem, for example, to have relied more heavily there than anywhere else on the cooperation of intermediaries who, if exposed, can be plausibly represented as having acted on their own initiative. In any event, the only hard evidence of Warsaw Pact member assistance to individuals associated with the Baader-Meinhof Gang points to Pankow and Prague. The arms destined for the non-Marxist Provisional Wing of the IRA that were seized at Schiphol Airport in Holland in late 1971 were of Czechoslovak origin and had been handled by a Czechoslovak firm. Even in the original "Carlos Affair," Cuba was the state actor most directly implicated. In short, the true dimensions of Soviet involvement remain extremely difficult to ascertain.

Nonetheless, one thing is clear. However much the Soviets might wish otherwise, their efforts to gain some handle on extremist activity have, together with their pursuit of less congruent objectives, done more to aggravate than to contain the current rash of transnational terrorist activity. The hard fact is that it is difficult to translate assistance into leverage or control when there are other available sources of support. Indeed, as the Soviets should by now have learned, any assistance provided to an extremist group under these circumstances risks simply increasing the recipient's potential for autonomous action.

A third actor deserving of separate comment is Cuba—not so much because of the extent of Havana's past activities in support of revolution and rebellion, but because there is mounting evidence (such as the statement issued at the conclusion of the regional Communist conference which was hosted by the Cubans in June 1975) that Castro's ambiguous policies have finally undergone a fundamental change in this regard. After years of hedging, the Cubans have now publicly espoused Moscow's recommended *via pacifica* strategy with respect to revolutionary struggle in Latin America—a development which bodes ill for those smaller militant formations that still rely heavily on Cuban support. It would appear that they will have to fall in line or face the risk of extinction. But many of Latin America's more active proponents of armed struggle are less vulnerable to Cuban retrenchment. Some are already highly self-sufficient. Of the remainder, those who are unable to tap the enormous war chests that have been accumulated by Argentine terrorist groups are likely to engage in more frequent ransom and resupply operations of their own. Partly because of this, and partly because Castro has made it abundantly clear that he does not intend to effect a parallel cutback in his support of armed revolutionary struggle outside of Latin America, the impact of Cuba's new posture on the overall level of transnational terrorism may be minimal.

The last and most elusive global variable to be addressed here is the *overall economic environment.* It can impact on the problem of terrorism in a number of subtle and, in some cases, countervailing ways. For example, *extra-cyclical world-wide economic strains*—such as those generated by the sudden quadrupling of oil prices—can so overtax the capabilities of local regimes as to invite domestic violence of a sort that could easily spill over national boundaries. Short of this, they can contribute to a general undercurrent of unrest by curtailing the resources that can be devoted to ameliorating societal ills.

Because the social and political effects of *cyclical trends* in the overall economic climate tend to be delayed and uneven, the potential consequences of short-term fluctuations do not lend themselves to generalization. Medium- to long-term trends, however, can affect both the potential and the opportunities for transnational terrorist activity in any given area. In so far as it affects industrialized countries, *rising economic prosperity* can, for example, facilitate the undetected movement of terrorist groups by fostering a heavy flow of tourist and commercial travel. It also attracts the large aggregations of emigre workers that not only make it easier for foreign terrorists to escape notice but provide a ready pool of manpower for their operational teams and support mechanisms. More broadly, a prolonged and general economic upturn can increase local potentials for political violence by causing popular expectations to far outpace governmental capacities to deliver. And in more affluent societies, at least, the attendant emphasis on materialistic values can alienate significant segments of the student and intellectual communities. Indeed, a combination of these last two destabilizing trends contributed, together with the factors cited earlier, to the emergency of a distinctly "revolutionary" political atmosphere in the late 1960s.

Conversely, *a prolonged economic decline* (something which some observers predict the world will experience for the next 20 years or more) has generally tended to dampen revolutionary ardor. Popular expectations decline, and people everywhere are preoccupied with the exigencies of day-to-day existence. But the world has much changed since its last broad economic slide. Whether the numbing effects of generalized adversity will be felt as strongly in the future is thus open to question. Their potential impact on the level of transnational terrorist activity is even more uncertain. The actors engaged therein are scarcely representative of the general population. They are few in number and elitist by nature. And given the proven strength of their convictions, they are likely to be among the most resistant to the psychological effects of untoward changes in the overall economic environment.

How Cost Effective?   The answer to this question depends on the vantage point of the observer. The achievement of disproportionately large effects from the employment of minimal resources is, of course, what political terrorism is all about. Its most serious drawback is that its consequences are, as the Soviets maintain, to a considerable degree unpredictable. It can alienate those groups whose sympathy was sought. Rather than disorient the masses, it can rally them to a previously unpopular government. It can galvanize a weak or wavering government into forceful counteraction. In short, tactical successes can, as in Jordan in 1970 and Uruguay in 1970-72, lead to strategic reverses of major proportions.

This risk is, however, easily accepted by those who dispose of no effective alternative methods for achieving their goals. Moreover, despite a number of sobering experiences, the overall balance sheet thus far provides the practitioners of transnational terrorism with grounds for considerable optimism.

Briefly put, the record shows that both transnational and international terrorists have generally been successful in avoiding capture (or, if caught, in escaping punishment) and in meeting at least some of their proximate objectives. For example, in a study of 63 major kidnapping and barricade operations executed between early 1968 and the late 1974, the RAND Corporation concluded that such actions were subject to the following probabilities of risk and success:

—87 percent probability of actually seizing hostages;

—79 percent chance that *all* members of the terrorist team would escape punishment or death, whether or not they successfully seized hostages;

—40 percent chance that all or some demands would be met in operations where something more than just safe passage or exit permission was demanded;

—29 percent chance of full compliance with such demands;

—83 percent chance of success where safe passage or exit, for the terrorists themselves or for others, was the sole demand;

—67 percent chance that, if concessions to the principal demands were rejected, all or virtually all members of the terrorist team could still escape alive by going underground, accepting safe passage in lieu of their original demands, or surrendering to a sympathetic government; and

—virtually a 100 percent probability of gaining major publicity whenever that was one of the terrorists' goals.[15]

Such hostage operations have resulted in the freeing of large numbers of prisoners, the payment of huge ransoms, and in one case where Austria was targetted, the changing of government policy. Until mid-1974, at least, the record for skyjacking was fully comparable. Out of 127 terrorist attempts to seize aircraft between March 1968 and early July 1974, only a dozen were abortive. Of the remainder, less than 10 are known for certain to have ended in the death or imprisonment of the terrorists. In a great majority of cases through 1972, the skyjackers were successful in securing full compliance with their demands. Thereafter, however, they generally received no more than safe haven, and for the past year and a half, skyjacking has been a distinctly losing proposition. Of the 6 attempts made between late July 1974 and the end of 1975, 4 were nipped in the bud and the other 2 brought sentences of death or life in prison to the terrorists involved.

Terrorist acts lacking a bargaining dimension (e.g., bombings and assassinations) have generally entailed a correspondingly lower degree of risk. All told, only about 267 individuals associated with transnational terrorist activity have been caught in the past five years. Of these, 39 were freed without punishment, 58 escaped punishment by getting safe conduct to another country, 16 were released from confinement on the demand of fellow terrorists, 50 were released after serving out their prison terms, and 104 were still in jails as of mid-September 1975. The average sentence meted out to those terrorists who have actually stood trial has been 18 months.[16]

How Disruptive? The human and material toll exacted by transnational and international terrorist violence over the past eight years has been relatively low. For example, although the total cost of such activity in terms of ransom payments and property damage has never been tallied, all indications are that it falls far short of the half billion dollars loss suffered to school vandals in the U.S. each year.

Closer track has been kept of the human casualties involved. Latest estimates place these at about 800 killed and 1,700 wounded—including the losses incurred by the terrorists themselves. To put these figures in better perspective, consider the fact that they fall somewhat short of the total casualties attributable to domestic terrorism in Northern Ireland alone during the same period or that Argentine terrorists and "counterterrorists" have managed to kill more than 1,000 of their countrymen since mid-1974. For a starker contrast, take Vietnam. There, in one year

(1968), Viet Cong terrorists were credited with assassinating 6,000 people and wounding 16,000 more. Comparisons with "normal" levels of domestic violence in the U.S. may also be useful. There were, for example, about 20,000 homicides—and more than 2,000 bombings—recorded here in 1975.

The juxtaposition of these statistics suggests that the dimensions of the problem posed by transnational and international terrorism are still quite small and that the increase in such activity since 1968, while marked, should have done little to undermine world order. But the disruptive impact of these terrorist incidents and campaigns has been magnified by the publicity they have received and by their interaction with other destablizing trends and forces. Thus, while the terrorists have made no revolutions and, by themselves at least, toppled no governments, they have:

—Embarrassed several governments and contributed to the effective collapse of a few (e.g., the initial Bordaberry Adminstration in Uruguay and the Isabel Peron regime in Argentina);

—Added an abrasive new dimension to both North-South and East-West relations;

—Contributed to the growing international status and fortunes of the PLO;

—Compelled some nations to temporarily abandon their law enforcement function (e.g., to release captured terrorists) out of fear of future retribution;

—Aggravated and accentuated the dilemmas generated within the existing international system by the emergence of a growing company of powerful non-state actors;

—Introduced strains in relations among those Western nations which, because of divergent national intersts, feel constrained to adopt differing positions with respect to specific incidents or broader terrorist-related issues;

—Reinforced the currently pervasive sense of global flux and disorder;

—Caused a large number of nations, including the US, to divert substantial resources to defense against terrorist attacks;[17]

—Adversely affected the quality of life in many open or formerly open societies.

In short, while scarcely cataclysmic, the spoiling effects of modern-day transnational and international terrorism have been substantial. Harking back to earlier discussion, this state of affairs is both a measure and, in large part, a consequence of increasing global interdependence. As the dimensions and complexity of the web of interstate and transnational linkages that together comprise the functional core of the "international system" have grown under the impact of technological advance, the reverberations of events—including terrorist attacks—which disturb or threaten its more important intersections have tended to become increasingly widespread and sharply felt. At the same time, the limits within which individual states can attempt to cope with such problems through unilateral action without risk of adversely affecting the interests of others have steadily narrowed. But, as previously observed, rather than encourage increasing interest in supranational solutions, the frustrations born of this *de facto* shrinkage of sovereignty have generated an unhelpful backlash of nationalism. And this, of course, has been one of the key factors that have affected the nature and effectiveness of the international community's response to the terrorist threat.

What International Constraints? With the exception of a number of bilateral agreements providing, *inter alia,* for a greater exchange of intelligence and technical assistance or, as in the memorandum of understanding concerning hijackers of aircraft and vessels that was signed by the U.S. and Cuba in 1973, for the prompt extradition of specified categories of terrorists, the international response to terrorism has been relatively weak and ineffective.

The UN's problems in grappling with *transnational* terrorism were cited and illustrated at the outset of this study. *International* terrorism, however, has proved to be a somewhat less contentious issue. Indeed, the Declaration on Principles of International Law Concerning Friendly Relations and Cooperation Among States which the General Assembly adopted without vote on 24 October 1970 asserts at one point that:

> Every State has the duty to refrain from organizing, instigating, assisting or participating in acts of civil strife or terrorist acts in another State or acquiescing in organized activities within its territory directed towards the commission of such acts, when the acts referred to in the present paragraph involve a threat or use of force.[18]

But even as an essentially unenforcible admonition, this rule of behavior is weakened and clouded by the greater emphasis that the Declaration accords to the "principal of equal rights and self-determination of peoples." The language employed in this regard implies that it is the overriding duty of all states to assist groups struggling for the realization of these rights in every way possible. For example, the Declaration avers that:

> Every State has the duty to refrain from any forcible action which deprives people referred to above in the elaboration of the present principles of their right to self-determination and freedom and independence. In their actions against, and resistance to, such forcible action in pursuit of the exercise of their right to self-determination, such peoples are entitled to seek *and to receive* support in accordance with the purposes and principles of the Charter. [Emphasis added][19]

There have, in addition, been a total of five international conventions adopted over the past 12 years that have dealt with one or another aspect (in all cases rather narrow) of the terrorism problem. These are as follows:

—The Tokyo Convention (Convention on Offenses and Certain Other Acts Committed on Board Aircraft): Signed in September 1963, it did not come into force until December 1969. It is a very limited accord which does no more than to set a few jurisdictional ground rules and to require the contracting states to (1) make every effort to restore control of the aircraft to its lawful commander and (2) arrange for the prompt onward passage or return of hijacked aircraft together with their passengers, cargo, and crew. As of this writing, 77 countries have ratified it.

—The Hague Convention (Convention for the Suppression of the Unlawful Seizure of Aircraft): Signed in December 1970, it came into force 10 months later. Its principal feature is that it requires (albeit with important discretionary exceptions) contracting parties either to extradite or to prosecute skyjackers. Seventy-four countries have ratified it.

—The Montreal Convention (Convention for the Suppression of Unlawful Acts Against the Safety of Civil Aviation): Signed in September 1971, it came into force in January 1973. Covering the sabotage or destruction of aircraft or air navigational facilities, it requires the contracting parties to make such offenses subject to severe penalties and establishes the same extradition-or-prosecution system for offenders as in The Hague Convention. Sixty-three countries have ratified it.

—The Organization of American States Convention (Convention to Prevent and Punish Acts of Terrorism Taking the Form of Crimes Against Persons and Related Extortion that are of International Significance): Signed in February 1971, it entered into force in October 1973 (the U.S. is a signatory, but not a party). With its emphasis on the prevention and punshment of crimes against persons to whom the state owes a special duty of protection under international law, it was a precursor of the UN convention concerning the protection of diplomats which is cited below. It also employs The Hague Convention extradite-or-prosecute formula. Only four of the thirteen signatory countries have ratified it.

—The United Nations Convention on the Prevention and Punishment of Crimes Against Internationally Protected Persons Including Diplomatic Agents: Signed in December 1973, it has yet to come into force. It requires the contracting states to establish certain specified acts against protected persons (or against the official premises, private accommodations, or means of transport of such a person) as crimes under internal law. Once again, The Hague Convention on extradite-or-prosecute formula applies. So far, only nine countries have ratified it.

Although they reflect international concern and at least a slim majority consensus that something must be done, these conventions presently do not, singly or in combination, constitute much of an effective constraint on terrorist activity. In the first place, many states—including a high percentage of those that have been particularly active in supporting revolutionary or national liberation groups—are not yet parties thereto. Secondly, the conventions lack teeth in that all make the extradition or prosecution of terrorists subject to discretionary escape clauses and none provides for the application of punitive sanctions against states that simply refuse to comply at all. Finally, the exclusive focus on skyjacking and the protection of diplomats leaves a good deal of terrorist activity outside the cognizance of international law.

But this, it would seem, is all the traffic will bear. The US has tried repeatedly to correct some of these deficiencies and has run into a stone wall of opposition on each occasion. For example, at the conclave sponsored by the International Civil Aviation Organization (ICAO) that formulated the final draft of The Hague Convention, the US delegation sought unsuccessfully to (1) limit drastically exceptions to extradition of hijackers, (2) establish hijacking as a common crime, and (3) exclude political motivation as a defense against extradition or prosecution of hijackers. Two years later, in September 1972, the US submitted a draft convention to the UNGA that was aimed at limiting the "export" of terrorism. But even though it established a number of restrictive criteria that would have to be met before its enforcement provisions became applicable, it was effectively stifled by opposition centering on the impermissibility of interference with the right of self-determination. The following summer, a proposal sponsored by the US and several other nations for a separate enforcement convention that would have backed the Tokyo, Hague, and Montreal documents with sanctions affecting the rights and services guaranteed under existing international and bilateral air service agreements was soundly defeated at the ICAO's Rome Conference and Assembly.

The obstacles which have blocked more effective international action are formidable. They have, as previously indicated, included the controversy over *justifiable* versus *illegal* political violence and broad resistance to such further infringements of national sovereignty as would be implied to any inflexible curtailment of the right to grant political asylum. Equally important, however, they have also included an understandable reluctance on the part of many nations otherwise ill-disposed toward terrorist activity to commit themselves to any course of action that might either invite direct terrorist retribution or provoke the application of sanctions by states that happen to be sympathetic to the terrorists' cause.

To make these observations is not, however, to imply immutability. It must be remembered, for example, that such progress as has been made in the field of multilateral countermeasures has, in each instance, been occasioned by reaction to some general or specific escalation of terrorist violence. (In this regard, hopes that Carlos' assault on the OPEC ministerial meeting in Vienna will have some sort of salutary catalytic effect may yet be borne out in practice.) There are, moreover, a host of other factors which could alter the attitudes and behavior of any of the state actors concerned. Hence, whether or not all the obstacles to a more effective international response that have been cited thus far will retain their present force in the decade ahead is a valid question—and it is one that is addressed below.

THE OUTLOOK

International Terrorism   Although it is possible that a few others may emulate the irresponsible behavior of Libya's Colonel Qaddafi, international terrorism seems unlikely to pose much of a threat to world order or US interests during the next few years. Even in its presently weakened state, the international system subjects states to a host of legal obligations and practical constraints that they can ignore only at considerable risk. The continuing force of these considerations is evidenced by the fact that international terrorism is no more prevalent today than it was in 1968.

Indeed, throughout the entire postwar era, both the weak and the musclebound have tended to view international terrorism as a policy tool to be used sparingly and (except when exercising their "right" of retaliation) discreetly when potentially effective alternative means are lacking. Moreover, while no apologia for such activity is intended, it should be noted that—with the exception of certain actions undertaken in connection with the Middle East conflict—its objectives have generally been defensive (e.g., the neutralization of hostile foreign-based groups or individuals) as opposed to the offensive and deliberately disruptive character of most transnational terrorism.

Nevertheless, the sporadic employment of government-controlled terrorist groups against Israeli targets both within and outside that country's borders raises some troublesome questions about what the 1980s may hold in store. And while their true sponsorship has yet to be firmly established, so do the recent Rejectionist Front-associated operations in Madrid and Vienna that were intended to bring pressure on moderate Arab regimes.

These questions center on the kind of adjustments in international behavior that may flow from ongoing changes in the distribution and component elements of national power and, no less important, from the growing array of economic, political, and technological restraints affecting the ways in which latent power can be translated into effective leverage. Are Arab actions a precursor of things to come? Is it, in fact, likely that, lacking or despairing of more conventional means for defending or advancing their international interests, an increasing number of states will opt to engage in—or to sponsor—terrorist activity?

In assessing this possibility, some observers have noted that because of the expense, the risks, and the constraints deriving from the patron-client relationships that are now involved, high-intensity conventional warfare—even of the local variety—may be becoming obsolete. On the other hand, although it is "permissible" under current international ground rules, low-level protracted conflict of the Vietnam type is not, as they point out, a very attractive alternative. For these reasons, they suggest that there will be a strong temptation for governments to employ terrorist groups as means of waging "surrogate warfare" against other nations. Brian Jenkins has expressed this notion as follows:

> Terrorists, whatever their origin or cause, have demonstrated the possibilities of a third alternative—that of "surrogate warfare." Terrorism, though now rejected as a legitimate mode of warfare by most conventional military establishments, could become an accepted form of warfare in the future. Terrorists could be employed to provoke international incidents, create alarm in an adversary's country, compel it to divert valuable resources to protect itself, destroy its morale, and carry out specific acts of

sabotage. Governments could employ existing terrorist groups to attack their opponents, or they could create their own terrorists. Terrorism requires only a small investment, certainly far less than what it cost to wage conventional war. It can be debilitating to the enemy. Prior to the 1973 Yom Kippur War, a senior Israeli officer estimated that the total cost in men and money to Israel for all defensive and offensive measures against at most a few thousand Arab terrorists was 40 times that of the Six Days War in 1967. A secret backer of the terrorists can also deny sponsoring them. The concepts of subversion sabotage, of lightning raids carried out by commandos, are not new, but the opportunities are.[20]

The case presented, however, is far stronger with respect to the probability of increasing resort to some form of surrogate warfare—which, as Brian Jenkins notes, is scarcely a new phenomenon—than for the corollary argument that this development is likely to be characterized by widespread adoption of terrorist tactics.[21] For one thing, the safety factor of deniability would all but disappear if a state were to engage in such activity on a regular basis. For another, barring total collapse of world order and consequent international anarchy (something that no state actor has reason to promote), international terrorism is highly unlikely to gain acceptance as an admissible form of behavior in the foreseeable future.

All told, in fact, it seems likely that the employment of terrorist groups in a surrogate warfare role will continue to be more the exception than the rule for some time to come. And if this proves to be the case, it follows that while there may be a slight upward trend in the annual total of international terrorist incidents, the scope of the problem in 1985 should not be much more serious than it is today.

Transnational Terrorism   On balance, the outlook with respect to transnational terrorism is less encouraging. On the positive side, the decline in the number of states willing to provide terrorist safe haven gives promise of being lasting.[22] It seems most doubtful that the currently shrinking aggregations of emigre workers will soon regain their former size, and this will probably have some small impact on the security and resources of terrorist groups operating in Western Europe. More importantly, political developments of a sort which presently seem to be at least possible could significantly reduce levels of terrorist activity in such current trouble spots as Northern Ireland, Argentina, and the Middle East.

But overall, the potential for domestic, international, and transnational terrorism is—as asserted at the outset of this study—almost certain to remain high. Furthermore, most of the broad environmental factors that have contributed to the feasibility, efficacy, and popularity of transnational terrorism in recent years will continue to operate with at least equal force in the decade ahead. The salience of some, in fact, seems bound to increase.

Barring some cataclysmic event which reduces mankind to a more primitive order of existence, technological advance, modernizing social and economic change, and growing global interdependence are, for example, essentially irreversible phenomena with an urgency and momentum which seems more likely to increase than to decline in the coming decade. And while their political consequences can, to a certain degree, be controlled by carefully-tailored policy decisions, they bode well to aggravate the terrorism problem by generating further increases in (1) divisive ethnicity and nationalism, (2) urban unrest, (3) terrorist capabilities, and (4) societal vulnerabilities.

In the political field, the widespread erosion of established institutions of authority that has both invited and facilitated terrorist activity in recent years shows no signs of abatement. For its part, the postwar international order seems likely to remain under challenge—and thus in flux—throughout the decade ahead. But the problem will probably continue to be most evident at the national level where increasing difficulties of governance hold forth the prospect of a further proliferation of ineffective and unstable regimes.

As a byproduct of the above, most non-state actors on the world stage will probably manage to escape significantly firmer national or international control for some time to come. Because of this, and because the values underlying the strong "social conscience" component of today's political environment seem likely to retain their current force, the chances are that national liberation and leftist revolutionary formations will continue to receive both moral and material support from a wide variety of transnational and international organizations as well as a potentially substantial flow of ransom and "insurance" payments from vulnerable multinational corporations.

At the same time, the trend toward greater international contact and cooperation among terrorist groups that has already markedly enhanced the operational capabilities of some of the organizations involved seems likely to gain further momentum. For one thing, lingering inhibitions born of sharply different goals and outlook are bound to decline in the face of continuing and widely-publicized proof of the advantages that can be derived from such a course. For another, the tough but scattered local counterterrorist campaigns that are sure to dot the political landscape throughout the decade ahead will each provide compelling new incentives for transnational cooperation.

Ominously enough, therefore, the wave of the future seems to be toward the development of a complex support base for transnational terrorist activity that is largely independent of—and quite resistant to control by—the state-centered international system. This does not mean, however, that the behavior of supportive state actors will become increasingly irrelevant. On the contrary, it suggests that unless the principal patrons of subversion and revolutionary violence cut back on the assistance they are furnishing to practicing or potential terrorists more drastically than currently available evidence as to their intentions gives grounds to expect, the deleterious impact of their behavior may be considerably greater than in the past.

The problem of extensive and sometimes sympathetic publicity is another aggravating environmental factor that promises to persist in many parts of the world. Not only has all the attention that has been focused on terrorism made it increasingly newsworthy, but the coverage and capabilities of the world's satellite communications systems have been steadily upgraded since 1968. Moreover, radio, television, and the press are bound to continue to reach an ever larger audience.

Although most Western media officials, at least, are by now fully aware of the danger of playing into terrorist hands, competitive pressures are strong and the line between responsible and irresponsible reportage or commentary is very fine. In short, self-censorship is unlikely to work very well. On the other hand, the only potentially more effective alternative—firm governmental management of the news—is, in time of peace, virtually out of the question in most Western democracies.

Another aspect of the information explosion that promises to continue to be troublesome is the diffusion of terrorist-adaptable technological know-how and—to a lesser degree—of possibly inspirational speculation about new and potentially ultra-disruptive terrorist tactics. Although the objectives of such literature may be (and most often are) above reproach, it can scarcely help but aggravate the problems posed by the development and wholesale deployment of sophisticated (and in many cases, man-portable weaponry; the world-wide proliferation of nuclear facilities; and the race, motivated by both political and economic considerations, to sell nuclear technology and modern armaments to developing countries. And these problems are serious enough as it is. Indeed, despite the attention that has been paid to nuclear safeguards and the physical security of sensitive installations and depots, the world seems to be moving toward a state of affairs in which the limits of any "technological escalation" of terrorist violence will depend more on the self-imposed restraints affecting the behavior of the groups involved than on lack of capability or opportunity.

It is, of course, the upper limits of the potential scale of terrorist violence that are of most concern. Individual terrorist groups already have the capability of manufacturing or otherwise acquiring a variety of weapons or agents of mass destruction. More will be in a position to exercise this option in the future. Just how likely is it that they will do so?

That the threatened employment of such awesome ordnance would have profound political and psychological effects is undeniable. But it must be emphasized that there are major hazards that would be involved for the terrorists as well. The most important of these (and the only probably primarily responsible for the failure of terrorists to make more of an effort to exploit mass destruction technology in the past) is the high risk of adverse public reaction—particularly in the event that the group involved were to end up in a position where it felt compelled to make good its threat.

Although a few terrorist groups have, in fact, resorted to indiscriminate mass murder, such instances have been relatively rare, and in each case thus far the human toll has been negligible in comparison to the casualties that would result from the broadcast of only a few ounces or less of a highly toxic agent or the detonation of even a small nuclear device. Basically, terrorists are in business to influence people, not exterminate them. Moreover, those that aspire to some sort of political legitimacy—and this means most of them—are generally quite sensitive to the need to take some care to avoid alienating local and international opinion.

The fact remains, however, that weapons of mass destruction cannot help but hold considerable temptation for militants whose basic strategy of violence centers on wringing maximum political leverage from publicity and fear. Hence, it seems prudent to assume that sooner or later some group is bound to take the plunge.

Because their very mention strikes terror into the hearts of many, nuclear weapons come first to mind. But the practical problems facing the would-be nuclear blackmailer are numerous and complex. Although nuclear devices are clearly no longer beyond terrorist reach, their acquisition (whether through theft or manufacture) is still—and for a few years yet will probably continue to be—a relatively demanding task. Once in terrorist hands, their emissions present anti-detection shielding problems not only during passive storage but, if deployed against specific targets, during the delivery and bargaining phases of the operation as well. Moreover, there is further room for trouble when it comes to establishing the credibility of the threat since the target authorities must be persuaded not only that the terrorists actually have a nuclear device but that it will probably work. Finally, all but the most fanatical terrorists might be given pause by the fact that if worst comes to worst, the destructive effects of such weapons are not manageable.

Thus, while the prospect of nuclear-armed terrorists can scarcely be dismissed, a more likely scenario—at least in the short term—would seem to be a terrorist seizure of a nuclear weapons storage facility or a nuclear power plant in a straightforward barricade operation. Such a group need not threaten a nuclear holocaust (although that possibility would be in the back of everyone's mind), just the destruction of the bunker or reactor with the attendant danger of radiological pollution. The threat would be inherently credible. The publicity would be enormous. And if their demands were to be denied, the terrorists would be in a position to tailor the amount of damage they actually inflicted to their appreciation of the existing circumstances.

A more pressing threat, however, would seem to lie in the field of chemical, biological, and radiological agents. In contrast to nuclear devices, many of these are presently relatively easy to acquire. Hence the danger that they could turn up in the hands of the sort of ultra-radical or psychopathic fringe group that would have the fewest compunctions about actually using them is very real. Moreover, since small—sometimes minute—quantities are usually all that are needed for potentially devastating effects, such agents also tend to be easy to conceal, easy to transport, and easy to introduce into the target area. Credibility poses few problems, for a small sample of the agent delivered by mail or left at some designated pick-up point should quickly dispel any doubts on this score. Finally, a number of these agents offer the additional advantage of being amenable to relatively selective targeting (e.g., the occupants of a single building or compound).

As implied in earlier discussion, any such dramatic escalation of terrorist violence as that suggested by these brief scenarios on weapons of mass destruction would be likely to touch off a new flurry of efforts to devise international countermeasures. Indeed, another convention or two would probably result. But just how much practical effect this would have is open to serious question.

Simply put, the net thrust of the forces at work within the international community promises to remain more centrifugal than centripetal throughout the decade ahead. Indeed, all indications are that rising nationalism and ethnicity, the developing nations' fundamental challenge to the existing world order, and the related proliferation of subnational and other non-state actors will continue to render the international system increasingly complex and uncertain. Moreover, the attendant diffusion and erosion of political authority will tend to be self-reinforcing. And under these circumstances, the degree of consensus needed to adopt and enforce meaningful counterterrorist accords will be more elusive than ever.

It follows that the recent stiffening of a number of nations' policies toward terrorists is almost certainly more reflective of relatively narrow and quite disparate tactical calculations—with respect, for example, to such things as improved domestic security arrangements, the current state of play in the Arab-Israeli conflict, or the latitude of action that may now be afforded by Third World divisions and the general unpopularity of certain terrorist groups—than of any broad upsurge of interest in a global approach. Nonetheless, this development is encouraging for it opens up new possibilities for bilateral and limited multilateral counterterrorist undertakings of a sort that have, in combination with unilateral measures, proved relatively effective in the past.

In sum, although it is unlikely to trigger a collapse of world order, transnational terrorism promises to pose a continuing and potentially gravely unsettling problem for the world community until such time— possibly years hence—that the international system gels into new and generally accepted contours. The frequency and intensity of violence will decline in some areas. The cast of characters will be constantly changing. In all likelihood, technological and organizational innovations in the security field will make terrorism a more risky affair. Yet at best the overall number of terrorist groups seems unlikely to decline—and the number of countries in which they are active appears destined to grow. Furthermore, because of their symbolic value, their availability, and the embarrassment they can create, the popularity of *American targets* will probably remain high.

Ironically, there may well be fewer *people* engaged in transnational terrorist activity some five years hence than there are today. But this prospect is not as encouraging as it sounds. For even if changes in the political environment or partial satisfaction of their objectives do encourage some of the larger and more "responsible" formations to eschew transnational violence, their place on the international stage is likely to be quickly filled by more militant splinter groups—not to mention a smattering of total newcomers to the game. And since (as amply demonstrated by the JRA, Carlos and company, and the PFLP) small terrorist groups can, when properly connected, mount all manner of highly disruptive operations, such a development could—through the introduction of additional increments of fanaticism—provoke at least temporary increases in the intensity of terrorist violence.

In any event, it seems likely that the constraints on terrorist behavior will, through international default, continue to depend primarily on (1) the terrorists' subjective orientation and (2) the policies and resources of the individual countries in which they operate. Of necessity, however, the impact of these will be uneven. Remember, too, that the inherent dynamics and logic of a campaign of terrorist violence are such that it has a natural propensity to escalate over time. Moreover, all but the most isolated terrorist groups will be able to draw on a common and cumulative media-fed pool of experience and inspiration. Hence, even if the cited constraints do result in some tapering off in the frequency of transnational terrorist incidents during the next few years, we should expect to witness steadily greater and more widespread sophistication in targetting, execution, and weaponry. And while, as suggested earlier, most groups will probably continue to be deterred by both moral considerations and calculations of the risks involved, the danger that a fanatic few might resort to weapons of mass destruction will increase accordingly.

IMPLICATIONS

Two basic messages emerge from the foregoing discussion. The first is that the phenomenon of widespread internationalized terror is not only likely to persist for at least the next several years, but also to evolve in ways that could pose a more substantial threat to U.S. interests—and, under certain circumstances, to world order—than in the recent past.[23] The second is that the factors bearing on this phenomenon and its political ramifications are so numerous and cut across so many jurisdictional and disciplinary lines that the development of more effective national and international countermeasures is likely to be a particularly demanding task.

Whether or not weapons of mass destruction are actually brought into play, the odds are that the impact of transnational and international terror will be more sharply felt in the US in the years just ahead. There is, for example, good reason to believe that at least a few foreign terrorist groups are planning to step up their attacks on American targets abroad in the near future. Moreover, the influx of foreign travellers and dignitaries expected in connection with such major US-sponsored events as the current Bicentennial celebrations and the 1980 Winter Olympics will inescapably afford a host of opportunities for dramatic terrorist action. Hence, despite the likelihood that the practical considerations that have so far generally deterred foreign-based terrorist groups from extending their areas of operation to US shores will retain their present force, there is a good chance that a few will succumb to the temptation to do.[24] Finally, no matter how tough and well-publicized a "no concessions" policy the US Government maintains, it seems likely that Washington will be targeted by terrorist demands somewhat more frequently in the future—partly to probe more fully the limits of US resolve, partly for sheer publicity or other psychological effect, and partly to foster intergovernmental or domestic tensions.

More importantly, perhaps, even if the problem of internationalized terror is not brought "closer to home" in the ways suggested above, it promises to impinge more directly on US interests and options with respect to a broad range of critical issue areas. For example, it is likely to:

—Figure as even more of an irritant in both East-West and North-South relations:

—Sharpen the dilemmas inherent in the politically and economically sensitive questions of arms sales and the transfer of advanced technology;

—Provide potential new grounds for strains in Washington's relations with its principal friends and allies;

—Reinforce some of the obstacles which currently impede efforts to find a mutually-acceptable way to cope with the dependence of Western industrialized countries on foreign energy sources; and

—Impose burdensome new demands on limited human and material resources.

Although, as emphasized in earlier discussion, the dimensions of the threat posed by international and transnational terror should not be overdrawn, the picture outlined above is sobering. Among other things, it suggests that the machinery and guidelines that the US and its allies have so far developed for dealing with the problem bear careful review.

There is no magic formula for endowing any given government's approach to the problem of terrorism with the direction, breadth, and coherence required to marshal the remarkably disparate talents and resources that are needed and to weave its response into the overall fabric of its domestic and foreign concerns. Indeed, any number of alternative courses of action could prove equally effective. Nevertheless, it bears emphasis that together with *timely intelligence and sound multi-disciplinary analytical support, flexibility* and *extensive coordination* (both inter- and intra-state) would seem to be critical to devising and implementing a counterterrorist strategy that is both internally consistent and minimally disruptive to national values and foreign policy objectives in terms of "hidden" social, economic, and political costs.

Obviously, such a strategy cannot be framed in isolation. Among other things, its architects would need ready access to top policymakers in both the foreign and domestic fields as well as to the advice of a broad range of government and non-government experts or interested parties. Moreover, the necessity to maintain some freedom of maneuver (born of the fact that every new terrorist incident is likely to have its unique aspects) is a particularly delicate problem—and one that can easily contribute to unnecessary misunderstandings. Hence, routine pre-crisis coordination of terrorism-related policies and contingency plans with all the key domestic and foreign actors whose interests and options they could affect becomes all the more important.

[1] These factors include weak and inefficient government, societal rivalries and inequities, social and economic dislocations stemming from the accelerating process of change, and high levels of frustration born of social immobility or feelings of relative deprivation. (The term relative deprivation is defined by its originator, Professor Ted Robert Gurr, as a "perceived discrepancy between the goods and conditions of life which members of a group believe are their due and the goods and conditions which they think they can in fact get and keep." *Why Men Rebel,* Princeton: Princeton University Press, 1970, page 319.)

[2] The committee, which in New York from 16 July to 11 August 1973, was also unable to reach agreement on either the causes of international terrorism or on measures which might be taken to prevent such activity. In consequence, its report was simply a compendium of disparate and conflicting views. To date, neither the UN General Assembly nor the Sixth Committee thereof has been able (or willing) to find time to consider it.

[3] Brian Jenkins, *International Terrorism: A New Mode of Conflict,* Research Paper No. 48, California Seminar on Arms Control and Foreign Policy (Los Angeles: Crescent Publications, 1975), p. 1.

[4] In his chapter entitled "Terror as a Weapon of Political Agitation" in *Internal War: Problems and Approaches* (edited by Harry Eckstein and published by Collier-Macmillan Ltd., London, in 1964), Thomas P. Thorton defines political terror as "a symbolic act designed to influence political behavior by extranormal means, entailing the use or threat of violence." Other particularly useful general analyses of political terrorism are to be found in Brian Jenkins, *op cit.;* Robert Moss, *Urban Guerrillas* (London: Temple Smith, 1972); Brian Crozier, ed., *Annual of Power and Conflict,* 1972-73 and 1973-74 (London: Institute for the Study of Conflict); Paul Wilkinson, *Political Terrorism* (London: Macmillan, 1974); Martha C. Hutchinson, "The Concept of Revolutionary Terrorism," *The Journal of Conflict Resolution,* Volume XVI, Number 3, September 1972, pp. 383-396; and Philip A. Karber, "Urban Terrorism: Baseline Data and a Conceptual Framework,"*Social Science Quarterly,* Volume 52, December 1971, pp. 521-533. The last-named author stresses the symbolic qualities of political terrorism and suggests that it can be analyzed in much the same fashion as other mediums of communication.

[5] Given the element of governmental patronage that is common to both, the boundary line between transnational and international terrorism is often difficult to draw. To the degree that it can be determined, the key distinction lies in who is calling the shots with respect to a given action or campaign. Hence, groups can and do drift back and forth across the line. For example, even a one-time "contract job" undertaken on behalf of a governmental actor by a group that normally acts according to its own lights qualifies as international terrorism.

[6] This figure excludes terrorist attacks on US and allied personnel and installations in Indochina. It also excludes most of the mutual assassination efforts and cross-border operations associated with the Arab-Israeli conflict. The only exceptions in this regard are incidents that either victimized noncombatant nationals of states outside the principal arena of conflict or were of such a nature that they became the object of international controversy.

[7] There are relatively few political groups in the world that are totally dedicated to terrorist violence. As used here, the term terrorist organization simply denotes a group that has employed terrorist tactics.

[8] Although international and transnational terrorist incidents are lumped together in these charts, the former were outnumbered by the latter by more than 20 to 1 and thus had little impact on the patterns reflected therein.

[9] In a series of well-coordinated actions (all but one of which were staged during the course of a single day: 6 September 1970), the PFLP hijacked four airliners and attempted to seize a fifth. One plane was flown to Cairo, where it was destroyed as soon as the passengers and crew had disembarked. The other three aircraft were diverted to a landing strip in the Jordanian desert. These were blown up on 12 September, but some of their passengers were held hostage for another 13 to 18 days.

[10] In the latter case, the Montoneros organization kidnapped Jorge and Juan Born, co-owners and directors of Bunge and Born Ltd., in September 1974 and held them for nine months. An additional condition for their release—which also was met—was the publication in several leading Western papers of a full page political "announcement" drawn up by their captors.

[11] The JCR is composed of Argentina's Revolutionary People's Army (ERP), Bolivia's National Liberation Army (ELN), Chile's Movement of the Revolutionary Left (MIR), Paraguay's National Liberation Front (FREPALINA), and the remnants of Uruguay's National Liberation Movement (MLN/

Tupamaros). Backed by the ERP's overflowing coffers, it has grown more active in recent months and has the potential for becoming an effective and dangerous organization.

[12] With Guevara's demise and subsequent decline in stature as a revolutionary theorist and tactician, the works of such leading advocates of terrorist violence as Fannon, Satre, and Marighela have assumed increasing importance as a major literary source of inspiration for ultra militants in many parts of the world.

[13] The PLO is a political umbrella organization embracing several Fedayeen commando groups. It was accorded recognition as the sole legitimate representative of the Palestinian people (at the expense of Jordan) by the 1974 "Islamic nonaligned" and Rabat summit meetings. In November of that same year, it was granted observer status by the UNGA. All told, some 50 states have allowed the PLO to open offices in their capitals. In addition, five UN-affiliated international agencies (ILO, WHO, UPU, ITU, and UNESCO) have granted it observer status.

[14] In their commentary on fedayeen activities, however, the Soviets have consistently been careful to distinguish between "permissible" attacks on "legitimate" targets inside Israel and "regrettable" incidents involving noncombatant third parties.

[15] As excerpted in *Terroristic Activity—International Terrorism:* Hearings Before the Subcommittee to Investigate the Administration of the Internal Security Act and Other Internal Security Laws of the Committee on the Judiciary, United States Senate, Ninety-Fourth Congress, First Session; Part 4; May 14, 1975 (Washington: US Government Printing Office, 1975), p. 240.

[16] "Terrorism: 'Growing and Increasingly Dangerous'," (Interview with Robert A. Fearey, Special Assistant to the Secretary of State and Coordinator for Combatting Terrorism), *U.S. News and World Report,* 29 September 1975, p.79.

[17] In the U.S. this has been reflected most clearly in the installation of an effective but costly airport security system and, following the Khartoum incident of 1973, in a supplemental $20 million appropriation provided to the Department of State for the sole purpose of improving the security of American diplomatic and consular installations abroad. The construction of a special bombproof courthouse in which to try the captured leaders of the Baader-Meinhof Gang was one of the more notable extra expenses that have been incurred by Bonn. By the time these proceedings are over, it is estimated that they will have cost the West German taxpayer more than $6 million. Even the liberal Swedes have become nervous since incurring the wrath of the JRA in March 1975 by arresting two members of that group and deporting them to Japan. In any event, they chose to take no chances when they hosted the Chilean Davis Cup tennis team some six months later. They converted the fashionable coastal resort where the matches were held into a veritable fortress protected by floodlights; fences up to 35 feet high; and a 1,300-man police force equipped with gunboats, helicopters, scores of dogs, and some 50 horses.

[18] *Yearbook of the United Nations: 1970* (New York: United Nations Office of Public Information, 1971), p. 790.

[19] *Ibid.,* p. 791.

[20] Brian Jenkins, *International Terrorism: A New Mode of Conflict, op. cit.,* p. 21.

[21] It must be remembered that under the definitions employed in this study, there are many kinds of covert subversive activity—including support of insurgent paramilitary forces and even sponsorship of highly discriminate sabotage operations—that would not of themselves constitute terrorism.

[22] Although this trend has been evident for some time, it was underscored in August 1975 when the JRA terrorists who had seized the U.S. Consulate in Kuala Lumpur not only had great difficulty in finding a state willing to grant them safe haven, but were even denied permission to transit nationally-controlled airspace by some Third World countries.

[23] Despite the frequency with which terrorists have attacked American citizens and property overseas, the US has been lucky in many ways. For example, foreign terrorist groups have for the most part eschewed staging operations on American soil—and those transnational terrorist incidents that have been authored here by domestic groups have generally been relatively minor affairs. Furthermore, the US Government has, as previously indicated, rarely been the target of terrorist demands. Hence, except for extensive (and readily accepted) airport security measures, the quality of American life and democratic freedoms has been little affected. And Washington has so far been spared the agony of having the lives of key political leaders or large numbers of innocents, be they Americans or foreigners, hang on its decisions.

[24] While it bears note, the parallel danger that commonly perceived opportunities for action in connection with such events could result in growing contact and cooperation between US-based and foreign terrorist groups falls outside the purview of this study.

Russell and Miller analyze data on several hundred terrorists from eighteen groups to develop a terrorist profile. Using eight categories (age, sex, marital status, rural versus urban origin, social and economic background, education or occupation, method/place of recruitment, and political philosophy), they produce a profile with some societal variations but with reasonable applicability. One of the most disturbing aspects of this analysis is the authors' conclusion that urban terrorists are gaining recruits from increasingly younger age groups.

Reprinted by permission from *Terrorism—An International Journal*, Volume 1, Number 1, 1977. Copyright © 1977 by Crane, Russak & Company, Inc.

Profile of a Terrorist

by CHARLES A. RUSSELL and BOWMAN H. MILLER

Throughout the past decade, a steady and continued rise in terrorist activity within many nations of the world has generated a flood of academic, military, and journalistic studies on this subject. In most of these analyses, however, the primary focus has been on the mechanics of terrorism rather than the individuals involved. As a result, such subjects as the rural-to-urban shift in the locus of most terrorist and guerrilla operations as well as the structure, organization, financing, weaponry, strategy, and tactics of various terrorist groups all have been explored in some detail. In recent years, equally careful attention has been given to the problem of transnational terrorism and the increasingly close interrelationships existing between terrorist organizations in widely separated geographic areas of the world. However, until the well-publicized exploits of the now infamous Venezuelan terrorist "Carlos" (Illitch Ramirez Sanchez), considerably less attention was given to an examination of the individuals involved in terrorist activity. Nevertheless, as pointed out in the summary remarks of Dr. Chalmers Johnson at the 25-26 March 1976 Conference on International Terrorism held in Washington, D.C., it is in this important area that additional knowledge is necessary.[1] Without knowledge as to the type of individual engaged in urban terrorism and those factors motivating his or her actions, coping with the problems of both national and transnational terrorism will be increasingly difficult.

While the following article does not pretend to close the important research gap outlined above, it does represent an effort to determine if there are truly common characteristics and similarities in the social origin, political philosophy, education, age, and family background of those individuals engaged in terrorist activities within Latin America, Europe, Asia, and the Middle East. Based upon a compilation and analysis of published data regarding over 350 individual terrorist cadres and leaders from Palestinian, Japanese, German, Irish, Italian, Turkish, Spanish, Iranian, Argentinan, Brazilian, and Uruguayan terrorist groups active during the 1966-1976 time span, an attempt is made to draw a sociological portait or profile of the modern urban terrorist.[2] To insure the greatest possible accuracy in this portrait, data were collected only on those individuals active in eighteen revolutionary groups known to specialize in urban terrorism as opposed to rural guerrilla warfare. Accordingly, among the Palestinians emphasis was placed on persons associated with the Popular Front for the Liberation of Palestine (PFLP) and the Black September Organization (BSO), whereas in Japan the Japanese Red Army (JRA), a group that has always operated outside that nation, was chosen. Within the Federal Republic of Germany, attention was given to the Movement Two June (M2J) and the Baader-Meinhof Group (BM), whereas in Northern Ireland the Provisional Wing of the Irish Republican Army (IRA-P) was the target. In Italy similar emphasis was placed on the Red Brigades (RB) and the Armed Proletarian Nuclei (APN), whereas in Turkey the People's Liberation Army (TPLA) of the early 1970s was selected. For Spain, the Basque Fatherland and Liberty Movement, specifically ETA-V, and the Marxist influenced Anti-Fascist, Patriotic Revolutionary Front (FRAP) were used. Finally, in Latin America, the Argentine Montoneros and the Trotskyite Revolutionary People's Army (ERP) in that country, the Brazilian groups following Carlos Marighella and the Uruguayan Tupamaros were of particular interest.

In organizing information regarding personnel in the above-mentioned groups, data have been summarized under eight general headings entitled age, sex, marital status, rural versus urban origin, social and economic background, education or occupation, method or place of recruitment, and political-economic philosophy. Within each category or heading, factors common to terrorists from various areas of the world are indicated as well as those that appear to vary depending upon national origin. The article concludes with a summary of commonalities and differences regarding terrorists from various geographic areas.

AGE[3]

Within the eighteen groups studied, the ages for active terrorist cadre members as opposed to leadership were remarkably consistent from group to group. Except for individuals affiliated with Palestinian, German, and Japanese organizations, the usual urban terrorist was between 22 and 25. Among the Uruguayan Tupamaros, a group particularly active in the 1966-1971 time frame, the average age of arrested terrorists was

24.1. In neighboring Brazil, where revolutionary elements were very active in the late 1960s, and in Argentina, wherein terrorism has almost become a way of life since the early 1970s, individual terrorist cadre averaged 23 and 24 respectively. For other Latin nations such as Spain and Italy, almost identical figures were noted. In Spain, for example, arrested members of the Basque Fatherland and Liberty Movement (ETA-V) average 23.2, and those associated with the Marxist-Communist Anti-Fascist, Patriotic Revolutionary Front (FRAP) were 24.6. Even in Iran, Turkey, and Northern Ireland, the same general pattern continued with ages averaging between 23 and 24. As indicated previously, only in Japanese, Palestinian, and West German groups was there an upward trend in cadre age. In Japan, based on arrested members of the Japanese Red Army, the average age was approximately 28. For those affiliated with the Popular Front for the Liberation of Palestine and the Black September Organization, data on identified and arrested terrorists indicates most were in their late twenties. In the case of the Baader-Meinhof organization and the Berlin-based Movement Two June, data on over 100 individual cadre members reflected an average age of 31.3.

While a precise explanation is not readily available regarding the significantly older status of at least the Palestinian and West German terrorist cadre members, one possible reason may lie in composition of the groups themselves. In both cases, the terrorist organizations in question are not composed primarily of university students, both graduate and undergraduate, as is the case for many of the groups studied. Instead, many members of both Palestinian and West German organizations are university graduates who since have become junior professional people, doctors, lawyers, and so forth. By virtue of this fact alone, their average age is higher than that of the almost purely student groups.

While age trends for members of many terrorist groups have been relatively stable over the last decade, there are recent indications, particularly among the Spanish, Latin American, Irish, Iranian and, Turkish organizations, the 22-to-25 age level may be dropping. In brief, it would appear that the often anarchistic-revolutionary philosophy heretofore largely a province of the university students has permeated into the secondary school level. Thus, arrests of Spanish ETA-V members in the spring of 1976 disclosed a number in their teens. Similar developments were evident in Argentina, Iran, and Turkey, while in Northern Ireland, some of the terrorists apprehended have been as young as 12 to 14. There also are signs that the age of Palestinian terrorists may be lowering. For example, those individuals involved in the 11 August 1976 attack on the Israeli El Al terminal in Istanbul's Yesilkoy Airport, for example, were 23 and 24.

Although terrorist cadres continue to fall into the early and mid-twenties, the leadership level of many terrorist organizations is usually much older. In Brazil, during the late 1960s and early 1970s, Carlos Marighella and his successors often were in their late 40s or early 50s. Marighella himself, a man generally considered as the leading theoretician of urban terrorism, was 58 at the time of his death in November 1969. Among Argentine, Uruguayan, and Italian terrorist elements, leadership is or was in its mid-30s or early 40s. In Argentina, Mario Santucho, founder and leader of the highly effective Revolutionary Army of the People (Ejército Revolucionario del Pueblo—ERP), was 40 at the time of his July 1976 death in combat with government forces. His chief lieutenants, Enrique Gorriarán, José Urteaga, and Domingo Mena (also killed in July), were only slightly younger than Santucho. In a similar manner, Raul Sendic, chief of the Uruguayan Tupamaro organization, was 42 when his group began significant operations in the latter 1960s, whereas Renato Curcio, leader of the Italian Red Brigades, was 35 at the time of his arrest in early 1976. Within the Palestinian groups, policy level leaders are often in their late 40s or early 50s. Similarly, in Germany, Andreas Baader, founder of the Baader-Meinhof organization, is 33 and many of his group's current or former leaders (Horst Mahler, 40; Christa Eckes, 46; Gudrun Ensslin, 36; and Holger Meins, 35) are in their late 30s and early 40s. Ulrike Meinhof, the cofounder and chief ideologue of the Baader-Meinhof group, took her own life at the age of 42 in May 1976 while on trial in Stuttgart.

SEX[4]

Despite minor variations among some of the groups studied, urban terrorism remains a predominantly male phenomenon. During the period examined (1966-1976), almost all significant terrorist operations (well over 80 percent) were directed, led, and executed by males. Within Latin American terrorist organizations (the Argentine Montoneros and ERP, the Brazilian successors to Marighella, and the Uruguayan Tupamaros), female membership was less than 16 percent (based on arrested-identified terrorist cadres). Among these organizations, the Tupamaros made perhaps the most use of females; however, with few exceptions, the role of these women was confined to intelligence collection, operations as couriers, duties as nurses and medical personnel, and in the maintenance of "safe houses" for terrorists sought by police and for the storage of weapons, propaganda, false documentation, funds, and other supplies.[5] Interestingly, the elusive Venezuelan terrorist "Carlos" (Illitch Ramirez Sanchez), an individual associated with Popular Front for the Liberation of Palestine operations in Europe, also used his female contacts in Paris almost solely for these purposes.[6] In Spanish, Italian, Turkish, and Iranian terrorist groups, this same predominantly support role for women has been noted.

Despite the support, as opposed to operational, roles assigned women in many terrorist organizations, there have been numerous well-known exceptions to this generalization. Thus, Leila Khalid and Fusako Shigenobu were highly effective leaders in the Popular Front for the Liberation of Palestine (PFLP) and the Japanese Red Army (JRA), respectively. Together, they were instrumental in arranging the initial PFLP training of JRA and West German cadres in Lebanon during the early 1970s. Today

Shigenobu still is considered the actual leader and operational brains behind the JRA. Within Latin America, Norma Ester Arostito was a co-founder of the Argentine Montoneros and served as chief ideologue of that group until her death in 1976. In Spain, Genoveve Forest Tarat played a key role in the December 1973 ETA-V operation that resulted in the assassination of Spanish Premier Admiral Carrero Blanco as well as the 13 September 1974 bombing of a Madrid restaurant (Café Rolando), which resulted in eleven killed and more than seventy persons wounded. In this same context, Margherita Cagol, the now-deceased wife of Italian Red Brigades (RB) leader Renato Curcio, appears to have played an important role in that organization and quite possibly to have led the RB commando team that freed Curcio from Rome's Casale Monferrato jail on 8 February 1975.

While these and many other women have carried out key leadership or operational roles in varied terrorist groups, most female terrorists continue to function in a supportive capacity. Significantly, this frequent relegation of women to a support role is not the product of male chauvinism but rather practical experience. In the minds of most terrorist leaders, and as demonstrated by actual operations, women are simply more effective than men in such supporting activities. Several women living together (yet acually operating a "safe house," weapons storage cache, or document fabrication facility) are infrequently seen by security personnel as something unusual. whereas a gathering of males in an apartment or house might well be viewed with substantial suspicion. Similarly, in the terrorist view, females—by virtue of their sex alone—are more adept at allaying the suspicions of security personnel. As a result, posing as wives or mothers, they often can enter areas that would be restricted to males, thereby obtaining useful intelligence information on government or business operations and activities.

Although women have functioned in a secondary role within most terrorist groups, they have occupied a very important position within the West German Baader-Meinhof organization as well as the Movement Two June. There, women constitute fully one-third of the operational, as opposed to support, personnel. In addition to the leading role of Ulrik Meinhof in founding the Baader-Meinhof group, nearly 60 percent of that organization and Movement Two June personnel at large as of August 1976 were women. Four of these women escaped from jail in West Berlin in June 1976. Several others were freed during the successful kidnapping of Peter Lorenz, Christian Democratic mayoral candidate in Berlin, by Movement Two June on 27 February 1975 and have since joined forces with the Popular Front for the Liberation of Palestine (PFLP). In the West German context, there appears to be no real terrorist division of labor based on sex.[7] Women such as Ulrike Meinhof, Gudrun Ensslin, Ingrid Siepmann, Hanna Krabbe, Gabriele Kroecher-Tiedemann, and Angela Luther all have been identified in leadership roles and as participants in robberies, burglaries, kidnappings, bombings, and other operations. In this context, Gabriele Kroecher-Tiedemann was responsible for the "execution" of Austrian police official Anton Tichler during the December 1975 attack on the OPEC oil ministers meeting in Vienna, whereas Ilse Jandt, a former associate of the Movement Two June, planned and personally carried out the assassination of German terrorist turncoat Ulrich Schmuecker in West Berlin on 5 June 1974.[8]

MARITAL STATUS[8]

The unmarried terrorist is still the rule rather than the exception. Requirements for mobility, flexibility, initiative, security, and total dedication to a revolutionary cause all preclude encumbering family responsibilities and normally dictate single status for virtually all operational terrorist cadres. Statistics regarding arrested or identified terrorists in Latin America, Europe, the Middle East, and Asia reflect over 75-80 percent of the individuals involved were single. In the Federal Republic of Germany and West Berlin the 80 percent figure is also accurate. Some of the few married individuals involved in German terrorist activities (Horst Mahler, Ulrike Meinhof, and Angela Luther) severed ties to spouses and children in order to pursue terrorist methods. Only in the case of the Uruguayan Tupamaros, a group that according to revolutionary theorist Regis Debray may have made the greatest use of women,[10] were a significant number (still less than 30 percent) of the terrorist cadre in a married status.[11] Of interest in regard to this group is the fact that the married status of many Tupamaros posed some significant operational problems for that group. In those instances where the wives of Tupamaros were arrested and subjected to interrogation, morale considerations almost compelled the group to seek their release. As a result, in operations such as the 8 March 1970 attack on the women's prison in Montevideo where the effort secured the release of thirteen women Tupamaros and was a propaganda/morale victory for the organization, the cost was high in casualties suffered by the attack team. Thus, the decision of most terrorist organizations to utilize unmarried or separated personnel appears sound from an operational point of view.

RURAL VERSUS URBAN ORIGIN[12]

As pointed out so well by Carlos Marighella, probably the most widely read, known, and imitated theoretician and practitioner of urban guerrilla warfare, the terrorist must be intimately familiar with the terrain in which he or she operates.

> What matters is to know every path a guerrilla can use, every place he can hide, leaving the enemy at the mercy of his own ignorance. With his detailed knowledge of the streets, and all their nooks and crannies, of the rougher ground, the sewers, the wooded ground . . . urban guerrillas can easily elude the police, or surprise them in a trap or ambush. If he knows the ground well . . . he can always escape arrest.[13]

In view of the above, it is not at all surprising that most urban terrorists are natives or long-time residents of metropolitan areas, particularly the cities in which they operate. Within Argentina, where the ERP and Montoneros have been so successful in urban operations during the past six years, approximately 90 percent of their members are from the greater Buenos Aires area itself. In Brazil, the bulk of Marighella's followers and imitators came from Rio de Janeiro, São Paulo, Santos, and Recife, whereas in Uruguay over 70 percent of the Tupamaros were natives of Montevideo, their primary area of activity. Within Iran, Turkey, Italy, and the Federal Republic of Germany, most terrorists are from urban areas, particularly Tehran, Ankara, Rome, Milan, Genoa, West Berlin, and Hamburg. Similarly, a significant number of the Japanese Red Army members, who operated so effectively with European-based members of the Popular Front for the Liberation of Palestine during the years 1972-1974, are from Tokyo, Kyoto, Osaka, or other Japanese metropolitan centers. Even in Spain this same trend is evident. There, however, although most members of the Communist-FRAP are from larger cities such as Madrid or Barcelona, members of the Basque ETA-V generally come from smaller centers in the Basque region such as San Sebastián and Bilbao. In addition to an urban background, several European terrorist groups have tended to focus operations within a specific region or city of origin or in familiar nearby areas. Thus, in Italy, the Armed Proletarian Nuclei (APN), which traditionally has operated in south and central Italy, focuses its activities in Naples, Reggio Calabria, and Rome while the Red Brigades, of northern Italian origin, have been most active in Milan, Genoa, Bologna, Turin, and Florence. Within Germany and Spain similar patterns are evident. In the Federal Republic, the Movement Two June—which originated in West Berlin—confined much of its activity to West Berlin, whereas the Baader-Meinhof organization, a group born in Frankfurt, operated primarily in the Frankfurt base area and surrounding cities. In Spain, with few exceptions, most activities of the Basque Fatherland and Liberty Movement (ETA-V) have been in the Basque provinces and particularly the area surrounding the city of San Sebastián. In contrast, the Anti-Fascist Patriotic and Revolutionary Front (FRAP), a group composed largely of Marxist students from Madrid and Barcelona, has tended to emphasize operations in their areas. Other identifiable patterns of this type are evident in Turkey (with the Ankara-based Turkish People's Liberation Army focusing on operations in that city) and in Iran (with the People's Strugglers and People's Sacrifice Guerrillas both stressing activities in Tehran and its environs).[14]

For the Palestinian organizations, particularly the Popular Front for the Liberation of Palestine, many members also appear to have been born in or lived for significant periods of time within major urban areas. In addition, many Palestinians, including some of those now affiliated with the PFLP, were educated abroad (in 1969 some 6,000 Palestinians were studying abroad).[15] Trained in European and various Middle Eastern universities located in such cities as Frankfurt, Stuttgart, Berlin, London, Cairo, Beirut, and Paris, these individuals were intimately familiar with urban life, normally spoke a foreign language and were able to integrate into and live within any metropolitan area without difficulty. The success of Palestinian terrorist operations in Europe over the past four to five years attests readily to this fact.

SOCIAL AND ECONOMIC BACKGROUND[16]

In conjunction with their urban origin or long-time residence in metropolitan areas is the predominantly middle-class or even upper-class background of many terrorist cadres and leaders. A statistical review of data on arrested-identified terrorists associated with the eighteen groups mentioned earlier reflects well over two-thirds of these individuals came from the middle or upper classes in their respective nations or areas. In most instances their parents were professional people (doctors, lawyers, engineers, and so forth), governmental employees, diplomats, clergymen, military officers, or sometimes even police officials. Although these parents were part of the existing social and economic systems, many of them had been frustrated in their efforts to use them as vehicles for upward social and economic mobility. Liberal in political outlook, they also frequently advocated significant social and political change.When these parental views were coupled with the radical socioeconomic doctrines so popular in most university circles during the 1960s, this combination of forces—added to general student distrust of "democratic institutions" as effective media for implementing social change—may have moved some young people toward terrorism and guerrilla war as rapid methods of achieving the desired change or obtaining the power to implement such changes.

While space limitations do not permit a detailed case by case analysis of the more than 350 terrorists studied, even a cursory look at the background of some group leaders and cadres demonstrates their middle-class origin. Thus, in the case of the Baader-Meinhof organization and the Movement Two June in the Federal Republic of Germany, over 65 percent of the membership was from the middle class. Baader himself was the son of a historian, Ulrike Meinhof the daughter of an art historian, Horst Mahler the son of a dentist, Holger Meins the son of a business manager, and Gudrun Ensslin the daughter of a clergyman. In the Japanese Red Army a similar pattern was evident. There, even the leading female member, Fusako Shigenobu, was the daughter of an insurance executive while cadre members and leaders such as Maruoka Osamu, Hidaka Toshihiko, Nishikawa Jun, and others also were products of a middle-class environment. The same is evident among the Uruguayan Tupamaros, whose membership rarely included individuals from the working class, and whose composition was over 90 percent middle- and upper-class students and young professionals. As pointed out very succinctly in November 1970 by then Uruguayan Chancellor Jorge Peirano Facio, "For each family of the upper social class there is a Tupamaro,"[17] In Argentina, the same general situation prevails with members of the Trotskyite ERP and the radical Peronist Montoneros from these same general social levels. Even in areas such as Turkey, Iran, and among the

Palestinian organizations, where one might expect some breakdown in the pattern, it remains generally consistent. Only in the ranks of the Provisional Wing of the Irish Republican Army (IRA-P) is there a real deviation from the norm. To a significant degree this may result, as pointed out in several excellent studies on this organization by the London-based Institute for the Study of Conflict, from the fact that Catholic families in Northern Ireland traditionally have been relegated, by political means, to the lower economic and social levels through a process of deliberate discrimination. Accordingly, it is not surprising to find that many cadre members and the leadership within the IRA-P are not drawn from the middle and upper classes. This situation, however, stands out as almost the sole exception to an otherwise general and consistent pattern.

EDUCATION OR OCCUPATION[18]

As might be anticipated from comments made in preceding paragraphs, the vast majority of those individuals involved in terrorist activities as cadres or leaders are quite well educated. In fact, approximately two-thirds of those identified terrorists are persons with some university training, university graduates, or postgraduate students. Among the Latin American terrorist groups, particularly the Uruguayan Tupamaros and the Argentine Revolutionary People's Army and Montoneros, the figure neared 75 percent. Within even such essentially nationalist organizations as the Basque Fatherland and Liberty Movement (ETA-V), over 40 percent of the identified leaders and cadre members who have been arrested had some university training and many were graduates. In the Federal Republic of Germany, the same pattern was evident with approximately 80 percent of the more than 100 identified terrorists involved with the Baader-Meinhof organization and Movement Two June having received at least some college education. For the latter group, the Free University of Berlin was a particularly fruitful recruiting ground.

Even in Turkey and Iran, university-trained terrorists were the rule rather than the exception. The Turkish People's Liberation Army (TPLA), a group responsible for the March 1971 kidnapping of four U.S. Air Force airmen in Ankara and the subsequent March 1972 kidnapping and execution of three NATO technicians, was composed almost totally of students from the Middle Eastern Technical University (METU) in Ankara. Leading the TPLA group involved in this operation was Denis Gezmic, a METU graduate. Within Iran, a substantial number of those involved in terrorist activities were persons with university backgrounds. In Tehran, for example, Resa Resa'i, the 2 June 1973 assassin of U.S. Army Lt. Colonel Lewis Hawkins, was a dentistry student at the time of this act. Other significant assassinations and terrorist acts in Iran, such as the attacks on the U.S. officers Price, Shaffer, and Turner, also were carried out in large part by Iranian university graduates.

For Palestinian groups, as pointed out by Dr. Paul Jureidini in his presentation on "Terrorism in the Middle East" at the Washington, D.C., Conference on International Terrorism, most leading terrorist cadres are not only products of a middle-class environment but also university students or graduates. As early as 1969, as mentioned previously, over 6,000 Palestinians were studying abroad, particularly in Europe. Exposed to the anarchist-Marxist ideas then so prevalent in European universities, and active as members of the radical Fatah-affiliated General Union of Palestinian Students (GUPS), individuals from this group constituted an important pool of educated manpower that was tapped frequently by ESO and PFLP recruiters.

Coupled with the generally high educational level of operational cadre members was an equally high level for group leaders. George Habbash, chief of the very active PFLP, is a medical doctor while his counterpart and frequent rival, Yasir Arafat, is a graduate engineer. Renato Curcio, founder of the Italian Red Brigades, is a sociology graduate while Roberto Santucho, now deceased, former leader of the Argentine People's Revolutionary Army, was an economist, and Raul Sendic, creator of the Tupamaros, is a lawyer. In the Federal Republic of Germany, Baader-Meinhof leader Horst Mahler (now imprisoned) is a lawyer, and Meinhof was a journalist, Ensslin and Luther teachers, and Jan-Carl Raspe a graduate sociologist. Practicing doctors and nurses also have been active terrorists in these West German groups.

Although spanning a rather wide educational spectrum, the formal training of both terrorist leaders and cadre members, in most groups, tended to focus on the humanities, with particular emphasis on law, history, economics, education, sociology, philosophy, and medicine. In contrast to this general arts and sciences curriculum, Iranian and Turkish terrorists tended to be educated in the more exact sciences, particularly in technical fields such as engineering. As a general exception to the entire educational pattern, however, is the Provisional Wing of the Irish Republican Army, essentially for the reasons set forth in the earlier discussion of social origin. "The Provisional IRA, and the extremist Protestant groups which arose in reaction to it, are the only terrorist organizations in the world which even in their leadership have practically no intellectuals."[19]

As stated previously, particularly in regard to Latin American terrorists, the dominant occupation among these individuals is now and always has been that of student. Often in their lower twenties, Tupamaros, Montoneros, ERP members, and the various followers of Brazilian revolutionary Carlos Marighella frequently have conducted terrorist operations almost as a direct part of their college curricula. Operating from university centers, which by law and tradition were immune from government search, over 70 percent of the arrested-identified terrorists in Argentina and Uruguary were students, and in Brazil the percentage was well over 50. When older individuals also were active in these groups, they usually were white-collar workers and professionals such as doctors, bankers, lawyers, engineers, journalists, university professors, mid-level government executives, and so forth. Outside Latin America, although the percentage of students identified as terrorists was somewhat lower, this occupation remained important. Smilarly, of the above professionals, lawyers, econo- mists, and medical doctors were particularly prevalent among European and Middle Eastern terrorist leaders and cadres. In like manner, uni- versities in West Berlin, Frankfurt, Heidelberg, and Hamburg in Ger- many and elsewhere in Europe have served as operational bases for ter- rorist efforts.

METHOD AND PLACE OF RECRUITMENT[20]

Considering the important role played by students and university graduates (or dropouts) in most terrorist movements, it is not surprising that many large universities have been and now are primary recruiting grounds for operational terrorist cadres. Quite often young men and women first encounter anarchistic and Marxist doctrines upon entrance into a university where the prevalence of such concepts is often coupled with a strong Marxist bias on the part of professors and administrators. When these developments are linked with frequent Marxist domination of student federations, it is not surprising that the university has become an ideological training ground for future terrorist cadres. Thus, for the Japanese Red Army, the universities of Tokyo, Rikkjo, and Kyoto have been very important. In Spain, both the Basque ETA-V and the Com- munist-supported FRAP have been staffed by graduates from the uni- versities of Madrid and Barcelona. Within Italy, the universities in Rome, Turin, and Bologna are fertile recruiting grounds for anarchist groups such as the Red Brigades. In Latin America, the National University in Montevideo, the University of Buenos Aires, and those in Brazil have supplied a substantial percentage of those individuals involved in urban terrorism. The pattern also continues in Iran, Turkey, and the Federal Republic of Germany. There, the universities in West Berlin, Frankfurt, Hamburg, Heidelberg, Munich, and Stuttgart have been the basic train- ing centers for many German terrorist groups. Finally, even in the case of the Palestinians, many of whom were educated abroad, universities were frequent recruiting bases. Only in Northern Ireland and to some extent in the Basque ETA-V, as well as among certain Palestinian groups, is the pattern broken. In each of these cases, however, terrorist recruit- ment often is based on the primary appeal of nationalism rather than an anarchistic and Marxist political philosophy. For those few terrorist groups that include both intellectual and criminal elements, the place of initial recruitment for the latter is often a prison. Thus, the Italian Armed Proletarian Nuclei (APN) frequently makes initial contact with a potential terrorist while he or she is still serving a prison sentence. By facilitating the release of such an individual or providing assistance to him or her after release, APN is able to assess the individual's potential for terrorist activity. If useful to the organization, such a person often can be recruited without much difficulty. In this manner, Martino Zicchitella, the ANP member killed in the 14 Dec 1976 assassination attempt against Rome's antiterrorist chief Alfonso Noce, apparently was drawn into the organi- zation. The same has been true for the imprisoned Baader-Meinhof cadres whose stated objective is to politicize fellow inmates for the continued revolution once freed from confinement.[21]

POLITICAL PHILOSOPHY[22]

The question of a political philosophy is a most difficult one to treat, particularly as a category, since it defies a statistical response. Using the basic definition of terrorism as a tactic used by weak groups against larger opposing forces in pursuit of political objectives, one can discard terrorism itself as meeting the criteria of a philosophy. Three basic ideological tendencies are at play among most major terrorist groups operating today; anarchism, Marxism-Leninism, and nationalism. It is the combination of these three in specific contexts that produces the variant left-extremist philosophies espoused by most terrorists today. Nationalism is rarely and important ingredient in such views. Of the eighteen organizations studied, it can be considered significant only in the case of three: the Basque ETA-V, the Irish Republican Army, and the Popular Front for the Liberation of Palestine. Even in these groups, however, it is strongly blended with Marxism. For most other organizations, such as the Japanese Red Army, the West German Baader-Meinhof group,[23] and the Movement Two June, the mixture is a combination of anarchism and Marxism with the latter as a predominant element.

Although basically Marxist, the majority of terrorist organizations today reject the passive outlook of orthodox Soviet communism in favor of the revolutionary violence advocated by Carlos Marighella. In return, the orthodox Communists normally reject terrorists as "bourgeois gangsters" who lack a political foundation and have abandoned the tested social and political Communist party structure in favor of shortsighted and often counterproductive "hooliganism." Accordingly, it should be no surprise that those terrorists discussed in this profile related more closely with the Trotskyite Fourth International than Soviet communism. "Trotsky's theory of 'permanent revolution' emphasizes, in its international aspects, the global nature of the phenomenon, the necessary links between revolution in one country with that elsewhere. Ethnic, cultural, and national distinctions will on this thesis be unable to withstand the revolutionary side . . . ."[24] Thus, in the final analysis, the philosophical underpinnings of most modern terrorist groups may be found in a loose synthesis of the views developed by Mao, Trotsky, Marcuse, Fanon, and particularly those of Marighella.

In summation, one can draw a general composite picture into which fit the great majority of those terrorists from the eighteen urban guerrilla groups examined here. To this point, they have been largely single males aged 22 to 24, with exceptions as previously noted, who have some university education, if not a college degree. The female terrorists, except for the West German groups and an occasional leading figure in the URA, JRA, and PFLP, are preoccupied with support rather than operational roles. More often than not, these urban terrorists come from affluent, urban, middle-class families, many of whom enjoy considerable social prestige. Like their parents before them, many of the older terrorists have been trained for the medical, legal, engineering, and teaching professions, among others, and may have practiced these occupations prior to their commitment to a terrorist life. Whether having turned to terrorism as a university student or only later, most were provided an anarchist or Marxist world view, as well as recruited into terrorist operations while in the university. It is within the universities that these young products of an affluent society were initially confronted with and provided anarchist or Marxist ideological underpinnings for their otherwise unstructured frustrations and idealism.

While no international trend is as yet readily discernible, there are indicators that in a number of countries including Argentina, West Germany, Iran, and Spain, as well as the region of Northern Ireland, urban terrorists groups—or the phenomenon of urban terrorism itself—is recruiting younger and younger adherents. Increasing numbers also are drawn from those who are undergoing vocational training in preparation for work in skilled trades, many of which are readily adaptable to terrorist requirements, e.g., electrician, gunsmith, mechanic, and printer. To what extent this development may alter the preliminary composite picture sketched in this article is a question deserving additional research and attention.

NOTES & REFERENCES

[1] Conference on International Terrorism, 25-26 March 1976, Department of State Auditorium. Washington, D.C. Conference panelists included representatives from the academic, industrial, journalistic, and governmental communities. Also present were speakers from the Federal Republic of Germany, Israel, and the United Kingdom.

[2] Most of the data used in this article was abstracted from general circulation English, French, German, Spanish, and Italian language newspapers, government documents, research publications, and so forth. In regard to Spain, Argentina, Brazil, Uruguay, the Federal Republic of Germany, and Japan, a substantial amount of government doumentation on terrorist personalities and groups also was available. For Turkish, Irish, and Italian terrorist organizations and individuals, however, data was obtained primarily from newspaper reports and academic studies. In the case of the several Palestinian groups discussed, the authors are particularly indebted to Dr. Paul Jureidini, Vice President, Abbott Associates Inc., Alexandria, Virginia. A speaker on "Terrorism in the Middle East at the above cited conference, Dr. Jureidini, a native of Lebanon, is the author of numerous classified and unclassified articles, research papers, and monographs on the Palestinian movement as well as consultant to several Department of Defense agencies. He is also a regular speaker at the USAF Special Operations School on Middle Eastern problems and insurgency.

[3] The most fruitful sources of age data on terrorist cadre were governmental reports such as the Spanish *Terrorismo y Justicia en España* (Madrid: Centro Espa de Documentación, 1975). Also useful were academic analyses and chronologies such as Ernesto Mayans, "Los trabajos y los días cronología" (a day-by-day account of Tupamaro operations from 1962 through 1971) in Ernesto Mayans (ed.) *Tupamaros: Antología Documental* (Cuernavaca: Centro Intercultural de Documentación, 1971). Also useful were Foreign Broadcast Information Service reporting and the following newspapers: *The New York Times;* The London *Times; The Economist: Informaciones, Ya, and ABC* of Madrid; *La Nación* of Buenos Aires; *O Jornal do Brasil; Le Monde;* the English language *Turkish Daily News* of Ankara; *La Stampa* of Turin; *Il Messagero; Corriere Della Sera* and *Il Gironale* of Milan; and *Die Welt* and *Frankfurter Allgemeine Zeitung* in West Germany.

[4] Ibid.

[5] See "El pape de la mujer" in *Los Tupamaros en Acción* (Mexico, D.F.: Editorial Diogenes, 1972), pp. 56-62. This book, with

a new prologue by Regis Debray, is a reprint of an earlier Tupamaro handbook published in Argentina under the title *Actas Tupamaras.*

[6] See "The Number 1 Terrorist", *Japanese Times Weekly* (Tokyo), 4 March 1975 and *Informaciones* (Madrid), 11 July 1975, pp. 2-3, articles entitled "Carlos, el terrorista es miembro de FPLP" and "la embajada cubana en Paris, complicada en el terrorismo", and the three-part series in *Der Spiegel,* 26 July, 2 and 9 August 1976.

[7] See also Dr. Hans-Josef Horchem, *Extremisten in einer selbstbewussten Demokratie* (Freiburg: 1975), pp 26 and 27. "Women are involved not only as helpers, informants, intelligence collectors but as active fighters who carry pistols up to 9 millimeter under their coats or in their purses which they readily use if necessary to avoid arrest . . . . Of the 22 activists of the RAF nucleus, 12 are women. Of the 20 activists who later augmented the RAF, eight are women. In the concept and activity of the RAF are also the result of an explosive emancipation of the participating female activists." (English translation by Bowman H. Miller)

[8] *Innere Sicherheit,* no. 27, Bonn, 14 April 1975.

[9] See item 3 above for general source materials.

[10] "Prólogo" by Regis Debray in *Los Tupamaros en Acción.*

[11] Ernesto Mayans, "Los trabajos y los días cronología".

[12] See item 3 above for general source materials. See also Rolf Tophoven, *Guerrilla ohne Grenzen*, p. 127; "30 preguntas a un Tupamaro", *Punto Final* (Santiago), 2 July 1968, pp. 5-8; Andy Truskier, "The Politics of Violence: The Urban Guerrilla in Brazil", *Ramparts,* vol. 9, October 1970, pp. 30-34; "La actividad terrorista in Bresil", *Este & Oeste* (Caracas), vol. 8, no. 132, December 1969, pp. 8-9; Charles A. Russell, James F. Schenkel, James A. Miller, "Urban Guerrillas in Argentina: A Select Bibliography", *Latin American Research Review,* vol. 9, no. 3, Fall 1974, pp. 53-89; *Il Messaggero* (Rome), 10 Feb. 1976; Hubert O. Johnson, "Recent Opposition Movements in Iran," Masters thesis: (University of Utah, June 1975), pp. 305-320,; Interviews with Dr. Paul Jureidini; *Terrorismo y Justicia en España;* Dr. Hans Josef Horchem, "West Germany: The Long March Through the Institutions" *Conflict Studies* (London: Institute for the Study of Conflict), no. 33, February 1973; Dr. Hans Josef Horchem, "West Germany's Red Army Anarchists" *Conflict Studies* (London: Institute for the Study of Conflict), no. 46, June 1974.

[13] Carlos Marighella, *For the Liberation of Brazil* (London: Cox and Wyman, 1971), pp. 74-75.

[14] "El jefe dela brigada antiterrorista herido en un atentado." *Informaciones,* 15 Dec. 76, pp. 10; "Conmoción en Italia tras los recientes actos de terrorismo" *ABC,* 16 Dec. 76, pp. 26; "Tupamaro a la Italiana", *Cambio 16,* 2-8 Feb. 76, pp. 49-50.

[15] Barbara Anne Wilson, *Conflict in the Middle East: The Challenge of the Palestinian Movement* (Washington, D.C.: Center for Research in Social Systems, January 1969), pp. 20-30, 35-36.

[16] See prior citations for source materials as well as Brian Crozier (ed.), *Ulster: Politics and Terrorism* (London: Institute for the Study of Conflict, June 1973). See also Hubert O. Johnson, "Recent Opposition", pp. 259, 305, 331, 333, and the two *Conflict Studies* by Dr. Horchem.

[17] Ernesto Mayans; "Los trabajos y los días cronología (1962-71) in Ernesto Mayans (ed.), *Tupamaros: Antología Documental.*

[18] See also Mayans, *Tupamaros;* Hubert O. Johnson, "Recent Opposition"; pp. 259-320, 331, 333, 334, *Arab World,* June 1973; "Secretly to Death", *Economist,* 3 June 1972, pp. 44; *Il Messaggero, Corriera della Sera, Il Giornale* 19 Jan. 1976; *Daily American* (Rome), 20 January 1976; *Le Monde,* 17 and 24 February 1972.

[19] Richard Clutterbuck, *Terrorismus ohne Chance* (Stuttgart: Seewald Verlag, 1975), p. 174.

[20] See also "La universidad de la Republica y el Marxismo", *Este & Oeste* (Caracas), vol. 14, no. 180, October-November 1974, pp. 1-6; "El problema de la Juventud Peronista", *Este & Oeste* (Caracas), vol. 12, no. 177, May 1974, pp. 1-5; "El ERP y la subversión de Extrema Izquierda en Argentina", *Este & Oeste* (Caracas), vol. 12, no. 177, May 1974, pp. 6-10.

[21] "El jefe de la brigada antiterrorista herido en un atentado." *Informaciones,* 15 Dec. 1976, p. 10.

[22] For a useful review of the political philosophy of terrorists and terrorist groups see Robert Moss, *The War for the Cities* (New York: Coward, McGann & Geoghegan Inc., 1972), ch. 1 "The City and Revolution, Political Violence in Western Societies and the Roots of Revolution," pp. 17-30; Edward Hyams, *Terrorists and Terrorism,* (New York: St. Martin's Press, 1974), pt I, "The Theorists," specifically chap. 1 through 4; and Paul Wilkenson, *Political Terrorism* (London: MacMillan Press Ltd., 1974), chap. 1 through 3.

[23] For detailed information on the political views of the Baader-Meinhof organization and leadership see *Dokumentation über Aktivitäten anarchistischer Gewalttäter in der Bundesrepublik Deutschland* (Documents on Anarchist Criminals in the Federal Republic of

Germany), a compendium of confiscated Baader-Meinhof writings seized during raids on terrorists' cells in July 1973 and on 4 February 1974, published by the German Interior Ministry (in German) during 1974.

24 Anthony Burton, *Urban Terrorism: Theory, Practice and Response* (New York: The Free Press of Glencoe, 1976), p. 109.

II THREAT POTENTIAL OF CONTEMPORARY TERRORISM

Contemporary terrorism has a threat potential which far surpasses its classical counterpart. This is brought to our attention daily by the news media, which often presents worst-case scenarios involving nuclear blackmail or toxic terrorism. Indeed, nuclear terrorism is considered by many to be the next step up the escalation ladder. Many governments are already preparing extensive preventive measures to make it impossible for terrorists to gain access to dangerous chemical and nuclear materials or to steal nuclear weapons. Difficulties associated with this problem area are discussed by Rosenbaum, who emphasizes the necessity for concerted international action. A follow-up article by Norman is included in this section to focus on preparations made by the United States to increase physical security of nuclear storage sites.

Other points of discussion are the more likely applications of contemporary terrorism as a military weapon, or in a broader sense, for surrogate warfare. These uses have inspired far less controversy than possible terrorist seizures of nuclear weapons or use of toxic chemicals, but may prove more dangerous.

Jenkins' concept of surrogate warfare may already be in operation. His prediction that, "We are going to see some high technology terrorism, made possible by new vulnerabilities and new weapons," is given further emphasis by Mallin, who describes terrorism's potential as a military weapon.

Threat potential associated with the type of terrorist attacks described here will create new difficulties for government representatives organized to counter terrorism. High technology terrorism will result in the necessity for greater collaboration between law enforcement and the military. This is particularly true for industrialized nations with large reserves of military manpower. New problems will arise in attempting to harmonize these efforts and these problems will be considered in the following section on response.

Jenkins provides a different view of terrorism's threat potential by projecting current trends in technology in order to assess what impact they may have on terrorist capabilities in the future. Many may recognize the technology-vulnerability relationship, but everyone may not accept Jenkins' argument that modern conventional warfare is becoming obsolete. For that reason his description of surrogate warfare is all the more valuable.

The following article is reprinted by permission from the Rand Corporation, Santa Monica, California, 1975.

High Technology Terrorism and Surrogate War: The Impact of New Technology on Low-Level Violence

by BRIAN MICHAEL JENKINS

Several questions occurred to me when I first began to think about the impact of technological developments on low-level violence. For example, how has new technology changed rural or urban guerrilla warfare? What kinds of new military technology have the struggles in Northern Ireland, Southeast Asia, or Latin America produced? What kinds of weapons are Palestinian commandos or IRA Provisionals now using? What kinds of technology are being developed to counter the activities of guerrillas and terrorists?

But instead of dissecting the inner workings of a letter-bomb or cataloging the new surveillance and detection devices that have been developed to locate phantom guerrillas in jungles or skyscrapers, or find hidden explosives, I decided to examine the topic in somewhat broader terms, looking at current trends in technology, both military and civilian, what they could mean in the long run to guerrillas and terrorists, and also what they could mean for the rest of us.

In the following paper, I would like to develop two independent but complementary ideas about the war in the future. First, I will argue that due largely to technological developments—the development of new weapons and the creation of new vulnerabilities in a society that is increasingly complex and dependent on fragile technology—modern guerrilla and terrorist groups are being afforded a growing capacity for disruption and destruction. Second, I will argue that what we now call modern conventional war, the kind that is declared and openly fought, is becoming obsolete for a variety of reasons. The decreasing profit of modern conventional warfare as an instrument of political pressure may persuade some nations to adopt terrorist groups or terrorist tactics as a means of surrogate warfare against another nation. The support of terrorists by any nation or group of nations in turn will further increase the terrorists' capacity for violence. It may also prevent effective international cooperation aimed at controlling international terrorism.

The balance of military power, defined in this instance simply as the capacity to inflict damage, will shift away from armies toward smaller armed groups that do not necessarily represent or confine their activities to any particular nation. National governments, of course, will retain a clear superiority in conventional military power, but will lose their monopoly over the means of large-scale violence as smaller groups gain more destructive power, which they can use in ways that make conventional military power of little utility. Modern terrorists have already demonstrated that small groups with a limited capacity for violence can achieve disproportionately large effects in the world. They have attracted worldwide attention to themselves and to their causes; they have caused worldwide alarm; they have compelled governments with a clear preponderance of conventional military power to negotiate with them, to grant them concessions, and to exert pressure on other governments to grant concessions.

The technological developments which are taking place now both in military weaponry and in civilian society, will have important military and political consequences. Their effect may be as profound as that created by the introduction of nuclear and strategic weapons a generation ago. As numerous small groups acquire an increasing capacity for major violence, warfare may be redefined and the rules of warfare modified. Our present concepts of security and defense may have to be altered. Armies, as we know them now, could become increasingly irrelevant as providers of national security. In the political realm, national governments threatened by increasingly violent terrorists may collectively turn to authoritarian measures as they seek to preserve domestic and international order. Some countries may not be able to satisfy or pacify dissident minorities and will come apart. The present system of international order based on a community of national governments may itself be jeopardized. The concept of nationhood itself could be altered.

This vision of the future is not meant to be alarmist or apocalyptic. The world is not likely to collapse into terrorist anarchy any more than it is likely to end in a single nuclear holocaust. Conventional wars are likely to remain at least the primary mode of armed conflict between nations. Conventional armies will be maintained. Conventional wars probably will produce more casualties than all the world's terrorists put together. The kind of war that is now waged by terrorists will not replace conventional war as waged by armies. Terrorist violence will coexist with conventional war, but it probably will become more destructive, and therefore will become more important.

THE LONG MARCH TO LOD

While terrorism itself is not a new concept, the kind of terrorism we see today is a derivative of twentieth-century theories of guerrilla warfare. Mao Tse-tung deserves the most credit for developing the modern theory of guerrilla warfare. He gave a coherent theory to what had been until then a set of military tactics employed by groups who lacked armies. In doing so, Mao formulated a series of relationships that differed from existing military strategies and earlier Marxist theories of revolution. He differed from the earlier Marxists in placing greater emphasis on military power. Political power depends on military power, or, as Mao put it, "political power grows out of the barrel of a gun." But Mao also recognized that his forces were at the outset numerically and technologically inferior to those of his opponent, and so also substituted political power for a *lack* of conventional military power. Guerrillas, because of their superior political motivation, strengthened by the political support of the Chinese peasants, Mao reasoned, could survive military reverses and wage a protracted military campaign to wear down their opponents.

Mao's concept of people's war freed strategists from thinking about warfare exclusively in terms of more soldiers and better armaments, and it allowed determined revolutionaries who lacked conventional military power to take on militarily superior forces with some hope of ultimately defeating them. In saying that guerrillas aimed for and depended upon the political mobilization of people who would be mere bystanders in a conventional military conflict, Mao introduced a relationship between military action and the attitude and response of the audience. This added a new dimension to conflict, which until then had measured achievement primarily in terms of the physical effect that any military action had on the enemy. Now it was being said that the effect that any violent action has on the people watching may be independent of, and may equal or even exceed in importance the actual physical damage inflicted on the foe. Terrorism is that proposition pursued to its most violent extreme.

Terrorism is violence for effect—not primarily, and sometimes not at all for the physical effect on the actual target, but rather for its dramatic impact on an audience. Developments in world communications, particularly in the news media, have expanded the potential audience to national and, more recently, to international proportions. By means of dramatic acts of violence, guerrillas can gain worldwide attention, and mobilize national and international support for their struggle. The relationship between actor and audience can be reciprocal. Radio and especially television allowed an expanding audience to "participate" vicariously in the guerrillas' struggle. Through the mass media, guerrillas could arouse, frighten, evoke sympathy, even create a bond with a distant audience. And the reactions of this audience could affect the outcome of the struggle. It is an idea that owes as much to Marshall McLuhan as it does to Mao Tse-tung.

Orthodox Marxists were willing to condone the massive use of terror to protect the revolution they achieved in Russia, but tended to be wary of sole reliance on military power, and especially of reliance on terrorism, to foment revolutions. Indeed, they still are. The early Maoists attached greater importance to the role of military power, but said little about the use of terrorist tactics. It is not in Marxist theory of revolution, Russian or Chinese, that a theory of antigovernment terrorism arises. It is in the postwar Jewish struggle in Palestine, and in the guerrilla campaigns against the colonial powers, that we first find campaigns of deliberate terrorism.[1]

Colonial insurgents defined colonialism itself as "violence in its natural state, and thus the only possible means of ending it was by greater violence."[2] (Some Marxists have used an idea similar to this to justify revolutionary terrorism, claiming that the existence of economic or social injustice was in itself a form of terrorism and that those who exploited the people, maintained order, or protected the government were on these grounds the original terrorists.) Greater violence was not only justified by the colonial insurgents, but the legitimate targets of violence were potentially broadened to include the entire colonial machinery: government officials whether high-ranking dignitaries or minor bureaucrats, whether civilian or military, policeman, plantation owners, colons, indigenous collaborators, just about anybody who participated in the colonial structure; which in its extreme could mean anybody who did not actively participate in the struggle to overthrow the colonial ruler. This narrowing of the category of innocent bystanders, who are theoretically immune from deliberate military attack under the traditional rules of warfare, paralleled the development of the twentieth century concept of total war. In World War II, for example, cities, factories, workers, anything connected with the enemy's "war machine"—and given the indiscriminate nature of modern destructive weapons, a good many bystanders, as well—were attacked. The fine line which divides total war from terrorism is that in the latter, bystanders are hit not by predictable accident, but often deliberately, in order to achieve greater shock effect.

The struggles for political independence were unique in the sense that colonialism after World War II was regarded as anachronistic and inherently immoral, not only by the colonial subjects, but also by many people in the ruling nations, and by a number of influential noncolonial governments, particularly the United States and the Soviet Union. As newly independent nations entered the United Nations, this attitude came to constitute the majority view in that forum. Public opinion at home plus that of the international community inhibited the governments of colonial nations from responding to insurgent violence with the even greater violence that they were militarily capable of inflicting. The harsh measures that had often been used to conquer and pacify distant subjects in the nineteenth century were simply unacceptable in the second half of the twentieth century.

Under these circumstances, the political mobilization and party organization considered necessary by the early Marxists, or the protracted military campaign described by Mao, were not prerequisites to achieving independence. In the wake of the First Indochina War and the bitter struggles in Indonesia and Algeria, colonial governments were anxious to avoid the military costs, the potential military disasters, the inevitable domestic political divisiveness, and condemnation by the international community that a protracted and debilitating military campaign against guerrillas in a distant colony could bring. The mere threat of such a struggle could often persuade colonial governments to retire gracefully. Colonial insurgents found terrorism to be an effective means of broadcasting their opposition to continued colonial rule, of embarrassing the colonial government, of gaining instantaneous worldwide attention, sympathy, and support, which in turn could be translated into international pressure on the colonial government, and of forewarning the colonial government of the kind of struggle it would face if it chose to resist.

Whether or not they realized it at the time, these colonial freedom fighters had developed the relationship between violent action and the audience to the point that they nearly deleted from the equation the military capabilities of their opponents. They could play to the audience, undertake acts of violence which were in themselves militarily insignificant but were designed to gain worldwide attention, then count on domestic political pressure and international pressure on the colonial government to help them achieve what they might not have been able to achieve militarily by themselves, namely, bring about the withdrawal of the opponent's army.

Guerrillas fought elsewhere in the world for causes other than independence from colonial rule but outside of Cuba few guerrillas fighting against an indigenous government were able to repeat the success of colonial freedom fighters. Colonial governments, despite their military superiority, had obvious psychological and political disadvantages, which indigenous governments did not. Moreover, withdrawal from colonies did not entail dismantling the government at home. Revolutionary guerrillas who took on indigenous governments found them far less willing to relinquish their power. Their frustration was especially keen in Latin America where, in the decade following the Cuban revolution, the numerous rural guerrillas who had hoped to emulate the success of Fidel Castro had in fact not managed to advance beyond the remote mountain tops and jungles where they had initiated their struggles. In frustration, they turned to the cities where they could carry the struggle directly to the seat of government, and in the process gain national and international attention. It was an objective for which terrorist tactics were ideally suited.

Urban guerrilla warfare thus provides an important developmental link between earlier theories of revolution and guerrilla warfare and today's international terrorism. Urban guerrillas deliberately sought national and international attention by dramatic acts of violence. They assassinated or kidnapped government officials, businessmen, and foreign diplomats. They staged spectacular bank robberies, set off bombs, and hijacked airliners. Other dissident groups quickly adopted these tactics, and went one step further by carrying their struggle to individuals and countries not directly involved in the conflict. Terrorism became truly international.

International terrorism is thus an offshoot, the newest branch in the evolution of modern revolutionary and guerrilla warfare theories. It elevates individual acts of violence to the level of strategy (and therefore is denounced by orthodox Marxists as adventurism). It denigrates conventional military power by substituting dramatic violence played for the people watching. It violates the conventional rules of engagement: it reduces the category of innocent bystanders to the point that there are no innocent bystanders. It makes the world its battlefield: it recognizes no boundaries to the conflict, no neutral nations.

HIGH TECHNOLOGY TERRORISM

The development of international terrorism has depended upon certain technological developments which have taken place in the past half century. Up to now, guerrillas and terrorists have been more imaginative in their tactics than most armies, and innovative to a degree that their clear military inferiority encourages creative thinking, but they have been technically crude. Their weapons have been limited for the most part to submachine guns and dynamite. Their successes in gaining their objectives are less the result of their own military capabilities than of new vulnerabilities in the society at large.

Modern technology has benefited terrorists most in providing them with almost instantaneous worldwide notoriety and attention through contemporary news reporting. International terrorism in large measure depends on, and is enhanced by, the capacity of the media to reach a worldwide audience. The extensive news coverage given to terrorist attacks satisfies the terrorists' aim of propagandizing their cause and it also results in a greatly exaggerated impression of the amount of violence that has occurred. Up to now, the actual toll of terrorists' actions, in lives lost, in personal injuries and in property damage has been small when measured against the world volume of violence. In the next ten to twenty years that is likely to change. Low-level violence, as contrasted with the high-level violence of modern conventional or nuclear war, is going to escalate. We are going to see some high technology terrorism, made possible by new vulnerabilities and new weapons.

New technologies create new vulnerabilities. Civil aviation is a perfect example. It is now possible to travel conveniently to almost anywhere in the world in a matter of hours. It is also possible for a single armed man to hijack a 747 jumbo jet and hold 300 passengers hostage at 37,000 feet. Our energy systems are fragile. Supertankers, natural gas pipelines, the transportation system for liquefied natural gas, offshore oil platforms, all seem especially vulnerable to physical attacks and deliberate disruption. Burning tank cars carrying lethal chemicals have already forced the evacuation of population centers several times. These fires were accidents, but their consequences would not be any different if they had been deliberately set. Recently a great deal of public attention has centered on the potential terrorist threat to nuclear power programs and nuclear weapons.

Nuclear power facilities will probably proliferate in the next few decades. The traffic in fissionable material and radioactive waste material will increase. The growth of civilian nuclear programs, plus the atomic weapons which we have stored around the world in vulnerable bunkers, raises a number of new possibilities for mass hostage situations and political extortion on a grand scale. There are, of course, nonnuclear alternatives for terrorists—cheaper, less dangerous ways to free political prisoners or to get a few million dollars than seizing an atomic reactor or attempting to build an atomic bomb. In most countries, terrorists need only seize an embassy or hijack an airliner. But, given the basic theory of terrorism—violence to gain attention, instill fear, and thereby gain political leverage—nuclear blackmail would seem to be, at least in theory, extremely attractive to terrorists.

People tend to be frightened by the mere mention of the word "atomic," whether it is intended for peaceful purposes or already in the form of weapons. It is the most potent, and to the general public, the most sinister force available to mankind. To create an atmosphere of alarm, terrorists using any sort of nuclear blackmail would have much of their mission accomplished in advance. A plausible nuclear threat would instantly provide them with a tremendous amount of publicity and considerable political leverage. To anyone faced with nuclear blackmail by terrorists, it might make very little difference whether scientists unanimously and publicly agreed that the probability that the terrorists actually could or would blow up a city was quite low. Who is going to believe them? Who would be willing to run the test? Even if the terrorists ultimately failed to carry out the threatened deed, the publicity they would gain would be tremendous.

The feasibility of a terrorist-posed nuclear threat is currently an issue of heated debate. Feasibility, of course, depends on what kind of nuclear threat one is talking about. It may be possible for a determined, well-trained group to steal a single tactical nuclear weapon from a storage site, although it would be technically difficult to successfully detonate one. But it may not be necessary to steal an atomic warhead to carry out nuclear blackmail. Some experts tell us that with sufficient technical skill, terrorists could also steal enough fissionable material and manufacture their own crude atomic bomb.[3] People with the necessary technical skill are said to number in the tens of thousands, and can be found at research facilities in a number of countries. The possession of radioactive waste material and its threatened use as a contaminant could also constitute a serious danger to public safety. Seizure of a nuclear reactor might bring the terrorists nothing more than a lot of publicity; they would not be able to turn it into a bomb; but even their threat to damage an expensive facility worth billions, or perhaps cause widespread panic might still place them in a powerful bargaining position.

Are terrorists likely to employ nuclear blackmail? After all, had they wanted to, terrorists could already have done a number of things which could produce widespread casualties. Apart from the technical difficulties involved, which are less than those involved in putting together an atomic bomb, why hven't terrorists threatened to contaminate a city's water supply? Certainly there must be some constraints, other than technical ones, against killing thousands. There are, of course, to begin with, moral ones. Despite the popular view of them, terrorists, for the most part, are not wanton killers. There are also practical arguments against mass murder. Killing a lot of people is seldom an objective of terrorism. High body counts do not necessarily further their objectives, and can provoke a damaging backlash. Moreover, such tactics are not very discriminating. Neither, of course, were the three Japanese terrorists who machine-gunned passengers at Lod airport in Israel, but we must remember that the idea of deliberately indiscriminate murder carried out in order to gain worldwide attention, along with the practice of going abroad to strike targets, are both relatively recent innovations. Most terrorists have operated on their own territory and have had to take some care not to totally alienate the local population. Indiscriminate violence can be dangerous, especially if you have to live among your victims. These constraints, however, do not preclude the possibility of a large-scale Lod by foreign terrorists or by local lunatics, and they do not preclude terrorists from attempting to threaten—as opposed to wanting to kill—a lot of people.

The creation of new vulnerabilities has been matched by the development of new weapons. We should first note that most of the major technological advances in warfare in the past half century have been in the areas of large weapons—tanks, artillery, aircraft, missiles, nuclear warheads, and in weapon guidance systems—radar, television, computers, lasers. The individual weapons of the infantryman have changed little. The modern foot soldier goes into battle armed with a semiautomatic or automatic rifle, perhaps a pistol, and some hand grenades. None of these weapons has changed much since World War II. Many of them have been in use for fifty or sixty years. Until quite recently, there have been few dramatic developments in personal weapons to parallel those made in larger weapon systems. Now that is changing. The curve of the individual soldier's capacity for destruction is zooming upward, propelled by the military research and development programs which are currently supported by the national governments of the industrially advanced countries, ironically those who will be most vulnerable if some of the weapons now being developed come into the hands of dissident groups willing to employ violence.

Individual weapons are now beginning to take some significant strides. The most important development from the viewpoint of guerrilla and terrorist groups is that major weapons and guidance systems are being miniaturized to the point where they can be carried and operated by one man with little training. As a result, we are now creating a new range of small, portable, cheap, relatively easy to operate, highly accurate, and highly destructive weapons which, when produced on a large scale for armies, will undoubtedly find their way into the hands of terrorists. Some of them already have.

One need only scan the defense journals to get an idea of the kinds of weapons that will be available to tomorrow's infantryman, and to terrorists and guerrillas the day after tomorrow. Weapons such as the U.S.-manufctured "Redeye" or the Soviet-built SA-7 or "Strela" will become increasingly available. Arab terrorists have been caught with SA-7s outside the Rome airport. Both "Redeye" and the "Strela" are shoulder-fired, antiaircraft missiles guided to their target by an infrared sensing device which homes in on the heat of a low-flying aircraft's engines. "Redeye" weighs under 30 pounds and is only about four feet long. It is already being replaced by "Stinger" which has a greater range and velocity and an improved infrared device giving it greater accuracy, but without any increase in size or weight.

The British have their own man-portable surface-to-air (or surface) missile called "Blowpipe." Instead of an infrared heat-seeking device, the small supersonic missile is guided by radio commands sent to it by its aimer. There is also the Swedish-built low-level, surface-to-air missile, the RB-70, which fires a supersonic missile kept on target by a laser beam guidance system that is reported to be virtually unjammable. It weighs under 180 pounds, breaks down into three smaller packages, and can be operated by one man with minimal training. As opposed to "Redeye" or "Strela," in which a heat-seeking missile flies up the exhaust pipe of the aircraft, the "Blowpipe" and the Swedish RB-70 can be fired head-on toward an approaching plane.

A number of man-portable antitank weapons employing sophisticated guidance systems have also been developed. The Soviet-built "Sagger," a wire-guided antitank missile, was used extensively in the "October War" in the Middle East. It is normally mounted in sixes on an armored car but it is not a large weapon, and one could be rigged to fire from some other platform. There are several Western counterparts to "Sagger," including the U.S. "Dragon," a wire-guided antitank missile. Weighing under 30 pounds, it can be carried and operated by one man. There is also the U. S. "Tow," the French/German "Hot," and the British "Swingfire." The French/German "Milan" is a smaller antitank weapon with a semiautomatic guidance system. It also can easily be carried and operated by one man. It is now being deployed by the West German army which expects to have 11,000 "Milan" missiles by 1977, and eventually 1200 launchers with 50,000 missiles.

A Belgian arms manufacturing firm has meanwhile developed a disposable, lightweight, silent mortar which can be used against personnel and also fires a projectile with a spherical warhead designed to produce a "shattering effect" suitable for the "destruction of utilities, communications, and light structures." The full field unit, which weighs only 22 pounds, includes the firing tube plus seven rounds. All seven rounds can be put in the air before the first round hits.

The increasing urbanization of Europe and the expectation that armies may have to do more of their fighting in cities has led to the creation of weapons designed for urban warfare which will also be ideal for use by urban guerrillas. Among these is the German-designed "Armbrust 300," an antitank weapon that has no backblast, making it possible to fire the weapon from inside a room—something no rocket launcher can do now. The Germans expect to produce the "Armbrust" in large quantities. Several firms are also manufacturing tiny—some less than 15 inches long—silent submachine guns.

There have also been important developments in propellants and explosives. A new projectile which can be fired from the existing U. S. M-79 grenade launcher, is capable of penetrating two inches of armor plate and igniting any fuel behind it. Mines smaller than a man's hand are available. Miniaturized detonating devices have made thin letter bombs possible. Nonmilitary developments such as day-date calendar watches, digital clocks, and long-lasting power cells have increased the possible time delays in setting off time bombs.

These weapons were designed for use against specific military targets, not for terrorists. The antitank weapons, for example, have the capability to penetrate thick armor but would not do as much explosive damage when fired against a building as, say, dynamite. Bullets are adequate to kill a man. Assassinations can be carried out with submachine guns or high-powered rifles. Since dynamite and machine guns are widely available and easier to get than the more advanced weapons, it is fair to ask why terrorists would be interested in acquiring such weaponry and, if they were, would they be able to do so.

In answer to the first part of that question, we should understand that guerrillas and terrorists now operate with the best individual weapons they can get their hands on. The fact that they now have to rely mainly on pistols and submachine guns, and rocket-propelled grenade launchers, is not evidence that they would not prefer to use something more advanced. Terrorists, those who actually do the shooting, often tend to be gun freaks or explosives freaks. It must be far more exhilarating to fire a guided missile and hit something than to fire a rifle. Terrorists may want the added firepower for its own sake, simply because it is advanced technology, regardless of its utility to them in all circumstances. They may acquire the weapons first, then think of the targets.

We should also understand that the military specifications of a hand- held antitank or an antiaircraft weapon may not be the same character- istics the terrorists are after. To reiterate, terrorism is violence for dra- matic effect. The mere possession of advanced weapons, demonstrated by their use, is in itself dramatic. The dramatic effect of an explosion in a government office building is exceeded by the dramatic effect of even a small hole in the national palace when that hole has been made by a sophisticated antitank missile, and it implies that the terrorists are a much more potent force. Finally, we must not overlook the potential utility to terrorists of easily concealable weapons that give their users great accuracy at long distances, thus increasing the chances of success while reducing the risks of capture.

Will they be able to acquire them? Obviously not as easily as they can now acquire machine guns and dynamite. Up to now, these advanced weapons would not have been available in large quantities, but if they are mass-produced and eventually widely distributed, the opportunities for diversion will inevitably increase. Sales competition among the arms man- ufacturers by itself may push the preceding generation of "obsolete" weapons to the international market. Arms control is difficult enough when satellites are able to photograph missile silos. It will be extraordi- narily difficult, perhaps virtually impossible, to keep track of hand-held missile launchers.

A major impetus in the West for increasing the destructive power of its individual soldiers has been the numerical superiority of the Soviet and Warsaw Pact armies. Manpower is more expensive in the West. The United States and its European allies have continually sought to offset the numerical advantage of their most probable adversaries with tech- nological superiority. That technological superiority is now being minia- turized and mass-produced to the point that every other soldier, poten- tially every other militiaman too, will eventually be able to kill a tank or bring down a plane.

Since the West does not consider itself the probable aggressor in any conflict with the Warsaw Pact countries, some believe that the deployment of these weapons will tend to discourage invasion and thereby stabilize the defense of Western Europe. Yet the notion that widely available, easy- to-operate, highly accurate and highly destructive yet portable weapons are going to stabilize the defense of any country deserves critical exami- nation. While the widespread deployment of such weapons could dis- courage a potential invader, it could also increase the problems of internal security, and thus destabilize Western Europe, especially if we examine the deployment of such weapons in the context of Europe's current economic problems, the resultant social unrest, and in some countries, increased internal violence.

We generally only discuss the consequences that the use of these weapon will have on the battlefield. This discussion usually proceeds in the form of rather neat pairs: new antitank weapons versus new designs in tanks, new surface-to-air missiles versus tactical aircraft, and so on. I have the feeling that we are somehow comfortable with these terms of debate. Projectiles go faster or have a higher probability of hitting and destroying their target, but the basic terms of warfare have not changed. For each item of new military technology there seems to be a counter-vailing military technology. It becomes disconcerting when we remove these new weapons from the battlefield and begin to think about their potential use against nonmilitary targets: portable surface-to-air missiles versus civil aviation, precision-guided antitank weapons versus speak-ers' podiums, motorcades, squad cars, supertankers, nuclear reactors, or national monuments.

There is, of course, a countervailing technology here, too. New sur-veillance and detection devices have been developed; we are made aware of some of them every time we board an airplane. But the full application of such technology implies great social control. We have accepted such controls for brief periods to deter certain crimes like hijacking. But we do not live in airports, nor do I think we would like to. Thus, though a countervailing technology may be there, its application could be costly in terms of human liberty.

TOWARD SURROGATE WARFARE

Let me now proceed to the second idea I want to discuss. Nations have acquired far more destructive armaments than terrorists can ever hope to have unless they are in power, but at the same time that nations have been improving their arsenals, it appears that they are finding fewer opportunities to employ them.

Modern conventional war is becoming increasingly impractical. It is too destructive. Nations entering into conventional warfare risk the most productive members of their population, their wealth through the de-struction of resources like industry and cities, the semi-permanent alter-ation of their landscape.

For most nations, modern conventional warfare is also too expensive. Few nations can afford modern sophisticated armaments. Most of them must rely on external backers for funds and materiel. But dependence on foreign support imposes constraints: The backers are likely to be super-powers who are likely to be on opposite sides. If a local war esca-lates, there is the danger that the backers themselves will come close to a direct confrontation, as we saw in the 1973 war in the Middle East. In that event, before risking a nuclear war which neither wants, they are likely to constrain their proteges, cutting off their supplies, if necessary.

World opinion imposes further constraints on a nation entering war. War is no longer regarded by the world community as a legitimate means of exerting political pressure. Warring nations can ignore world opinion up to a point, but when that point is reached—more importantly when the major powers agree that the war has gone far enough, that the risk of a major world war is real—then ceasefires are imposed.

Domestic constraints also must be taken into account, perhaps to a greater degree in democracies than in totalitarian states. The intense nationalism that supported nineteenth century wars, World War I, and World War II, has declined. Televised wars simply don't appeal to the people at home.

A nation planning to wage a modern conventional war thus must plan to achieve its military objectives fast, before it runs out of tanks, before the cost of the war seriously disrupts its economy, before world opinion can be mobilized to condemn the aggression or support a ceasefire, before the superpowers decide between themselves that the fighting should end, before the public at home turns off and domestic opposition to the fighting mounts. *Blitzkrieg,* always militarily attractive, has become an economic and political necessity. In recent years we have witnessed several military offensives in which the advancing armies have raced the clock: the Israeli offensive in 1967, the Indian invasion of East Pakistan in 1971, the Egyptian offensive against Israel in 1973, the Israeli counteroffensive in which the last few hours of fighting were crucial, and the Turkish invasion of Cyprus.

Imposed ceasefires, however, do not resolve national conflicts the same way that surrender does. They stop the shooting temporarily, but leave two hostile armies in the field, neither of which is totally exhausted. Even in retreat, these armies may hold on to the notion that a few months or a few years' respite enforced by a ceasefire will suffice to restore their srength, and that they will take to the field again at a future date. And so we have seen a number of repetitive wars between the same sets of adversaries: the four wars between Israel and the Arab countries in 1948, 1956, 1967, and 1973; the three wars between India and Pakistan in 1947, 1965, and 1971; and two periods of fighting in Cyprus in 1963 and 1974.

None of these wars, or rather none of the larger troop engagements that erupted from a lower level of continued hostility, lasted very long. Leaving out anticolonial insurgencies and the war in Vietnam—because it is a protracted conflict and difficult to fix the date when it began or predict when it may end—there have been twelve major military conflicts involving two or more nations since World War II. Their average duration was less than six months. The nine conventional military conflicts that have occurred since the Korean War lasted an average of nineteen days. For the most part those wars ended in ceasefires that were encouraged, arranged, or imposed by the major powers.

The present alternatives to a short conventional war are nuclear war, which most nations fortunately still lack the capacity for, and protracted war, such as we see in Indochina. Protracted wars are debilitating military contests in which staying power is more important than firepower. They are "poor men's wars" fought sometimes for generations, necessarily with long periods of military stalemate. The level of fighting peaks and declines with the availability of resources, and often with the seasons. Military victory loses its traditional meaning as strategists debate whether not winning means losing or not losing means winning.

Conventional war and its present alternatives, then, are less and less attractive as a means of settling international disputes. Indeed, in a recent article in *Foreign Affairs,* Louis J. Halle posed the question, "Does war have a future?" He concluded that "the time has probably gone, perhaps forever, when the formal resort to war, duly declared and openly conducted, was an accepted practice among organized societies . . . " With a few caveats, Halle also concluded that "the day of general wars, directly involving great powers on both sides, may also be past."[4]

I tend to agree with Halle's conclusions even though there have been two conventional wars since the publication of his article: the October 1973 war in the Middle East and the recent conflict in Cyprus. Both of these fit the pattern which I have described. They were short, ceasefires were imposed, and they ended somewhat inconclusively. The probability of renewed fighting—a fifth round in the Middle East or a third round in Cyprus—remains high.

In the final paragraph of his article, Halle avoided drawing any overly optimistic inferences from his conclusions. He foresaw the continuation of conflict in forms other than conventional war: guerrilla warfare, incidents and interventions involving the use of armies, the clandestine use of military power, widespread and continual disorder—what we might indeed still call low-level violence.

Finding modern conventional war an increasingly unattractive mode of conflict, some nation may try to exploit the demonstrated possibilities and greater potential of terrorist groups, and employ them as a means of surrogate warfare against another nation. A government could subsidize an existing terrorist group or create its own band of terrorists to disrupt, cause alarm, and create political and economic instability in another country. It requires only a small investment, certainly far less than what it costs to wage a conventional war; it is debilitating to the enemy, and it is deniable. A number of national governments already provide financial support, weapons, training, and other forms of assistance to groups waging war against other governments because they support their cause. There is little evidence, however, that they actually direct terrorist operations. The concept of surrogate warfare—sabotage and subversion—is not new, but the opportunities for destruction and disruption by small groups, as terrorists have demonstrated, are increasing.

In sum, I believe we are going to see more examples of war being waged by groups that do not openly represent the government of a recognized state: revolutionaries, political extremists, lunatics, or criminals professing political aims, those we call terrorists, perhaps the surrogate soldiers of another state; examples of war without declaration; of war without authorization or even admission by any national government; of war without invasions by armies as we know them now; of war without front lines; of war waged without regard to national borders or neutral countries, of war without civilians; of war without innocent bystanders.

THE POLITICAL CONSEQUENCES

Society's new vulnerabilities and the new weapons that may become available to guerrillas and terrorists have greater significance when they are placed in the political context of our present era in which people seem increasingly unwilling to accept authority, increasingly willing to challenge it. It recalls an earlier period in history, that roughly from 1775 to the mid-nineteenth century, which like our own era, was also a period of defiance marked by widespread revolutions in Europe and in the Americas directed against existing political and social customs. It was a period, not unlike the past two decades, marked by the dissolution of several empires and the creation of many new states.

The similarities between the revolutionaries of this earlier period and the guerrillas and terrorists of our own era—note how a hundred years can make extremist gunmen into respectable revolutionaries—are also fascinating. Like many of the young, educated (a characteristic many of them seem to share) members of modern urban guerrilla and terrorist groups, the earlier revolutionaires were romanticists. They were dedicated to causes considered in their time extreme. As romanticists, they had a tendency we again notice now to exult in dramatic, theatrical violence, bloodshed, and death. Their political utopias tended to be vague. And they too cooperated with each other internationally: Europeans came to fight in the American Revolution. An American helped write the new French constitution and American officials in the Spanish colonies were regarded as subversives, which sometimes they were. Englishmen died fighting in the Greek war of independence. Garibaldi fought at the side of rebels in Argentina before launching his own campaign in Italy.

The increasing vulnerabilities in our society plus the increasing capacities for violence afforded by new developments in weaponry mean that smaller and smaller groups have a greater and greater capacity for disruption and destruction. Or, put another way, the small bands of extremists and irreconcilables that have always existed may become an increasingly potent force. This could have profound political consequences. Nations maintain their credentials in the last resort by maintaining their monopoly over the means of violence.

Repression may become an irresistible temptation to national governments trying to protect their own citizens against violence by a small minority and to preserve domestic and international order. Even democratic governments may find themselves compelled to resort to harsh security measures that curtail civil rights. Repression, by itself, will not always work. Governments unable to protect their citizens against violence carried on by small groups, and unable or unwilling to resort to the measures required to stamp them out, may be forced to make tactical concessions. Ultimately they may be compelled to make political accommodations that end the violence.

If the power to destroy becomes more diffuse because of technological developments, political power may also become more diffuse as it must be divided among others who have the power to disrupt and destroy. In the simplest sense this could mean the creation of more nations. Unable to reconcile the competing demands of armed extremists, some nations will come apart and be subdivided into several smaller new nations. This will happen not just because guerrillas or terrorists have acquired modern weapons; it seems to be happening anyway, but the acquisition of modern weapons will accelerate the process in some cases, and cause internal security problems in some nations that otherwise might not have been subjected to centrifugal forces. New weapons may generate new causes or, at least, prevent peaceful reolution of old conflicts.

A breakup of some nations would confirm a long-range historical trend toward smaller national units, a trend that has continued since the dissolution of the major empires which existed in the nineteenth century. Imperial expansion in the second half of the nineteenth century was in part made possible by the vast technological superiority, primarily in weapons, of a few nations. The empires were dissolved in the mid-twentieth century, for the most part peacefully, but, as I mentioned before, significantly after wars in Indochina, Indonesia, and Algeria demonstrated that the alternative to getting out gracefully was a lengthy and costly colonial war. The breakup of the great empires into smaller national units has continued beyond independence. When the French left Indochina, it was officially three nations; it is now four, and in reality, it is six or seven. British India was one, on independence it became two, and now is three. Malaysia and Singapore were united upon independence; now Singapore is independent.

At its creation in 1945, there were 51 members of the United Nations; by 1960 there were 82; by September 1973 there were 135; there are now [1975] 138 nations in the United Nations and 15 or 20 nations which are not members. Unless there is a renewed trend toward imperialism, or unless the international system is totally reorganized, by the end of the century it would not be surprising to see two hundred or even three hundred politically independent communities in the world, the vast majority of them mini-states.

Much of today's terrorism is carried on in the name of oppressed ethnic minorities—demanding their own territory or self-rule. Ethnicity seems to be vying with nationality as the legitimate basis for government and representation in the world community. As a result of ethnic pressures, Cyprus and Jordan each may be divided. India, Iran, Iraq, Pakistan, Burma, Indonesia, Yugoslavia, Spain, and Ehtiopia to name a few, also face strong centrifugal pressures from dissident ethnic minorities.

The concept of nationhood may itself be changed as international forums such as the United Nations admit the representatives of armed entities which are not nations. We may eventually see two types of representatives in the UN: those of nations in the traditional sense, with boundaries, capital cities, and national armies, and those of groups which are not nations, do not always have a precisely defined national territory, but do have some sort of armed force of their own. The two kinds of political communities may overlap.

The resultant international system is likely to resemble the political complexity of Renaissance Italy in which major kingdoms, minor principalities, tiny states, independent city republics, Papal territories, and bands of *condottieri* engaged in incessant, but low-level, warfare with one another. Medieval Europe, and India in the seventeenth and eighteenth centuries also come to mind.

The extremists who fight in behalf of political ideologies are not necessarily going to be satisfied by the creation of some new countries. Neither are those who fight for grievances or causes shared only by a handful, or for purely personal motives; they may lack constituencies to sustain them and therefore will remain small and ephemeral, but they too will be capable of greater violence during their brief lifespan.

The world that emerges is an unstable collection of nations, ministates, autonomous ethnic substates, governments in exile, national liberation fronts, guerrilla groups aspiring to international recognition and legitimacy via violence, and a collection of ephemeral but disruptive terrorist organizations, some of which are linked together in vague alliances, some perhaps the protégés of foreign states. It is a world in which the acronyms of various self-proclaimed revolutionary fronts may take their place in international forums alongside the names of countries. It is a world of formal peace between nations—free of open warfare except, perhaps, for brief periods—but of a higher level of political violence, of increased internal insecurity.

I am speaking here of a qualitative change in politicially motivated violence, not necessarily a quantitative one. Low-level violence may increase and become more troublesome while conventional wars become fewer and shorter. The overall number of casualties may decline. Indeed, a future world of many Ulsters could turn out to be far less violent in total casualties than the past sixty years during which approximately 23 million soldiers and between 26 and 34 million civilians died in two major wars. When it comes to slaughter, the "civilized" nations of the world can do it on a far grander scale than those we now call "terrorists."

In conclusion, I think it would be silly for us to glibly assume that the consequences of these recent technological developments in weaponry which greatly increase the individual soldier's capacity for destruction will be confined to the battlefield. The technological developments in individual weaponry are likely to have greater impact off the battlefield where they may be employed against the increasing vulnerabilities of our society, as it becomes more modern, more complex, and more dependent on technology. It would be a gross overstatement to say that anarchism has or will become technologically feasible. But the capacity to disrupt and destroy is becoming more diffuse. The destructive power which, in the past, was possessed only by national armies is descending to the level of small bands, without governments or the necessity of maintaining large sympathetic constituencies which constrain their actions. This could lead to a corresponding diffusion of political power, and perhaps a still greater diffusion of political violence. It suggests a world in which Prince Kropotkin is far more likely to feel at home than Clausewitz or Metternich.

[1] For a more thorough discussion of modern terrorism, see the author's *International Terrorism: A New Mode of Conflict,* Santa Monica, California: California Arms Control and Foreign Policy Seminar, forthcoming.

[2] Frantz Fanon, *The Wretched of the Earth,* New York: Grove Press, 1963.

[3] Books and articles forewarning or describing the potential terrorist threat to nuclear weapons or possibility of terrorists manufacturing their own nuclear weapons are legion. Among the most useful are Theodore B. Taylor and Mason Willrich, *Nuclear Theft: Risks and Safeguards,* N.Y.: Ballinger 1971; R. B. Leachman (ed.), *Preventing Nuclear Theft: Guidelines for Industry and Government,* N.Y.: Praeger Publishers, 1972; AEC Study Group, *Special Safeguards Study* (also referred to as the "Rosenbaum Report"), April 1974.

[4] Louis J. Halle, "Does War Have a Future?" *Foreign Affairs,* Vol. 52, October 1973, pp. 20-39.

Focusing on terrorism as a military weapon, Mallin concentrates on one of the more significant tactical components of the surrogate warfare discussed by Jenkins. He, too, considers terrorism to be a new form of warfare. Problems identified by Mallin highlight the continuing need for greater collaboration between police and military forces on an international basis.

The following article is reprinted from *Air University Review*, Volume XXVIII, Number 2, January-February 1977.

Terrorism as a Military Weapon

by JAY MALLIN

Terrorism is a disease of modern society. It is a virus growing in an ill body. The effects of the virus can sometimes be ameliorated, but there is no certain cure.

The causes of terrorism are diverse; often one cause overlaps another or several causes. There is the social cause: Uruguayan young people denied their rightful place in a society that was stagnating. There is the racial cause: black and Indian militant groups in the United States. And, of course, there is the political cause: Israelis seeking independence from Great Britain; Cubans seeking freedom from Dictator Batista and then from Dictator Castro; Algerians seeking independence from France; northern Irish Catholics seeking to destroy British rule, and, conversely, Irish Protestants seeking to neutralize the Catholics.

Each instance was or is one of armed conflict—in a word, of war. Whether the cause be social discontent or national aspirations, a larger or smaller segment of a population wars on another segment or on a foreign adversary. The feasible weapon is terrorism. A military observer, Colonel William D. Neale, noted, "Terror, it is obvious, is a legitimate instrument of national policy."[2]

The complexity of causes of terrorism, the diverse ideologies that have employed terrorism, the multitudinous arms and tactics available to terrorists—all these factors have made terrorism one of the most complicated problems of the times. Certainly the scope of the problem defies understanding by any single discipline. Terrorism is a tangled skein of varied human motivations, actions, hopes, emotions, and goals.

A conference on terrorism and political crimes held in 1973 made the following conclusion, among others:

> The problem of the prevention and suppression of "terrorism" arises in part because there is no clear understanding of the causes leading to conduct constituting "terrorism." The International Community has been unable to arrive at a universally accepted definition of "terrorism" and has so far failed to control such activity.[3]

Terrorism cannot be explained by psychologists who construct facile theories. It cannot be countered by police who view terrorism as simply one more type of criminal activity: identify the criminals, arrest them, throw them in prison or perhaps shoot them, and the problem is solved. Terrorism cannot be handled by conventional military men who scoff at it as being beneath their notice.

The academician who wishes to study terrorism with academic dispassionateness finds theories, explanations, and chronological statistics but little else. Penetrating interviews with genuine terrorists, for example, are of minimal availability.

Terrorism *is* a tangled skein, and any observer attempting to unravel and separate one thread leaves himself open to criticism, justified criticism. "You say terrorism is a military weapon. What about the kidnappings solely for financial gain in Italy and the brigandage in Argentina motivated by monetary profit?"

Precisely. The skein is a mess of threads; it may not be possible to separate any one of them cleanly. Nevertheless, the effort is worth attempting if it contributes a pinpoint of light in what is certainly a long, dark tunnel. This article will attempt to focus on one thread: terrorism as a military weapon.

In September 1972 the world was stunned to learn that the Twentieth Olympic Games, a symbol of international harmony, had been attacked by political terrorists. A group of urban guerrillas belonging to the Palestinian Black September movement had forced their way into the Israeli quarters at the Olympic Village and seized nine hostages. The guerrillas issued a number of demands, including one for the release of 200 Palestinian prisoners in Israel. Day-long negotiations took place between the guerrillas and the West German government, and eventually the government appeared to accede to the Palestinian demands. An accord was reached whereby the terrorists, together with their hostages, were to be taken to an airport and there provided with air transportation to Egypt. At Fürstenfeldbruck Airport, however, German snipers opened fire on the terrorists, and in the resulting battle all Israeli hostages died, as did four guerrillas, a police officer, and a helicopter pilot.

Thanks to the sophistication of modern communication systems, people in many lands were kept abreast of developments minute by minute. Americans watched television in fascination as events unfolded before their eyes. When the final holocaust occurred at the German airport, shock, horror, and revulsion swept the civilized world.

The question was repeatedly asked, what did the Palestinians hope to gain by their action? Did not the kidnappings—and the resulting killings—do their cause far more harm than good? The actions of terrorists, however, cannot be measured in the way other acts of war or revolution are appraised. Urban guerrillas do not march to the same drum that regular soldiers or even rural guerrillas march to. Colonel Neale stated:

> Terroristic violence must be totally ruthless, for moral scruples and terror do not mix and one or the other must be rejected. There can be no such thing as a weak dose of terror. The hand that controls the whip must be firm and implacable.[4]

Although not generally viewed as such, the Olympic action was nevertheless fundamentally a military move. Having failed in three conventional wars to defeat the Israelis, the Arabs and Palestinians resorted to unconventional tactics: specifically, terrorism in the border zones and against Israeli installations in foreign lands. If the Arab leaders had not themselves been conventional, they might have utilized unconventional tactics much earlier—perhaps more successfully than were their efforts to defeat the Israelis in "regular" warfare.

Basically, terrorism is a form of psychological warfare (frighten your enemy; publicize your cause). Seen within this context, the Olympic attack achieved its purpose. Kidnapping the Israeli athletes did no military harm to Israel. As a psychological blow, however, it probably boosted Palestinian morale, and it certainly spotlighted worldwide the Palestinian cause. It encouraged future moves by Palestinian terrorists—the historical record attests to this. As a psychological blow the Olympic attack demonstrated that wherever Israeli figures of prominence went abroad, whether they be diplomats or athletes or whatever, they were susceptible to terrorist attack. _A._

War is armed conflict, and armed conflict is the province of the military. Terrorism is a form of armed conflict; it is therefore within the military sphere. When diplomats fail, soldiers take over. When soldiers fail, terrorists take over. The political terrorist, however, is a soldier, too. He wears no uniform, he may have received little or no training, he may accept minimal discipline, his organization may be ephemeral—but he is a soldier. He engages in armed conflict in pursuit of a cause. His weapons are the gun and the explosive. His battlefield is the city street, and his targets are the vulnerable points of modern society.

Certainly not all terrorists are soldiers. Not all terrorism is military. For purposes of this article, it is postulated that terrorism is military when: _B._

● It is utilized as a substitute for "regular" warfare, as in the case of the Palestinians against the Israelis.

● It is used in conjunction with other military activities, as in the cases of Cuba (against Batista) and Vietnam (against the Saigon administrations).

● It is used as the chosen weapon of conflict by a population segment against another segment and/or a foreign power, as in Northern Ireland.

Terrorism is sometimes believed to be synonymous with urban guerrilla warfare. Urban guerrilla warfare, however, is a broader term: it encompasses urban terrorism but other actions as well, i.e., ambushes, street skirmishes, assaults on official installations, and other types of hit-and-run urban combat. Also, it may be noted that terrorism is not confined to urban zones: it can be conducted in rural areas as well, as was notably the case in South Vietnam.

Thus, terrorism in certain circumstances is conducted as a military tactic. The purpose of military action is often to achieve political goals. "For political aims are the end and war is the means ... " stated Clausewitz.[5] In some instances terrorism is a part of the means, or is *the* means.

Terrorism as a tactic can be traced back to ancient times. Today's terrorists take human hostages; Incas of old seized the idols of the people they had conquered and held these as hostages to ensure that the defeated would not rebel. Terrorism as a tactic of urban guerrilla warfare dates back to the struggles in the past century and in this century to Russian revolutionaries against the czars. The concept of terrorism as a military instrument, however, is comparatively new. One of the papers developed at the first National Security Affairs Conference, held at the National War College in 1974, noted:

> Despite Mao's emphasis on the relationship between guerrilla warfare and the rural peasant, despite the doctrinaire vision of armed, revolutionary conflict culminating on the open battlefield, and despite the role of rural warfare in the most important revolutions of the past half-century, the rapid urbanization of much of the world now suggests new opportunities, and hence new strategies for revolutionary warfare, and, in particular, a new attitude toward the role of the city as the ultimate revolutionary battlefield.[6]

For the political militant, urban guerrilla warfare offers clear advantages over rural guerrilla warfare. If he is a city youth, he can remain in the cities and need not meet the rugged demands of rural and hill fighting. In the cities there is an abundance of potential targets. The countryside offers few targets. In the cities there are opportunities for militant actions (such as the placing of bombs) that do not necessarily entail direct personal conflict with the police. In the countryside guerrillas must eventually prove themselves by combat with units of the regular army. Rural guerrilla warfare requires a great deal of physical exertion with few gratifying results over a long period. In urban areas guerrillas can commit spectacular acts that garner great publicity and, then, if they have not been identified by the authorities, can return to "normal" lives until the time comes for their next violent action.

The growing technological complexity of our times increases the vulnerability of modern life. Not only does technology engender vulnerability, it also develops more sophisticated weapons that can kill or endanger more people and do more damage. Professor Zbigniew Brzezinski aptly referred to "the global nervous system";[7] Swedish Premier Olof Palme, at the United Nations, discussed "technology's multiplication of the power to destroy."[8]

One has but to look about a modern city and he will see a plethora of targets. Aqueduct pumping stations and conduits, power stations and lines, telephone exchanges, post offices, airport control towers, radio and television stations—all these form part of a city's nervous system. Terrorists can shoot at policemen, rob banks, sabotage industrial machinery, kill government officials, incapacitate vehicles, and set bombs in theaters and other public localities. Destruction of an enemy's cities is an accepted strategy of modern warfare; whether it be accomplished by aerial bombers or by land-bound terrorists is merely a matter of means. The National War College paper previously noted also pointed out:

> The destruction of a hydroelectric system, the crippling of a central computer bank, the acceleration of a social disorder by racist and counterracist assassination, the undermining of an economy by the pollution of an entire wheat crop . . . all these are but mere samples of the kind of violence which would lend itself to strategic manipulation. Although disguised in the name of revolution or rebellion, such violence could be decisive in terms of distracting a nation, or isolating it, or even paralyzing it. It would be, in effect; a new form of war.[9]

As postulated, terrorism could be used in conjunction with "regular" military activities. Or it could be used as a substitute. Colonel Seale R. Doss sets forth in the aforementioned paper that, "with the rapidly shifting alliances and animosities of the modern world, no nation could be quite sure in any case just which foreign power had (or even *if* some foreign power had) sponsored its disasters, for such violence would lend itself, like underworld money, to political laundering."[10]

Because terrorism as an instrument of war is a relatively new concept, there has been little doctrinal categorization or interpretation of, or doctrinal direction for, this type of warfare specifically. The three foremost warrior-theoreticians of guerrilla warfare, Mao Tse-tung, Vo Nguyen Giap, and Ernesto "Che" Guevara, virtually ignored this method of combat. Giap has said only that *"to the counter-revolutionary violence of the enemy, our people must definitely oppose [place in opposition] revolutionary violence,"* and that *"the most correct path to be followed by the peoples to liberate themselves is revolutionary violence and revolutionary war."*[11] (Emphasis is Giap's.) By "revolutionary violence" Giap probably meant all available means of warfare, including terrorism.

Guevara alone approached the subject of urban guerrilla warfare as a specific type of combat, and then he did so only in brief. In his book *La Guerra de Guerrillas* he provided limited recognition to what he called "sub-urban warfare." The sub-urban guerrilla group, he stated, should not carry out "independent actions" but rather should "second the action of the larger groups in another area." As for terrorism itself, Guevara said, "We sincerely believe that that is a negative weapon, that it does not produce in any way the effects desired, that it can turn a people against a determinate revolutionary movement and that it brings with it a loss of life among those who carry it out far greater than the benefits it renders." Guevara separated terrorism from assassination, which he felt was "licit" although only in "very selective circumstances," namely, against "a leader of the oppression."[12]

La Guerra de Guerrillas has served as a basic instructional book for Latin American guerrillas. It has, however, no instructions for urban guerrilla warfare. This is especially interesting in view of the fact that the urban guerrilla movement played as important a role, perhaps a more decisive role, than did the rural guerrillas in the 1956-1958 Cuban civil war. Fidel Castro and Guevara preferred, however, to promote the mystique of the rural guerrilla. They had been rural guerrilla captains, and it did not suit the historic position they envisioned for themselves to grant recognition to the urban clandestine movement that participated so significantly in the conflict.[13]

There was a practical consideration as well in the Castro-Guevara effort to develop the mystique of the rural guerrilla. Almost as soon as Castro came to power in Cuba, that small country launched an extensive program of subversion, with most of the effort concentrated on creating *fidelista* guerrilla movements in rural areas of Latin America. Castro and Guevara sought to duplicate their own guerrilla operation: launched from abroad, it had functioned in isolated rural areas. Guerrilla warfare, declared Guevara, is "the central axis of the struggle" in Latin America.[14] So deeply did Guevara believe in the guerrilla mystique that eventually it led him to his death in Bolivia. It was only after repeated failures, including Guevara's death, that Castro turned his attention to urban movements.

A perusal of other military instructional literature reveals a similar dearth of attention to urban guerrilla warfare. North Vietnamese Lieutenant General Hoang Van Thai's *Some Aspects of Guerrilla Warfare in Vietnam*[15] deals entirely with rural combat. The *Handbook for Volunteers of the Irish Republican Army*[16] is a fine basic book on rural guerrilla warfare, and much that it says is applicable to urban guerrilla combat, but it does not touch on this specifically despite the long utilization of urban terrorist tactics by the Irish Republican Army (IRA). Bert "Yank" Levy's *Guerrilla Warfare*[17] has a brief chapter on "the city guerrilla," but the book is primarily about rural guerrilla warfare. Spanish General Alberto Bayo's *One Hundred and Fifty Questions to a Guerrilla*[18] and Swiss Major H. von

Dach Bern's *Total Resistance*[19] also have material useful to an urban guerrilla, particularly in regard to sabotage activities, but again the books are concerned mainly with rural guerrillas.

The only document specifically dealing with urban guerrilla warfare that has received international recognition was written by a Brazilian politician-turned-terrorist, Carlos Marighella. Marighella wrote the *Minimanual of the Urban Guerrilla* for use by Brazilian terrorists, but its instructional contents are valid for guerrillas in any city in the world. Marighella stated:

> The urban guerrilla is an implacable enemy of the government and systematically inflicts damage on the authorities and on the men who dominate the country and exercise power. The principal task of the urban guerrilla is to distract, to wear out, to demoralize the militarists, the military dictatorship and its repressive forces, and also to attack and destroy the wealth and property of the North Americans, the foreign managers, and the Brazilian upperclass.[20]

Marighella declared: "The urban guerrilla is a man who fights the military dictatorship with arms, using unconventional methods . . . . The urban guerrilla follows a political goal . . ."[21]

It is interesting to note that just as Mao, prophet of rural guerrilla warfare, believed that type of combat was secondary to "regular" warfare,[22] Marighella, prophet of urban guerrilla warfare, envisioned urban combat as supplementary to rural guerrilla combat. He stated that the function of urban guerrilla warfare was "to wear out, demoralize, and distract the enemy forces, permitting the emergence and survival of rural guerrilla warfare which is destined to play the decisive role in the revolutionary war."[23]

As for terrorism specifically, Marighella said, "Terrorism is an arm the revolutionary can never relinquish."[24] It is also a weapon the military cannot ignore.

Anyone writing about terrorism labors under the difficulty that it has not been possible for anyone to develop an entirely satisfactory definition of terrorism. Mainly this is due to the fact that there is no precise understanding of what the term "terrorism" encompasses. There are too many gray areas of violence and of intimidation that may or may not be labeled as terroristic. Whether any particular area of activity or specific act is indeed terroristic largely depends on the circumstances within which this is undertaken. Example: Is sabotage a form of terrorism? Seeking an answer, we go full circle, for whether sabotage is terroristic depends on the definition of terrorism.

Therefore, in this article the following working definition is offered:

> Political terrorism is the threat of violence or an act or series of acts of violence effected through surreptitious means by an individual, an organization, or a people to further his or their political goals.

Under this definition sabotage committed for political purposes is indeed a form of terrorism.

Perhaps there is no such thing as "military terrorism." Or perhaps this is merely a semantic lack. At any rate, terrorism is one form of military activity that can be utilized by an organization or a people in pursuit of their political goals. Terrorism is a military weapon.

(Most often, terrorism consists of a series of acts of violence. All terrorism is criminal in the eyes of the government that is assailed. But there may be "criminal terrorism" in which the violence is committed purely for monetary, not political gain. Frequently this type of terrorism will disguise itself as political terrorism, especially in situations wherein genuine political terrorism is rampant, e.g., the Argentine situation.)

Terrorism as a military arm is a weapon of psychological warfare. The purpose, as the very word indicates, is to engender terror in the foe. The terror thrust encompasses the following ingredients:

- Terrorism publicizes the terrorists' political cause.
- Terrorism demonstrates the capability of the terrorists to strike blows.
- Terrorism heartens sympathizers of the terrorists' cause.
- Terrorism disconcerts the enemy.
- Terrorism eventually—the ultimate goal—demoralizes the enemy and paralyzes him.
- Conceivably, in certain circumstances, terrorism could deter potential allies of the terrorists' target country from assisting that country. ("If you provide aid to our enemy, we will unleash our terror tactics against you, too.")
- Sabotage causes material damage to an enemy's vital installations; the damage, in turn, has a psychological effect on the foe and on the populace. It frightens the foe and emboldens the ally.

Terrorists function within an area controlled by the enemy whether it be a metropolis or an airliner in flight. The terrorists either:

- Represent a significant portion of the population (as in the case of a struggle against an unpopular dictator), and their actions are applauded, even when they cause discomfort to the population (as when rebels knocked out a substantial portion of Havana's electric and water systems during the Cuban civil war).[25]
- Do not receive any significant amount of popular support and are generally condemned as outlaws (the minuscule ethnic militant groups in the United States are an example).
- Or, are foreign or foreign-supported and are seeking to destroy the enemy's control structure or to achieve some other political result (as in the case of the IRA bombs in restaurants and other public places in London).

Whereas in Case One the terrorist may try to minimize civilian casualties in order not to turn the population against him, in Case Three the more casualties there are the better the terrorist feels his goals are served: he is applying ruthless pressure against his enemy, and the number of casualties is a measure of his success. In Case Two, whether the terrorist concerns himself over civilian casualties is largely determined by whether his fanaticism is tempered by mercy.

At what point does terrorism become the concern of the "regular" military? For a military establishment that is *attacking,* terrorism can be used as a substitute for conventional warfare or in conjunction with conventional warfare and/or rural guerrilla warfare. For a military establishment that is responsible for *defending* an area or a country, the military role in the handling of a terrorist problem is determined by local circumstances: Is the government of the country under attack run by civilians or by the military? What constitutional and other legal responsibilities and restrictions are placed on the military? What useful capabilities do the military have that the police do not have?

The level of intensity of terrorist activity appears to be a determinant of military response more than any other factor. In most national cases military activity has been largely limited to guard and military intelligence duties in support of the police authorities. In other cases, however—notably in pre-Israel Palestine, Cyprus, Algeria, Uruguay, Argentina, and Northern Ireland—the military took over primary responsibility for combating terrorists because the police were overwhelmed.[26] In those cases cited where the military sought to maintain foreign control over populations, it is significant that the independence struggles were nevertheless successful (except in Ireland, where the conflict continues). In the two countries where indigenous military have sought to suppress major terrorist movements, the military were successful in one instance (Uruguay), and the outcome is as yet inconclusive in the other (Argentina). One may reasonably gather from this that terrorism is an effective weapon when used by a substantial portion of a population against foreign occupation troops. As a weapon against indigenous authorities supported by a military establishment, its efficacy is open to question. Terrorism appears to have succeeded only in such cases wherein it was used in conjunction with other military tactics (Cuba, South Vietnam).

There appear to be three fundamental functions of terrorism as a military weapon:

● Psychological warfare—Demoralize the enemy (his government, armed forces, police, even the civilian population) through assassinations, bomb explosions, agitation, and so on. The Viet Cong utilized the entire arsenal of violence in their campaign in South Vietnam.

● Material destruction—Destroy or damage the enemy's utilities, communications, and industries. Destruction by sabotage, particularly against specific targets limited in size, can be as effective as destruction by air raid.

● Economic damage—Engender a state of psychological unease and uncertainty in a city or a country and commerce dries up, investment funds vanish. The deterioration of the Cuban economy during the 1956-58 revolution was a major factor in the downfall of the Batista regime.

Terrorism utilized as a military weapon, whether by a foreign power or by domestic insurgents, is somewhat akin to air raids: it is warfare conducted in the enemy's rear. In both cases the tactic aims at destroying the foe's installations, killing his officials and battering his morale. Lamentably, in both cases the deaths of civilians are an additional result, unacknowledged as a goal but nevertheless often deliberately sought.

If, then, terrorism is a military weapon—a weapon to be used for a military goal: the defeat of an enemy—how much recognition of this weapon has been extended by "regular" military establishments? Traditionally the regular military have looked askance at any type of unconventional warfare. This remains true today even though the line of differentiation between conventional and unconventional warfare grows increasingly blurred. In the cases of the British, Israeli, Argentine, and Uruguayan armies, the military have been forced by circumstances to recognize their responsibility in dealing with terrorism. Reality has legitimatized the bastard, military terrorism, in fact if not in name. The daring Israeli commando rescue of 102 airline-hijack hostages at Entebbe, Uganda, in July 1976 was a dramatic example of the utilization of military power in a counterterror endeavor.

In South Vietnam terrorism was a major problem facing the American and South Vietnamese forces. Nevertheless the main responsibility for combating it was turned over to civilian intelligence organizations, such as the Central Intelligence Agency. In general, of the military branches only the U.S. Marines recognized the military importance of Viet Cong terrorism and sought not only to conquer territory but to hold it and to provide security for its inhabitants.[27] It is interesting to note that the U.S. Joint Chiefs of Staff's *Dictionary of Military and Associated Terms* finds no place for the words "terror" or "terrorism."[28]

U.S. military interest in terrorism appears to be minimal. The fact that one of the panels at the National War College's National Security Affairs Conference dealt with "New Forms of Violence in the International Milieu" was encouraging. There have been lectures and panels at the Institute for Military Assistance at Fort Bragg, North Carolina, and a protection-against-terrorism manual for U.S. military personnel being sent overseas has been written there. The *Air University Review* has published a number of relevant articles. This attention, however, must be considered inadequate in view of the enormity of the problem. Major General Edward G. Lansdale, USAF (Ret) has warned:

> We live in a revolutionary era. My hunch is that history is waiting to play a deadly joke on us. It did so on recent graduates of the Imperial Defence College in London, who now find themselves facing the savagery

of revolutionary warfare in Northern Ireland. It did so on Pakistani officers under General Niazi, who undoubtedly wish now that they had learned better ways of coping with the Mukti Bahini guerrillas. It is starting to do so on Argentine graduates of the Escuela Nacional de Guerra in Buenos Aires, who are waking up to the fact that Marxist ERP guerrillas intend to win themselves a country with the methods of the Tupamaros next door.[29]

There are existing situations and possible situations which counsel greater understanding of terrorism by the U.S. military. American military personnel have already been subjected to terrorist attacks in countries as diverse and far apart as Iran and Guatemala. It is not inconceivable that an international terrorist organization might decide, for tactical and ideological reasons, to strike at U.S. military personnel and even installations in a number of countries. (NATO, concerned over the spread of terrorism, conducted through the intelligence agencies of its member states a study of an international terrorist organization that is believed to operate globally.)[30]

The United States provides military equipment and guidance to a substantial number of friendly countries. Of what use is tank warfare doctrine to an army confronted with a major terrorist problem? Are U.S. Military Advisory Groups prepared to provide the assistance needed? Another scenario: U.S. forces are stationed in a foreign country, perhaps as part of an international peace-keeping force, and the local rebels resort to terror tactics. Are the U.S. military prepared to cope with such a situation?

There are additional scenarios that might require military involvement in terror situations within the United States itself, much as troops were required at critical moments during the civil rights struggle of the sixties. Recognizing the constitutional and historical limitations on the military and recognizing that a terror level akin to those in Argentina and Northern Ireland is not likely to develop in the United States within the foreseeable future, one can, nevertheless, postulate situations in which the military would have to exercise counterterror capabilities. Two possibilities:

- Terrorists seize the Capitol in Washington while Congress is in session. Or they take another major edifice in an American city. Handling the crisis is beyond the means of the police.
- Terrorists have a nuclear weapon or a mjaor bacterial weapon. They hold the weapon in a heavily guarded building in the center of a city, and they threaten to devastate the city if their demands are not met. Again the situation is beyond the capability of the police.

Hypothetical situations, yes. But terrorists have seized buildings in other countries, and the U.S. government is concerned over the possibility of terrorists obtaining a nuclear bomb. These situations could occur within the United States. The U.S. military would do well to prepare to assist if they are called upon to do so.

Beyond that is the necessity of recognizing that in today's world terrorism is often a military weapon. General Robert E. Lee said of the Confederacy's own guerrillas, "I regard the whole system as an unmixed evil."[31] Evil or not, guerrilla warfare has been employed by innumerable combatants down through the ages, always bedeviling the regulars. Disdaining it will not make it go away. Disdaining terrorism will not make it go away, either. Unhappy though it may make the graduate of the Imperial Defence College or of the Escuela Nacional de Guerra, or of the U.S. Military Academy, it is a tactic that must be dealt with. Far better that the U.S. military be prepared than that they, too, be caught by surprise. Tactics must be studied, doctrines must be developed, defenses must be constructed. For, as one writer stated, "Step by step, almost imperceptibly, without anyone being aware that a fatal watershed has been crossed, mankind has descended into the age of terror."[32]

NOTES & REFERENCES

[1] Richard M. Ketchum. *The Winter Soldiers* (New York, 1973). Washington prescribed the "rifle dress" for his troops because it was associated in the minds of the British with the apparel worn by skilled rifleman.

[2] Colonel William D. Neale, USA (Ret), "Terror—Oldest Weapon in the Arsenal," *Army*, August 1973.

[3] M. Cherif Bassiouni, editor, *International Terrorism and Political Crimes* (Springfield, Illinois, 1975).

[4] Neale, op. cit.

[5] H. Rothfels in *Makers of Modern Strategy*, Edward Mead Earle, editor (New York, 1970).

[6] Colonel Seale R. Doss in *Defense Planning for the 1980's & the Changing International Environment* (Washington, D.C., 1975).

[7] "The U.S. and the Skyjackers: Where Power Is Vulnerable," *Time*, 21 September 1971.

[8] "The City as Battlefield: A Global Concern," *Time*, 2 November 1970.

[9] Doss, op. cit.

[10] Ibid.

[11] Vo Nguyen Giap, *The South Vietnam People Will Win* (Hanoi, 1965).

[12] Ernesto Guevara, *La Guerra de Guerrillas* (Havana, 1960).

[13] See Jaime Suchlicki's *University Students and Revolution in Cuba, 1920-1968* (Coral Gables, Florida, 1969); Ruby Hart Phillip's *Cuba, Island of Paradox* (New York, 1959); Jay Mallin's *Fortress Cuba* (Chicago, 1965).

[14] Guevara, "Guerrilla Warfare: A Method," *Cuba Socialists*, September 1962.

[15] Foreign Languages Publishing House (Hanoi, 1965).

[16] Issued by General Headquarters, 1965.

[17] Panther Publications (Boulder, Colorado, 1964).

[18] Twenty-eighth edition (Havana, 1961).

[19] Panther Publications (Boulder, 1965).

[20] Carlos Marighella, "Minimanual of the Urban Guerrilla," *Tricontinental* (Havana, November 1970).

[21] Ibid.

[22] "When we say that in the entire war (against Japan) mobile warfare is primary and guerrilla warfare supplementary, we mean that the outcome of the war depends mainly on regular warfare, especially in its mobile form, and that guerrilla warfare cannot shoulder the main responsibility in deciding the outcome." From "On Protracted War" in *Selected Military Writings of Mao Tse-tung* (Peking, 1963).

[23] Marighella, op. cit.

[24] Ibid.

[25] Mallin, op. cit.

[26] Robert Taber, *The War of the Flea* (New York, 1965); *Challenge and Response in Internal Conflict* (three volumes, Washington, D.C., 1967, 1968).

[27] William R. Corson, *The Betrayal* (New York, 1968).

[28] Washington, D.C., 1972.

[29] Major General Edward G. Lansdale, USAF (Ret), "The Opposite Number," *Air University Review*, July-August 1972.

[30] "Radical Nations Aid, Finance Global Terror, NATO Thinks," *Miami Herald*, 6 February 1976.

[31] Bruce Catton, *A Stillness at Appomattox* (New York, 1953).

[32] Paul Johnson, quoted in David Fromkin's "The Strategy of Terrorism," *Foreign Affairs*, July 1975.

Potential perpetrators of nuclear terrorism and the problems of nuclear proliferation are described by Rosenbaum in this article. To preclude the possibility of nuclear terrorism, Rosenbaum recommends that society declare war on terrorism, strengthen nuclear safeguards and the International Atomic Energy Agency, and form a cartel to regulate international nuclear trade.

This article is reprinted by permission from *International Security,* Volume 1, Number 3, Winter 1977. Copyright is held by the President and Fellows of Harvard College.

Nuclear Terror

by DAVID M. ROSENBAUM

A SHORT STORY

On September 14, 1981, 100 kilograms of plutonium are hijacked en route from a plutonium storage area in France to a fuel fabrication plant in Italy. In order not to alarm the public, the French and Italian governments decide to keep the incident a secret while they try to recover the plutonium. On October 20, after more than a month of fruitless search, the other governments of NATO are informed of the theft. They all agree to keep the information secret to avoid public panic.

On December 24, the White House and major newspapers and broadcasting networks receive a letter stating that the World Peace Brigade will explode a nuclear weapon within the next two days. No one has ever heard of the World Peace Brigade.

On Christmas, a nuclear explosion of approximately seven kilotons explodes on the crest of the Blue Ridge Mountains sixty miles west of Washington, D.C. The news spreads quickly around the world. The President appears on national television and explains to the nation all he knows about the circumstances of the blast and the theft of the plutonium in Europe. He tries to calm the public by explaining that no one was killed by the blast.

The next day, a new letter from the World Peace Brigade is received at the White House. It makes the following demands. The United States must immediately renounce all its defense and security agreements. It must pull back all troops and equipment from overseas within six months and immediately stop all sales and shipments of arms. The number of people in the Armed Forces must be cut to 75,000 within one year. The United States must turn over fifty billion dollars a year to the United Nations to be used in specified Third World countries. A list of acceptable countries is appended to the letter. TQHE President must pardon all black and Spanish-surnamed prisoners in federal institutions within the next three months.

The letter says that nuclear weapons have been hidden in three of the largest cities of the United States and will be exploded if all of the demands are not met.

What options do the President and the United States have? They cannot threaten to retaliate if a nuclear weapon is exploded in a United States city, because they do not know at whom to direct the retaliation. Thus all of our massive investment in nuclear retaliatory forces is of no avail. Even a crude small nuclear device need be no bigger than an office desk. The chance of finding one which has been cleverly hidden somewhere in a large metropolitan area is small. If one searches a particular metropolitan area and does not find a weapon, what can be concluded? What is more, since the World Peace Brigade has already demonstrated that it took the plutonium and is capable of making nuclear weapons from it, it does not actually have to make any more weapons. No additional bombs may be hidden anywhere. But we could never be sure.

Will we choose to evacuate our largest cities? For how long? Will we choose to ignore the demands of the note? Once people are informed of the contents of the note, as they will have to be since the terrorists could release it at any time, will people still choose to live and work in our cities?

If the demands of the note are acceded to, what will stop more demands from being made? Won't the Government of the United States be permanently under the command of a small unknown group?

The writers of the note do not have to expose themselves to find out whether their demands have been carried out. They can simply read the newspapers.

Will democratic institutions be able to stand the strain of such a situation? Indeed, will any present governmental institutions, democratic or totalitarian, be able to withstand such demands?

At least since biblical days, guerrilla warfare has been a weapon of the few against the many, the weak against the strong. Here we see the logical conclusion, the helplessness of a nation of hundreds of millions of people and millions of weapons against a handful of men. If strategic nuclear warfare between major nations is avoided, nuclear terrorism may be one of the most important political and social problems of the next fifty years.

A FEW FACTS

The April 1975, *Bulletin of the International Atomic Energy Agency* (IAEA) estimates the cumulative production of plutonium (Pu) in the civilian

power cycle to be 20 metric tons (MT),[1] in 1975; 200 MT in 1980; and
more than 700 MT in 1984. Much of this will not be separated from
spent fuel, but in this country alone approximately 1.7 MT of Pu and 6.8
MT of uranium (U_{235}) now exist in separated form in the civilian cycle.[2]

It takes around 7 kilograms (kg) of Pu, 10 kg of plutonium oxide
(PuO_2), 25 kg of metallic uranium (U_{235}), 35 kg of highly enriched uranium oxide (UO_2), or somewhere around 200 kg of intermediately enriched UO_2 to build a crude nuclear explosive. The quantities needed
might be increased by a factor of two if less skill is assumed for the
weapon builders, but this uncertainty will not make any difference in our
conclusions. For convenience we will call fissionable material which can
be used to make nuclear weapons "special nuclear material" (SNM) and
the amount of fissionable material needed to make one crude nuclear
weapon a "weapons quantity" (WQ). Thus, 10 kg of PuO_2 = 1WQ, and
25 kg of U_{235} = 1 WQ. In these terms more than 2,800 WQs of Pu were
produced in world civilian power cycles by 1975 and more than 28,000
WQs will have been produced by 1980. In the United States alone, more
than 500 WQs of Pu and U_{235} presently exist in separated form in the
civilian power system.

In addition, large amounts of plutonium are produced for military
use around the world. Some suggestion of the quantities involved is given
by newspaper reports of a classified July 1976 report on Energy Research
and Development Administration safeguards. A newspaper report[3]
quotes a House of Representatives subcommittee staff summary as saying
that "More than 50 tons of nuclear material, much of it refined to weapons grade, cannot be accounted for by the 34 uranium and plutonium
processing plants in the country." And that "the Government is unable
to find at least 6,000 pounds of material of weapons grade." Thus, at
least 75 WQs are unaccounted for. This, of course, does not prove that
any material has been taken.

To make the problem even worse, it seems that the protection afforded United States nuclear weapons is not all that could be desired. In
the September 25, 1974 *Congressional Record,* Senator Pastore, Chairman
of the Joint Committee on Atomic Energy, said "If a terrorist—and it is
not that difficult breaking into one of these depositories—takes one of
these bombs and it is heralded all over the world, I am telling everyone
that we are going to be in a bad way."

Nuclear material and knowledge are spreading around the world. In
his July 1976 annual report to the Congress on Arms Control and Dis-
armament, President Ford estimated that by 1986 nearly forty countries
will have produced enough plutonium from their nuclear power reactors
to make nuclear weapons. He also said that about twenty countries already
had the technical competence and material to produce nuclear weapons.

People with the skills needed to build crude nuclear weapons are easily
found in the general technical community. Someone with experience in
calculating fast neutron systems would be useful, as would a physical
chemist and an explosives expert. There are thousands of people around

the world with sufficient nuclear experience and tens of thousands of people with the appropriate skills in physical chemistry and explosives. Thus most established organizations, given enough time, should be able to acquire appropriate people.

One kilogram of uranium or plutonium is about the size of a golf ball. A typical one-kilogram brick of marijuana is about 12″ X 6″ X 24″, or about twenty times as large. If we intercept less than ten percent of the more than 4,000 tons of marijuana smuggled into the United States each year, it is clear that we, or any country with reasonably open borders, has little chance of intercepting a few "weapons quantities" of SNM. Even Communist countries, which line their borders with electrified barbed wire, minefields, search lights, and machine guns, have serious problems with smuggling. Thus, nuclear weapons or SNM stolen anywhere are a threat to countries everywhere.

TYPES OF THREATS

This section contains a brief review of three types of nuclear threats: threatened or actual use of plutonium as a poison; threatened or actual sabotage of nuclear facilities; and threatened or actual use of nuclear explosives.

Plutonium as a posion   It is true that plutonium is a deadly poison, but it is far from the most deadly poison. Not only are biological and chemical toxins such as anthrax and botulism at least as deadly and easier to obtain, but many other radionuclides, available under much less stringent conditions, are far more deadly. For these reasons, I will not discuss further the use of plutonium as a poison.

Sabotage   Like other types of installations, nuclear facilities can and have been sabotaged to cause economic loss or to prevent their operation. Insofar as such attacks do not threaten the loss of many human lives, they are in no way unique. Attention here is restricted to the types of threatened or actual sabotage of nuclear facilities which might cause many deaths.

The sabotage of nuclear facilities for power generation, fuel reprocessing, fuel fabrication, plutonium storage, spent fuel storage, and high-level radioactive waste storage might endanger the lives of many people. In some parts of the world, such as the Soviet Union, these facilities are ringed with barbed wire and protected by machine guns. In the United States and many European countries, however, nuclear power plants have traditionally been accorded only a slightly higher level of security than fossil fuel generating plants. Some other parts of the fuel cycle usually receive a higher level of protection, but the level varies greatly from country to country.

There are two main types of sabotage threats against these facilities. The first concentrates on producing the casualties and loss of property associated with the sabotage. The second involves holding a facility hostage in return for some political or financial goal.

Since attackers can pick the facility, time, and weather of their choice, thousands of deaths might be caused by the sudden sabotage of an appropriate nuclear facility. One certain result of such an incident would be a substantial increase in the amount of protection afforded such facilities in the country attacked and probably in the whole world. Thus such an act would be much more difficult to duplicate. Since actual and not potential damage is involved, the only desired consequences could be those which would follow from the damage itself. While property damage and deaths are often motives for terrorist action, the economic and human loss would not seriously damage the military, political, and economic strength of a large advanced country and would be much less than that caused by many natural disasters such as the recent earthquake in Tangshan, China.

The most likely motive for sudden sabotage is a desire to slow down or eliminate nuclear power in the country attacked, or in a large part of the world. The Western world already generates a substantial portion of its electricity with nuclear power and this proportion seems likely to increase sharply by the end of the century as the supply of fossil fuel diminishes. The elimination of their commercial nuclear power would, therefore, be a significant blow to the economic and long-range military strength of many nations. Countries which see it in their interest to weaken the Western democracies and certain types of terrorist groups might find this possibility very attractive. Criminal organizations, while having no direct motive, could be hired to help.

An operation of this kind is likely to be too difficult for any single individual. Environmental groups, however militant, have shown absolutely no propensity for violence on this scale.

A nuclear facility near a metropolitan area could be captured by a terrorist group which threatened to cause an explosion releasing large amounts of radioactive material into the atmosphere. If the facility contained more than a WQ of easily useable SNM they might, given sufficient time, even construct a nuclear explosive on the site. Properly used, such an explosive could greatly increase the amount of radioactive material dispersed and the area over which it was dispersed.

Whatever the terrorists' demands, it would almost certainly take many hours and perhaps several days before the negotiations could be completed and the demands met or rejected. This would allow time for many, perhaps most, of the people to be evacuated from the area, and would thus reduce the threat to one of property damage.

Nuclear Explosives   Nuclear weapons are the most efficient devices for killing ever devised. The vast quantities of nuclear weapons already possessed by nations pose a threat to the continued existence of human life.

No method now potentially available to small groups is anywhere near as lethal as even a crude nuclear weapon. This is not only because of its explosive force, but also because its small size and mobility make it possible for the group to choose a time and place which will maximize the harm done. It has been estimated that one million people might die if a 20 kiloton nuclear weapon was exploded on Wall Street at noon on a buisness day.[4]

A nuclear weapon can not only kill many people, but it is extremely useful for blackmail as the scenario at the beginning of this article illustrates. Thus its use is likely to be attractive to hostile foreign nations, terrorist groups, criminals, or combinations of them. The weapon might be obtained either through the theft of an already constructed weapon or through the theft of SNM and the manufacture of a weapon from it.

A terrorist group which successfully steals a nuclear weapon or more than one "weapons quantity" of SNM may be able to extort sizable gains just by proving that it took the material and claiming that it is able to set off a nuclear explosion. It is difficult to see what assurance could be offered to the public that the claim was false.

A great deal of thought has gone into designing United States nuclear weapons to make it extremely difficult for an unauthorized person to cause them to explode as nuclear weapons. They are designed on a fail-safe basis so that no one individual, even one who has been trained to "arm" them, will be able to cause a nuclear explosion. The other nations who already have nuclear weapons and those who will come to have them in the future may not have given the same amount of attention to this problem. On the other hand, other nations may protect their nuclear weapons much better than Senator Pastore's comments indicate that we have protected ours.

One wonders whether one or more nuclear weapons have already been stolen from the United States world-wide inventory, or whether we would even know, in a timely manner, whether a nuclear weapon was missing. Perhaps there is a secret "materials unaccounted for" (MUF) associated with nuclear weapons as well as SNM.

POTENTIAL PERPETRATORS

It is useful to examine briefly the types of potential terrorists: their history, their goals, and their methods of action. A recent MITRE Corporation study which I directed covers this subject in much more detail.[5]

Foreign Government Organizations—The Soviet Union As an Example

In spite of its enormous investment in détente, its need for Western food and technology, and even the possibility of starting a war, the Soviet Union might conduct terrorist activities in the United States.

Early in World War II when its existence was imminently threatened, the Soviets organized extensive intelligence networks in the United States and Great Britain which stole vital information about radar, anti-submarine devices, and nuclear weapons. Exposure of this espionage and the resulting public outcry might have prevented the United States from entering the war, or changed the Western world's attitude such that the postwar structure of Europe would have been radically altered. Yet the Soviet Union took this chance.

Soviet détente with Great Britain preceded and was the opening wedge to its détente with the United States. In 1970, for example, Soviet exports to Britain were twice their imports from Britain and more than six times their exports to the United States. The Soviets also needed their expanding relations with Great Britain to provide them with access to the latest Western technology. In 1971, after the defection of a key KGB member of the Soviet Trade Mission, the British Government expelled 105 representatives of the Soviet Union for being intelligence agents. This ended the Soviet-British détente for several years. The *Daily Mail* on October 2, 1971, said, "The most sensational revelation may be that the Russians planned to sabotage vital installations even during peacetime."

This should come as no surprise since not only has the Soviet Union carried out far worse activities around the world, but many other countries including our own have been involved in similar operations. Countries which attempt to overthrow the governments or murder the leaders of countries with which they are at peace, are unlikely to be deterred from other acts on the basis that failure will disturb the status quo.

Actually, the consequences of getting caught seem to be quite small. Libya, for example, has continually financed Palestinian terrorist operations against other Arab and OPEC nations with whom it presumably has the closest ties. The recent wave of sabotage and bombings in Egypt; the invasion of the Sudan; the Palestinian kidnapping of the OPEC oil ministers and the Palestinian occupation and murders in the Saudi Arabian embassies in Paris and the Sudan were all planned or financed by Libya. Nevertheless, the Libyans continue to be a member in good standing of both the Arab League and OPEC and the Libyan foreign minister has been prominent as a mediator in the 1976 Lebanese war.

These examples should make it clear that foreign governmental organizations are a serious potential threat to nuclear installations, SNM, and nuclear weapons, either directly or through financing, training, planning, and rewarding of terrorist or criminal groups.

Insurgents and Terrorists There have been many insurgent groups throughout history who have been reluctant to take life and have targeted only specific individuals or groups for destruction. Among such groups in recent times were the original Irish Republican Army (1916-1921), the Jewish underground movements in Palestine, and Castro's revolutionaries in Cuba. Most "revolutionaries" now, however, seem to consider indiscriminate slaughter a primary tactic and one of which they are proud.[6] Palestinian operations such as the Lod Airport massacre, which killed mostly Puerto Rican Catholic pilgrims, the massacre of Israeli athletes in Munich, and the slaughter of school children in Maalot are illustrative. In each of these incidents, the perpetrators were proclaimed as heroes by the sponsoring organizations. It is clear that such groups would not be deterred from nuclear terrorism by the fact that thousands of innocent and uninvolved people might die.

Since the Phillistines supported David against King Saul, there has always been a great deal of cooperation among insurgent groups and between them and nations with parallel interests. The United States revolution received support from France; the Irish revolutionaries received support from the German Government and many private groups in the United States; Castro supported revolutionary movements throughout Latin America after taking power in Cuba.

In recent years the increased ease of transportation and communication has made this sort of cooperation far more extensive. The Palestinian terrorists, for example, have been financed and equipped by Saudi Arabia, Kuwait, Iraq, Libya, Algeria, the Soviet bloc, and China, among others. They have received training from such wide-spread countries as North Korea, Syria, and Cuba. They have links with terrorist organizations around the world including the Tupamaros in Uruguay, the Quebec Liberation Front, the Irish Republican Army, the Basque Liberation Front, the Baader-Meinhof Gang in West Germany, the Turkish Popular Liberation Front, and the Japanese Red Army Group.

Terrorist groups often stage joint operations. The Lod Airport Massacre in May 1972, for example, was carried out for the Popular Front for the Liberation of Palestine by members of the Japanese Red Army Group armed with Soviet weapons who had been trained in a Palestinian camp in Syria. Members of the Japanese Red Army Group, the Irish Republican Army, the Tupamaros, and the Baader-Meinhof gang have all been trained in Palestinian camps.

The most modern portable military arms are available on the world market. Even in this country such weapons are easy to get. A classified document recently released by Representative Les Aspin of Wisconsin reports that during the period of 1971 to 1974 approximately 6,900 weapons and 1.1 million rounds of ammunition were lost or stolen—enough to equip ten combat battalions or 8,000 men. The stolen weapons include M-16 rifles, M-60 machine guns, M-76 grenade launchers, and M-3 submachine guns. In addition, there have been many thefts of light anti-tank weapons in the past few years and terrorists have acquired Soviet-made SA-7 Strella rockets—a one-man, portable heat-seeking anti-aircraft rocket. The extensive use of the most modern weapons by all the groups involved in the current Lebanese fighting will undoubtedly make these weapons available to terrorists around the world.

Criminals Criminal organizations, some of which have extensive international ties, are potential sources of nuclear terrorist activities. Among the most prominent are the Mafia, originally a Sicilian organization, which dominates organized crime in Italy and the United States, and the Corsican Brotherhood which dominates organized crime in France. These

organizations are involved in drug smuggling, gambling, prostitution,
loan-sharking, and narcotics.

All crime in the United States is not "organized," nor is the Mafia the only organized group. There are Chinese, Cuban, Puerto Rican, Mexican, and Black groups with power in specific localities. Nevertheless, the Mafia represents a substantial economic, political, and operational organization. Its twenty-six "families" contain more than 6,500 members across the nation and control a much larger number of men. They have connections around the world.

Organized crime can put together sizable teams, including specialists with the latest information and equipment. The famous Boston Brink's robbery of January 17, 1950, for example, involved eleven men, almost a year of planning, and thorough attention to detail. Through observation with binoculars from adjacent roofs, the number, routine, and placement of every Brink's employee was charted. The lock cylinders from the five doors between the street and the vault were removed, keys made for them, and replaced. A copy of the alarm system for the building was obtained by burglarizing the offices of the company which installed the alarms. The plans were then returned. A new truck was stolen from a car dealer two months prior to the robbery and hid in a private garage until it was used. Afterwards, it was cut into small pieces, placed in burlap bags, and scattered about a dump yard. The details of the robbery from the approach to the building to the final getaway were practiced over and over again. The robbery went off without a hitch and the members of the gang were caught only because of a subsequent falling out among them over the division of the spoils.

Organized crime in this country has been extraordinarily successful in stealing cargo. Over one billion dollars is taken each year in the trucking industry alone. Most of this theft occurs at truck terminals and involves employees of the various companies, but hijacking is also a serious problem. The sophistication of hijackers has increased to the point where they take loaded trucks before they can be driven away from the loading dock and seize entire terminals and warehouses. It is not unusual for hijackers to take an order from a customer, hijack the specified goods, and deliver it directly to the customer's warehouse for a flat fee.

A New York City police intelligence officer commenting on the smuggling of cigarettes into New York City said, "Organized crime is complete from one end to the other. The driver, the warehouse facility, the salesman, the office help, the territory and everything else. We think probably they are responsible for about 20 percent of all cigarettes sold in the City of New York."[7]

Organized crime has infiltrated many legitimate businesses. A great many businesses have employees who act as agents for bookies or numbers racketeers. It is through these people that bets are placed at the plant. This sometimes leads to debts which cannot be paid, loan sharking, and other more serious interactions with organized crime.

138   In addition to infiltrating businesses, organized crime often captures control of them. This may give criminals access to and control over material and situations which would otherwise be impossible. Imagine, for example, if a "financial investment firm" in the control of organized crime bought a company which had a license to transport SNM. Perhaps this has already happened.

The border between criminal and revolutionary operations is always fuzzy and revolutionary organizations often have arrangements with criminal organizations. Individuals move from one type of organization to the other. It would be easy for a revolutionary group or a country to contact organized crime and hire it to steal and deliver SNM.

It is sometimes said that organized crime would not engage in such an operation because it is too patriotic. This is not said by anyone with much knowledge about organized crime because it is extremely brutal, solely bent on profit, and without scruples.

It is sometimes said that organized crime would not engage in nuclear terrorism because exposure of its role would generate such bad publicity that its already extraordinarily profitable operations would be jeopardized. This argument is based on two fundamental misunderstandings. In the first place, an organization which makes an enormous and highly publicized profit from selling heroin to our youth is unlikely to be deterred from anything by the thought of bad publicity. In the second place, organized crime is not that organized. While there is a structure and a certain amount of control, there is also a great deal of individual freedom for people both in and associated with organized crime. For a sufficient amount of money, an appropriate group could be recruited even without the approval of the top organized crime leaders.

There is already a great deal of contact among governmental, terrorist, and criminal organizations around the world. It would not be surprising if the first serious incident of nuclear terrorism involved cooperation between two or three of these types of organizations.

NUCLEAR PROLIFERATION IN A WORLD OF TERRORISM

The Effect of Additional National Proliferation   Nuclear proliferation is inevitable. Ten years from now more than six countries will have nuclear weapons. Taiwan, South Korea, Pakistan, and Israel, for example, have large hostile armies on their borders and these countries will probably develop nuclear weapons for the same reason we have them: deterrence. The problem, therefore, is not what can be done to completely stop the proliferation of weapons among nations, but rather what can be done to slow proliferation and increase the benefits and limit the harm from the acquisition of nuclear weapons by new nations.

The acquisition of nuclear weapons by additional nations is only one of many important problems the world faces and certainly not the most serious. Most of the possible danger to mankind from national proliferation is already present. The addition of several more countries to the game is not likely to increase that danger greatly.

There may even be some counterbalancing advantages to further national proliferation. It is widely believed that the possession of nuclear weapons and appropriate delivery systems by the United States and the Soviet Union has lessened the chance of a war between them. I see no reason to think that this same effect will be any less true for other pairs of countries that possess nuclear weapons. In addition, states without nuclear weapons will be less likely to engage in warfare with states that have them. Both of these effects are likely to lessen the frequency of wars.

With the exception of West Germany and Japan, none of the states that do not now possess nuclear weapons are capable of acquiring large numbers of thermonuclear weapons and long-range delivery systems before the end of this century. Thus any of nuclear weapons by states not now possessing them ("new nuclear states") is liable to involve a few small weapons used locally. While still having the potential of large-scale death and destruction, this sort of use is not likely to cause the sort of eschatological catastrophe characteristic of nuclear war between superpowers.

Because of their enormous psychological and destructive effects, nuclear weapons will tend to make wars shorter. Since a large part of the casualties in most wars are due to long-term effects on the population, reducing the length of wars should help to reduce casualties. The current struggle in Lebanon, in which more than a third of the population has either been killed or wounded, or has left for exile, is a perfect example.

Wars involving new nuclear states may have more casualties and deaths than they would if neither side had nuclear weapons. On the other hand, they may not; since the wars will be shorter, have more tendency to be settled by negotiations, and nuclear states may be deterred from using their weapons by the possibility of retaliation from the enemy or from a larger nuclear power. When, after the Egyptians' initial success in the Yom Kippur War, it looked as if the Israeli Army might be routed, the Soviet Union moved nuclear weapons into the port of Alexandria. These weapons, which could have been installed on the medium-range Soviet missiles already in Egypt, were presumably there to deter any possible Israeli use of nuclear weapons as a last resort.

If wars involving new nuclear states are fewer and shorter than they would otherwise be and only a small percentage of them involve the use of nuclear weapons, it is not certain that on the average the world will suffer more deaths and injuries than it would if no new country ever got nuclear weapons. However, this uncertainty is not present in the case of acquisition of nuclear weapons by some types of subnational groups.

The Effect of Subnational Proliferation There are subnational groups, such as the Kurds, the Christians in the southern Sudan, the Eritreans, the Nagas in Northeast India, and the Shans, Karen, and Kachin in Burma, which while not now sovereign states have long occupied a region in which they are a large majority, and who are now fighting for independence. Many other groups such as the Tibetans, Ukranians, Czechs, Croats, and East Germans also have a geographically defined territory and a desire for more freedom from outside controlling groups. Insurgent groups representing such peoples have many of the same constraints that nations have and may be deterred from nuclear terrorism by the possibility of severe retaliation against their own people.

The problem is quite different for small groups which represent an ideology, a people who do not live in a contiguous geographical area, or a small segment of some ethnic group. These types of terrorist groups may see the sabotage of nuclear facilities as a way to weaken a hated country and the acquisition of even a crude nuclear device as the perfect terrorist weapon: a chance to hold an entire nation hostage.

Some Examples of National Vulnerability   The Soviet Union is particularly vulnerable to nuclear proliferation and terrorism. The last two nations to explode nuclear devices lie along its southern border and South Korea, Pakistan, and Iran are likely to acquire nuclear weapons in the future. Since Taiwan and Israel are also reported to have or to be building nuclear weapons, the Soviet Union might find itself with seven nuclear weapons states on or near its southern border within the next decade. The Svoiets' problem is even worse because many of the minorities which live along its southern border extend into the neighboring countries. Soviet borders are not completely sealed and many of these minorities continue to have a great deal of legal and illegal contact with their ethnic brethren on the other side. If a revolutionary group based in one of these minorities were to acquire SNM or a nuclear weapon within one of the countries on the Soviet border they might be able to smuggle it across. Thus the spectre of nuclear terrorism is as real for the Soviet Union as for ourselves and we share a common interest in trying to prevent it.

China also faces a potentially dangerous problem from nuclear terrorism. The Soviet Union and India already have nuclear weapons and South Korea, Taiwan, and Pakistan are likely to develop them. Thus China may soon be surrounded by five nuclear weapons states. Given China's preponderance of nuclear weapons and delivery systems, India, Pakistan, Taiwan, and South Korea are unlikely to use nuclear weapons against China in a war. But any of them, particularly Taiwan, might attempt to use nuclear terrorism to bring down the Communist regime. Such terrorism would be done in the name of some group not obviously associated with the sponsoring country. Given the ability of Taiwan to infiltrate people and supplies into China and the possibility that the Soviets might use terrorism employing people from one of the ethnic groups which bridge the Chinese-Soviet border, it seems that the Chinese Government should also have a strong interest in international measures against nuclear terrorism.

The danger of nuclear terrorism is probably greater for Israel than for any other country. Israel is already a prime target for a large number of Arab and other allied terrorist groups. Libya has offered very large sums of money for strategic quantities of SNM and is trying to assemble Arab nuclear scientists to develop an indigenous nuclear capability. If

Colonel Qaddafi were to acquire nuclear weapons, it is very likely that he would try to use them against Israel. In addition, since Palestinian terrorists and their allies operate in most of the developed and many of the semi-developed countries of the non-Communist world, SNM or nuclear weapons stolen anywhere pose an immediate and direct threat to Israel's existence.

Western Europe has already suffered a number of instances of nuclear-related sabotage. In 1975, in France, for example, two incidents of sabotage were reported. On August 15, two bombs exploded at the 70 megawatt Experimental Heavy Water Plan at Brennilis. The Breton Liberation Front-Breton Liberation Army claimed credit for the attack. More than three months earlier two bombs exploded at the nuclear power plant under construction at Fessenheim. The saboteurs put the bombs in exactly those places which would cause maximum delay in the construction. A French newspaper article said, "It is certain that the perpetrator of the crime must have been perfectly acquainted with the site and must have had experience and mastery of the explosives and some understanding of the technology of the installations at which he aimed."[8] Seventy minutes before the bombs exploded, a telephone call gave warning and claimed credit for the Meinhof-Puig Antich Group. This group had never been heard of before.

Western Europe has even more open borders and many more active revolutionary and terrorist groups than the United States. It also has a stronger tradition of revolutionary and terrorist violence than the United States. The reasons that make the United States vulnerable to nuclear terrorism are even more pronounced in Western Europe.

Considering its size and diversity, the United States has had little internal political violence. Even our "revolutionaries" have been remarkably benign. Furthermore, neither of the countries we border are likely to develop nuclear weapons. Nevertheless, we face very serious dangers from nuclear terrorism. Our far from adequate concern for protecting our facilities and SNM from the potential threats previously discussed make them fairly easy targets. Our concern for civil liberties makes it difficult to do the sort of intelligence work which might warn us of a substantial proportion of such attacks. The United States is still the undisputed leader of the world's democracies. As such, it is a primary political target for totalitarian regimes and the scores of terrorist groups which are trained and supported by them. It might also be a target for other domestic and foreign groups, but these are likely to be much less capable and thus less of a threat.

Almost every country in the world has problems with ideological and ethnic groups who are unhappy with their lot. While small underdeveloped countries with no nuclear facilities or weapons are less likely to be targets of nuclear terrorism than more developed countries, no country is completely safe from the threat. Every nation will have to learn to live with the possibility of nuclear terrorism in its own way, just as they have learned to live with the far grimmer prospect of all-out nuclear warfare.

The Effect of Nuclear Terrorism Societies have invariably preferred order, even repression, to anarchy. Even large revolutionary groups usually set up governmental structures of their own. Thus societies which experience many casualties from an act of nuclear sabotage may very well react by strengthening the protection of these facilities and expanding police prerogatives rather than giving up nuclear power. Terrorist attacks on airlines, for example, have strengthened airport protection rather than significantly diminishing air travel.

It is possible that societies which are blackmailed or attacked by terrorists possessing nuclear weapons will experience radical changes in governmental form, perhaps in the direction of extremely rigid totalitarianism. Societies which are already totalitarian may experience their own radical changes, perhaps splintering into a number of smaller states.

On the other hand, nuclear terrorism may be less of a strain on societies and their institutions than is often thought. When the Black Death hit its peak in Europe in 1348, more than 75 percent of the people died within a few months in some regions. One quarter of the total population of Europe was killed during the Great Epidemic.

During the Great Plague of London in 1665, at least a quarter of the people died. It was reported that in the last week of August alone, more than 5 percent of the population was killed. The next year almost the entire Old City of London was burned to the ground.

Out of the 8,500,000 people in Ireland when the potato blight struck, 12 percent died of starvation and disease and 19 percent emigrated.

While these catastrophes had noticeable social consequences,[9] in no case did they change the fundamental political and economic systems, or even bring down a national government. Nuclear terrorism is unlikely to cause catastrophes of this magnitude. It is quite possible, therefore, that nuclear terrorism will only bring down more quickly those political institutions which are already collapsing. The only way that nuclear terrorists could cause a disaster of eschatalogical proportions is if a terrorist weapon touched off an all-out nuclear war. Indeed, this might be the purpose of such an explosion.

Insurgency and terrorism are forms of warfare. Major powers have based their security against nuclear attack on the concept of retaliation. This concept has no relevance to attack by a small unknown group.

However pervasive and ruthless the secret police; however deep the barbed wire and mine fields and guard posts along the borders; however rigid and constant the attempts to control the minds of children and adults; every system develops weaknesses over time. The number of terrorists with nuclear weapons need be so small and the damage they can inflict is so large, that internal security measures alone will not be sufficient for any country. These are compelling reasons for countries, particularly states with nuclear weapons, to cooperate very closely with both their friends and their enemies in meeting his problem.

Perhaps the best analogy to terrorism is not warfare but plague. While the weakening of its enemies might bring a country some temporary advantage, such infection is impossible to contain within national borders. The advent of nuclear terrorism will probably force more profound changes in international than national politics.

WHAT CAN BE DONE

Nuclear terrorism is not the only problem in the world, nor is it the worst one. Sixty million people died last year. Thus, unless nuclear terrorism brings on an all-out nuclear war, neither further nuclear proliferation nor any form of nuclear terrorism are likely to make a dramatic change in the annual number of deaths. Starvation might. The rapid expansion of world population coupled with either dramatic weather changes (such as may now be upon us) or some new plant disease could kill many times more. So could a new human disease. The swine flu killed more than twice as many people in the winter 1918-19 than were killed in all the fighting of World War I. The introduction of some entirely new disease through the genetic manipulation of virus or bacteria might kill hundreds of millions.

The problem of nuclear proliferation is tied to the proliferation of civilian nuclear power and the spread of nuclear knowledge. The problem of nuclear terrorism is tied to all three. However, these ties are fairly weak. At least six countries have already made tens of thousands of nuclear weapons and, as far as is known, not one weapon has been made from SNM taken from a civilian nuclear power cycle. Our own first nuclear weapon was made with plutonium from a small special-purpose air-cooled reactor hidden under the University of Chicago football stadium. It would be much easier today for a country to build a small special-purpose reactor to make plutonium than it was then. Thus, even shutting down all civilian nuclear power would not stop nuclear proliferation and might not even slow it down very much. Nuclear terrorism will remain a serious problem no matter what we do.

Some Suggestions That Might Make Things Worse

Cut Off Promised Enrichment Services Many people have suggested that we cut off enrichment services to countries such as France and Germany if they do not stop all sales of fuel cycle facilities. The idea seems to be that for the next several years they will have to depend on us for fuel enrichment or shut down some of their nuclear power plants. Since they would be unwilling to do this, the argument goes, they will have to do what we want.

It is unlikely that countries like France and Germany will bow to this sort of blackmail. More important, this argument contains the seeds of global disaster. The great cataclysm that hangs over the head of mankind is not nuclear proliferation or terrorism, but all-out nuclear war between superpowers. Germany and Japan have the technical capability to manufacture superpower-sized arsenals of hydrogen bombs and intercontinental ballistic missiles. Their failure to do so is a political decision, not a technical one. They lie at the edge of the Communist empires and if they come to doubt America's commitment to defend them from attack, they will certainly take steps to enable them to defend themselves. If we break our agreements with them and threaten them with serious economic harm, it could result in the dissolution of NATO, the full rearmament of Germany and Japan, and the end of democracy in those two countries. The dissolution of NATO would be the Soviet's greatest victory since World War II, and the possibility of the nuclear armament of Germany and Japan might lead the Soviet Union to take steps which could bring on World War III. If Germany and Japan acquire a full arsenal of hydrogen bombs and long-range delivery systems that, in itself, will greatly increase the chance of global disaster.

Multinational Regional Fuel Reprocessing Centers The idea behind multinational regional fuel reprocessing centers is that because many nations are involved, no one nation will be able to secretly steal plutonium from the facility. This may or may not be true, but the dangers from such a system far outweigh any benefits it might have.

Multinational regional reprocessing centers have to be located somewhere. Two years ago when I asked one of the early advocates of this proposal where he would locate the regional center in the Middle East, he said Lebanon. So much for predictions of national stability.

No matter where the center is located, it will be subject to actual if not legal expropriation. What will we do if the center is expropriated for some "good" reason? Will we invade? Most likely we will protest and learn to live with it, particularly if the expropriating country agrees to have the facility inspected by the IAEA. We can avoid the possibility of expropriation only by locating centers in countries which already have reprocessing plants and large nuclear forces and thus have no incentive to expropriate the facility.

Who will provide the security for such a multinational center? Who will control the computers which keep track of how much material is supposed to be there? The international staff. But with few exceptions, the staffs of international organizations act as agents for their home countries not as international civil servants. Thus, very little organizational loyalty or discipline is possible. The security at such an installation will be very bad and it will be a much easier target for terrorist groups than would a facility protected by the police forces of any one nation.

An international reprocessing center will provide excellent training for the nationals of all the countries who staff it. Countries will send specialists for this very purpose. It will thus help to spread the knowledge needed to build and operate large reprocessing centers.

If, on the other hand, the facility is located in a country which already has a large supply of nuclear weapons and if that country supplies the guard force and all the technical personnel, then in what sense will the center be international? It is certainly a good idea to slow down the spread of fuel cycle facilities, but this is an awful way to do it.

Declare War on Terrorism It is useful to draw a distinction between insurgency and terrorism. By terrorism I mean the purposeful killing of untargeted and uninvolved people as a major mode of operation. Insurgency is a legitimate form of warfare but terrorism, like piracy, is the enemy of all nations. Terrorists, like pirates, must be treated as international criminals and attacked wherever and by whomever they are found.

Before Jefferson became President, a sizable part of our annual national revenue was paid to Morocco, Algiers, Tunis, and Tripoli, either to ransom prisoners or to allow free passage for our ships in the Mediterranean. Jefferson sent a fleet to Tripoli to attack the Bey instead of paying him. That ended the problem. There is no other answer to terrorism.

We must form an alliance against terrorism with as many nations as possible and actively strike at terrorist training camps and headquarers wherever they may be located. Sooner or later, perhaps after the advent of nuclear terrorism, most of the nations of the world will join in this effort. But there are some steps we should take immediately. Congress should pass legislation banning all aid or trade with any nation that supports or harbors terrorists. We should encourage and assist actions like the Entebbe rescue and attacks on terrorist leaders, headquarters, and training bases. Let us give terrorism no respite and no sanctuary until this plague is brought under control.

Form a cartel The free market is not a very useful model with which to understand the international nuclear trade. Rather our total monopoly is just beginning to be challenged by a few other countries. Naturally, the challengers must offer more attractive propositions in order to break into the market. The United States Government has spent so many billions of dollars for so many years developing and subsidizing our native nuclear technology that it is difficult for other nations to offer much lower prices. Thus there is a strong incentive for them to offer things that the United States cannot or will not offer. Many of these things have implications for the proliferation of SNM and nuclear weapons. Canadian heavy water reactors do not need enriched uranium; France and Germany have been willing to sell enrichment, fuel fabrication, and reprocessing plants. These countries want to control the spread of SNM and nuclear weapons, but they also want a larger piece of the action.

The problem can only be made worse by threatening other exporting nations, but it can be handled rather easily by guaranteeing them an appropriate share of the market. Let us form a cartel of nations which export nuclear facilities, divide the market according to some mutually agreed upon formula, and agree that no one will export a fuel cycle facility.

Complaints will be raised by economic purists, some buyer nations, and by American nuclear exporters who will have to take a smaller share of the market than they have been traditionally used to. In fact, such a step will be in their interest, since without it American nuclear exports may be cut off completely for political reasons. The Organization of Petroleum Exporting Countries (OPEC) has shown that after the first wave of criticism passes, members of a successful cartel are treated with a good deal more respect in the international community than they were before. Purchasers of nuclear power plants from the cartel should be assured that the cartel will exchange new fuel for old for the life of the plants. Buyers would thus have no need for reprocessing plants, regional or otherwise, as long as the cartel's price for fuel was low enough. For this reason the price for fuel should be kept very low, while raising the price of power plants to make up for it if necessary.

Although multinational regional reprocessing centers are a bad idea, reprocessing centers run and protected by a single country which already has or could easily obtain large numbers of nuclear weapons is a good one. Such members of the cartel should provide enrichment and reprocessing under contract from the cartel. Each of the plants would be owned, operated, and protected by the nation on whose territory it resided. Plutonium separated from the reprocessed fuel would be used to enrich fuel for power plants operated by cartel members.

Support the IAEA   When the IAEA looks for diversion of SNM the most it is likely to find are indications and suspicious acts rather than absolute proof. IAEA inspectors have found many such indications and acts in the past, but the IAEA has never taken action on any of them. This will probably continue to be true.

The IAEA is unlikely to detect even moderate amounts of diversion by a nation which sets out to deceive it, and it has no authority over the physical security of SNM anywhere. All in all, the fact that the nuclear facilities of a country are under IAEA inspection is unlikely to give great comfort to a knowledgeable person who is suspicious of the country's intentions.

The question, however, is not whether the IAEA can stop nuclear proliferation; the question is whether it is worth the money we and other countries are putting into it. The amount of money is quite small and the answer is clearly yes. The IAEA should be strengthened because it is another imperfect, sensible instrument which helps make things better than they would otherwise be. It would be just as unwise to close it down as it would be to delude ourselves about its very serious and intrinsic imperfections.

Strengthen Safeguards   The United States led the world in producing nuclear weapons and civilian nuclear power. We must lead the world in protecting nuclear weapons, installations, and SNM. While our protection of nuclear installations and SNM is better than it was a few years ago, it is still entirely inadequate. We should greatly strengthen this protection and expand and formalize the help we give to other nations in this area.

They will welcome it because no nation, however radical, wants its own facilities destroyed or its own SNM taken. Just the fact that we strengthen our own safeguards will exert great pressure on other governments to do the same.

CONCLUSION

The world has the potential to become ever more beautiful, just, and humane. It will certainly become more dangerous. There is no safety in static defenses and controlled scientific advancement is a contradiction in terms. Our only safety lies in becoming ever more capable of handling the increasing dangers.

Frightening as they are, further nuclear proliferation and nuclear terrorism are not our worst problems and even the immediate shutdown of civilian nuclear power around the world will not protect us from them. If it is human life we are trying to save, starvation may be a bigger problem and the countries which export large amounts of food depend heavily on energy to grow it. The world may need all the energy it can conserve and generate. Although no amount of energy may make it possible for us to stop mass starvation indefinitely, certainly the possibility of saving tens of millions of human lives a year is important. Those upper-middle class people who wish to cut off the world's long-term possibilities for energy growth may have a good deal to rationalize if they succeed and this success results in the deaths of tens of millions who might otherwise have been saved.

NOTES & REFERENCES

[1] 1 metric ton = 1,000 kilograms = 2,200 pounds.

[2] Nuclear Regulatory Commission figures.

[3] *The New York Times,* August 6, 1976, article by David Burnham.

[4] Calculated by Theodore Taylor, Private Communication.

[5] *The Threat to Licensed Nuclear Facilities,* MTR-7022 (Washington: The MITRE Corporation, September 1975).

[6] It is worth noting that countries often use similar tactics. In World War II, for example, all sides conducted widespread bombing of civilian areas.

[7] The Department of Justice and Department of Transportation, *Cargo Theft and Organized Crime: A Desk Book of Management and Law Enforcement.* (Washington: Government Printing Office, 1972).

[8] Extract from the French newspaper *Le Gaeule Ouverte,* June 9, 1975, M. Goulet.

[9] For example, in 1348, 50,000 Jews were burned alive in Burgundy alone, because it was believed that the Black Death was due to their poisoning the wells.

Norman reports on specific improvements being made by the U. S. Department of Defense to upgrade the security of nuclear storage sites. Norman's interview with Joseph J. Liebling, Deputy Assistant Secretary of Defense for Security Policy, recounts United States plans which add 20,000 more security troops and spend an additional 400 million dollars to provide a credible deterrent to terrorists.

Our Nuclear Weapons Sites: Next Target of Terrorists?

by LLOYD NORMAN

With the threat of nuclear blackmail by international terrorists now a real possibility, the U.S. Defense Department is taking steps to beef up security at the some 1,500 nuclear weapons-storage sites it maintains around the world. Especially vulnerable, either to a terrorist grab or to enemy ground attacks, are the more than 100 such sites in NATO Europe—where the United States keeps about 7,000 tactical weapons—and those in South Korea, where about 1,000 warheads are reportedly stored.

If even one small nuclear weapon from this stockpile, each with an explosive yield of one kiloton (equivalent to 1,000 tons of TNT), fell into the hands of a terrorist group or a criminal mob, the world would quake as hostage under the threat of nuclear murder.

"We are living in probably the wildest period in history when we have to be prepared for the one-in-a-million possibility that a zealot or some one with a deranged mind could get hold of an atomic bomb from somebody's stockpile or from a weapon in the field or while it was being transported." said Joseph J. Liebling, Deputy Assistant Secretary of Defense for Security Policy. He is an internationally known expert on military security matters and strategic technology trade control.

"Safeguarding our nuclear weapons against theft or assault is getting high priority these days because of the possible threat," Mr. Liebling said. "The Defense Department in fiscal 1978 is planning to add 20,000 more troops to improve the security of nuclear weapons-storage sites and about $400 million is being spent on anti-intrusion sensors, warning systems and hardening the sites.

"We are moving the quick-response troops to hardened control centers on the sites so they can react fast to warning from a security patrol or the sensors."

The storage sites are usually concrete-and-steel underground "igloos" surrounded by double anchor-chain fences with sophisticated sensors (IDS, or intrusion-detection systems) which react to noise, magnetism, movement or seismic effect (earth tremor). The igloos are flood lighted at night and constantly guarded. Besides the guards at each site there are "reaction" or alert forces in nearby hardened buildings ready to defend the site when the alarm sounds.

The troops guarding the sites are called "dedicated"; they are specially selected for the assignment and they have to pass tough physical and mental reliability tests.

"We have to operate under the assumption that there could be an attempt made to penetrate a nuclear weapons site by terrorists or criminals," said Mr. Liebling. "Thus far we have not been able to identify or trace any attempts to break into a site to terrorists or criminals. Some attempts have been made to climb a fence or to cut a fence, but the possible intruders were frightened away. They may have been pranksters or people bent on some mischief, but they were not determined or sophisticated enough to go through with the attempted break-ins."

Mr. Leibling said that terrorists who want world attention and who are driven by some political cause would be most likely to plot the capture of atomic bombs. He suggested that they might employ criminals in their operations, but ordinary professional criminals probably would not take the risks of nuclear theft.

"The threat from terrorists is very significant," he said. "They have taken hostages, they have hijacked airplanes to propagandize their cause and now, with sophistication of terrorists far greater than ever, they may go for an atomic bomb.

"They have some highly trained people. These are fanatics motivated by an ideology. Their objective is to gain world attention for their cause, and what's more significant or terrifying than a nuclear weapon? It is frightening to contemplate what leverage they would have against a government by threatening catastrophic devastation.

"Thus far, there has been no incident of any penetration or attempt to enter a nuclear site to obtain weapons by any specific terrorist organization."

Secretary Liebling said he could not discuss intelligence studies that might identify terrorist groups who might make such an attempt. His refusal may have been prompted by the reluctance of intelligence agencies to disclose whether they are maintaining surveillance over political extremists.

"Modern technology has added to the sophistication of the terrorists' methods and techniques," Mr. Liebling said in a recent talk. "Weapons like the small, man-portable missile, the Russian SA-7 or the Redeye [infrared antiaircraft missile], which are particularly dangerous in the hands of terrorists, could be available through the black market or irresponsible governments.

"It is perhaps inevitable that more of these [types of] weapons will fall into the hands of terrorists. It has added to our vulnerability by providing the terrorists with targets of increasing attractiveness, and an assault upon them will draw the attention of the press, will embarrass the government, will be used for blackmail and will wreak havoc with the populace.

"I have in mind nuclear installations, public utilities and refineries, uranium enrichment plants, chemical plants, for example, as well as facilities and installations in support of national defense. Terrorist attacks on such facilities would be chaotic. With horrifying regularity these people who are desperate in their political aims are escalating to find the world stage they need to champion their cause."

So far, added Mr. Liebling, terrorists have taken the path of least resistance and gone after fairly easy targets like airliners, trains, people and buildings.

"These reckless people, because of their desire for world attention, may at any time decide to attempt an incident that could severely affect the national security of the United States," he said.

The secretary said that in response to this possible threat the U.S. government has launched "a massive program involving technology and research to adopt standardized sensors and intrusion-detection devices." Studies are being made of fencing, lighting, sensors using sound, magnetism, pressure, television and seismic devices for detecting intruders. The nuclear sites are protected by standard nine-gauge, two-inch-square chain-link fences with underground braces and a barbed-wire Y at the top. Cutting the wire or digging under it sets off an alarm.

The double-perimeter fence is monitored in some places by guards in a tower and by a control center that watches the detection systems. These patrols are augmented by the quick-response forces: specially trained military police or security troops who have passed emotional stability and reliability tests as well as the usual physical and mental tests. Secretary Leibling said they are given special instruction in guarding nuclear weapons sites.

The quick-response troops are equipped with armor vests, M16 rifles, M60 machine guns and M79 grenade launchers. They can be rushed to the atomic weapons "igloos" by jeep or helicopter if the site of the pentration is some miles from the control center. These ready troops can be augmented, if necessary, by combat forces from nearby military posts.

"In one drill the local command deployed a battalion of troops by helicopter in a matter of minutes," Mr. Leibling recalled.

As chairman of the Defense Department's physical-security review board, which sets uniform policy and standards for safeguarding military installations. Mr. Leibling said the board found that "our security concept for the protection of nuclear weapons required updating and that standardized safeguard criteria were necessary."

Concepts of the 1960s and earlier were "man-oriented," he said, depending upon sentries in the protected area to detect intruders. Intrusion-detection devices were used to determine attempted penetrations into storage areas. The studies showed that a more effective system would emphasize electronic equipment to alert the system to an attempted intrusion, with the manpower being used primarily for response forces.

The detection devices would be posted around the perimeter to give early warning. Security troops would be dispatched quickly from the control center that monitors the television and other detectors. Guards who were used previously to patrol the fences are now assigned to the tactical-response forces that can be deployed with a heavier concentration of firepower in the area under attack. Armed roving patrols augment the detection system.

Aside from terrorists and criminals, Secretary Liebling was asked, what security measures are available to guard nuclear weapons overseas from a takeover by the host government or by a revolutionary force that overthrows the government? Or, what happens if communist forces roll over an area that has U.S. nuclear weapons-storage sites?

For these worst-case situations, chairman Liebling said cryptically, "We have contingency plans, but those are not my responsibility. We are concerned with safeguards against theft, unauthorized access, or attempts to damage or destroy nuclear weapons by criminals or terrorists or some irrational person. A large-scale military attack is a separate problem."

A nuclear weapons expert said that "in an extreme situation we have contingency plans that provide for destruction of the weapons if they are in imminent danger of capture. We have the materials and procedures for destruction."

Defense Department directive No. 3224.3, on physical security equipment research, refers to "anticompromise emergency destruct (ACED) as a means which will prevent the recovery of national security information and material under emergency or no-notice conditions. With due regard for personnel and structural safety, the ACED system shall reach a stage in destruction sequences at which positive destruction is irreversible within 60 minutes at shore installations, 30 minutes in ships, and three minutes in aircraft, following a decision to destruct."

That's the last resort, for example, were an ally to suddenly turn on us and try to grab our nuclear weapons.

The nuclear weapons expert, asked if a terrorist could use a ready-made captured or stolen atomic bomb, said, "It depends on whether it is an old-type weapon or a new one. The old ones might be taken apart by someone with expertise and he might be able to separate the pieces and

reconstruct them. He could not detonate the bomb itself, however, because he would have to know the precise voltages and the necessary set-
tings for that bomb.

"If he broke into a nuclear weapons igloo he might be confronted by
various packing cases and he would have to assemble the components.
The weapons are constructed in such a way that they contain internal
safeguards against unauthorized use or misuse. It takes two people with
the proper instruction to arm the weapon.

"The newer nuclear weapons are more sophisticated. They are controlled by a so-called PAL—permissive-action link. If certain actions are
not taken in the proper sequence, the link won't be closed and the bomb
won't work. Some weapons have numbered dials like a safe and two men
have to set the dials correctly before the weapon is armed.

"Without the permissive-action link the bomb is a dud. It won't explode with nuclear force. You might set off an explosion of the chemical
explosives, but that would not trigger an atomic explosion. It requires
very exact timing of the explosion to get the critical mass for nuclear
fission."

A sophisticated terrorist organization with competent engineers might
be able to dismantle a stolen atomic bomb and rebuild it and possibly
make it work, but the odds appear to be against that happening.

If the ready-made bomb is relatively new—fabricated in the late 1960s
or later—it probably has the coded persmissive-action link, one of the
requirements ordered by President John F. Kennedy. The terrorists
would have to obtain the ultra-secret codes to make the bomb go. And
that would be highly unlikely unless they had some insiders to help.

The possibility of an insider in a nuclear weapons area being involved
with a terrorist or criminal group cannot be discounted, but defense officials said measures have been tightened to "screen out" people who
might be unreliable. The "human reliability" program was designed to
do this, and so far, officials said, "There has been no lapse that has
exposed any weapons to unauthorized use."

As an example of the screening-process results, the former Joint
Atomic Energy Committee of Congress in 1975 disclosed that the U.S.
Navy in Europe, from April, 1972, to March, 1973, disqualified 213 enlisted soldiers (no officers) out of some 14,000 persons involved in handling nuclear weapons (which included 2,450 officers, 11,520 enlisted
soldiers and 36 American civilians).

Of the 213 dropped by the reliability tests, 83 were for drug abuse,
18 for alcohol abuse, 52 for undesirable performance of duty, 26 for
disciplinary problems, 12 for mental disorders and 22 for character traits
(indebtedness, dishonesty or improper conduct).

The U.S. Air Force, from July through 31 December, 1972, disqualified one officer and 134 airmen out of 9,140 persons in the nuclear
weapons program in Europe (including 1,470 officers and 7,670 airmen).
Of those disqualified, 28 airmen were dropped for drug abuse; the others
were rejected generally for medical or psychiatric reasons or both, the

Air Force told the joint committee.

The U.S. Navy command in Europe told the committee that in 1972 four sailors were disqualified for nuclear weapons duty—two for "personal beliefs," one for drug abuse and one for disciplinary reasons.

The rejection of "unreliable" GIs for the nuclear weapons program was prompted by fears that troops involved in drugs, heavy indebtedness or other improper conduct would be vulnerable to blackmail or bribery by foreign agents trying to gain access to nuclear weapons.

Four years ago, Sen. John O. Pastore (D-R.I.), who retired last year, and Sen. Howard H. Baker (R-Tenn.) visited "special ammunition sites" (atomic weapons storage) in Europe because they were concerned. Sen. Baker said later "that nuclear weapons in NATO were vulnerable to terrorist attack and that some of these weapons were located in areas where they were susceptible to being overrun in the event of surprise attack." Their report, censored for security, was made public in April, 1975.

Senators Baker and Pastore urged at the time that the number of storage sites (described generally as more than 100) in Europe be reduced and security tightened at those remaining. The Defense Department told the senators in April, 1975, that 20 percent of the nuclear weapons sites had been closed during the two years since 1973 and that another ten to 15 percent would be closed by 1976.

Sen. Pastore in his 1975 statement said that the "Defense Department has taken steps to improve the security and protection of nuclear weapons in NATO" in the two years after their inspection in 1973. He said, however, that despite "considerable improvements" more needed to be done and he recommended that even more sites be closed and that the number of weapons in Europe be reduced, especially where their usefulness "is highly questionable."

He noted that some nuclear weapons for 155-mm and eight-inch guns were stored near the forward defense line only about ten miles away from Soviet or Warsaw Pact troops who might overrun them. He also observed that "nuclear weapons sites appeared to be vulnerable to terrorist attacks; that certain nuclear weapons sites appeared to be particularly vulnerable to surprise attack by communist forces, and that certain nuclear weapons might not be usable in the event of war."

The senators, in their comment, said that "today a new threat has emerged. In recent years, terrorism has become a means to achieve political ends." Their survey showed that "meticulous checking" of visitors to nuclear weapons sites would detect impostors but would be useless against terrorists who would try to shoot their way into a site.

The senators recalled that at one site (not identified for security reasons) the nuclear weapons were stored in the basement of a building with offices not guarded by a double-perimeter fence. A guard had been assigned to the entrance ramp to the basement only on the very day the senators visited the area. On an earlier visit, in November, 1972, the steel door to the basement was open and "it appeared that terrorists could probably at least reach the basement door without detection."

Emergency-destruction demolitions for that site were located about a 25-mile round trip from the barracks building where the nuclear weapons were stored. If the nuclear weapons had to be destroyed before they fell into hostile hands, it might take as long as an hour to deliver the explosives needed to destroy them.

In another instance, the senators learned that nuclear weapons for quick-reaction-alert fighter-bombers had to be moved on a public road about 300 yards, exposing them to possible capture. They also noted that the nuclear sites are easily identified because of the spotlights that are kept burning all night. They said that local newspapers and a communist magazine had identified the locations of some of the sites.

The senators noted that suspected intruders had been fired upon at two weapons sites but that none had been apprehended. They suggested that these suspects were probably trying to "case" the weapons areas.

Pentagon officials said more determined and organized terrorist efforts to steal a ready-made nuclear weapon cannot be ruled out. But they said safeguards at nuclear storage sites in Europe and elsewhere have been tightened substantially since the congressional inspections four years ago.

"With the improvements now under way the security at the sites should deter virtually any break-in attempt." one official said.

III RESPONSE OF THREATENED SOCIETIES

The past several years have demonstrated that while all nations are vulnerable to attacks by contemporary terrorism, democracies are especially threatened because their socio-political environment has permitted terrorists to exploit laws designed for the protection of citizens. Yet, responses to terrorism by the industrialized societies have remained within the rule of law in most cases.

There are several exceptions involving industrializing nations, which have destroyed democratic governmental processes while overreacting to terrorism. As our suspicions grow regarding the motives of nations which are actively supporting terrorism, we may discover that this is part of a grand design to further global revolutionary objectives. In spite of this possibility, the response by threatened societies must remain within the rule of law while going to the limit of what the law allows.

Moynihan, in this fashion, considers terrorism a weapon directed against the international community, with the democracies being a primary target. Indeed, if contemporary terrorism can subvert the democracies, there remain only those states which respond frequently with an official terrorism that is difficult to distinguish from that which started the action-reaction cycle. If we are to control terrorism and retain individual freedoms, it will be necessary to train appropriate police and law enforcement units to cope with this threat. These units must be organized and equipped at least as well as terrorists and, when authorized and when necessary, supported by military forces.

Because complete information on how governments are organized to respond to terrorism cannot be revealed for security reasons, the discussion in this section focuses on subjects where policy and response are best known. These include

158   *skyjackings, hostage situations, and bombings. Wolf addresses very directly the overall problems of response and concludes with a thought-provoking battle plan which has a Counter-terrorist Assessment and Response Group as one of its key features. Bell examines the United States response to skyjacking, which leads to consideration of the major problem of hostages. The articles by Mickolus and Beall demonstrate the problems in organizing governmental policy and explain some of the tactical complications of hostage negotiations.*

The role of intelligence has been under heavy attack due to the argument that intelligence gathering too frequently compromises the rights of individual citizens. Cooper does not adopt this position and cogently explains why and how the intelligence function should be organized to aid in the struggle against terrorism.

The United States position of not bargaining with terrorists is well known. Wider acceptance of United States policy by the international community will ultimately be a major source of defeat for contemporary terrorism.

Moynihan explains his view of terrorism through a discussion of Israel's response to terrorist attacks. He considers terrorism to be a weapon of totalitarianism directed against all democratic states. Prescribing an international force to combat this threat, Moynihan urges haste to prevent terrorists from taking advantage of nuclear technology.

The following article is reprinted by the permission of Senator Daniel P. Moynihan.

The Totalitarian Terrorists

by DANIEL P. MOYNIHAN

It was not an exercise of power; it was an act of courage. It was what there was left to do when every other hope was abandoned.

It happens I was something of a stage prop in the drama as it unfolded. I was to be in Jersusalem Monday, July 5, to give the commencement address at the Hebrew University. I arrived in Tel Aviv Friday, July 2. Meetings had been arranged: the minister of defense, the foreign minister, the former United Nations ambassador—a long list, including most of the persons who would make the decision between Friday night and Saturday afternoon. An atmosphere of capitulation was maintained throughout: of men waiting for others to decide their nation's fate and with little to do in the meantime. Appointments with visiting honorary-degree recipients were both kept and publicized—possibly just a trifle more than necessary, but this is a retrospective impression. When I boarded El Al at Kennedy on Thursday night, the New York *Post* proclaimed: ISRAEL YIELDS. Arriving at Tel Aviv, I encountered a government that seemingly had.

This was not all contrivance. Israel *had* yielded, and the point is not to be forgotten. She would give up the prisoners, or most of them. There was hope that the French would negotiate the best deal possible. All that Israel asked was the lives of her citizens.

By Friday, however, even capitulation began to look problematic.

Uganda was collaborating with the terrorists. This had not been in the American press, but it was all Defense Minister Shimon Peres could talk about on Friday afternoon. Amin had met the plane, had embraced the terrorists, had put soldiers to guard the hostages, was supplying the hijackers with everything they needed. The list of prisoners demanded in exchange for the hostages presented problems. There had been no response from the Swiss. The French had already released the woman they were alleged to hold. The Kenyans disclaimed any knowledge of the Ugandans on the list. The assumed condition that any exchange would take place on neutral territory had been rejected.

Peres's preoccupation, however, was the onset of what he saw as organized collaboration among the hijackers. Here was the PLO joined with the Baader-Meinhof group. Some suggested that representatives of the Carlos group were among the terrorists who met the plane at Entebbe. The groups had all opened bases in Yemen. Russia supplied the arms. Was the First Terrorist International upon us?

Peres is, after all, defense minister, and such issues are his proper concern. As for Entebbe, Peres has colonels to deal with day-to-day things. We left the subject. "By Sunday," he said, "it will be all over." Another of the details forgotten on the spot, only later recalled.

At breakfast on Saturday Yigal Allon, the foreign minister, went over the facts, now worsening. Terrorism is a disease, he fair to pleaded. Does not the West know this—that the disease spreads? His voice was raised; the words came faster. Then—again this is only now recalled—he remembered himself and a kind of passivity took over. Why were we hurrying away? Stay for another cup of coffee. In the lobby a television crew was waiting. I told the New York Jewish joke about the man standing on a street corner when a complete stranger comes up and knocks him down. "Why did you do that?" the man asks, "I've never tried to help you." Allon laughs more than necessary, thinking (I thought then) of Entebbe airport, which the Israelis had helped build. Again, later, it occurs to me that he may have been thinking of what was *about* to happen at Entebbe.

Terrorism was Rabin's message as well, on Monday, when it was all over. His government had taken the most awful risks. They had succeeded. Jerusalem was joyous. But the prime minister of Israel mostly pondered what would come next. International terrorism had become a greater menace than anyone had foreseen. It had become an instrument of totalitarianism, a means of bringing countries to their knees. The technology of terrorism had only begun. Terrible dangers were to come.

For Israel, of course, there would be the predictable orgy at the United Nations. They were not quite in the mood to be overconcerned by this. "Better," said Abba Eban, "to be disliked than pitied." But they did repeatedly ask—did the West understand what was happening?

Hijacking is as new as aircraft are new. The Federal Aviation Administration records the first occurrence in the world in 1931 and none thereafter until 1947, when there was another. If you care for statistics, you can find three cycles since then: the late forties, with a peak of 7; the rise in the late fifties, peaking at 11 in 1961; then the late sixties, surging to a peak of 87 in 1969. Each peak was higher than the previous one. The General Assembly pronounced on the subject in 1970 and a Hague convention on "Suppression of Unlawful Seizure of Aircraft (Hijacking)" was drawn up and came into force. It was ratified by the United States in 1971, by Uganda in 1972. A special assistant to the secretary of state was created to deal with the issue. At a time when the Supreme Court was telling the police what not to do until the lawyer arrived, and striking down the death penalty. Americans, at airports festooned with signs declaring hijacking to be punishable by death, got accustomed to being frisked by total strangers in the employ of private corporations.

Rabin is right: The issue is totalitarianism, and the question for the democracies is whether they will see this.

It is an old issue, or a new one, depending on your time perspective. For certain, it is a modern issue. It begins, as does so much else, with Robespierre and the Terror in France. Right at the outset two principles were invoked which are the antithesis of liberalism, and against which liberal society has had to struggle ever since.

The first principle is that an elite shall judge the direction of society, consulting no one, responsible to none.

The second principle—vastly the more dangerous—is that no one is innocent of politics. Terrorism *in principle* denies the distinction between state and society, public and private, government and individual, which is at the heart of liberal belief. For the terrorist, there are no innocent bystanders, no private citizens. Terrorism altogether denies that there is any private sphere, that individuals have any rights or integrity separate from or beyond politics.

Such a denial is, of course, a creed of the well-educated and the well-to-do—proclaiming the cause of the masses, but never remotely connected with them. Orwell saw this, and the insight liberated democratic socialism from a then seemingly ineluctable tie to the totalitarians. It is a desperately dangerous disease. The Baader-Meinhof group—bombing, burning, murdering its way across Germany—is judged by Helmut Schmidt, the Social Democratic chancellor of the Federal Republic, as "the most serious challenge in the 26-year history of our democracy." (As with the Japanese groups, the German terrorists have been utterly antinomian, aching for the outrageous. members of the group bombed Berlin's Fasanenstrasse Synagogue, which had been burned by the Nazis in 1938, one member explaining that people such as they had to get over their *Judenknax,* their "thing about the Jews.")

And it is scarcely just German, or Japanese, or French, or Palestinian. In one sense the disease is already pandemic. In his BBC interview Solzhenitsyn spoke of the parallels between the West today and Russia of the nineteenth century: the same "universal adulation of revolutionaries . . . if not a cult of terror in society, then a fierce defense of the terrorists." We have had our taste of it here, and more; our conditioning. If you don't think that is so—and meaning no offense—ask when was the last time you were told that "if you aren't part of the solution, you're part of the problem." People who say such things mean well, but they aren't thinking well. The liberal society entitles the citizen to be intelligently uninvolved. This is in no sense an obstacle to social reform. More often it is the condition of reform—the circumstance, that is—which enables relatively small numbers who know a good deal about a situation and care about it to bring about change. Totalitarians who declare that everyone must care typically produce societies in which no one does. If this seems nit-picking, it only suggests how vague our liberalism has become—and how vulnerable.

The U.N. will do nothing about terrorism. Paul Johnson, former editor of the *New Statesman,* wrote last fall, in the context of the resolution declaring Zionism to be a form of racism, that the U.N. was rapidly becoming "the most corrupt and corrupting organization in the history of human institutions." To condemn Israel for the Entebbe rescue, as the U.N. will seek to do, will only deepen that corruption, and do so in the face of the judgment of mankind that what the Israelis did was honorable and brave—and done for all of us.

The point is that Israel has become a metaphor for democracy. The determination of the totalitarians and the despotisms to destroy Israel is transparently directed at all of us. Equally, the terrorist assault against Israel has become a metaphor for the general challenge to liberal societies everywhere, a challenge employing the most direct totalitarian means.

A century ago, in a lesser but not dissimilar situation, Gladstone warned that the "resources of civilization" against its enemies had not been exhausted. We shall see.

One thing is certain. The Israelis acted in self-defense under thoroughly established international doctrine, whose *locus classicus,* as international lawyers say, is the *Caroline* case. In the 1830s Irish-Americans had a way of invading Canada from time to time, hoping to exchange it for Ireland. In 1837, they occupied Navy Island, Canadian territory, where they were supplied and reinforced by the steamer *Caroline,* which came over from the American side of the Niagara River. On December 29 of that year, a British force from Canada entered the United States, set fire to the *Caroline,* and sent her over Niagara Falls. During the skirmish two American citizens were killed. The British minister in Washington, five weeks later, stated the British position in these terms:

> The piratical character of the steamboat *Caroline* and the necessity of self-defense and self-preservation, under which Her Majesty's subjects acted . . . would seem to be sufficiently established.

The United States did not then contest the strength of the British position. But five years later, when the British action had become the cause of another incident between the two countries, Secretary of State Daniel Webster did call upon the British to show that they had acted from "necessity of self-defense, instant, overwhelming, leaving no choice of means, and no moment of deliberation."

This has become the classic definition, confirmed by the International Military Tribunal at Nuremberg.

The essential point is that *the right of territorial integrity is never absolute.* This is clearly established law. The U.N. majority will insist otherwise, seeking to punish not only Israel, but also Kenya, the one nation that had the moral courage to stand with Israel during its ordeal. The question for the Western democracies, and most especially for the United States, is whether we will now have the moral courage to say what is true, which is that Israel acted in the exercise of the legitimate right of self-defense, and that what Israel did others can do as well.

What is needed in fact is an international force. If it is not to be that of the United Nations, which it should be, then let it be that of the democracies—which it *can* be. And it had better be soon, for the terrorist with the nuclear weapon is near at hand. If you listen hard, you can hear the countdown.

Advocating a response to terrorist acts within the rule of law, Wolf describes how specific laws may deter terrorism and evaluates responsibilities of the news media and police task forces. Wolf proposes a Counterterrorist Assessment and Response Group and a comprehensive battle plan to meet the terrorist threat.

This article is reprinted by permission from *Orbis,* a journal of world affairs, published by the Foreign Policy Research Institute, Volume XIX, Winter 1976, #4.

Controlling Political Terrorism in a Free Society

by JOHN B. WOLF

Skyjackings, abductions, bombings, wanton slayings and the seizure of hostages and government buildings are among the tactics employed by political terrorists, whose victims range from helpless school children, religious pilgrims, vacationing travelers and business executives to diplomats, government officers and dignitaries. In the first three months of 1975, acts of terrorist brutality came in swift succession: in New York City in late January; then in Israel, West Germany and Argentina as the winter progressed. During the spring and early summer, terrorist epsiodes included the seizure of the West German Embassy in Stockholm, the abduction of American students in Tanzania and the kidnaping of a U.S. military officer in Lebanon.

Later, terrorist acts perpetrated in December proved to be the most awesome of the year. During that month armed East Asian terrorists, attempting to gain worldwide recognition of South Molucca's right to independence from Indonesia, held a total of forty-nine hostages on a hijacked train in northern Holland and in the Indonesian Consulate in Amsterdam. Also, shortly before Christmas, a cell of Irish Republican

Army (IRA) gunmen surrendered to British police after being involved in a protracted hostage situation in a residential section of London.

STRATEGIC CONSIDERATIONS

Political terrorism may be defined as the threat or use of deliberate violence, indiscriminately or selectively, against either enemies or allies to achieve a political end. The intent is to register a calculated impact on a target population and on other groups for the purpose of altering the political balance in favor of the terrorists. Thus, terrorist activities, when directed against democratic states with a plethora of minority groups, or against states that contain historically antagonistic peoples—Israel, Northern Ireland, Cyprus and Zaire, for example—seem to be aimed at discrediting the existing government by provoking it to concetrate its coercive power on a particular segment of the population with which the terrorists try to identify.

Phrased another way, the terrorist's strategic intent is to destroy the confidence a particular minority group has in its government by causing that government to act outside the law. Always, terrorist strategy aims not to defeat the forces of the incumbent regime militarily—for the terrorist this is an impossible task—but to bring about the moral alienation of the masses from the government until its isolation has become total and irreversible. The terrorist therefore strives to implement a protracted campaign of violence designed to make life unbearable for a democratic government as long as his demands remain unsatisfied. Unfortunately, some governments submit to terrorist demands, thereby obtaining a temporary respite, in preference to risking a counter-terrorist campaign that might serve only to isolate them further from large segments of the population. Later, many of these same governments find themselves confronted with additional terrorist demands.[1]

Although expensive in terms of both human life and property, the most effective counterstrategy for a liberal democratic society seems to be one that ignores these demands, since submission to terrorists only serves to reinforce their behavior. Attempts to reason with individuals committed to the principle of "direct action" (bombings, kidnapings and the like) as the only effective way to bring about the instant change they demand are extremely risky. Furthermore, many terrorists are impatient, impulsive young people who are infused with an unrealistic idealism bordering on the irrational, and who consequently view all mechanisms of peaceful change with contempt.

COORDINATION AND COOPERATION AMONG TERRORISTS

The rapid progress of technology in the past decade has contributed its share to the growth and danger of terrorism worldwide. Equipped with fraudulent credentials of excellent quality, terrorists use regularly scheduled jetliners to transport themselves by way of circuitous routes to the target area; there, prearranged contacts with other terrorist organizations provide them with site information, surface transportation, plastic explosives and automatic weapons. Safe-house networks, which afford cover and concealment for covert activities, have been established for their use in American and European cities. Additionally, there is some evidence that elaborate "exchange attack systems" and "joint action commitments" have been concluded among terrorist groups of various nationalities.[2] The Cuban Intelligence Service, believed to be dominated by the Soviet KGB, is allegedly responsible for the development of a liaison network used by some American and European terrorist organizations.[3]

The first signs of an international exchange and pooling of weapons and information among terrorist groups emerged about five years ago, when information filtered into the press about American Weathermen, IRA gunmen and Turkish Dev Genc terrorists attending summer training sessions at Palestinian commando bases. In May 1972 additional evidence came to light when members of Japan's Red Army Group, acting in behalf of the PLO, removed weapons from their suitcases and opened fire on a group of pilgrims at Tel Aviv's airport. Moreover, Cuba has trained both Palestinian and Irish terrorists and has established secret relations with the Quebec Liberation Front (FLQ) and various German terrorist groups.[4]

TUPAMARO TACTICS AND THE POLICE OFFICER

The urban guerrilla tactics of Uruguay's Tupamaros and the widespread publicity generated by their more spectacular propaganda actions have made them the most emulated revolutionary group in the world. The Weathermen, the West German Baader-Meinhof Gang, the Symbionese Liberation Army (SLA) and other groups all imitate Tupamaro methods. The established Tupamaro propaganda tactic of hijacking trucks from food stores and dispensing their contents to slum dwellers, for example, was used by the SLA about two years ago when it demanded that a multimillion-dollar food handout be undertaken in selected California cities.

Most terrorists choose targets similar to those favored by the Tupamaros: large international corporations with facilities in Third World countries, diplomats and other representatives of North American and West European states, and police officers, whom they regard as tools of the "capitalist forces of repression." Also, techniques for urban operations have been demonstrated by the Tupamaros to others who now realize that the urban terrorist "can work through so many thousands of people [that] . . . the enemy is made to feel him as an impalpable presence, until every ordinary pedestrian seems like a guerrilla in disguise."[5]

Terrorists know that this uncertainty has a profound psychological impact on the police officer, who is constantly open to harassment and feels he can trust no one, as a seemingly innocuous person or event may deal him a fatal blow. Added to the police officer's anxiety is the extreme frustration he experiences in trying to implement terrorist-control measures without incurring the ire of the citizens he inconveniences.

Under these circumstances, the police agencies of democratic states should anticipate an escalation in the number of direct terrorist attacks, which will probably include attempts to disarm, kidnap and assassinate police officers. They must train their officers to react rationally and objectively, even in that most trying situation when a fellow policeman is slain by a terrorist. Otherwise they play into the hands of the terrorist, who aims at breaking police morale and discipline, especially when a member of the news media is present. The Black Liberation Army (BLA), which killed police officers "because of their color, which was neither black nor white, but blue," tried (but failed) to employ these tactics successfully against the New York City Police Department in 1972.[6]

Police Education and Integrity   Although terrorists usually avoid communication with the police, except to obtain information on plans and events from individual policeman or through police informants working as double agents, they actively seek to identify and exploit the "contradictions, weaknesses and fissures" of the police force. Police commanders should be aware that acts of intimidation and reprisals, genuine or fabricated, will be manipulated by terrorists such as the BLA, who are also known to carry out "revolutionary justice" by executing selected police officers. The Tupamaros, particularly, are convinced that this "vigilante approach to police brutality gives excellent fruits and must not be abandoned."[7]

Police agencies, therefore, should develop and implement a comprehensive program of in-service training geared to provide every police officer with the skills in interpersonal relations and survival that are needed to cope with this aspect of political terrorism. Furthermore, "since the policing service in a free society is almost entirely a personal service, every condition in a police organization and its environment is traceable in a large measure to the acts of policemen and to the success or failure of their operations."[8] Hence, internal investigation units must be established or expanded in order to monitor police integrity; through a process of periodic inspections, failures and errors can be identified and corrected before they become serious and subject to manipulation by terrorists, who are always on watch for ways in which to discredit the police.

THE LAW AND THE DETERRENCE OF TERRORISM

Nationwide Uniform Penal Codes   There is some evidence that both the court and correctional components of the American criminal justice system lack a well-developed and coordinated program designed to handle the terrorist who operates within our free society. Managers of these components seeking a solution to this problem would do well to take note of the British approach to terrorism. Once confronted with terrorism, the British strengthen social sanctions and act on the supposition that counterterrorist operations should be a part of normal police work and not a kind of social engineering.[9] This approach seems more sensible than the current American method, which is to undertake long-overdue preventive measures as a consequence of immediate terrorist pressure; indeed, the American response is counterproductive since it can be manipulated by terrorist propagandists to aid their cause. A prerequisite to the adoption of the British approach is nationwide enactment of uniform penal codes, which many of the fifty American states presently lack. Pending before Congress [1976], a 753-page bill known as S.1 would give the nation its first real criminal code: Bill S.1 seeks to restore the death penalty for certain federal crimes by amending federal law to take account of the Supreme Court's 1972 decision, which held that the death penalty was unconstitutional because it was capriciously imposed.

The Discretionary Death Penalty   On August 5, 1975, the United States moved toward legal uniformity with the enactment of Public Law 93-366, which reimposed the death penalty—subject to a special hearing and assurance by a jury that there were no mitigating circumstances—in hijacking cases involving death. This law should now be extended to cover other acts of terrorism and should no longer be restricted to hijackings, which are on the decrease. Although no one knows the exact deterrent value of capital punishment, a discretionary death penalty is of benefit if it saves the life of even one person.

The discretionary death penalty has other advantages worthy of consideration. Factual information pertaining to a terrorist organization's infrastructure or membership is not usually forthcoming from the terrorist who has received an unequivocal and unrevokable death sentence. Whereas the mandatory death penalty stops the flow of information, the discretionary death penalty can actually encourage it. Furthermore, if the penalty for aircraft hijacking, for example, is a mandatory death sentence, the terrorist has little to lose by killing everyone aboard. And yet, even capital punishment is not a deterrent for some terrorists, the totally fanatic, who are already prepared to die as martyrs to their cause.[10]

Improved Court Management   It is important that terrorists be brought to trial within sixty days after apprehension so that maximum benefit may be derived from the discretionary death penalty laws. Consequently, court management procedures and policies must be devised to reduce the delay—presently eighteen to twenty-four months—between the apprehension and trial of those few terrorists who finally do stand before a jury. Terrorists are acutely aware that only a few of the Arabs responsible for the hijackings, kidnapings and execution of hostages over the past few years have suffered meaningful punishment after capture. Many, incarcerated for extended periods pending prosecution, were freed in compliance with the demands of their compatriots, who meanwhile held innocent people as hostages. It was this sort of extortion that forced the West Germans to release the three surviving members of the Munich team of killers late in 1972.

West Germany has also been subjected to numerous demands and onslaughts by resurgent members of the Baader-Meinhof Gang who seek the release of their leaders and about thirty gang members captured in 1972.[11] Clearly, terrorists must be made to realize that if found guilty they will be swiftly punished, and that demonstrations, petitions or violence in their behalf will be futile.

Ransom Laws A federal law making it illegal to pay ransom could serve as another deterrent to terrorism. True, it would be most difficult, perhaps counterproductive, to prevent people from paying ransom to obtain the release of loved ones. But, at a minimum, income-tax law could be revised so that American corporations could no longer deduct ransom payments as business expenses. If this measure should prove impracticable, perhaps the companies themselves will come to recognize that ours is a difficult world and will make nonpayment of ransom a matter of corporate policy.

Terrorist propaganda tactics, such as the SLA demand for distribution of food to the poor in the Patricia Hearst case, can help to create a "Robin Hood" mystique.[12] Therefore, Congress might also consider passage of a law making it a crime for a third party to receive the benefits of a ransom payment.

THE HOSTAGE PROBLEM: WHAT IS TO BE DONE?

The Official Hostage Policy of the United States For law enforcement officials around the world, terrorism and its effects have become a recurrent nightmare, particularly when "nonnegotiable demands" are issued for the release of prisoners, ransom money, or safe passage to another country. Is the safety of hostages to be secured at any cost? Or must their lives be risked to discourage other terrorists and save future victims? Forced to confront the problem through a heavy overlay of politics, emotion and history, different countries have found different answers. The Israelis argue that hijackings and other extortion attempts would escalate if they complied with terrorist demands. This refusal to deal with terrorists is a difficult decision, however, for Israel is also concerned with the hostages' well-being. It is nevertheless a necessary choice: when one sees assassins released by the authorities in order to protect hostages, it becomes obvious that terrorists will thrive on the common decency of peoples and governments.

America's official hostage policy closely resembles that of Israel; namely, "no deal" with terrorists. The United States formulated her policy in 1973 when several persons, including an American diplomat, were kidnaped by Arab terrorists in the Sudan. At the time, President Nixon declared that the United States would not meet any demands to secure the release of the hostages, on the grounds that this would encourage political kidnapings and other terrorist acts. The U.S. diplomat was killed, but the federal government has not strayed from its decision to refuse to yield to extortion or blackmail anywhere in the world. A corollary to this policy is that it is the host country's responsibility to assure as far as possible the safety of American diplomats and American citizens in its jurisdiction.[13]

The argument against acquiescence is persuasive. Still, there is little hard evidence that the tough approach is best. Psychiatrists have found, in fact, that political terrorists are often paranoid schizophrenics with overt suicidal tendencies—a deadly species. To this kind of mentality, death is not the ultimate punishment; it is the ultimate reward. Consequently, law enforcement agencies should realize that in many cases a terrorist does not take hostages in order to achieve some preconceived goal; rather, he dreams up a goal in order to take hostages.[14] He seeks a pretext to stage a production for all the world to see.

"The Hostage Must Live" Concept One big gap in the existing American public-security system—one which should be narrowed if terrorists are to be discouraged from operating in this country—is the lack of a nationwide uniform hostage policy. Generally, the hostage policy adhered to today by local and state police departments is in substance that "the hostage must live." This is in direct opposition to official federal policy, but it seems unlikely that in practice the two policies would come into conflict. If, for example, Arab terrorists hijacked an airliner at Kennedy International Airport and demanded the release of Sirhan Sirhan in exchange for the lives of the hostages they held, the entire event would fall within the jurisdiction of the federal government. The FBI would handle enforcement within the FAA's jurisdiction, and a federal official would most probably reject the demand to free Sirhan, who is held in San Quentin Federal Prison.[15]

If, to take another example, a terrorist group seized a hostage within New York City and demanded safe passage to the nearest international airport, the New York City police, in compliance with the city's hostage policy, would submit to the demand, assuming that the only alternative would be the hostage's death. Once the terrorists and their hostage entered FAA jurisdiction, what would happen is not clear. Would the federal authorities who take over jurisdiction bargain with the terrorists, or would they refuse to deal? It is assumed that they would not deal, and that New York City's hostage policy would be negated. But no one knows for certain how such cases of overlapping jurisdiction will be handled. Consequently, discussions should be held among federal, state and large-city officials in order to resolve all possible points of conflict and confusion.

THE RESPONSIBILITY OF THE NEWS MEDIA

The political terrorist depends on supportive publicity to help him convince the public of the urgent need to correct societal conditions that he finds wanting. He must therefore get across the point that moderate measures and the extended democratic process are not sufficient to bring about the immediate change and social equality he demands. To this end, he must beguile the press into seeing his use of terrorist tactics as a clear response to the denial of basic freedoms to a politically identifiable group that must be "liberated." Without credible publicity skewed to this consideration, he risks rejection of his activities as illogical and intolerable behavior and could find himself temporarily neutralized.

Thus, a public relations assessment is a prerequisite to any terrorist plan and serves as the factor controlling its intensity, direction and duration. This evaluative process is called, in the rhetoric of the Tupamaros, a diagnosis of the *coyuntura;* that is, "the political, economic, military and organizational conditions of both the society and the social movement."[16] In this context, the release of the British ambassador to Uruguary, Sir Geoffrey Jackson, after his capture by the Tupamaros in January 1971, suggests that his captors realized that there was nothing further to be gained and much to be lost by killing or retaining the ambassador. The news media were already well acquainted with the Tupamaro program, the British government would give nothing to save Sir Geoffrey's life, and at the time they kidnaped him the "Robin Hood" Tupamaros were already a Uruguayan institution.[17]

Since freedom of the press is basic to our concept of a free society, however, it is difficult to devise any kind of restraint that would be accepted voluntarily by the news media. The media have, on occasion, reported terrorist activities in such a way that the practitioners were encouraged to believe they were extremely important persons. A greater degree of cooperation between federal intelligence agencies and the news media, in the form of an educational effort, might alert all concerned to the contagious nature of terrorism and to the fact that terrorists are not reformers and idealists but criminals, who should be treated as such in news releases.

In crisis situations television crews should practice objective reporting, free of embellishment, so that they do not exacerbate a situation the police are attempting to control. They might also voluntarily agree not to provide their audiences with specific locations of violence until it has been contained by the police. This practice would reduce the large numbers of people drawn to such sites by news reports, thereby creating additional problems of crowd control and taxing already overextended police manpower—or even serving the terrorists directly by expanding a mob already under their control.[18]

All in all, the media might strive to strip terrorists of their self-delusions, instead of providing them with several million dollars' worth of free publicity. To protect against this sort of inadvertent cooperation by the press, the British have subjected their newspapers to the "D-notice" system, under which the press is notified prior to publication when a particular news item could violate security laws.[19] For a free or "open" society like the United States, however, media self-restraint and not the institution of censorship seems to be the best approach. This openness is one of our strongest weapons, for it accelerates mutual understanding and reduces barriers to rapid social development.

Although pressured by news publicity to respond dramatically to a terrorist situation, the police of a free society must be careful not to overreact and enhance the terrorist's popular image. An example of carefully calculated police response to terrorism is provided by events on the island of Bermuda in March 1973; namely, the murder of the governor general, Sir Richard Sharples, and his aide. Although the media reported the possible implication of a politically motivated insurgent group known as the Black Cadre, the British felt that a team of detectives from Scotland Yard should investigate the matter calmly and prepare the normal reports. These police reports were then used to assess the situation and shape future response if any should be required. Meanwhile, the Black Cadre did not benefit from any publicity it might have been seeking, nor were its activities considered by the media as a formidable factor in Bermudian affairs.[20]

Essentially, the value of the task force approach is that it concentrates specially trained manpower on a single case. In May 1975 the West German government created a terrorism-control branch within the national police, the Federal Criminal Office, to search for members of the Baader-Meinhof Gang who are still at large. A few years earlier the New York City Police Department had also used the task force approach in order to counter and eliminate attacks by the BLA on its personnel. In the latter case, a team of detectives was assigned to collect information on individuals associated with the BLA and to coordinate the activities of police officers working undercover within that terrorist group. Only detectives actively involved in the investigation were privy to all field reports, and sensitive information was consequently not leaked to the press.[21]

In the United States today, a few police vice-control units have considerable expertise in the ties among organized-crime figures on which the syndicate relies to extend its criminal conspiracy. Many of these organized-crime structures and networks are akin to those maintained by political terrorists. Consequently, police methods used in organized-crime control might also be used effectively against terrorists. For years the police have tried unsuccessfully to eliminate the Mafia; they have not failed because their methods are ineffective but because it is difficult to conduct a prolonged intelligence operation unjustified by the kind of performance statistics that elicit higher budgetary appropriations. Thus, only a few detectives in a handful of large, urban police departments have the training and experience needed to control organized conspiracies or to handle the public security aspects of municipal-police intelligence operations.

THE CABINET COMMITTEE WORKING GROUP

After the 1972 Munich tragedy, which illustrated that international terrorism had reached the point where innocent people anywhere could be victimized, President Nixon directed Secretary of State Kissinger to chair a Cabinet Committee whose assignment would be to identify the most effective ways to prevent both domestic and international terrorism. Responding to the president's order, the secretary of state formed such a committee and established a Cabinet Committee Working Group, composed of senior representatives or agency heads of the groups represented in the Cabinet Committee. Although members of the working group are in close contact as issues arise and incidents occur, the committee itself rarely meets.[22]

The working group's function is (1) to ensure collaboration among U. S. agencies and departments with domestic and foreign responsibilities and (2) to recommend countermeasures that can close gaps in the security screen around Americans at home and abroad, as well as foreigners in the United States, whom the agencies represented in the working group help to protect. With respect to the task of protection, the working group relies heavily on the customary local and federal agencies. Thus, it is kept informed by the FBI of the international potentialities or implications of domestic terrorist groups and uses the CIA as an important tool in foreign incidents.

The working group devotes most of its efforts to the collection of information on terrorism, which it uses to improve deterrent procedures in the United States and overseas, and in this area it performs quite well. It is active in pressing for the ratification of important multilateral conventions on hijacking and for the adoption of International Civil Aviation Organization standards designed to improve the security of international airports worldwide. The group also works with the United Nations; however, its discussions with groups of UN members often get bogged down in debate over the issue of justifiable versus illegal violence.

Unfortunately, working group members do not handle terrorist matters on a continual basis but rather provide input into the group from their respective agencies and obtain information in return only as incidents occur. Task forces have thus been established by the group to study incidents after they take place; this was the case with the unsolved murder of the Israeli attaché in Washington (July 1973) and the assassination of two Turkish diplomats in Santa Barbara, California (January 1973). Some events occur so quickly, however, that the working group does not respond. In cases where the group becomes involved, its task force is disbanded once the incident is over.[23]

THE COUNTERTERRORIST ASSESSMENT AND RESPONSE GROUP

Although the American public is largely against surveillance, data banks, dossiers or any other facet of a long-term intelligence operation, intelligence is still the only way we can learn about terrorist plans and predict terrorist acts. Consequently, there is a definite need for legislation to establish a Counterterrorist Assessment and Response Group at a high level of the national government. The activities of this group would supplement the work of the Cabinet Committee Working Group and serve as an immediate information resource for other authorized agencies. It would not duplicate the work of the CIA, which is restricted by law from performing internal security functions. Nor would it supplant the FBI, which does not collect intelligence abroad or employ analysts with sufficient expertise in international politics to function in a strategic public security capacity. This new group would be staffed with people who know how to gather and analyze public security information from both domestic and foreign sources for regular dissemination to law enforcement agencies on a "need-to-know" basis.[24]

The Counterterrorist Assessment and Response Group should contain three primary units: an assessment unit, a teaching unit and a response unit. The *assessment unit* would receive information on terrorists from members of the Cabinet Committee Working Group, municipal law enforcement agencies and the response unit. It would then process this information for its own use and for dissemination in strategic reports to other agencies. The *teaching unit* would provide training for local law enforcement agencies in subjects relating to terrorism that are not currently taught by the FBI. Initially, the teaching team would concentrate on developing the skills of persons assigned to existing public security intelligence units, which were established by many large urban police departments when they realized that their detective bureaus could not handle the work.

The *response unit,* composed of experts in such disciplines as management, law enforcement, psychology and public relations, would travel to the site of a terrorist act whenever an American citizen or corporation is involved. Although fully respectful of the sovereignty and sensitivities of other nations, the jurisdictions of other agencies and, of course, the wishes of the victim, the response team would urge other governments to accept all the American resources that could be put at their disposal, including intelligence and communications. Additionally, the response unit would collect specific field information for the assessment team on foreign terrorist groups with the capability to infiltrate highly trained teams into the United States.

Computerized Information Systems To accomplish its mission, the Counterterrorist Assessment and Response Group would have to provided with data from sophisticated information systems such as the CIA's "Octopus" bank. "Octopus," a computerized file maintained at the CIA's headquarters in Langley, Virginia, can match television pictures of known terrorists and their associates against profiles contained within the system. The television pictures are taken in various overseas airports, bus terminals and other transportation centers. In microseconds, "Octopus" can analyze a picture along with the information already in its file on targets in the area and the equipment and skills required to attack them successfully. Within a few minutes after the analysis, a radio alarm can be transmitted to a counterterrorist team who can in turn apprehend the terrorists. Thus detected and accused of criminal intent, terrorists have often been "flabbergasted at being presented with plans they hadn't yet made."[25] To be sure, the use of television and other forms of surveillance in a free society must be carefully controlled and tightly monitored. Also, the managers of these information systems must be extremely careful that they are not used for purposes abhorrent to a free society.[26]

LIAISON BETWEEN FEDERAL AND LOCAL LAW ENFORCEMENT AGENCIES

Federal agencies, though aware of the threat posed by terrorism, have found it most difficult to cooperate, even with other federal agencies, to put it down. It is understandable, therefore, that they have been unable to develop any lasting and mutually beneficial liaison with local police departments. A properly organized and legally empowered Counterterrorist Assessment and Response Group could help to remedy this situation, since its teaching and assessment teams would be working constantly with municipal police agencies.

American law enforcement's deficiency in the realm of cooperation is plainly evident. Eighteen federal strike forces have been established to combat Mafia-dominated organized crime throughout the United States. The record of these forces can be described charitably as "mixed," and until recently U.S. attorneys have urged their dissolution on the grounds that the various federal agencies pooled in the strike forces tend to compete with and distrust each other. Among the federal agencies normally grouped into these strike forces are the FBI, the Drug Enforcement Administration, the Immigration and Naturalization Services, and the Alcohol. Tobacco and Firearms Division of the Treasury Department. Many of these agencies are also included in the Cabinet Committee Working Group.

There is some justification, however, for this competition and mistrust. One strike-force attorney, asked by a reporter to show FBI charts on the Mafia, replied sardonically, "They'll hardly show them to us." When asked why, the attorney replied, "Well the bureau has the attitude that one day you're a prosecutor, and the next day you're a defense attorney." This is frequently true of the young attorneys who work in the federal strike forces and in the U.S. Attorney General's Office, where a prosecutor's term averages three years.[27]

LOCAL POLICE FORCES AND PUBLIC SECURITY INTELLIGENCE

In a free society, a public security intelligence unit must be particularly responsive to the legal principles and public policies that develop with respect to the collection, storage and dissemination of domestic intelligence. At the same time, it is imperative that such activities be continued because they are critical components of other operations undertaken to control both terrorists and covert, organized criminal groups. Intelligence operations also enable law enforcement agencies to make the informed judgments and preparations required to police adequately the disorders, meetings, rallies, parades and strikes that take place in their jurisdiction. Therefore, to ensure that this vital task is completed without violation of civil rights, certain measures must be carried out.

All police working in intelligence units, including undercover agents, must be given intensive instruction in relevant constitutional principles, especially those embodied in the First, Fourth and Fourteenth amendments. This training should take place on initial assignment to the unit and periodically thereafter. It is urgent, also, that intelligence units draft, adopt and enforce guidelines and procedures for the recording and storage of information in public security files and for the intra- and extra-departmental dissemination of these data. Perhaps the most critical of the guidelines are those having to do with the use of informants. The steps to be followed in the processing, registering and payment of informants must be clearly spelled out, and all intelligence units must have a legal adviser who will evaluate and continually review the unit's procedures to see that they keep up with current legislation and judicial decisions. It is important, too, that a Criminal Source Control Office be created to legitimize and ensure the most efficient use of intelligence obtained from informants.

In order to control political terrorism, police intelligence units must have strategic and tactical analytical capabilities, as well as traditional field-information collection units and sources. These requirements can be met by establishing public security intelligence modules. The module concept works in the following manner. A team of field investigators and a public security desk analyst work together as a unit, concentrating on a specific area of concern, such as right-wing or left-wing extremist groups; this enables police officers to become expert in a specific problem within a relatively short time.[28] The module would also facilitate the instruction of public security analysts by the Counterterrorist Assessment and Response Group.

Once a public security intelligence module is established, it is important that the supervisor keep its activities focused on the strategic aspects of its area of concern (for example, such things as target analysis or propaganda techniques in the case cited above). At the same time, he must ensure that its work is current and yields recommendations with regard to tactics. Thus, each module should be organized according to study area (dignitary protection or terrorist groups, for example) and not according to function (strategy or tactics). Also, the various modules should be placed within the framework of a unified intelligence division to which all intelligence, department-wide, is directed. Information can then be exchanged efficiently—a goal further facilitated by uniform filing techniques that enable cross-referencing among all areas of concern.[29] It follows that another task for the Counterterrorist Assessment and Response Group could be to establish a uniform, nationwide reporting and classification system to expedite intra- and extra-departmental dissemination of terrorist information. The system used by the FBI's National Crime Information Center might serve as a model for such standardization.

Because of the complex political, economic, sociological and psychological factors surrounding the problem of terrorism, many police officers lack the education and training needed for proficiency as public security desk analysts. Consequently, urban police departments with a shortage of desk analysts should obtain qualified specialists from outside sources. Local or regional colleges and universities can often provide suitable personnel, and the Counterterrorist Assessment and Response Group could help to train them.

The police department's patrol division should remain the primary collector of "street information." Complementing this service, a uniform field-reporting system, compatible with data processing equipment, should be designed and implemented. Such a system will make it possible to process reports of terrorist incidents and terrorist plans without delay.

In order to enhance the ability of the ordinary patrolman to gather information on groups with terrorist potential, a series of pertinent lectures should be added to in-service training programs. In addition, recruit-training schedules should include a block of time devoted to political terrorism. The development of curriculum and related materials could be accomplished by the Counterterrorist Assessment and Response Group. All of these educational programs would supplement, not replace existing programs conducted by other agencies (for example, the training in protection of dignitaries provided by the Secret Service).

A BATTLE PLAN TO MEET THE TERRORIST THREAT

Confronted with proliferating and increasingly sophisticated terrorist groups at home and abroad, on the one hand, and the necessity to maintain the basic constitutional freedoms and safeguards that are the hallmark of a democracy, on the other, the United States must develop new programs and policies to combat political terrorism. In America today, by virtue of a process of governmental debate and freedom of the press, it is fortunately almost impossible to undertake a program of pure repression. If we examine the political culture within which Americans function, it is evident that there exist well-defined convictions about what the government may or may not legitimately do and a broad consensus on the fundamental rights of man. Our democratic system is thus both a necessary and a sufficient limitation on the use of repressive force. Moreover, any illegal action by a democratic state is undertaken with peril since it can be manipulated by the terrorist to serve his own purposes. But Americans' desire to maximize individual freedom also blinds them to the dangers presented by political terrorism and at times prevents them from seeing the necessity for deterrent action.

Consequently, the federal government should embark on an educational program designed to inform the public about all aspects of political terrorism, particularly the difficulty of combating it within a free society. Once made aware of the seriousness and extent of the problem, the American people might give their support to the institution of uniform penal codes, the discretionary death penalty, improved court manage-ment programs, laws constraining the payment or receipt of ransom, and other measures necessary to control terrorism. Such a program would also help Americans to understand the rationale behind the government's official hostage policy and thus accept it as a painful necessity. The program would be aimed additionally at heightening the news media's awareness of terrorist tactics intended to obtain publicity and public sympathy and could serve to warn the policeman on the beat to guard against being manipulated by the terrorist into violating his code of conduct.

Apart from educational measures, the government should expand the scope of the Cabinet Committee and its working group and battle for legislation that would establish a full-time, highly specialized Counterterrorist Assessment and Response Group as described above. Units of this new group would perform several vital tasks: education of police agencies' public security analysts, assessment of the domestic and international aspects of terrorism, development of a consolidated terrorist-information system, study of significant terrorist incidents around the world, and support of the Cabinet Committee and its working group. Once the counterterrorist group is established, however, it is mandatory that proper safeguards be implemented and that procedures be established to regulate its computerized intelligence system. Moreover, the group must make its information available to local law enforcement agencies and to other federal agencies.

Meanwhile, it is imperative that public security operations be continued by local police agencies and that they be made responsive to the legal principles and public policies developing in the United States today. Police intelligence units should be upgraded in the areas of personnel selection and training, information-handling techniques and organization. Furthermore, the men and women of the press and in Congress who relentlessly investigate the activities of the American intelligence community must take care not to undermine the effectiveness of the CIA as a global collector of information on terrorist matters, or that of the FBI as the nation's primary guardian of internal security.

In our highly politicized age it would appear that the dangers posed worldwide by political terrorism are likely to continue into the immediate future. Americans must therefore be prepared to cope with terrorist acts that will almost certainly occur in their cities. No doubt some will argue that there is no way to guard against the unknown and the unseen and will oppose the expenditure of tax dollars for preventive measures. This sort of fatalism can result in terrorist incidents that might otherwise have been prevented—incidents that will be both costly and internationally embarrassing. It would be foolish to pretend that the tide of sabotage, extortion, bombings and hijackings can be totally turned back. But if we are not to surrender to lawlessness, we must expand present efforts to make terrorism less effective and less attractive as a political weapon.

[1] Martha Crenshaw Hutchinson, "The Concept of Revolutionary Terrorism," *Journal of Conflict Resolution,* September 1972, pp. 383-396.

[2] John B. Wolf, "A Mideast Profile: The Cycle of Terror and Counterterror," *International Perspectives,* November/December 1973, pp. 29-30.

[3] Marta Rojas and Mirta Rodríquez Calderón, *Tania: The Unforgettable Guerrilla* (New York: Random House, 1971), pp. 32-79.

[4] John Barron, *KGB: The Secret Work of Soviet Secret Agents* (New York: Reader's Digest Press, 1974), p. 22.

[5] Raymond M. Momboisse, *Blueprint of Revolution—The Rebel, the Party, the Techniques of Revolt* (Springfield, Ill.: Charles C Thomas, 1967), p. 282.

[6] Robert Daley, *Target Blue* (New York: Delacorte Press, 1973), pp. 402-445.

[7] Arturo C. Porzecanski, *Uruguary's Tupamaros: The Urban Guerrilla* (New York: Praeger, 1973), p. 21.

[8] O. W. Wilson, *Police Administration* (New York: McGraw-Hill, 1972), p. 197.

[9] Lucian, W. Pye, *Aspects of Political Development* (Boston: Little, Brown, 1966), pp. 129-131.

[10] U.S. House, Committee on Internal Security, *Terrorism, Hearings,* 93rd Congress, 2nd Session, May 8, 14, 16, 22, 29-30, June 13, 1974, Part 2, pp. 3222-3223.

[11] Melvin, J. Lasky, "Ulrike and Andreas," *New York Times Magazine,* May 11, 1975, pp. 73-79.

[12] U.S. House, Committee on Foreign Affairs, *International Terrorism, Hearings,* before the Subcommittee on the Near East and South Asia, 93rd Congress, 2nd Session, June 11, 18-19, 24, 1974, pp. 68-69.

[13] *Terrorism,* Part 2, pp. 3133-3138.

[14] Gerald Arenberg, *Hostage* (Washington: American Police Academy, 1974), pp. 22-26.

[15] *Ibid.,* p. 15.

[16] Porzecanski, p. 11.

[17] Sir Geoffrey Jackson, *Surviving the Long Night—An Autobiographical Account of a Political Kidnapping* (New York: Vanguard Press, 1973), pp. 208-211.

[18] In June 1975, within ninety minutes of the crash of an Eastern Airlines passenger jet in New York, NBC was on the scene with electronic cameras ("minicams"). Half an hour later, the NBC broadcast of the event was being watched by nearly three times the normal 6:00 p.m. auidence (1.5 million versus 500,000). John Corry, "Many Moods at Scene of Crash," *New York Times,* June 25, 1975, p. 1.

[19] Alvin Shuster, "Secrecy Veils British Intelligence Service," *ibid.,* October 28, 1974, p. 7.

[20] John B. Wolf, "Terrorist Manipulation of the Democratic Process," *Police Journal,* April/June 1975, p. 110.

[21] Albert A. Seedman and Peter Hellman, *Chief* (New York: Avon Books, 1975), pp. 419-498.

[22] The members of the Cabinet Committee are the secretary of state, the attorney general, the secretary of defense, the director of the FBI, the director of the CIA, the secretary of the treasury, the secretary of transportation, the president's assistants for national security and domestic affairs, and the U.S. ambassador to the United Nations. The working group includes the senior representatives of Cabinet Committee members listed above and nineteen other agencies; other participants are included on an *ad hoc* basis. *International Terrorism,* pp. 13-14.

[23] *Ibid.,* pp. 13-30.

[24] *Terrorism,* Part 2, pp. 3086-3190.

[25] Miles Copeland, *Without Cloak or Dagger: The Truth About the New Espionage* (New York: Simon & Schuster, 1970), pp. 16-24.

[26] "Palestinians Planning to Review Tactics," *New York Times,* November 24, 1974, p. 3.

[27] Mary Breasted, "Gallos vs. Columbos: Brooklyn's War Without End," *ibid.,* September 22, 1974, p. 6.

[28] Howard A. Metzdorff, "The Module Concept of Intelligence Gathering," *Police Chief,* February 1975, pp. 52-53.

[29] Arthur Grubert, "New York City Task Force," in International Narcotics Officers' Association, *14th Annual Conference Report* (New York: International Narcotics Enforcement Officers Association, 1974).

Although directed at recent conditions in the United States, Cooper's analysis of problems confronting an intelligence community striving to cope with the terrorist threat has far wider application. After describing weaknesses which intelligence agencies must overcome, Cooper discusses counterintelligence functions essential for combating terrorism successfully.

This article is reprinted by permission from *Chitty's Law Journal*, Volume 24, Number 3, 1976, Toronto, Canada.

Terrorism and the Intelligence Function

by H. H. A. COOPER

Much of what goes awry in intelligence functions can be laid to secret, subjective judgments about the establishment of priorities for intelligence-gathering, the selection of the kinds of information to be gathered, a failure to analyze gathered information adequately and a stubborn failure to reappraise decisions over time. The intelligence function should be subject to the same policy procedures as any other important government enterprise.—*Watergate Special Prosecution Force Report*[1]

INTELLIGENCE CRISIS

The United States is currently wracked by what may be not inaptly entitled, the "Intelligence Crisis." There has, on the one hand, been a colossal mismanagement of many aspects of the most costly intelligence gathering apparatus the world has known to date, while on the other, there has been a shrewd, highly organized drive, on a national scale, to curb, dismantle and destroy the intelligence gathering capacity of law enforcement and other agencies.[2] This is a bitter and not wholly unexpected reaction to the insensitivity and ineptitude shown by some who have clearly extended, quite arrogantly, their mandate beyond what is allowed by law. The zeal of this strange alliance arrayed against the intelligence community, is as understandable in an election year as it is frightening. It seems, nevertheless, unlikely to achieve its objectives and there are already signs that the pendulum is swinging, with gathering momentum, the other way. Before this counter-reaction is complete, it seems helpful to take a brief look at some of the problems involved in the intelligence function, as it is broadly understood, and, more particularly, the need for the development of a sound, efficient and well regulated intelligence capacity to combat the growing threat of domestic and international terrorism.[3]

Perhaps the first observation to be made is that there are a wide variety of activities somewhat carelessly lumped together under the general title of intelligence. Many of these functions are not strictly intelligence activities at all, that is, they are not concerned with the collection, processing, analysis and transmittal of information obtained concerning the activities of individuals, groups, events, and things kept under surveillance. Their only real associations with intelligence are their covert nature and the fact that the activities in question are frequently engaged in by regular intelligence agencies as a part of or adjunct to the work in which they are more appropriately employed. It is these covert operations, which are concerned more with doing something to those kept under surveillance than merely finding out about their activities, that have given the intelligence community such a bad name during the last few years. While such activities have always been known, particularly through the medium of the novel and the film, they have not, until recently, been the subject of general, public concern; it was something the "other side's" agencies did, never our own. The point is worth the closest examination.

THE SPY

The traditional role of the spy, to use an exact if somewhat tarnished term, was to find out something about the operations of a friend or adversary which were not manifest and which needed to be correctly understood in order to make an informed policy decision. Nations, like individuals, like to keep some matters strictly to themselves and, human nature being what it is, curiosity led to steps to find out what was being concealed. In time of conflicts, the spy has always had a vital role to play. Napoleon said of Schulmeister that one spy in the right place is worth 20,000 men in the field and many a commander of lesser ilk would agree only too readily with this assessment. The spy, a romantic figure for some, a despised, contemptible creature for others, has his (and her) place in history. It may well be that with the advent of modern technology, the day of the old-time spy, whose daring, personal gathering of information was so essential to the conduct of operations in both war and peace, is over. Intelligence gathering in this electronic age has become dehumanized. Perhaps it would be more accurate to state that the human element has remained but that it has grown more fallible and more diffident before the incursion of the computer and the other marvels of the electronic age.

The possibilities for intrusion into the private lives of almost all who inhabit this planet are astounding to those who have thought of intelligence gathering in terms of what was possible a mere two decades ago. The thought of the monitoring, analysis, tabulating, and review of all telephone communications taking place, at any instant anywhere in the world, raises not only the hackles of civil libertarians and conservative, constitutional lawyers, but is extremely depressing to those who are engaged in the more personal, more primitive, old-style espionage. Our surprise is perhaps surprising; we are, after all, but a mere eight years away from that world of 1984 of which George Orwell so percipiently warned us at a time when it seemed like aeons into the future. Yet man is never content that the machine is the master. The intelligence community has slowly learned to adapt. The use of this fascinating gadgetry has spurred many on to excess. The gathering of more and more information by better and better means has become an end in itself. It has been well said that:[4]

> Files contribute to the mystique of professionalism. The reduction of a mass of material into subversive classifications, of events into a chronological sequence, of names by alphabetical order, can somehow clothe a body of questionable data, assembled by the most arbitrary and unreliable standards, with a special aura of objectivity and professionalism. The serried ranks of file cabinets joined the microscope, camera, and electronic transmitter as valuable instruments of scientific investigation. In short, the process by which material is organized inevitably comes to serve as a mask for its relevance or probative value.

Is this curious transformation of the intelligence community and its self-perception not a special manifestation of what McLuhan perceived, in more general terms, nearly a decade ago?[5]

True intelligence work, notwithstanding the dangers and initiative involved, is essentially passive. The traditional spy is an observer who reports on what he has perceived so that someone else may make an operational decision on the basis of the information he has provided. The disturbing change in intelligence work that has taken place in the last few years is well illustrated by a statement of Brooks McClure in hearings before the Committee on the Judiciary of the United States Senate. He said:[6]

> The techniques of police intelligence—penetration of suspicious groups, dossier-keeping, cultivation of informers, undercover activities in general—disturb the average citizen. These are seen as underhanded methods, and there is frequently concern—sometimes justified by events—that they will be misused. The whole aura of "secret police" is disagreeable.

To say that the average citizen is disturbed by what he has learned about the broad range of activities which are now seen to take place under the general umbrella of intelligence is perhaps an understatement; the majority of those who think about the matter at all are frankly shocked. Tales of assassination and attempted assassination at home and abroad do not make pleasant reading in a country accustomed to think of itself and its people as a tolerant, law-abiding democracy. The "dirty tricks" of Watergate, so inept and amateurish, are now seen as the tiny tip of a massive, stranded iceberg, which is gradually revealing more and more of its concealed shape to the horrified gaze as time and tide recede. All this is having a devastating effect on legitimate law enforcement as well as on the wider functions of national defense for which the intelligence community must provide.

Essentially, what has been offended is people's sense of propriety. The intelligence community has overstepped the bounds. While few can ever aspire to receiving their country's highest honors for espionage work, in general, its utility is recognized even by those who find both the idea and the methods employed distasteful. In particular, in the United States, the credibility of the Federal Bureau of Investigation, perhaps one of the most professional law enforcement agencies in the world, has been badly damaged by the revelations regarding some of its covert operations.[7] Some of these are seen, on reflection, even to strong supporters of the Bureau as being as reprehensible as the activities they were designed to counter. This sullying of a fine, well-deserved reputation is as sad as it was unnecessary. The unfortunate result has been that public opprobrium generated by unacceptable responses to certain activities has spilled over into a general condemnation of the intelligence function as a whole. This is a misguided and short sighted view which can be highly damaging both to law enforcement capabilities to control and prevent conventional crime as well as to the larger interest of domestic and transnational security.

INTELLIGENCE v. COUNTER-INTELLIGENCE

What is clearly necessary, as a first step, is the drawing of a careful distinction between the true intelligence function, the collection, processing, analysis, and transmittal of data, and the more active, covert operations which comprise, in a general way, what has come to be known as the counter-intelligence function. Both give rise to their own peculiar problems when regulation is considered. Both, in essence, are vital, though, to many, repugnant functions. The real issue concerns the limits we should place upon both classes of activity and what form of regulation of each is practicable and desirable. It is suggested here that the confusion which obtains in our thinking about these matters has greatly complicated the finding of adequate solutions. Somewhere between the extreme poles of those who argue, on the one hand, that no oversight of any of these operations should be allowed and those who, on the other, argue that no operations of any kind should be allowed without oversight, a satisfactory solution has to be found. Once the functional distinction suggested here has been made, the task of regulation or, more properly, that of developing acceptable policies becomes much easier.

The extent to which the true intelligence function in the sphere of conventional law enforcement, is limited by law will depend upon the normative structure of the system under examination. In the United States, the Fourth Amendment of the Constitution and the Omnibus Crime Control and Safe Streets Act of 1968 are indications of what will be tolerated, although these have not proved, in the past an entirely weather-proof hedge against abuse. In Canada, the Protection of Privacy Act, 1974, has a similar, inhibiting effect on many law enforcement practices involving the development of what may be termed preventive intelligence. A strong body of opinion would argue that there should be no electronic surveillance at all for domestic intelligence purposes.[8] Meanwhile, others would argue, with scarcely less diffidence, that there should be no electronic surveillance for conventional law enforcement purposes either. Those who would argue the latter point advert to the slight impact, in terms of convictions, of costly surveillance operations mounted in recent years. This is to ignore, altogether, the use made, incidentally, of the information obtained for proper law enforcement purposes, although it was not appropriate for submission as evidence in a legal proceeding.

Broadly speaking, it would seem that electronic surveillance will be tolerated in our society provided that it is related to specific criminal acts or activities of an extremely serious nature; that it is used within a clearly delineated time and spatial framework; that its use be subject to judicial review and prior sanction: and that there be no less intrusive law enforcement techniques available for obtaining the information sought. It might properly be enquired, if this technique is to be subject to judicial approval before it is used, whether other, less sophisticated but no less intrusive techniques involving ordinary, unaided human surveillance, or the use of informers, ought not to be subject to similar, prior judicial sanctioning and approval. Most law enforcement agencies would be aghast at the prospect. Perhaps it is the fault of our system that these attitudes prevail, in that, the judiciary, in such situations, is seen as the adversary of law enforcement and the staunch defender of the citizen. Certainly, such a position were it more than impressionistic, would do little credit to either segment of our criminal justice system. Other countries, particularly those which have a system of examining magistrates similar to the French juge d'instruction have no such difficulties of role confusion. Elsewhere, judicial supervision of the investigatory function can and does work well where it is conscientiously carried out.[9] It is extremely doubtful, however, if the role assigned to the Judge under the Anglo-American system of law would permit of a more active *a priori* judicial participation in the intelligence function, and it is undesirable that this should be sought, having regard to the challenge it would present to the doctrine of the separation of powers.

That some sort of control is highly desirable, if not absolutely essential, seems to be agreed on all sides.[10] This would seem to point to it being undertaken by the legislature through one of its committees. Policies and procedures could be established for the conduct of the intelligence function, and the standards set by the legislature as a whole might be adopted by the committee as a measure of the performance of the agencies over which they have a review function. Such committees and their staff should be small, secure against leaks and thoroughly independent. Their functions should be to facilitate the sensible gathering of necessary intelligence, both domestic and international, in an efficient, economical way while guarding sternly against unwarranted intrusion into the lives of ordinary law-abiding citizens for political or other purposes. It is as well to remind ourselves that those engaging in criminal activities have no constitutional right to protect the privacy of those activities from legitimate law enforcement scrutiny. At times, we become frenetically over-defensive of some of the most curious freedoms, as when we law-abiding folk resist, vigorously, the introduction of a general identity card, which would facilitate living in so many of its complexities,[11] notwithstanding that we are more than content to carry wallets full of commercial credit cards that serve many of the same purposes. There are many who argue stridently for the upholding of the constitutional right to bear arms without let or hinderance, meaning without registration and licensing, who do not feel the slightest qualm at submitting themselves to rigorous testing before a license, complete with personal particulars and photograph, is issued to them to enable them to drive a motor vehicle.

What then of counter-intelligence, that vague, presently ill-defined area of activity embracing infiltration, entrapment,[12] and so called "dirty tricks" of all kinds? How much of this should we regulate? How much of this should we allow? The matter is of crucial importance when we think of such operations in the context of terrorism, domestic or transnational. What are the permissible limits in a democratic society of counter-intelligence programs? We must take a courageous look at these areas, although many would urge us, in the name of national security or the national interest not to do so. We could certainly close our eyes and ears more comfortably to some of these activities that are conducted in our name, much as many must have done in Nazi Germany. It is all too easy to fall or be driven into uncivilized ways. In the matter of our responses to terrorism, there are some uncomfortable comparisons with Nazi Germany that we ought, for our own clarification, to make. Assassination or "termination with prejudice" as it is called in the now familiar jargon, is no new weapon against terrorists, or, indeed others who have become candidates for extermination. The revelations of the Nazi counterterror in Denmark as recorded in the Nuremberg Proceedings have a surprisingly modern ring about them:[13]

> From New Year 1944 onwards a large number of persons, most of them well known, were murdered at intervals which grew steadily shorter. The doorbell would ring, for instance, and one or two men would ask to speak to them. The moment they appeared at the door they were shot by these unknown persons. Or, someone would pretend to be ill and go to a doctor during the latter's consulting hour. When the doctor entered the room, the unknown shot him. At other times, unknown men would force their way into a house and kill the owner in front of his wife and children, or else a man would be ambushed in a street by civilians and shot.

The attractive simplicity of such a solution, especially in times of great stress or fear, should not blind us to its consequences for our civilization. While the death penalty may or may not be an appropriate response to acts of terrorism,[14] pretrial capital punishment, as it is still practised in some parts of the world, is not.

Experience shows that a serious terrorist problem can almost never be handled satisfactorily short of using military means and military techniques. There may always be circumstances in a true, warlike confrontation where killing is both necessary and legally justified. Pre-emptive domestic killings by counter-intelligence agents, however dangerous the individual eliminated, cannot be justified; that they can be shown to be necessary is merely an exercise in subjective judgment. Such activities are a sign of weakness rather than strength. There is a great danger of the military need becoming the civilian creed. Subject to this caveat, it may be observed that every country that has successfully coped with terrorist threats to its existence has had to have recourse to its armed forces. Counter-intelligence measures, especially the techniques of infiltration of terrorist groups, played a large part in the successes achieved by the British in Malaya and Kenya, and have been used effectively by other countries elsewhere.[15] The terrorist cell and hermetic command structure are expressly designed to protect against such penetration which is greatly feared.[16] Such methods must be considered necessary, effective and legitimate. Reasonable policy guidelines can be laid down so as to prescribe the limits within which the agencies entrusted with these operations might function. Such guidelines would neither inhibit proper operations nor render them ineffective by revealing vital information to those against whom they are directed. What is recommended here is that the functions of counter-intelligence and its oversight be clearly separated, administratively, from those relating to what has been called the true intelligence function. Only in this way can proper policy determinations be made and the unfortunate contamination, as was experienced in the FBI cointelpro, produced by some of what may be necessary under the heading of counter-intelligence, be avoided.

Both intelligence and counter-intelligence activities are of the utmost importance in combating terrorism. Brian Crozier, an earnest advocate of the intelligence arm, has expressed the dilemma of the democratic state well:[17]

> The problem for the open society is how to have, build up and pre-
> serve this essential tool of defence—which in the long run is indispensable
> for the protection of ordinary people—and not so outrage the liberal
> conscience that the legitimate exercise of state power is frustrated.

The President's Commission on CIA activities within the United States expressed much the same thoughts:[18]

> Individual freedoms and privacy are fundamental in our society. Con-
> stitutional government must be maintained. An effective and efficient in-

telligence system is necessary; and to be effective, many of its activities must be conducted in secrecy. Satisfying these objectives presents considerable opportunity for conflict. The vigorous pursuit of intelligence by certain methods can lead to invasions of individual rights. The preservation of the United States requires effective intelligence capabilities, but the preservation of individual liberties within the United States requires limitations or restrictions on gathering of intelligence. The drawing of reasonable lines—where legitimate intelligence needs end and erosion of Constitutional government begins—is difficult.

Difficult though it may be, the task should never be regarded as insuperable. It is when measures must be taken to protect the state from within that the main difficulty arises and the problems inherent in the development of a proper preventive intelligence capability are greatest.

While the use of espionage, internationally, is at least more palatable to a majority, the use of intelligence, counter-intelligence and the development of the sort of preventive intelligence capability that is necessary to take effective measures against domestic terrorism still sticks in the craw of many. That there have been mismanagement and excesses in this area is unquestionable. That many whose activities can hardly be described as criminal have suffered intrusions upon their privacy and even harassment cannot be denied. None of this can, however, be made the foundation for an attack upon the development of a properly controlled preventive intelligence gathering capacity. The human defects in operation are not destructive of the theory in any way but are simply due to bad management which should be properly laid at the door of those responsible, something few administrations have the courage to do.[19] Control and oversight are essential to the proper functioning of intelligence. They should be neither feared nor resisted by any competent, intelligence-gathering agency. They are clearly the tasks of the legislature and should be addressed with courage and responsibility. It is necessary that our society does not deny itself, in the current welter of misdirected emotion, the defenses which might enable it to indulge in such luxuries for the foreseeable future.

NOTES & REFERENCES

[1] Washington, D.C. United States Government Printing Office, 1975

[2] The Nation-Wide Drive Against Law Enforcement Intelligence Operations. Hearings before the Sub-Committee to Investigate the Administration of the Internal Security Act and other Internal Security Laws of the Committee on the Judiciary, United States Senate, September 18, 1975, Washington, D.C. United States Government Printing Office, 1975.

[3] Brian Crozier, Director of the Institute for the Study of Conflict, London, England has written (Skeptic: The Forum for Con-

temporary History, No. 11, January-February 1976, pp. 44-53 at page 46):

Three separate processes are involved in intelligence-gathering: (a) establishing detailed background dossiers on active and potential terrorists and those who might lend them support and compiling organization charts to show the command structures of underground organization; (b) creating an efficient retrieval system so that this information can be passed on swiftly to the men in the field as they need it; and (c) developing 'strategic intelligence' into 'operational intelligence' through local contacts that will make it possible to lay hands on the right man at the right time.

[4] Donner, Frank J. *Political Intelligence: Cameras, Informers and Files,* in Privacy in a Free Society. Final Report of the Annual Chief Justice Warren Conference on Advocacy in the United States, June 7 to June 8, 1974. Sponsored by the Roscoe Pound American Trial Lawyers Foundation, pages 56-71, at page 67.

[5] McLuhan Marshall. War and Peace in the Global Village. New York: McGraw-Hill, 1968.

[6] Terroristic Activity: Hostage Defense Measures. Hearings before the Sub-Committee to Investigate the Administration of the Internal Security Act and other Internal Security Laws of the Committee on the Judiciary United States Senate, Part 5. July 25, 1975. Washington, D.C. United States Government Printing Office, 1975 at page 293.

[7] Some of the more spectacular errors of judgment have already been extensively covered in the national and international press. It is to be feared that some of the lesser excesses are yet to be fully revealed and dealt with. See, for example the Union. San Diego, January 11, 1976 under the title *FBI Reaps Doubtful Harvest from Sowing Discord.*

[8] *See, for example,* the recommendations of the distinguished participants to the Annual Chief Justice Earl Warren Conference on Advocacy: *supra,* note 4. It is worth observing that President Lyndon B. Johnson issued a confidential memorandum on June 30, 1965 which began (Cited in Domestic Intelligence Operations for Internal Security Purposes, Part 1. Hearings before the Committee on Internal Security. House of Representatives, Washington, D.C. United States Government Printing Office, 1974 at page 3391):

> I am strongly opposed to the interception of telephone conversations as a general investigation technique.

[9] *See, for example,* the important powers given to the Italian Investigating Magistrate under the law of April 8, 1974. *See* L'intercettazione telefonica e il diritto alla riservatezza. di Ciolo. Vittorio and di Muccio, Pietro. Milan: Giuffre Editore, 1974.

[10] Mr. Clarence Kelley, Director of the Federal Bureau of Investigation has said (Trial, January/February, 1975 at page 27):

> Our zeal to protect individual privacy must tempered with the concern for an effective system of criminal justice.

[11] The very modest and sensible proposal by the United States Passport Office to rationalize the form of the present United States passport was greeted by near hysteria by many who carry the current passport with no such fears that it infringes on some fundamental liberties. One can only wonder at the mentality and motives of such people.

[12] On this, see the interesting comment in 76 Yale Law Journal, no. 5, April 1967, pages 994/1019.

[13] *See,* International Military Tribunal, Trial of the Major War Criminals, Volume VII, Proceedings 5th February-19 February, 1946. Nuremberg, Germany, 1947 at page 45.

[14] Most of those who are charged with the immediate responses to terrorist activity would agree that their task is immensely complicated where the death penalty for terroristic acts is in force and enforced. Dr. Frederick J. Hacker, an internationally respected authority on terrorism, has said before the House of Representatives Committee on Internal Security (Terrorism, Part 1. Hearings before the Committee on Internal Security. House of Representatives, Washington, D.C. United States Government Printing Office, 1974, page 3014):

> I do not know whether you want me to give my views on the death penalty altogether, but that has been a long-going debate and I understand a great many constitutional issues have been exposed. I would say, in regard to terrorism, specifically, it is inappropriate to raise that question because on balance as you very well put it, for terrorism, it would not do very much. Therefore, on balance I might say the danger is greater that the potential terrorist might even be attracted and that that has been shown over and over again.

It is interesting to note that despite the tremendous political pressures and the terrorists' campaign which has proceeded in the United Kingdom, the death penalty has not been re-introduced. It seems that Sir Robert Mark, the head of Scotland Yard, would certainly agree with this in relation to the tactical problems presented by the response to terrorism.

[15] Especially in Brazil and Uruguay where extremely serious urban guerrilla movements were broken by the Military.

[16] *See, for example,* Legal Street Sheet, number 6, entitled, *Security-How not to get Busted.* Published by the National Lawyers Guild and cited in Terroristic Activity, Hearings before the Sub-Committee to investigate the Administration of the Internal Security Act and other Internal Security Laws of the Committee on the Judiciary, United States Senate, September 23, 1974, Washington, D.C. United States Government Printing Office, 1974 at pages 8 and 9.

[17] A theory of conflict. New York: Charles

Scribner's Sons, 1974 at page 154.

[18] *See,* Report to the President by the Commission on CIA activities within the United States, Washington, D.C. United States Government Printing Office, 1975.

[19] It is, perhaps, noteworthy that of all the excesses that have been revealed in relation to the counter-intelligence programs in the United States there have not, as yet, been any legal proceedings taken against those responsible for infraction of the law. Undoubtedly, some have been subject to disciplinary proceedings and have suffered loss of office. *See, for example,* the report in the Union, San Diego, California, January 16, 1976 under the title *FBI Informer Identified to Save Lives.* The Church Committee of the United States Senate has called for the appointment of a special prosecutor: *see,* New York Times, February 6, 1976.

*Bell examines the United States response to the challenge of protecting
civil aviation from terrorist attacks. Recognizing the success of United
States policy, Bell argues strongly in favor of decisive government responses that will convince terrorists not to attack targets of maximum
value to the state.*

The following article is reprinted by permission from *Orbis,* a
journal of world affairs, published by the Foreign Policy Research
Institute, Volume XIX, Winter 1976, #4.

The U.S. Response to Terrorism Against International Civil Aviation

by ROBERT G. BELL

In *Why Men Rebel,* Ted Gurr writes, "The most fundamental human
response to the use of force is counterforce. Force threatens and angers
men. Threatened, they try to defend themselves; angered, they want to
retaliate."[1] Terrorism, by its deliberate disregard for moral and legal
norms, selective targeting of innocent parties and ruthless exploitation of
human fear provokes a response more vengeful perhaps than any form
of force. Yet in modern society, in which government possesses a monopoly on the organized use of force, victims of terrorism cannot act as
vigilantes; they must turn to the state for redress.

Jordan Paust defines terrorism as

> the purposive use of violence by the precipitator(s) against an instrumen-
> tal target in order to communicate to a primary target a threat of violence
> so as to coerce the primary target into behavior or attitudes through in-
> tense fear or anxiety in connection with a demanded power (political)
> outcome.[2]

This definition offers a cogent distinction between the act of terrorism and its intended effect. "Instrumental targets" may be either persons or matériel—power stations or water supply systems, for example. The "primary target" is normally a state, but it may be a bloc of states or a faction within a state.

In most incidents of terrorism, the victims are powerless to affect the outcome of the deadly game played between terrorists and the state. Thus, the essential dynamic of terrorism is the value relationship between victims and the state. Any society that regards each human life as inviolate cannot ignore terrorists who bomb, kidnap or hijack its members.

The value relationship between victim and state is most likely to occasion accommodation in democratic societies. Since democratic governments act both in the name and at the discretion of the people, they must yield state interest to the more tangible expedient of the safety and well-being of a single citizen. In the words of one author, "The immediate value of the individual life outweighs the ulterior interest of the group."[3] While there are a number of strategies for negotiating with terrorists, a democratic government must compromise when faced with the imminent murder of the victims. Israel is the exception that proves this rule. For the Israelis, war with terrorists is a constant reality, and they are willing to support government policies that place the state interest first. Elsewhere, no such siege mentality exists.

For the terrorist, then, success will initially be forthcoming if he selects a target of maximum value to the state and demonstrates that he is willing and able to use violence until his demands are met. In the long run, however, this same high-value relationship between victim and state will work against the terrorist. Repeated attacks against a designated category of targets (e.g., diplomats, business executives, airline passengers) will compel the state to organize a defense-in-being. At a certain threshold, overcoming the state's point defense of the target will become too costly for the terrorist, and he will move on to different, "cheaper" targets of opportunity.

Nowhere has this pattern been better demonstrated than in the campaign against international civil aviation. As a vital and vulnerable component of world commerce and communications, aviation was a natural target for terrorist attack. The terrorist campaign threatened not only the passengers and material value of the aircraft and cargoes, but also the fundamental public confidence that flying was safe. International air travel is a highly visible, relatively glamorous aspect of the contemporary era; as such, the bombing and hijacking of airliners was guaranteed to attract widespread publicity. In many cases, publicity for a cause is a principal, if not the paramount, objective of a terrorist attack.

From 1960 through 1975, there were 439 hijacking attempts on American and foreign aircraft.[4] In the 1960s, most hijackings were not political in nature; the hijackers were fleeing from prosecution, attempting criminal extortion or acting out of mental derangement. Nevertheless, lessons learned during this decade were to prove invaluable when hijacking assumed a decidedly terrorist character in the 1970s. Beginning with the September 1970 hijacking and destruction of four airliners by members of the Palestine Liberation Organization (PLO), international civil aviation was assaulted by a succession of increasingly murderous attacks.

The attempt to shoot down an El Al 707 with a missile in January 1975 was generally believed to have brought commercial aviation to the brink of disaster. Surprisingly, statistics indicate that the terrorist campaign had in fact crested in 1972. In that year, there were 62 hijacking attempts worldwide. In 1973, the number dropped to 22 and it has since averaged 25.5. The greater significance of the missile attack was that it revealed the extent to which the defense of international civil aviation had been organized. By 1975, extraordinary means were required for terrorists to get to the aircraft. Since weaponry equivalent to the Soviet-made Strela SA-7 anti-aircraft missiles is not readily available, most terrorists have moved on to more vulnerable, unprotected targets.

This article examines the U.S. role in countering the terrorist campaign against civil aviation. With the most comprehensive aviation network in the world, the United States has the largest stake in maintaining the security of this mode of travel. Moreover, U.S.-flag airliners have been victimized more often than the carriers of any other country. More than 40 per cent of the hijackings around the world since 1960 have involved American aircraft. Predictably, the United States assumed leadership of the international response to aerial terrorism.

Has the U.S. effort been a success? Proponents of the American response point out that since 1973 there has not been a single successful hijacking of a U.S. flag airliner. Worldwide, there were only seven successful hijackings last year, compared with seventy in 1969. Today, newspapers chronicle what seems to be a "mopping-up operation." Cuba has returned hijackers to the United States for trial, and several hijackers recently have surrendered voluntarily. On November 21, 1975, the FBI arrested this country's first hijacker—a fugitive for fourteen years.[5]

The December 29, 1975, bombing at La Guardia Airport again focused national attention on the security of civil aviation. Sixty-two persons were killed or injured when a bomb estimated to be equivalent in force to twenty-five sticks of dynamite exploded in a baggage claim area.[6] In the wake of this tragedy, the government organized a task force to recommend new airport security measures. There is admittedly only so much that can be done. That the terrorists placed the bomb *outside* the airport's secure area illustrates that they will always take the path of least resistance. More than anything, though, this incident is notable for its random quality. Had the bomb been placed at a football stadium, the task force would likely have been studying the problem of safeguarding sports spectators.

What has really been accomplished? Around the world the overall incidence of terrorism is on the rise. Rather than seizing airliners and holding passengers hostage, terrorists in 1975 seemed to prefer storming embassies. This development prompted bolstered security measures for diplomats and other officials abroad.[7] A predictable consequence has been a new shift in terrorist targets—most recently to trains (Holland) school buses (Afars and Issas), and conferences (Vienna). In each case the attack was novel and the target was totally undefended.

Certainly, the American success in preserving the security of international civil aviation has been commendable, but it is not enough. The essential lesson of the U.S. experience in the war on aerial terrorists is that point defense of the latest target alone will not suffice. Unless the broad and fundamental causes of terrorism themselves are addressed, governments will remain one step behind the terrorists. As long as states cede the initiative, the power of counterforce will necessarily be limited.

THE EVOLVING AMERICAN POLICY

Unlawful interference with aviation dates to Bedouin seizures of French aircraft for ransom in the 1920s and the world's first hijacking in Peru in 1931. Official American interest was not aroused, however, until the late 1940s. In July 1947, three Rumanians commandeered a state-owned DC-3 in flight and landed it in Turkey. During the next three years fourteen other East European airliners were hijacked across the Iron Curtain, seven landing in the U.S. zone in Germany. In each case, the authorities granted political asylum and imposed no punishment. The fact that crew and passengers were killed in the course of some of the incidents was of minor interest to a public more inclined to regard the hijackers as heroic freedom fighters.

In 1948, a man named Diego Cordova assaulted three people while on board a U.S. airline fight over the Caribbean Sea. This incident exposed a gap in U.S. municipal law concerning crimes of violence committed over the high seas. Public Law 82-514, approved on July 12, 1952, closed the gap by authorizing the federal government to prosecute similar crimes. This act was the first in a succession of federal laws intended to protect air travelers.

The United States experienced its first hijacking on May 1, 1961, when Antulio Ramirez-Ortiz commandeered National Airlines Flight 337, en route from Miami to Key West, and ordered the crew to fly the plane to Cuba. Four subsequent hijackings within a sixteen-day period that year (two of which were successful) convinced the government that this would not remain an isolated phenomenon.

The initial U.S. response to hijacking combined legal and technical (physical security) countermeasures. Public Law 87-197, approved September 5, 1961, made "aircraft piracy" a federal crime punishable by death or not less than twenty years' imprisonment.[8] This law, superseding P.L. 82-514, provided for the application of federal criminal law to acts of assault, maiming and murder occurring on board aircraft engaged in air commerce.

In 1962 the Federal Aviation Administration (FAA) deputized twenty of its Flight Standards Branch employees as U.S. marshals and utilized them on board designated high-risk flights.[9] Unlike the later, highly publicized "Sky Marshals" program, the FAA kept this first armed guard program secret. This decision was consistent with the low-profile policy that governed the anti-hijacking program until 1968.

At this early date in the war against hijackers, the FAA hoped that hijacking could be stopped by legal deterrence. It accepted the airlines' contention that passengers should not be alarmed or inconvenienced by highly visible security measures. In fact, between 1962 and 1967 there were only seven hijacking attempts. Thus, for the traveling public the possibility of being hijacked seemed remote.

At the international level, a corresponding sense of complacency prevailed. Although the United States had first recommended study of the legal status of crimes committed on board aircraft to the International Civil Aviation Organization (ICAO) in the wake of the Cordova incident, there the matter languished until 1959. In that year, the ICAO Legal Committee counseled the promulgation of an international convention to address the subject. In preparatory drafts presented to the committee in 1962, the United States proposed that the convention obligate the state in which the hijacked aircraft landed either to prosecute the hijacker in accordance with its domestic laws or to extradite him according to applicable treaties.[10]

The committee deleted this provision from it final draft to the full ICAO membership; consequently, the resulting Convention on Offences and Certain Other Acts Committed on Board Aircraft (the 1963 "Tokyo Convention") included no forceful threat of punishment to deter hijackers. Article 11, the so-called hijacking clause of the convention, simply states that contracting states shall take measures to restore control of the aircraft to the aircraft commander, permit its passengers and crew to continue their journey, and return the aircraft to its owners.[11]

The Tokyo Convention was of value because it resolved key jurisdictional questions, strengthened the concepts of free movement and commander's powers, and established a precedent for multilateral action against hijackers. But it did not go into effect until it was ratified by the twelfth state (the United States) in 1969. This leisurely rate of ratificatin reflects the general tolerance with which governments regarded the infrequent hijackings of the mid-1960s.

Official disinterest was dispelled sharply in 1968. In that year alone eighteen aircraft were hijacked, and the FAA began to consider physical security measures to keep hijakers off planes. A task force under the direction of Dr. Evan W. Pickeral identified thirty-five behavioral characteristics common to past hijackers and, in 1969, conducted a successful test of a simplified behavior profile with Eastern Airlines. The test established that if all airlines applied the profile to all boarding passengers, less than 5 per cent would fit the profile and require searching.[12]

Although the number of hijacking attempts on U.S. aircraft soared to forty in 1969, the FAA chose not to order the airlines to apply the profile. Further, it rejected the more stringent measure of requiring the physical or electronic search of *all* passengers: the priority interest still was passenger convenience, rather than fail-safe passenger security.

Priorities shifted dramatically in September 1970, when Palestinian guerrillas seized and destroyed four airliners. Three were blown up at an airstrip in the desert after the passengers had been exchanged for imprisoned members of the PLO. The fourth aircraft exploded minutes after landing at Cairo Airport—and only seconds after the last passenger had scrambled to safety. With electrifying suddenness, the terrorists had shattered all prior assumptions about hijackers' motivations and made obsolete previous strategies for protecting air travel. This incident presaged new thresholds of violence and danger for the coming decade.

For the first time, the hijackers' objective was not to use the aircraft for a flight to freedom or to ransom its passengers for cash, but rather to exploit the vulnerability of aviation for political ends. The obvious ruthlessness of the terrorists and their fanatical dedication to their cause posed a danger not likely to be deterred by the threat of punishment alone. Clearly, new measures were needed to keep terrorists off planes. On September 9, 1970, President Nixon directed the FAA to implement a large-scale Sky Marshals program. Initially, military personnel were employed in this role until civilian armed guards could be trained.

On the international level, a new sense of urgency infused ICAO deliberations regarding a second anti-hijacking convention. When the International Conference on Air Law was convened at The Hague in December 1970, delegates from seventy-four states signed the resultant Convention for the Suppression of the Unlawful Seizure of Aircraft.[13] Where the Tokyo Convention had omitted specific anti-hijacking measures, the Hague Convention declared:

> The Contracting State in the territory of which the alleged hijacker is found shall, if it does not extradite him, be obliged, without exception whatsoever and whether or not the offence was committed in its territory, to submit the case to its competent authorities for the purpose of prosecution.[14]

This article was the subject of great controversy at the conference. In preparatory drafts, the United States had proposed mandatory extradition for all hijackers.[15] When it became obvious that this idea would not be supported, the U.S. delegation backed a proposal calling for either the extradition *or* the prosecution of all hijackers, including those acting out of political motivation, only to have it defeated by states intent on preserving the traditional sovereign right to grant asylum. The delegates finally accepted substitution of the expression "without exception whatsoever" in lieu of the more explicit "whatever the motive for the offence."[16]

Despite this tactical setback, the United States was pleased with the results of the conference. Article 4—the "universal jurisdiction clause"—ensured that, regardless of where the offense was committed, each contracting state would have to establish its jurisdiction to prosecute when the alleged hijacker was present in its territory and it did not extradite him.[17] Although the convention proclaimed only that the case be submitted for prosecution, to have *required* prosecution would have constituted unacceptable interference with the criminal procedures of the individual states. Finally, Article 2 dictated "severe penalties" for convicted hijackers. The Hague Convention was ratified by the required number of states and entered into force on October 14, 1971.

The Montreal Convention for the Suppression of Unlawful Acts Against the Safety of Civil Aviation likewise was drafted in the face of escalating terrorist violence. An extraordinary assembly of ICAO met in Montreal in June 1970 to hammer out deterrent controls for acts of sabotage—such as the bombings that had destroyed a Swiss airliner and damaged an Austrian airliner in February 1970.[18] The resulting draft built on the provisions of the Hague Convention, even before that convention had been put into final form. Such was the exigency of the moment. The Montreal Convention was adopted on September 23, 1971. Its provisions on sabotage constitute a valuable complement to the anti-hijacking provisions of the Hague Convention.

The international legal framework for combating terrorism against civil aviation, as established in these three multilateral conventions, was predicated on three fundamental assumptions. First, most states would accede to the protocols. Second, contracting states would faithfully execute their responsibilities under the conventions, particularly those dealing with extradition and prosecution. Third, the international aviation community could influence "responsible" behavior by states not party to the conventions.

Subsequent terrorist incidents severely shook the fragile hopes engendered at the conferences. During a ten-day span in May/June 1972, Japanese agents of the Popular Front for the Liberation of Palestine massacred twenty-five tourists at Lod Airport in Tel Aviv, two Americans hijacked a Western Airlines 707 to a heroes' welcome in Algiers, and ten Czechoslovakians hijacked a Czech airliner to West Germany, murdering the pilot. From 1970 through 1972, there were 203 hijacking attempts throughout the world.

In the wake of this explosion of violence, advocates of strengthened countermeasures focused on the issue of "sanctuary." Repeatedly, hijackers landed in countries sympathetic to their cause and received little if any punishment. Since these recalcitrant states seemed immune to world public opinion or diplomatic persuasion, hard-liners demanded "enforcement" of the conventions against states that dealt lightly with hijackers. Their proposals met with considerable resistance for political and economic reasons, however, and the initiative stalled.

This diplomatic deadlock was not acceptable to the U.S. Air Lines Pilots Association (ALPA), whose members were beginning to regard each flight as a combat mission. In a letter to President Nixon, ALPA's president declared, "It is our firm conviction that aerial piracy will not cease until there is absolutely no place to go—no place [the hijacker] could land without the sure knowledge that he will be apprehended and tried either in that country or the country from which he departed."[19]

Acting on ALPA's initiative, the International Federation of Airline Pilots Associations (IFALPA) announced that its members would institute a global stoppage of air service on June 19, 1972, if the United Nations failed to implement measures supplementary to the existing conventions, "including enforcement measures against states offering sanctuary and failing to prosecute hijackers."[20] When the deadline for the suspension of service passed without adequate UN or ICAO response, eighteen European, South American and Pacific airlines stood down. U.S. airline pilots were prohibited from joining the strike by a court restraining order; nonetheless, many U.S. pilots refused to fly.[21]

The pilots' boycott sparked renewed diplomatic efforts toward the convening of an enforcement assembly. ALPA's president commended the U.S. State Department for "doing all they could to stir the ponderous international machinery into unprecedented action."[22] Where states had failed to act or had procrastinated in adopting adequate countermeasures, IFALPA had demonstrated that private pressure group tactics could supply the necessary incentive.[23]

Nineteen hundred seventy-two had also been a busy year on the home front. Within a forty-eight-hour period during the first week of March, bombs exploded or were discovered in time on aircraft in New York, Las Vegas and Seattle. Declaring a resolve to "meet this blackmail on the ground as vigorously as we have met piracy in the air," President Nixon ordered the Department of Transportation to implement tougher security measures.[24] Transportation Secretary Volpe announced that airport operators would be required to establish secure zones and granted the FAA authority to review and approve all airport security plans.[25]

In September 1972 the director of air transportation security for the FAA listed the objectives of the government's program: "One, keep unauthorized, concealed weapons off the airplanes; two, have the airplanes free of bombs and incendiary devices; three, have the aircraft serviced in a secure airport environment."[26] However, without mandatory electronic screening or a physical search of all embarking passengers and their carry-on luggage, the first objective could not be guaranteed. Although there were twenty-six hijacking attempts against U.S. aircraft during the first ten months of 1972, the FAA continued to resist pressures to implement new security requirements.

That year's twenty-seventh hijacking provided an impetus previously missing. On November 10, three hijackers took command of a Southern Airlines DC-9 over Alabama. During this particularly harrowing incident the pilot was forced to fly for two days criss-crossing the southern United States and refueling at several different airports. Only his consummate professionalism averted a major disaster when he was forced finally to take off for Cuba, even though marksmen had shot out the airplane's tires.

Responding to a surge of criticism from Congress, the press and ALPA, the government on December 5, 1972, announced new security requirements, to be effective in thirty days. Airport operators were directed to (1) station armed law enforcement officers at passenger check points, (2) search all carry-on items, and (3) screen all passengers with electronic devices as a condition to boarding.[27] There has not been a single successful hijacking of an American airliner since these requirements were implemented.

The Memorandum of Understanding on Hijacking of Aircraft and Vessels and Other Offenses, signed by the United States and Cuba on February 15, 1973, was the result of years of painstaking negotiations. It was of value both as a symbol of a "thaw" in Cuban-American relations and as a deterrent to hijackings. This last point must be qualified somewhat, however, for the agreement's provision mandating extradition or prosecution is not ironclad.

The memorandum recognizes

mitigating circumstances in those cases where the persons responsible for the acts were being sought for strictly political reasons and were in real and imminent danger of death without a viable alternative for leaving the country, providing that there was no financial extortion or physical injury to the members of the crew, passengers, or other persons in connection with the hijacking.[28]

In explanation, Secretary of State Rogers said, "It does not affect the right of asylum. What it does mean is that you cannot commit *major* crimes on the way to asylum."[29] This subtlety is of little relevance to the airline pilot faced by a terrorist committing the *minor* crime of pointing a gun at his head. The pilot probably will not be comforted by the knowledge that the hijacker will be denied asylum in Havana if he pulls the trigger.

THE ICAO ROME CONFERENCE

The diplomatic offensive waged by the American delegation at the 1973 ICAO Conference in Rome denoted the high-water mark in U.S. leadership of the response to terrorism against international civil aviation. The American objective at this time remained the total reduction of attacks on aviation. The strategy was to eliminate all terrorist "safe havens" by establishing ICAO sanctioning authority.

However, the first blow to the American plan was struck even before the conference began. In preliminary subcommittee sessions the United States had campaigned arduously for the creation of an independent ICAO commission that could impose sanctions against states acting contrary to the principles of the Tokyo, Hague and Montreal conventions. These sanctions would include suspension of air service by all ICAO states to the offending state.

Led by France and the Soviet Union, most states maintained that economic sanctions could be imposed only by the UN Security Council. A French official explained, "We thought that such a formula, which basically implies sanctions against states outside the framework of the procedure set up by the United Nations Charter, raised very difficult problems."[30] The full Legal Committee rejected the American proposal and substituted a milder draft presented by several Scandinavian countries. The so-called Nordic proposal envisaged a two-phase ICAO response when a state failed to adhere to the provisions of the conventions: "fact-finding" and "recommendations."[31]

The conference agenda also included debate on three proposed amendments to ICAO's charter—i.e., the 1944 Chicago Convention. France proposed incorporating the Hague Convention verbatim into the Chicago Convention, omitting the Montreal Convention entirely and adding mandatory expulsion for any member not ratifying the amendment once it entered into force. A British-Swiss draft proposed the inclusion of the substantive provisions of both the Hague and Montreal conventions and would have obligated all ICAO members to deny use of their airspace to any member acting contrary to the amendment. The third proposal represented a compromise between the above. It omitted sanctions altogether and required incorporation of the Hague and Montreal conventions *if* the amendment *and* the two conventions were ratified by two-thirds of the memberhsip.[32]

The United States maintained that the amendment approach was not a timely response to the problem. Previous amendments had taken years before entering into effect due to the lengthy process of ratification. A State Department official warned, "Unless an independent convention is adopted . . . there will be no new international law measures to combat hijacking and sabotage for a period of five or ten years, if ever."[33]

The second blow to the U.S. plan came on August 10, 1973—just two weeks before the conference. The Israelis, with an appallingly poor sense of timing, forced down a Lebanese commercial airliner in order to search for Palestinian guerrilla leaders suspected of being on board. Echoing the August 15 UN Security Council resolution condemning the Israeli action, Lebanon, supported by the entire Arab bloc, opened the conference with a demand that Israel be ousted from ICAO.[34]

For the United States, it was now evident that ICAO would not promulgate further enforcement provisions, and it was possible that the Arabs might weaken the three multilateral conventions already agreed on. In addition, there was a real danger that Israel would be stripped of its ICAO membership. Paradoxically, the American delegation that had pressed for the conference with such forcefulness was now constrained to scuttle it. Although the United States did succeed through difficult diplomatic maneuvering in retaining Israel's membership, the conference adjourned without having adopted a single substantive addition to existing international legal machinery intended to deter terrorism.

Since the disappointing collapse of the Rome Conference, the United States has regarded the multilateral approach as closed. In 1974, Congress passed Public Law 93-366, entitled The Anti-Hijacking Act of 1974. This legislation authorizes the president to suspend air service to any foreign nation that he determines is encouraging aircraft hijacking by acting in a manner inconsistent with the Hague Convention, or that he determines is used as a base of operations or training by terrorists who attack aircraft. Further, the act authorizes the secretary of transportation, with the approval of the secretary of state, to revoke the operating rights of foreign air carriers that fail to adhere to the standards and practices of ICAO for air transportation security. To date, this authority has not been exercised.

ANALYSIS

The American effort to orchestrate the response to terrorism against international civil aviation was limited by a number of factors, from sovereign rights to legal and social norms—not to mention costs.

The Right of Asylum   The American response has contended consistently that hijacking must be regarded exclusively as a criminal matter. Endorsing U Thant's assertion that hijackings are crimes of a "totally different category" which must be judged for their "criminal character and not their political significance," Secretary of State Rogers declared, "Political passion, however deeply held, cannot be justification for criminal violence against innocent persons."[35] A Department of State official had said earlier, "We have concluded that the hijacker of a commercial airliner carrying passengers should be returned regardless of any claim that he was fleeing from political persecution."[36]

The U.S. argument for mandatory extradition or prosecution was rebuffed by three counterarguments. First, the United States seemed to be adhering to a double standard, since it has historically welcomed those fleeing from political repression. Critics of the American position could not believe that Washington would return all political refugees who reached the United States via hijacking. Second, the threat posed by hijacking did not warrant surrendering the sovereign right to confer asylum in any and all cases. And third, for many Third World states, political terrorism is the "last resort" for militarily powerless peoples in their struggle against colonialism or imperialism.

The U.S. error was one of extremism. As noted by John McMahon:

> ... if an international agreement requiring extradition or prosecution is to function in deterring the forcible diversion of aircraft, it must be a compromise between the preservation of the state's right to grant refuge to individuals who flee from prosecution and the need to discourage hijackers.[37]

Too liberal a position on asylum will not stop hijacking, McMahon says, while too strict a requirement for extradition will be unacceptable to most states.

The parable of the sun, the wind and the man in the coat comes to mind. At ICAO, the United States acted like the wind, trying to force the Arab states into agreeing to punish all hijackers—to no avail. Then, like the more subtle approach taken by the sun, the Arab states themselves

realized that the dilemma could be avoided simply by blocking their run-
ways and denying hijacked aircraft permission to land. This quiet revolution in policy was perhaps the single most decisive advance in dealing
with the problem of sanctuary.

Does the Threat of Punishment Deter?   The U.S. effort to eliminate "safe
havens" was based on the assumption that once the terrorists knew they
would be prosecuted in all cases, terrorism would stop. This presumption
ignores two realities. First, in many cases terrorists are so fanatically dedicated to their cause that they are fully prepared to accept capture. The
second reality facilitates this inclination: imprisonment of terrorists occasions follow-on terrorist action to free those in jail. The vast majority
of terrorists imprisoned during this decade are now free. One commentator suggested the probable necessity of an international prison to protect
states from terrorist blackmail.[38]

Inadequate Support of Foreign Technical Prevention Programs   While the
United States has led the world in its utilization and support of technical
security measures, it could do more. The issue is one of cost. Although
a share of the cost can be passed on to travelers in the form of surcharges
on air fare, the initial capital investment in large-scale technical security
systems requires special financing.
    In this regard, the United States has been stingy. With few exceptions,
it demands full reimbursement for services rendered, including the sa-
laries of experts loaned to foreign countries to survey aviation security
systems at their major airports. What is needed are financial initiatives,
manifested in direct grants or loans or a special ICAO Technical Assistance Fund to aid member states in installing effective security systems.
    The willing participation of a large number of countries in present
U.S. technical prevention assistance programs demonstrates their genuine
interest in protecting civil aviation. As of 1975, eleven governments had
requested inspection of their aviation security systems by FAA experts;
representatives of seventeen nations had attended the Department of
Transportation Aviation Security Training Course in Oklahoma City; and
more than fifty countries had received audio-visual programs on such
subjects as explosives security and in-flight hijacking defense tactics.[39]
Among the participating states are many generally regarded as sympathetic to terrorists: for example, Syria, Jordan, Egypt, France and Saudi
Arabia. In addition, through the State Department's Bilateral Air Transportation Security Information program, the United States consults with
all foreign governments and foreign air carriers on the full range of anti-
hijacking techniques.[40] Thus, the United States has laid the foundation
for international cooperation in the technical prevention field; with a
more farsighted policy, the cost of worldwide security could be met.

The Costs and Appropriateness of Intelligence Operations   Aggressive intelligence operations can effectively pre-empt terrorist attacks; however,

there are limitations to this method of counterterrorism. The first is cost. It is extremely expensive to maintain surveillance of all known or suspected terrorists. After the massacre at the Munich Olympic Games in 1972, the United States established an extensive surveillance-and-screening program designed to intercept terrorists before they could enter the country.[41] Although the State Department had been pleased with the results of the program, it scrapped Operation Boulder in March 1975. The coordinator for combating terrorism explained that the program had not been "cost effective."[42]

A second problem is that of scope. Contemporary terrorism is transnational in character. Mass communications allow terrorists on one continent instant access to information and ideas relating to successful terrorist tactics on another continent. Often, states are attacked "by proxy": terrorist organizations may employ "foreign" agents in a particular operation or obtain weapons from yet another foreign source. As a consequence, counterterrorist agents must demonstrate an equal facility in crossing international boundaries. Agencies such as Interpol provide a valuable clearing-house for information regarding terrorist activities.

The final restraint on intelligence operations is that of legal and social norms. I.M.H. Smart comments:

> Government in a democracy is expected to conform, in its behavior, to the general norms of the society. Thus, a democratic government which persistently adopts violent means of responding to terrorism . . . may achieve local success in the short term, but at the longer term expense of providing other groups within the society with a basis for claiming to use violence legitimately in their own interest.[43]

As has been demonstrated by the recent exposés of the CIA, democratic societies may determine that illegal or unconscionable activity by intelligence agencies poses a threat greater in the long run than that of the agencies' targets.

CONCLUSION

This review has shown that the American effort to stop attacks on civil aircraft was in no way perfect. The government's recognition that mandatory electronic screening was necessary came far too late. The American contention that states should relinquish their right to grant political asylum in cases of aerial hijacking was rejected by the international community. The attempt to obtain an enforcement convention turned into a diplomatic fiasco.

Yet, all in all, it worked. Today, hijackings are out of the headlines. The public now is aroused only when it is suggested that security measures be dismantled. The frequency of hijacking attempts has declined to acceptable levels.

To some extent, hijacking declined of its own accord. Terrorists increasingly had to compete with the hijacker "who commits the crime simply to get his name into the newspapers or television, in a last desperate effort to become someone."[44] A saturation of media coverage led to public apathy, robbing the terrorist act of its publicity effect. Finally, the UN General Assembly's acceptance of the PLO as a legitimate entity compelled the guerrillas to act in accordance with a new code of responsibility. On January 29, 1975, the PLO announced that it had decided to treat hijackings as crimes and execute any hijacker whose actions led to loss of life.[45]

Nonetheless, these influences were minor compared with the myriad countermeasures arrayed by the international community against the terrorist, even though they were not always coordinated or in line with the American plan. Often, actions taken unilaterally by states benefited the community at large. For example, when Iran executed a political dissident who had hijacked a *domestic* flight, it served notice on terrorists everywhere that Iran was not a promising place to start or end a hijacking. Some states ceased to provide sanctuary to hijackers after they learned that the terrorists could prove to be a nuisance or embarrassment. States that secured their airports in order to protect their national airline also protected foreign carriers. Without the "push" provided by the United States at home and abroad, however, it is probable that international civil aviation would still be imperiled.

The price of future aviation security is constant vigilance; defenses cannot be relaxed. At best, though, these defenses can succeed only in diverting the terrorists to other targets. Without a fundamental resolution of the rivalries, strife and injustices that spawn terrorism, the future promises recurring violence. In the case of international civil aviation, the United States won one battle, but the war with terrorism goes on.

NOTES & REFERENCES

[1] Ted Robert Gurr, *Why Men Rebel* (Princeton, N.J.: Princeton University Press, 1970). p. 232.

[2] Jordan J. Paust, "Terrorism and the International Law of War," *Military Law Review*, Spring 1974, pp. 3-4. Although current literature reflects wide disagreement on the proper definition of "terrorism," Paust's is the most comprehensive. It requires a "terror outcome," recognizes that terrorists may be governmental or nongovernmental actors, and limits terrorism to political acts.

[3] I.M.H. Smart, "The Power of Terror," *International Journal*, Spring 1975, p. 230.

[4] All statistics regarding dates, numbers and persons involved were provided by the Federal Aviation Administration (FAA), current as of January 1, 1976.

[5] *Washington Star*, November 22, 1975, p. 6.

[6] *Aviation Week & Space Technology*, January 5, 1976, p. 22.

[7] *New York Times*, November 16, 1975, p. 7.

[8] Again, there is wide disagreement on the terms "air piracy," "hijacking" and "skyjacking." Alona E. Evans in "Aircraft Highjacking: Its Causes and Cure," *American Journal of Internal Law*, October 1969, observed, "Aircraft piracy is not 'piracy' in the classical sense or as defined by Article 15 of the 1958 Geneva Convention on the High Seas, which refers to piracy by aircraft in the following terms: illegal acts of violence, detention, or any act of degradation, committed for private ends by the crew or passengers of . . . a private aircraft, and directed against another ship or aircraft.'" P.L. 87-197, as presently amended, defines "air piracy" as "any seizure or exercise of control by force or violence or by threat of force or violence or by any other form of intimidation and with wrongful intent, of an aircraft within the special aircraft jurisdiction of the United States [49 USC 1472(i)(2) (Supp. IV,

1974)." Congress has declared that the meaning of the law should in no way be influenced by precedents or interpretations relating to piracy on the high seas. U.S. House, Committee on Interstate and Foreign Commerce, *Crimes Aboard Aircraft in Air Commerce*, Report No. 958, 87th Congress, 1st Session, 1961.

⁹ Interview with Don Myers, chief of Air Security Branch, FAA New England Region, February 11, 1975.

¹⁰ Stanley B. Rosenfield, "Air Piracy: Is It Time to Relax Our Standards?," *New England Law Review*, Fall 1973, p. 96.

¹¹ ICAO Doc. 8364, *TIAS No. 6768; 20 UST 2941*.

¹² See above, note 9.

¹³ ICAO Doc. 8920, *TIAS No. 7192; 22 UST 1641*.

4 *Ibid.*, Article 7.

¹⁵ Gerald F. Fitzgerald, "Toward Legal Suppression of Acts Against Civil Aviation," *International Conciliation*, November 1971, p. 43.

¹⁶ Ibid., p. 58.

¹⁷ *Ibid.*, p. 56.

¹⁸ Nancy D. Joyner, *Aerial Hijacking as an International Crime* (Dobbs Ferry, N.Y.: Oceana, 1974), p. 216.

¹⁹ John J. O'Donnell, "Suspension of Service: Pilot's Answer to Hijacking," *Air Line Pilot*, July 1972, p. 7.

²⁰ *Ibid.*, p. 44.

²¹ *Ibid.*

²² *Ibid.*, p. 45.

²³ Alona E. Evans, "Aircraft Highjacking: What Is Being Done?," *American Journal of International Law*, October 1973, p. 669.

²⁴ White House Press Release, March 9, 1972.

²⁵ *DOT* (Department of Transportation) *News*, FAA News Release, March 17, 1972.

²⁶ "Airport Security," speech by James T. Murphy to the Airport Operators Council International, September 6, 1972.

²⁷ *DOT News*, Office of the Secretary Press Release, December 5, 1972.

²⁸ *Department of State Bulletin*, March 5, 1973, p. 261.

²⁹ *Ibid.*, p. 251. (Emphasis added.)

³⁰ *New York Times*, August 29, 1973, p. 74.

³¹ Arthur W. Rovine, "The Contemporary International Attack on Terrorism," *Israel Yearbook on Human Rights*, Vol. 3, 1973, p. 21.

³² Charles N. Brower, "Aircraft Hijacking and Sabotage: Initiative or Inertia?," in *Department of State Bulletin*, June 18, 1973, p. 874.

³³ *Ibid.*, p. 875.

³⁴ *New York Times*, August 29, 1973, p. 74.

³⁵ William Rogers, "A World Free from Violence," *Department of State Bulletin*, October 16, 1972, p. 429. The assertion by U Thant is from the *New York Times*, September 15, 1970, p. 17.

³⁶ *Department of State Bulletin*, March 10, 1969, p. 213.

³⁷ John P. McMahon, "Air Hijacking: Extradition as a Deterrent," *Georgetown Law Journal*, June 1970, p. 1150.

³⁸ Chester L. Smith, "The Probable Necessity of an International Prison in Solving Aircraft Hijacking," *International Lawyer*, April 1971, p. 274.

³⁹ DOT/FAA (ASE-5), "U.S. Assistance to Other Nations," 1/3/75.

⁴⁰ Department of State AIRGRAM, A-1288 "Exchange of Information on Anti-Hijacking Techniques," February 12, 1973.

⁴¹ *New York Times*, April 24, 1975, p. 7.

⁴² *Ibid.*

⁴³ Smart, p. 230.

⁴⁴ Roberta Wohlstetter, "Kidnapping to Win Friends and Influence People," Surry, Autumn 1974, pp. 39-40.

⁴⁵ *New York Times*, January 30, 1975, p. 1.

Mickolus applies a new approach to analyze the age old tactic of hostage-taking and effective government response. Through the use of statistical techniques, Mickolus examines hostage incidents which occurred during the period from 1968-1975 and reveals trends which might have otherwise been overlooked. Finally, he evaluates these trends as they relate to the ongoing policy debate concerning the value of negotiating for hostages.

This article is reprinted by permission from *Orbis*, a journal of world affairs, published by the Foreign Policy Research Institute, Volume XIX, Winter 1976, #4.

Negotiating for Hostages: A Policy Dilemma

by EDWARD F. MICKOLUS

In the past decade the world has seen the rise of a new type of actor on the global stage: the international terrorist group. To gain headlines and increase public awareness of their cause, these bands have engaged in the assassination of government leaders, the sabotage of critical facilities, the bombing of embassies and foreign corporations, assaults on military installations, skyjackings, kidnapings of diplomats and businessmen, and takeovers of embassies to hold their staffs for ransom. The latter three situation-types, which involve the taking of hostages, will be the concern of this article. How great a problem do we face? Are there any trends we can discover? Is the problem worsening? Can any nation consider itself safe from such attacks? Are certain nations being singled out for terrorist assaults of this kind? What groups are engaged in this activity? What is it they want? Finally, what can and should we do when faced with such situations?

THE SCOPE OF THE PROBLEM

The barricade-and-hostage scenario produces the first situation-type in which a nation or corporation may find itself faced with the question of negotiating for hostages. In it we find terrorists seizing one or more

TABLE I. Yearly Number of Incidents Involving the Seizure of Hostages[1]

Year	Total	Barricade & Hostage	Kidnaping	Aerial Hijacking
1968	1 (1)	0	1 (1)	0
1969	3	0	3	0
1970	35 (7)	1	27 (6)	7 (1)
1971	13 (2)	1	11 (2)	1
1972	25	3	11	11
1973	46 (2)	8	29 (1)	9 (1)
1974	23	11	10	2
1975	51 (1)	18	31 (1)	2
Totals	197 (13)	42	123 (11)	32 (2)

[1] Unsuccessful attempts are shown in parentheses.

hostages but making no attempt to leave the scene of the crime. Negotiations are carried on with the perpetrators themselves effectively being held hostage, unable to leave the scene when they choose. This situation frequently climaxes an incident in which the seizure of hostages is not the terrorists' primary aim: e.g., a bank holdup in which the robbers are discovered by the authorities before they are able to escape, whereupon the group seizes any persons who happen to be handy, or an attack on an airport lounge or a residence, in which hostages are seized in order to secure the free passage of the terrorists—or murderers—away from the site.

The second type is the more stereotyped kidnaping, in which a diplomat or businessman is taken to an underground hideout and held for monetary ransom, release of prisoners, publication of the group's manifesto, and the like. Our third type is a special case of aerial hijacking. We can distinguish among those situations in which the hijacker is merely seeking a means of transportation to a nation giving him asylum (the old "Take this plane to Cuba" skyjacking), situations in which the hijacker forces the pilot to land the plane, releases passengers and crew, and blows up the plane without making any ransom demands (engaged in for shock value), and incidents in which the skyjacker makes specific demands on governments or corporations, threatening the safety of the passengers and crew. This last type of hijacking is included in our discussion.[1]

We can see some trends in occurrences like these in Table I, which gives a breakdown of yearly incidents from 1968 through 1975.[2] Kidnapings are by far the most prevalent hostage incident, showing a wavering but increasing trend-line over time. In 1975 more kidnapings were perpetrated than in any other year in recent memory. Moreover, the probability that the kidnapers will successfully seize a hostage has grown dramatically since the beginning of the 1970s. A steady rise in barricade-

TABLE II. Site of Hostage Incidents by Country, Region and Type 209

Location	Barricade & Hostage	Kidnaping	Aerial Hijacking
Latin America			
Argentina	1	38	1
Brazil	0	6	0
Bolivia	0	4	0
Colombia	0	4	2
Costa Rica	0	0	1
Dominican Republic	1	2	0
Guatemala	0	4	0
Haiti	1	0	0
Mexico	0	3	1
Nicaragua	1	0	0
Paraguay	0	1	0
Uruguay	0	9	0
Venezuela	0	2	1
Atlantic Community			
Austria	2	0	1
Canada	0	2	0
France	3	2	1
Greece	2	0	0
Ireland	0	1	0
Italy	0	1	1
Netherlands	3	0	1
Northern Ireland	0	2	0
Spain	1	2	0
Sweden	2	0	1
Switzerland	0	0	1
Turkey	0	4	2
United Kingdom	3	1	0
United States	1	0	2
West Germany	1	1	2

and-hostage incidents includes no known failures to take hostages in eight years, and an annual record was established in this category during 1975. The situation changes with respect to aerial hijackings. Improvements in security procedures made in 1973, together with the unwillingness of countries to grant asylum to hijackers, have led to this type of incident becoming a rarity. Overall, we have seen an erratic rise in the total number of such terrorist incidents, marked by the increased probability of successfully seizing hostages.

Table II shows where the incidents occurred[3] and is summarized regionally in Table III.

Barricade-and-hostage incidents are most widespread in the Atlantic Community and the Middle East, and aerial hijackings also fit this pattern.

TABLE III. Site of Hostage Incidents by Region and Type

Region	Barricade & Hostage	Kidnaping	Aerial Hijacking	Total
Latin America	4	73	6	83
Atlantic Community	18	16	12	46
Middle East	13	12	6	31
Africa	1	20	1	22
Asia	6	4	5	15
Total	42	125	30	197
Middle East				
Algeria	1	0	0	
Bahrain	0	0	1	
Dubai	0	0	1	
Egypt	0	0	1	
Iran	0	1	0	
Israel	6	0	1	
Jordan	1	2	0	
Kuwait	1	0	0	
Lebanon	2	9	2	
Sudan	1	0	0	
Tunisia	1	0	0	
Africa				
Angola	0	3	0	
Chad	0	1	0	
Ethiopia	0	11	0	
Somalia	0	1	0	
South Africa	1	1	1	
Spanish Sahara	0	1	0	
Tanzania	0	1	0	
Uganda	0	1	0	
Asia				
Bangladesh	1	0	0	
Burma	0	1	0	
India	0	0	2	
Japan	0	0	1	
Malaysia	1	0	0	
Nepal	0	0	1	
Pakistan	1	0	0	
Philippines	1	2	1	
Singapore	1	0	0	
Thailand	1	1	0	

Such incidents can be considered a curiosity in Africa, but they are beginning to be suffered in Asia and Latin America. The pattern does not hold for kidnapings, for Latin America is plagued by 60 per cent of the

TABLE IV. Hostages by Region and Nationality 211

Region	Incidents with One Nationality	Incidents with Multiple Nationality	Total
Asia	10	10	20
Africa	3	3	6
E. Europe	3	0	3
Middle East	12	14	26
Latin America	12	8	20
W. Europe & U.S.	116	42	158
Other	4	23	27

world total. Argentina is clearly a special case, with kidnapings of domestic or foreign business leaders becoming almost a daily occurrence.[4] Ethiopia accounts for most of the African kidnapers, because of numerous raids on U.S. installations by the Eritrean Liberation Front. Lebanon has seen a dramatic increase in kidnapings in 1975, with more than 100 attempts being reported in one November weekend during the battle for Beirut. No discernible variances appear for Asia or the Atlantic Community, but it is notable that the communist nations are absent from the table. Aside from this major exception it appears, in looking at the recent historical pattern, that no nation can consider itself completely safe from some such attack.

But while they are apparently willing and able to strike in virtually any nation, terrorists have been somewhat selective in whom they choose to take hostage, as shown in Table IV.

Nations ranking high in per capita GNP, with large amounts of capital invested overseas, are more frequently chosen as hostage contributors. The United States finds itself singled out in one-third of all incidents. Nationals of the poorer countries who are seized are ordinarily their government's ambassador to another country, or a manager or president of a multinational corporation's subsidiary. Again, the communist nations are rarely terrorist targets, the exceptions being Yugoslavians attacked by Croatians and the Soviet ambassador being attacked by MANO, an Argentine right-wing group. Hence, although at times nationals of Third World nations are taken as hostages, the problem is primarily one for Westernized, capitalist nations.

Table V shows the regional location of nations, corporations and other entities that have been targets of terrorist demands, as well as whether or not they have been the sole target of demands in a given incident.

Despite the United States susceptibility as a provider of hostages, the U.S. government is rarely the target of demands. Terrorists have tended to single out corporations or make unspecific demands (e.g., "We want $4 million for his safe return") when holding Americans. Again, we find communist and African governments virtually exempt from demands.

TABLE V. Targets of Demands by Region and Type

Region	Sole Target	One of Many Targets	Total
Africa	1	1	2
Asia	9	3	12
Latin America	26	2	28
Middle East	11	10	21
Western world	30	24	54
Other (e.g., corporate, un- specified	51	5	56

Even terrorist groups have not been immune: in 1970, the Jewish Defense League demanded that the PFLP (Popular Front for the Liberation of Palestine) release hostages it was holding at Dawson Field. Western nations most frequently are involved when the terrorists single out more than one target for demands.

THE POLICY DEBATE

With this background, what should be the response of a government when faced with a hostage situation? The choice has been somewhere on a continuum ranging from never negotiating, which is the stated policy of the United States and Israel, to giving in to the terrorists' demands. Each approach is based on implicit theories regarding the driving mechanisms of terrorist behavior, but such theories have never been adequately spelled out. Various propositions have been used or can be used to justify the State Department's "no ransom" position; the same is true for a flexible response position, in which the characteristics of the situation determine whether negotiation can solve the problem. In both cases the proponents point to the advantages of their approach and the overriding disadvantages inherent in the competing view.[5]

The "No Ransom" Position In essence, this viewpoint holds that all terrorists will respond in the same way to perceived positive or negative reinforcements. In order to deter further attacks, one must not give in to what they demand; thus one makes future operations not worth their while. Arguments supporting this position may be outlined as follows.

(A) Terrorists are all the same, prompted by a generally leftist ideology, and they employ the same tactics. They tend to have the same views toward their own lives and the lives of others, i.e., little respect for either. They cannot be trusted to keep their part of the bargain and will kill the hostages no matter what the government's response. They may even increase their demands if the government complies with the original bill of particulars. There is no reliable guarantee that the kidnapers will release the hostages if their demands are satisfied.

(B) Due to their links, we are seeing the creation of a Terrorist International. When we deal with one terrorist group holding hostages, we are actually rewarding all members of this general conspiracy. Consider the evidence:

(1) They have the same funding sources, including the Soviets, Chinese, Arabs, Cubans, North Koreans and each other.

(2) They have held many worldwide meetings, among them the recent meeting in Trieste of a score of European separatist groups, the confederation of four major Latin American guerrilla groups, and the frequent meetings of the PLO, which at times has served as the forum for ten separate groups.

(3) They have conducted many joint operations, such as the skyjacking and barricade-and-hostage episodes engineered by the Japanese United Red Army and the PFLP, as well as kidnapings engaged in by coalitions of the MR-8, ALN and VPR in Brazil.

(C) Even if we were to grant that terrorists are not all alike, we are unable to get enough data at the scene of an incident to help us determine how we can gear our bargaining to these differences.

(D) In a form of the contagion hypothesis or demonstration effect, we can state that capitulation to the group presently facing us will only encourage others to engage in future, similar acts. Terrorists are motivated by the prospect of reward, and what we must do is remove the source of reward by refusing to pay monetary ransom, release prisoners or grant asylum. For example, Guatemala, Spain and numerous multinational corporations have granted the demands of terrorists, only to be faced with mounting demands in subsequent situations.

(E) In isolated incidents, however—especially those receiving the most publicity—the converse has been true; some governments and corporations that gave in to demands have not been faced with further incidents. Nevertheless, these cases have led to a building up of the expectations of the terrorists, who now believe that the overall tendency of their targets will be to grant demands.

(F) Article 29 of the Vienna Convention on Diplomatic Relations states: "The person of a diplomaic agent shall be inviolable. He shall not be liable to any form of arrest or detention. The receiving state shall treat him with due respect and shall take all appropriate steps to prevent any attack on his person, freedom or dignity." The best way to uphold our duties and responsibilities under this convention is to remove the temptation to kidnap diplomatic officers by denying rewards for such behavior.

(G) It is morally wrong to give in to the demands of groups engaging in terrorist acts that range from the Munich massacre to the machine-gunning of innocent persons in airport lounges and the random bombing of buildings. Orderly societies cannot long endure when leaders encourage this resort to violence to settle political differences. Our national prestige vis-á-vis other nations will be damaged if we negotiate with such murderers, and our people will lose faith in their government's ability to protect them from such attacks.

(H) Although this point is rarely mentioned, one should consider the government's responsibility to protect political prisoners. Do the terrorists wish to liberate those whose release is demanded, or is some other motive involved? In the von Spreti kidnaping, the Guatemalan government claimed that four of the guerrillas named in the demands were on the kidnapers' death list for disclosing information to the government. Abu Daoud, who allegedly revealed a great deal of information about the Black September organization, was frequently mentioned in the demands of subsequent hostage-takers. In the recent barricade-and-hostage incident in Malaysia, several members of the United Red Army refused to leave prison, claiming that the perpetrators were members of a rival faction.

(I) Finally, stated policy cannot countenance giving in to the demands of terrorists. While we may have to face the gruesome consequences of many incidents, including the loss of hostages' lives, before terrorists come to believe that we are serious in not negotiating under any circumstances, it is absurd to believe that any other policy could act as a deterrent. While we may lose the lives of a few people now, we are saving the lives and the sense of security of our citizens in the long run.

The Flexible-Response Position   In a nutshell, the flexible-response view questions the fundamental assumptions of the "no ransom" policy and advocates an *ad hoc* response to each instance. Based on an essentially different analysis of the motivations of terrorists, the function of deterrence and the value of hostages, its propositions include these judgments.

(A) Terrorists are not all the same, and they cannot be expected to react in the same way during hostage situations:

(1) They differ in ideology and purpose in their choice of terrorism. What we are dealing with is a group of people who have chosen a common tactic. We cannot infer from this that their motivations are commonly held. To illustrate, we could classify terrorists in the following manner.

Group Type	Examples
Separatists, irredentists	Basques, Eritreans, IRA, Corsicans
Fedayeen	PFLP, Black September, Al Saiqa
Ultra-left anarchists	Japanese Red Army, Baader-Meinhof Gang and its splinters
Latin guerrillas	ERP, Montoneros, ALN
Criminal gangs	Mafia; groups who publicly cloak their actions in political rhetoric, but whose real purpose is personal gain
Psychotic individuals	The security guard who seized the Israeli embassy in South Africa in 1975
Hoaxes	Brian Lea's kidnaping in Uganda

(2) Terrorists differ in their tactics. Interestingly, many of the major groups have not engaged in hostage-taking—e.g., the Weathermen in the United States, the Baader-Meinhof Gang in West Germany and the Argentine Anti-Communist Alliance. Moreover, it appears that some groups tend to "specialize" in one type of incident (the ERP has a taste for kidnaping businessmen), whereas others have an expanded repertoire and employ various tactics (e.g., the PFLP and Black September). These differences may be due to the group's ideology, the availability of targets, regional cultures of violence, societal norms, group strength in terms of firepower, logistics and personnel, public support for the group (real or perceived), security systems of potential targets, and the preferences of the group's leaders.[6]

(3) They do not hold the same views on the sanctity of life. Some are genuinely suicidal and totally indiscriminate in their choice of victims; others are willing to sacrifice all their demands for safe passage from the scene of the crime. Among the variables we can consider in determining the terrorists' views are these. Are they apt to practice the incremental release of hostages—i.e., do they allow wounded, sick, women and children to leave the scene of the incident? In previous incidents, was a warning given by the group before the bomb exploded, or did they attempt to kill as many people as possible? Were booby traps involved in the bombings? Were letter-bombs, which involve the least public risk to the terrorists, used? What kinds of victims were selected (e.g., Latin American groups rarely kidnap women or children)? What was the timing of the incident: was the bomb set to go off at midnight, or during the noon rush hour, guaranteeing many casualties?

(4) Terrorists rarely double-cross bargainers by increasing their demands, and they also rarely kill hostages without provocation. Of even greater rarity is the killing of hostages after demands have been granted. Terrorists have their own credibility to protect and can assume that their behavior in an incident will have an effect on the expectations and behavior of government negotiators in any future incident. If they renege on their part of the agreement, they can be sure that the government will not concede in the next incident.

(B) The links between groups do not necessarily lead to commonality of tactics, strategy, perceptions or motivations:

(1) In the past decade, not even a third of the groups who have engaged in incidents of transnational terrorism have attended relevant international meetings.

(2) Even the PLO, composed of groups of common nationality with a common purpose, has suffered from splintering and fighting among factions who disagree on tactics, strategy, the sanctity of life, types of demands, methods of negotiation, and so on.

(3) Many terrorist groups were established to fight "primary" terrorist groups. Examples of such pairings include the Ulster Defense Association versus the IRA, the Anti-ETA versus the Basque nationalists, the Jewish Defense League versus the PLO, the Argentine Anti-Com-

munist Alliance versus ERP and numerous other Argentine leftist groups.

(4) Nation-states have many links, such as trade and communications, but they do not necessarily share the same outlooks and may even go to war because of these multiple ties.

(C) Data obtainable at the site of an incident can provide clues as to how we should conduct our negotiations. Relevant considerations may include previous behavior of the group in similar situations, logistical constraints, age and sex of the perpetrators, existence of communication with the group's headquarters, choice of the government's negotiation-team representative or intermediary, size of the attack force, number of terrorist groups involved in the incident, choice of targets in terms of their symbolic value, as well as the nationality of the victims, targets and terrorists.

(D) The contagion hypothesis rests on shaky evidence. At present, we are unable to test whether terrorist groups are aware of "no ransom" policies or whether they base their behavior on knowledge of such policies. Furthermore, many governments have publicly stated beforehand their refusal to deal with groups who take hostages yet have been faced with incidents on their soil, involving their nationals as perpetrators or as targets. Such nations include Argentina, Israel, Turkey, Uruguay, West Germany and Japan, not to mention the United States, whose strict "no ransom" policy has not saved its nationals from being the most sought-after hostages.

(E) Governments have a moral duty to protect their nationals and should make every effort to secure the safe release of hostages. We should not sacrifice innocent individuals to prevent incidents that might not occur. Governments may feel that if tranquillity can be achieved—even temporarily—by the release of a few prisoners, they are justified in negotiating. The prestige of a nation, both at home and abroad, will most certainly be smirched if hostages are killed due to government inaction.

(F) Terrorists care most about what happens to them after an incident, rather than whether or not their demands are fulfilled:

(1) They are concerned about what happens to the attack squad, and they may be deterred from further incidents if the group is harshly dealt with as a consequence of their actions. More and more it is argued that the death penalty should be imposed on those who engage in such actions, both as a deterrent and to ensure that those who are captured cannot engage in even worse actions in the future. Many terrorists who have been released from prison as a result of demands being met have indeed engaged in subsequent terrorist acts.

(2) They are concerned about the fate of the group as a whole, and may reconsider sequels if a nationwide crackdown on terrorist activity is instituted. Since Uruguay and Canada were able to wipe out the Tupamaros and the FLQ, respectively, they have not been victimized by radical incidents.[7]

(G) The granting of asylum is a time-honored practice in Latin American international law. Government leaders recognize that one day they

TABLE VI. Terrorists' Publicly States Motives   **217**

Stated Demands	Barricade & Hostage	Kidnaping	Aerial Hijacking
Release political prisoners (only)	15	23	16
Monetary ransom (only)	1	41	8
Release prisoners and monetary ransom	3	8	5
Publish manifesto	0	8	1
No demands mentioned	1	15	0
Questioning and/or instruction of hostages	0	7	0
Retaliation	0	2	4
Other (including free passage from scene of incident, specific political changes)	18	12	6

may be requesting asylum, when and if they are ousted from power in a revolution. It is not in their personal interest to restrict this practice in any way, and any proposals to place a global or regional ban on the granting of asylum to political prisoners (either the terrorists instigating the incident or the prisoners whose release is demanded) will be met with great resistance in Latin America. Hence, we are unable to deny potential terrorists this avenue of reward.

(H) Terrorism has frequently been called the politics of desperation, the last refuge of the weak. Thus, while the actions of the terrorists themselves are reprehensible, and should be condemned, are the grievances they express necessarily at variance with concepts of justice? In many societies, the possibility of ventilating grievances is denied to certain groups. Resort to radical actions may be the only way these individuals can articulate their interests. Is it possible that we are approaching the problem incorrectly? Instead of attacking the manifestations of the problem—i.e., the expressions of despair—should we not rather tackle the underlying causes of terrorism: poverty, injustice, inequality, lack of political participation, and the like?

(I) The fundamental question to be answered in the "no ransom" versus negotiation argument is this: does deterrence deter? In other words, what are the rewards to terrorists who seize hostages? Are they seeking the ransoms they demand publicly, or do they aim at other goals? In Table VI, we note the demands publicly stated either to government and/or business negotiators or to the hostages themselves. As is immediately evidenced, not all incidents involve the public demand of ransom. But this does not tell the whole story. The granting of stated demands may be only an added bonus to terrorists. Even if they believe that all governments and corporations will adhere to their publicly stated "no ransom" policies, they might continue to engage in hostage operations for a number of reasons:

(1) Those who demand the freedom of prisoners may be attempting to focus adverse publicity on the government. The kidnapers may be endeavoring to show that it is impossible for the government to release the prisoners, because they have been poorly treated, tortured or secretly executed. The prisoners demanded may also have been involved in events highly embarrassing to the government, and the terrorists may wish to jog the public's memory of such episodes and thus increase hostility to the government.

(2) Those who demand ransoms may likewise be attempting to put their targets in a bad light. Many terrorists have demanded "Robin Hood" ransoms, in which a corporation is requested to provide food and other goods and services to a segment of the nation's poor, rather than hand over money for the terrorist organization's coffers. Targets faced with this type of demand are placed in a disconcerting position— public exposure of their refusal to aid in fulfilling a charitable goal. Even if the ransom *is* intended to bolster the organization's own funds, refusal of such demands makes the target appear to value money more than the life of the hostage.

(3) Many attacks have been made in retaliation for governmental moves against terrorist organizations. This is especially evident in the cycle of assassinations conducted by and against members of the Israeli security agency and the Black September organization. Some kidnapings in Latin America have also been undertaken solely in retaliation for government actions against terrorists.

(4) The group may engage in kidnaping to publicizie its overall ideology. Terrorism attracts great interest from the media, and the views of those who have taken over an embassy can be expected to fill the headlines. While some nations may be able to bar press coverage of these incidents for a time, curbs on a free press are bound to meet with strong resistance in many countries. The terrorists will be determined to get their message across in some way, and their real targets may be the audiences of the Western media covering the incident.

(5) Some kidnapings may be attempts to disrupt society's expectations of security and order. Those who engage in particularly brutal incidents are publicly stating that there are no lengths to which they will not go to fulfill what they believe to be justice. Such terrorists will not be deterred by the prospect of receiving no tangible reward, and a "no ransom" policy may simply doom the hostages.

(6) The terrorists may be deliberately attempting to provoke government repression against themselves. A government's countermeasures must generally by applied nationwide if it expects to hit all of the group's cells. Unfortunately, many innocent individuals will be harmed by such measures, and they can be expected to resent such incursions on their liberties. It is the terrorists' hope that his animosity will surface and that the government will be faced with a nationwide revolutionary movement

with broad popular support.

(7) The hostage may himself have some value to those who have seized him. The literature on terrorism frequently asserts that the targets of such incidents transcend those who are its immediate victims, and that one hostage is just as good as another. But the group may believe that this particular hostage has information of value to them, whether it be government intelligence about the group, classified information about weapons systems, or knowledge of his corporation's links with negative reference groups (e.g., secret funding of the corporation by foreign intelligence organizations or any military research under way). Depending on the substance of the information, the group may then use it as propaganda against the corporation or government, or employ it in other operations.

(8) The incident may represent the individual's personal affirmation of solidarity with the norms of the terrorist group. Especially in operations involving more than one terrorist group, the perpetrators may feel that the group will consider them traitors if they settle for anything less than the original set of demands. Should be the government call their bluff, the group's credibility will be damaged if they do not carry out their threats to kill the hostages.

(9) Finally, Régis Debray, one of the major theoreticians of Latin American guerrilla warfare, argues that the threat of kidnaping is part of the urban terrorist's overall strategy. Such operations must be considered in the wider context of the revolutionary struggle. In *Revolution in the Revoltuion?* he argues that such a threat

> immobilizes thousands of enemy soldiers . . . ties up most of the representive mechanism in unrewarding tasks of protection: factories, bridges, electric generators . . . —these can keep busy as much as three quarters of the army. The government must, since it is the government, protect everywhere the interests of property owners; the *guerrilleros* don't have to protect anything anywhere.[8]

By tying up the opposing forces, the guerrilla's job is made that much easier, and the balance of effective fighting forces is more nearly equal.

(J) If the "no ransom" policy was able to stop all hostage incidents, what would the terrorists do? Since they are fundamentally opposed to certain targets, it is doubtful that they would close up shop entirely. Rather, they could engage in other types of action not involving the taking of hostages, which might be even less desirable. For example, they could attempt to assassinate former potential hostages, an operation that takes less time than a kidnaping, leaves them less vulnerable to the strengthened security measures taken to stop kidnapings, and still has most of the advantages of a hostage situation, including the publicity they want. Many threatened assassinations have been avoided by those who have agreed to pay off the extorter's demands. The threat to bomb symbolic facilities may also be engaged in, with the bombing being carried out if extortion is not paid.

In broad outline, we have seen the problems faced by the policymaker who must live in a world plagued by international terrorism. Each position—"no ransom" or negotiation—is supported by convincing arguments but is also loaded with inherent disadvantages to be overcome. In recent months we have witnessed tests of the two positions, with mixed results. At one end of the spectrum, the French engaged in a shoot-out with Somali terrorists, which meant death for the terrorists but also hostage casualties. The British and Dutch took a wait-and-see attitude and were able to stall the IRA and the South Moluccans, respectively, into surrender. The Ethiopians refused to give in to ELF demands and witnessed the kidnaping of citizens of Italy, Taiwan and the United States. The Austrians again gave in to Palestinian demands.

The answer may lie somewhere between a stated "no ransom" position and a pragmatic view of on-the-scene bargaining. It may be that we should aim at creating a new self-image for the terrorists by gaining their commitment to what can be presented as humanitarian policies, such as releasing some of their prisoners or allowing food and medical aid to be supplied. If the terrorists would agree to making incremental moves in this direction, we might be able to keep up the process of commitment and eventually make possible the release of all hostages. Such tactics appear to have been successful when applied, and may represent an optimal mix of the advantages claimed for the two positions we have discussed.

NOTES & REFERENCES

[1] In general, one finds that more hostages are taken in aerial hijackings and barricade-and-hostage situations; kidnapers usually limit themselves to one or two persons. However, in late June 1958, Raúl Castro kidnaped forty-seven Americans and a number of other foreigners in a series of raids in Cuba.

[2] Our survey includes only those events that transcend national boundaries, whether through the nationality or foreign ties of the perpetrators, their location, the nature of their institutional or human vicitms, or the mechanics of their resolution. Episodes of interstate terrorism (e.g., kidnaping by government intelligence agents) are not included. Seizures occurring during the Vietnam conflict are also excluded.

The data were obtained from chronologies provided by the U.S. Department of State, the Federal Aviation Administration, the U.S. Information Agency, the RAND Corporation, and the U.S. Senate and House of Representatives; staff reports prepared for congressional committees; *Facts on File;* reports found in the Associated Press ticker; the *New York Times,* the *Washington Post,* the *Chicago Tribune,* the *Detroit Free Press, The Economist,* and various books on terrorism. Due to omissions in the reporting of some incidents, grand totals for the tables presented may be incomplete. The 197 incidents cover the period extending from January 1, 1968, through December 31, 1975.

[3] The location of an incident is considered to be the place in which it began. In the case of hijackings, the location is the nation in which the plane last touched ground before the hijackers made their presence known. In cases where the embarkation point is not known, the location is considered to be that nation in which the plane landed and the negotiations took place. If both of the above guidelines are inapplicable, the nation of registry is used.

[4] In the period under survey, Uruguay claimed nine kidnapings but has not had a problem of international kidnaping since it was able to destroy the Tupamaro organization.

[5] No one individual or agency recommends all of the propositions mentioned below. It would be false to maintain that people advocating one of the positions necessarily agree with all of the arguments that can be cited to support it. Rather, this exercise is designed to serve a heuristic function in bringing to light some ramifications of these positions that often go unstated.

[6] The nationality patterns found in groups engaging in such actions can be summarized as follows:

Nationality of Groups Claiming Responsibility by Region	Type of Incident			
	Barricade & Hostage	Kidnaping	Aerial Hijacking	Total
Latin American	3	48	7	58
Middle Eastern	24	9	13	46
Western	4	14	3	21
Communist nations	1	0	1	2
African	0	17	0	17
Asian	9	4	3	16
Other	3	36	7	46

In broad terms, it appears that Latin American and African terrorists prefer to attempt standard kidnapings, where they can rely on extensive underground organizations. Middle Eastern groups, who have taken their operations beyond the immediate borders of the Arab-Israeli conflict, have been forced to use tactics leaving them open to attack by security forces. Such actions have, however, allowed them to take many more hostages, which may be an added incentive.

[7] However, many reservations attend to arguments regarding guaranteed punishment of specific acts. First, if we wish to save the hostage, a certain death penalty for the kidnaper gives him no reason to spare the captive's life. Second, the consequences of governmental repression of public freedom should be considered; such repression may be precisely what the terrorists are seeking. Finally, if the roots of the terrorist's grievance are deep, he may believe that even death is better than the existence he and his people now lead. The prospect of apprehension and punishment may not be an effective deterrent in such contexts.

[8] Régis Debray, *Revolution in the Revolution? Armed Struggle and Political Struggle in Latin America* (New York: Grove Press), p. 75.

Beall deals with the tactical *aspects of hostage negotiations, in contrast to the previous selection by Mickolus. Beall provides a sample planning sequence and a hostage situation model to illustrate how law enforcement could plan and react to hostage-taking situations. In addition, he emphasizes the need for international exchange of information on this subject.*

The article is reprinted by permission from *Military Police Law Enforcement Journal*, Volume III, Number 3, Fall 1976.

Hostage Negotiations

by MARSHALL D. BEALL

Taking hostages to enforce compliance with a specific set of demands is probably one of the oldest devices known to man. Hostage taking is found in ancient Greek and Norse sagas as well as Roman mythologies and history.[1]

It can be traced not only by calendar but also through each culture and generation. By tracking the historical development of hostage taking, it is possible to note an evolution of purpose from "an agreement to secure a peace treaty to contemporary international jurisprudence called unilateral coercive assault."[2] This evolution is shown in these historical examples: "During the Middle Ages, Emperor Barbarossa used 300 hostages in securing a peace treaty with Milan in 1158." Again, the traditional use, and perhaps a noble one, of hostage taking. However, in 1193 hostage taking began to change from a gentleman's agreement to secure a treaty to one whose motive was based on economics, money. "Richard the Lion-Hearted had to come up with 67 hostages as a security for payment of the remaining ransom." Hostage taking soon mutated from solely a money making proposition to a political weapon. "In 1740 Fredrick the Great had two Russian noblemen taken into custody as hostages to make Russia release Baron von Stackelberg, a German agent." The Russians in turn became adept in using this device as a political stratagem. "In 1920 the Soviet government ordered the arrest of many German citizens as hostages. In this way the Soviets obtained release of their agent, Karl Rodak, who had been arrested in Germany on charges of political agitation."[3]

Hostage taking has also been used during the intervening years as an instrument to secure bridges, troop trains and even troop formations against espionage activities in an occupied land. This use was particularly effective during the Franco-German War of 1870-1871 where Germany used preventive hostages, prominent French citizens, as protection against sabotage of key facilities. Preventive hostages were also used by the British Commander-in-Chief, Lord Roberts, during the Boer War.[4] Thus, until recently the use of hostage taking appeared to be a practice reserved for sovereign nations and city-states.

However, today, extremists of all political ideologies and criminals seeking to escape have discovered that taking hostages is often a highly effective tactic in the battle against superior forces.[5] From 1968 to 1973, there have been over 400 individual acts of international terrorism. Many of these acts involved taking hostages.[6] Interestingly enough, only those individual acts of crossing national borders to commit terrorism were counted. Local acts of terrorism and hostage taking were not included. For example, during the same timeframe, New York City reported 120 hostage situations in 1968 and over 300 in 1973.[7]

Generally, there are two explanations for the rapid increase and popularity of hostage taking. The first of these is the intense international publicity given to hostage-taking situations by the news media. This publicity not only triggers imitative acts but also provides detailed guidelines for planning such acts.[8] The second explanation could be that society itself is not only becoming more violent but is accepting violence and the threat of violence more readily.[9]

Other authors, in an attempt to explain the recent rise in hostage-taking incidents, zero in on two other factors: the spectacular ways of committing the crimes and the frequency with which they occur.

Along with understanding the various theories that explain this recent increase in hostage taking, law enforcement officials must program for future occurrences to include systematic police responses. These responses will require the forecasting of assigned or assumed missions, courses of action, procedures, and priorities based upon current operations and capabilities of the police agencies. Currently the international law enforcement community is in the phase of *reacting* spontaneously to each incident, attempting to free the hostages and capture the criminals. The problem of little or no police planning is further compounded by terrorist groups, which have developed technologies and information-sharing networks far more advanced than those of law enforcement agencies. These groups maintain an active underground information network for the sharing of technical information, money, personnel, and weapons. But, there is no existing network specifically established to enable law enforcement administrators to share information on hostage-taking incidents on an international level. As a result, when dealing with hostage takers, the police are facing the unknown.[10] Planning for hostage nego- tiations in this country is, with a few exceptions, crisis-oriented. Few police departments have any written policies dealing with hostage-negotiation situations.

The implication is clear; planning must take place since, according to Conrad Hassek,[11] the hallmark of any police reaction in a kidnap/hostage-situation must be the blending of tactical responses and behavioral know-how. This requires the development of team tactics using blocking and containment forces. It requires the use of behavioral experts coordinated by cool-headed and professional leadership. These functions and their execution demand continuously developed estimates, analyses, and studies to insure that plans are refined and current. To assist in planning development, two models have been devised: the 8-step planning sequence at Table 1 and a Typology Hostage Situation Model at Table 2. As noted in Table 1, the first step in hostage planning is the gathering

TABLE 1. Eight-Step Planning Sequence *C.*

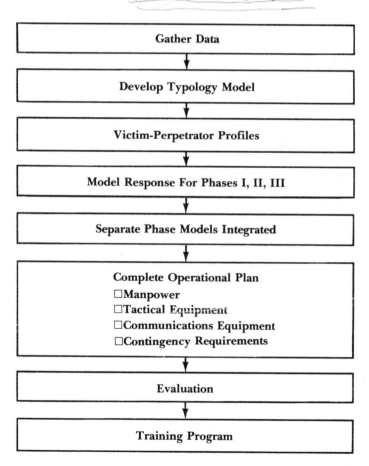

TABLE 2. Typology Hostage Situation Model [Incident Description: Armed Robber Attempting to Escape From First National Bank]

Tasks	Subtasks	Phase
Procedures of becoming barricaded	Attempt to rob bank failed when silent alarm activated. Hostage, female bankteller, taken when police patrol arrived.	I
Procedures for initial police response	Back off. Await reinforcements. Attempt initial contact with hostage taker. Begin to isolate area. Prevent overreaction. Attempt to determine hostage-taker motivation.	I
Establish inner perimeter	Established by Emergency Service Personnel. Relieve responding patrolmen. Isolate to prevent escape and to provide for safety of innocent people in immediate area. Receive briefing from initial responding patrolmen.	II
Establish outer perimeter	Use uniformed patrolmen to control traffic and crowd, to patrol frozen area, and as mobile reserve force.	II
Create command post	Locate near scene of action to provide necessary command and control. Must be covered and concealed from direct-fire weapons. Large enough to house commander, hostage negotiator, comunications equipment, research or intelligence personnel (Think Tank).	II
Negotiating teams	Receive briefing by responding patrolmen. Establish negotiating shift teams. Open initial communications with hostage taker. Develop patterns of questions.	II
Actions and events	Communications opened with hostage taker. Determine number of hostages and hostage takers. Also determine demands to include a request to go mobile and to receive .45-cal pistol. Request denied.	III
Examine outside factors that assist or interfere with police operations including public information	All available black and Spanish members of the Department mingle with the crowds and keep open dialogue with local residents to preclude spreading of false rumors. Local radio station broadcasting incident pinpointed police maneuver elements. Hostage taker was able to bring weapon fire to bear upon Emergency Service Personnel, he had a radio and was able to determine police movements. Three Muslim ministers volunteered their services to exhort hostage taker to surrender.	III
Method of concluding the incident	Hostage taker killed as negotiation failed. Hostage taker gave ultimatum to negotiator. Also, he gave time limit for when he would kill the hostage. Decision made by negotiator, on scene commander, Deputy Chief, and Chief to use SWAT. Hostage rescued unharmed.	III
Special equipment required	Electronic tracking devices. Public address system. Night-viewing devices.	III

of facts on a particular incident. This incident can be one of historical significance or a review of a local hostage situation. Once the facts of the episode have been analyzed and correlated, then they should be literally "plugged in" to the Typology Hostage Model. At Table 2 is an example of a type model devised for a trapped, armed robber who takes a hostage. The facts of the particular incident are the subtasks that support the police responses or the tasks. These tasks are constant in all cases in that they represent actions or proven techniques of response to a hostage situation. The list of tasks may be augmented as we analyze lessons learned and increase our knowledge. Once the model has been completed for a particular incident, then others of the same classification or grouping must be studied and applied to the model. By following this systematic procedure of incident analysis, a planner will begin to note similarities from which reasoned police response may be programed. Also, before law enforcement administrators can adequately prepare defensive operational plans to deal with criminals who seize hostages, the police must be aware of the socio-psychological characteristics of the hostage takers. Thus, it is necessary to classify perpetrators into categories.[12]

Generally, hostage takers may be divided into three broad categories: the politically motivated, mentally unbalanced, and the criminal deviant. The most common hostage taker in the United States is the criminal deviant. This category also includes the sociopath.

Initially, the **criminal deviant** is perhaps the most volatile and dangerous to both hostages and police. Until the situation is stabilized and contained by police and both sides settle down to a pattern of negotiation, the possibility of injury or death is very real. The immediate response of law enforcement in such a situation should be to contain and stabilize and to engage in no acts that might provoke a response against the hostages by a nervous gunman.[13] Examples found under this broad category of hostage taker include the trapped, armed robber, who seized a hostage to aid his escape, and the professional criminal, who often on the spur of the moment during the course of a crime takes a hostage when he finds his escape routes blocked. Usually, the professional criminal is the easiest type of hostage taker to deal with. He is considered a relatively rational thinker who, after assessing the situation and weighing the odds, in most cases, comes to terms with the police and refrains from unnecessary violence or useless killing.[14] The sociopath, on the other hand, represents a potential bombshell in any hostage situation because of impulsive behavior and total lack of concern for others. Appeals to him must always be couched in terms of what is best for him. Studies concerning the sociopath seem to indicate that the sociopath personality is responsible for an excessive number of crimes. He also makes up a significant percentage of our prison population. If this be the case, it is logical to assume that he represents a significant number of those who engage in hostage taking, particularly the trapped, armed robber and the prison rioter.[15]

The **mentally unbalanced** or psychotic hostage taker, according to John A. Culley,[16] offers the police a somewhat more complex problem. He tends to be irrational and, therefore, less predictable; he harbors great inner frustration and conflict. He may even feel a degree of pleasure from his precarious predicament, as he now finds himself important and the center of attention, a position that may be unique in his life. To further hamper an already intricate negotiation process, the mentally unbalanced hostage taker cannot be appealed to on a rational basis because he does not view the world in a rational way. Furthermore, a second relatively frequent mental aberration is a form of severe depression where the only logical answer to life's stress and pain is murder-suicide. Thus police must formulate appropriate responses in order to deal with a severely deranged person who firmly believes he is threatened or persecuted by others and sets out to take revenge upon them.[17] Stalling for time in handling a mentally deranged hostage taker has generally proved successful for the "psychotic is emotionally tense and expends a great deal of psychic energy that eventually wears him down.[18]

The problem of dealing with the first two categories of hostage takers is further magnified when one considers the estimated number of these types in our population. Using the 1970 census figures, psychotic individuals make up one percent of the population, or about two million persons, criminals, maladjustive groups (includes sociopaths, drug addicts, and alcoholics) seven percent or about fifteen million.[19]

The **politically motivated offender** is clearly the most dangerous hostage taker. He views himself as the antithesis of a criminal, he is a patriot, and a freedom fighter.[20] When caught in a criminal act many of them rationalize their behavior by claiming to be revolutionaries who are merely seeking social justice.[21] In many cases, the trapped, armed robber will imitate the political terrorist. However, this political zeal seems to be more of an ego bolstering device rather than a deeply held commitment.[22]

Attempts to establish a profile on the politically motivated hostage taker is difficult since he operates in supersecret, hard-to-infiltrate small groups. Though, generally speaking, the 1970's terrorists are young and educated. They have clearly succeeded in providing that a fanatical band of dedicated guerrillas can wreak havoc vastly out of proportion to its members.[23]

The key to the effectiveness of the political terrorist, as well as the felon, is the target, the hostage. The terrorist must find targets that will demonstrate publicly his opposition to foreign wars, racism, or some other cause.[24] To do this, the hostages must provide the necessary shock effect. The targets of the new strain of terror are innocents. It is their involvement that makes the phenomenon so frightening and from the terrorists' point of view so effective. "The victims are purely instrumental," says Dr. Frederick Hacker, a Los Angeles psychiatrist specializing in the study of terrorism. The terrorists don't care whether the victims are innocent or not. In fact, if they are innocent, they become better bargaining tools.[25]

The hostage is also the key element of the police response, since all efforts are directed toward his safe release. Yet, the safety of the hostage many times depends upon the relationship or degree of rapport established between the hostage and the hostage taker. The danger is greatest

when the culprits are political fanatics and, as a result of great national,
cultural, and social differences and insufficient time, rapport cannot be
established between the culprits and the hostages.[26] Perhaps a good example of what can happen when this transference of feeling does not
take place is provided by the Khartoum incident where Palestinian terrorists, on 1 March 1973, attacked the Saudi Arabian Embassy. During
negotiations, the terrorists, after having their demand for release of Sirhan Sirhan and a number of international criminals and terrorists refused, killed three diplomats, two Americans and one Belgian.[27] However, when time does allow for this transference of feeling, time usually
becomes an ally of law enforcement. The more time a felon spends with
the hostage, the less likely he is to take the hostage's life because they
become acquainted and develop feelings for one another. Furthermore,
this stalling for time also allows the police an opportunity to prepare for
different eventualities and permits the felon to make a mistake.[28] Nevertheless, what may appear to be an advantage to law enforcement officials
may soon disappear upon conclusion of the hostage incident. In a number
of cases, the hostages only reluctantly charged the culprits in criminal
proceedings, despite at least initial danger to their lives, long confinement,
and shocking experiences. The hostages admit that they were influenced
by the personalities of the culprits.[29] This transference of feeling to the
point of victim cooperation, or at least empathy, has been addressed in
many articles dealing with hostage taking. Conrad V. Hassel, Special
Agent for the Federal Bureau of Investigation, in his article "The Hostage
Situation: Exploring the Motivation and Cause" stated "almost all victims
had admitted to this phenomenon to some degree." Special Agent Hassel, using the terrorist as his model, continues in his discussion of this
mutual identification factor by stating several possible reasons for this
influence: "The politically motivated hostage taker in particular may
spend long hours in discussion and rationalization of his cause with the
victim. It has been found that this, plus the possibility of imminent death,
is a crude, unintended, yet effective type of brainwashing. It may cause
the victim to reassess his values and lifestyle."

Two examples are provided that amplify this occurrence. First, a stew-
ardess who was skyjacked to Kuwait in December 1973 on a Lufthansa
airplane emphasized, "They were so nice that I can hardly believe that
they are really that kind of people. The stewardesses said good-bye to the
terrorists with a handshake and almost a kiss.[30] The second example
occurred on 19 April 1971. "Fernand Muller, who had previously been
in jail many times, lured an elderly lady into his flat in Zurich, Switzerland,
and only released her at 4 a.m. on 23 April 1971. Despite the constant
fear and danger to her life, the woman did not leave the house right
away, but stayed another half-hour during which she tried to take Muller
with her because she feared he was going to commit suicide."[31]

This phenomenon of transference of feeling was later dubbed the
"Stockholm Syndrome" after an incident which occurred in Stockholm,
Sweden, in 1973. After the release of the hostages from the Stockholm

bank vault the victims expressed a strong attachment to their captors, to the point of refusing to testify against them.[32] The effect of this syndrome must be kept in mind by law enforcement officials, especially when attempting to predict or plan for victim response to a hostage situation. Empirical evidence from the field may prove false the assumption that a hostage will take an opportunity to escape. In fact, most hostages have found themselves to be extremely docile and cooperative with their captors, sometimes to the point of failing to take advantage of carelessness or mistakes on the part of their captors.[33] It has also been determined through field experience that, surprisingly, when men are hostages, their reactions are predictable. As a rule, they will not put up direct resistance. But women's reactions are absolutely unpredictable and often confuse the culprits. During a bank robbery in Hilden, Germany, on 31 January 1974, a culprit yelled to a female bank employee, "I want money. I'm going to blow up the savings bank." The employee calmly replied, "Don't do anything foolish. Come here and take the money." The perplexed culprit let the employee go and ran out of the bank.[34] Also, women hostage takers appear to be more difficult to deal with for they have on occasion been more persistent and cruel, and they do not always surrender as easily as men. Women also are inclined to have hostages killed for reasons of safety.[35]

Analyzing human motivation and determining the degree of commitment is indeed difficult, for much of the knowledge required to predict human reaction is lacking. However, by continually studying and developing profiles, a record can be established that will give law enforcers the best possible chance for predicting victim/hostage-taker response. From this best-possible-chance analysis, adequate plans can be developed that will provide an adjunct to the previously developed typology model. By studying these two systems, a general pattern of action-reaction should begin to appear. This pattern will give a reasoned approach to specific hostage-negotiation situations. This approach is in keeping with the recommendations of the **International Symposium on Cases Involving Hostages** conducted 3-5 February 1975 and sponsored by INTERPOL in Paris, France. These recommendations included these specific items:

—Develop training programs.
—Develop tactical responses.
—Gather facts on all known hostage-taking incidents. This should include categorizing by type as well as by commonalities and differences.
—Develop typologies for each type of incident that will provide necessary data to develop a frame of reference for each type of incident and to assist in developing hostage-incident operational plans and training programs.
—Profiles should be developed in conjunction with incident typologies on both criminals and victims.[36]

The success of any hostage plan and/or action hinges on a team approach in which overreaction is carefully avoided, especially during the initial confrontation.

Hostage situations usually are divided into three phases: Phase I, the initial confrontation/reaction; Phase II, Special Reaction Team plus trained negotiating teams to relieve patrol units and assume containment missions; Phase III, stabilization and negotiations.

In dealing with a hostage situation, the policeman is dealing with a mind barrier. He will have to discover the hostage taker's intentions and objectives. In most cases, time has been an ally and an asset. It works in the law's favor. The more time that elapses, the more time the hostage taker will have to think about his hostage and his predicament.

What is the future of hostage taking? Perhaps blackmail will grow to be a gigantic thing if it is not resolutely brought to a stop. Today, we are already familiar with the threat of sending letters containing deadly bacteria. It is not unrealistic to think that in a few years there may be atomic-bomb blackmail.

Police agencies around the world must be prepared for this and any other hostage eventuality. Preparation for the future, then, must include analyzing each hostage-taking occurrence, preparing a police response, and putting it to the acid test until a set of responses has been developed that will give the best possible chance for defeating hostage-taking situations.

NOTES & REFERENCES

[1]Wolf Middendorff, "Taking Hostages and Kidnapping," *Kriminalistik*, December, 1972, p. 1.

[2]Ibid., p. 2.

[3]Ibid., p. 1-2.

[4]Ibid., p. 2.

[5]Richard W. Kobetz, "Hostage Incidents the New Police Priority," *Police Chief*, May 1975, p. 32.

[6]Conrad V. Hassel, "The Hostage Situation: Exploring the Motivation and Cause," *Police Chief*, September 1975, p. 2.

[7]Richard W. Kobetz, "Hostage Incidents," p. 32.

[8]Ibid., p. 34.

[9]Richard W. Kobetz, "Hostage Incidents," p. 34.

[10]Ibid.

[11]Conrad V. Hassel, "The Hostage Situation," p. 7.

[12]Richard W. Kobetz, "Hostage Incidents," p. 34.

[13]Conrad V. Hassel, "The Hostage Situation," p. 7.

[14]John A. Culley, "Hostage Negotiations," *F. B. I. Law Enforcement Bulletin*, October 1974, p. 5.

[15]Conrad V. Hassel, "The Hostage Situation," p. 12.

[16]John A. Culley, "Hostage Negotiations," p. 5.

[17]Conrad V. Hassel, "The Hostage Situation," p. 11.

[18]John A. Culley, "Hostage Negotiations," p. 5.

[19]Thomas Strentz, "The Sociopath," F. B. I. Academy, Quantico, Virginia, 1974, (unpublished paper) p. 3.

[20]Conrad V. Hassel, "The Hostage Situation," p. 3.

[21]John A. Culley, "Hostage Negotiations," p. 5.

[22]Conrad V. Hassel, "The Hostage Situation," p. 5.

[23]"The Morality of Terrorism," *Newsweek*, 25 February 1974, p. 21.

[24]David E. Steele, "A New Countersniper System," *Law and Order*, October 1971, p. 52.

[25]"The Morality of Terrorism," *Newsweek*, p. 21.

[26]Wolf Middendorff, "The Victimology of the Taking of Hostages," *Kriminalistik*, April 1974, p. 2.

232 [27]"Killers of Khartoum," *Time,* 12 March 1973, p. 23.

[28]John A. Culley, "Hostage Negotiations," p. 3.

[29]Wolf Middendorff, "The Victimology of the Taking of Hostages," p. 4.

[20]Ibid., p. 3.

[31]Ibid., p. 4.

[32]Conrad V. Hassel, "The Hostage Situation," p. 13.

[33]Ibid., p. 15.

[34]Wolf Middendorff, "The Victimology of the Taking of Hostages," p. 2.

[35]Wolf Middendorff, "Taking Hostages and Kidnapping," p. 19.

[36]Richard W. Kobetz, "Hostage Incidents," p. 34.

IV EMERGING PATTERNS OF CONTEMPORARY TERRORISM

Emerging patterns of contemporary terrorism are made more difficult to identify because of terrorism's unpredictability. *Indeed, the most frightening aspect of this criminal menace is that it is unlikely to remain the same. Internationally, governments are still in a position where much of the time they can only* react *to terrorism's initiatives. Reversing this situation without drastically altering concepts of democratic government becomes increasingly difficult. We are now approaching a point where those changes which contemporary terrorism has already wrought within our own societies must be evaluated before opting too easily for "1984" solutions.*

Many of the emerging patterns that Jenkins spells out in his balance sheet are already apparent: alliances between terrorist groups, more destructive acts, and surrogate warfare. Anable expands on the close collaboration between international terrorist groups and describes the key role of several radical governments, further updating Jenkins' prognosis. But before overreacting by ascribing to terrorists more power than they actually wield, we are well advised to consider Laqueur's well-worded cautions.

It is not reasonable to state that society is either winning or losing the struggle with contemporary terrorism, although tremendous successes have been achieved. The durability of these victories may be seen in retrospect to be campaigns in a much bigger war. In this sense, the articles by Stiles and Cooper are very disturbing. Stiles, for example, considers contemporary terrorism particularly threatening because in the coming years it may force basic changes in the nation-state as we know it. Cooper voices concern about changes already made in many states which have spawned the growth of an official terrorism with "brave new world" characteristics. Considering many terrorist failures, Cooper speculates on what they will do next.

In gauging the success of terrorism, Jenkins reviews the six purposes which terrorism strives to achieve and the feeble response of the international community. Jenkins forecasts several trends of terrorism including alliances between terrorist groups, increasingly destructive acts, and surrogate warfare. Each of these trends is becoming clearly distinguishable and we must begin to concern ourselves with Jenkins' closing comment on how such trends may affect current concepts of democratic government.

This article is reprinted by permission from The International Institute for Strategic Studies, as originally published in *Survival*, Volume XVII, Number 4, 1975.

International Terrorism: A Balance Sheet

by BRIAN JENKINS

Terrorism is often described as *mindless* violence, *senseless* violence, or *irrational* violence. If we put aside the actions of a few authentic lunatics, terrorism is seldom mindless or irrational. There is a theory of terrorism, and it often works. To understand the theory, it must be understood first that terrorism is a means to an end, not an end in itself. In other words, terrorism has objectives, although those who carry out acts of terrorism may be so dedicated to violence that even they sometimes seem to miss this point.

Unless we try to think like terrorists, we are also liable to miss the point, for the objectives of terrorism are often obscured by the fact that specific terrorist attacks may appear to be random, directed against targets whose death or destruction does not appear directly to benefit the terrorists' cause. It is hard for us to understand how the killing of Olympic athletes in Munich or the hijacking of a Lufthansa airliner in Rome will ease the plight of Palestinians in the Middle East, or how blowing up an office in Manhattan will help topple a dictator in Latin America. But the objectives of terrorism are not those of conventional combat. Terrorists do not try to take and hold ground or physically destroy their opponents' forces.

While terrorists may kill, by our standards sometimes wantonly, and while they may threaten a lot of people, the objective of terrorism is *not* mass murder. Terrorists want a lot of people watching and a lot of people listening, not a lot of people dead. A credible threat, a demonstration of the capacity to strike, may be from the terrorists' point of view often preferable to actually carrying out the threatened deed, which may explain why, apart from the technical difficulties involved, terrorists have not done some of the terribly damaging and terrifying things they could do, such as poisoning a city's water supply, spreading chemical or biological agents, or other things that could produce mass casualties.

THE PURPOSES OF TERROR

Terrorists attempt to inspire and manipulate fear to achieve a variety of purposes. Terrorism may be aimed simultaneously at several objectives: specific tactical objectives made explicit by the terrorists, and broader strategic objectives, which may be implicit in the choice of tactics or targets. First, individual acts of terrorism may be aimed at wringing specific concessions, such as the payment of ransom, the release of prisoners, or the publication of a terrorist message, under threat of death or destruction. Terrorists may seek to improve their bargaining power by creating a dramatic hostage situation to coerce a government into fulfilling certain demands.

Second, terrorism may also be aimed at gaining publicity. Through terrorism, the terrorists hope to attract attention to their cause and project themselves as a force that merits recognition and that must be reckoned with. The publicity gained by frightening acts of violence and the atmosphere of fear and alarm created cause people to exaggerate the importance and strength of the terrorists and their movement. Since most terrorist groups are actually small and weak, their violence must be all the more dramatic and deliberately shocking.

Terrorist attacks are often carefully choreographed to attract the attention of the electronic media and the international press. Taking and holding hostages increases the drama. If certain demands are not satisfied, the hostages may be killed. The hostages as individuals often mean nothing to the terrorists. Terrorism is aimed at the people watching, not at the actual victims. Terrorism is theatre.

To illustrate this point, let me use an example that we have recently become familiar with in the United States—the Symbionese Liberation Army (SLA). There seem to be two SLAs. One of them appeared on television or in the newspapers almost daily. Everyone has seen the seven-headed cobra symbol; thousands have listened to SLA tapes. An enormous number of police and FBI agents were mobilized trying to find it. It excited and entertained, if not terrified, the people of California. Then there is the other SLA—the *real* SLA. It once had a dozen or so members, now perhaps three. It has to its credit one murder, one kidnapping, a food distribution financed by and extorted from the family of the hostage, one bank job, and a few stolen cars—hardly a crime wave. The difference between the two SLAs is the difference between the actual amount of violence and the greatly amplified effects of that violence.

There are other examples in which terrorism has been used to magnify the importance of the cause and the stature of the group. Insurgents fought in Angola, Mozambique, and Portuguese Guinea for 14 years using the standard tactics of rural guerrilla warfare. The world hardly noticed their struggle, while an approximately equal number of Palestinian commandos employing terrorist tactics have in a few years become a primary concern to the world.

Third, terrorism may be aimed at causing widespread disorder, demoralizing society, and breaking down the social order. This objective is typical of revolutionary, nihilistic, or anarchistic terrorists. Impatient at the reluctance of the 'people'—on whose behalf the revolution is to be carried out—to join them, terrorists may condemn society's normal rules and relationships as intolerable complacency. If the benefits of political obedience are destroyed, if the complacency of uninvolvement is not allowed, if the government's ability to protect its citizens (which is after all the origin and most basic reason for the existence of government) is demonstrated to be ineffectual, if the government can be made to strike back brutally but blindly, and if there is no place to hide in the ensuing battle, then, it is presumed, the 'people' will join the opponents of that government and a revolution will be carried out. Such a strategy often backfires. With no immunity from random terrorist violence, even sympathizers may turn against the terrorist violence, even sympathizers may turn against the terrorists and support the government's moves to destroy them.

Fourth, terrorism may be aimed at deliberately provoking repression, reprisals, and counter-terrorism, which may ultimately lead to the collapse of an unpopular government. In the past such terrorism has frequently been directed against government security and law enforcement personnel, but there are also examples of deliberately outrageous acts, the kidnapping of a foreign diplomat, for example, or random violence against civilians designed to embarrass a government and compel it to react with a heavy hand. The government may thus be induced by the terrorists to self-destruct.

Fifth, terrorism may also be used to enforce obedience and co-operation. This is the usual purpose of state or official terrorism, or what is frequently called 'institutional violence', but terrorists themselves may also employ institutional violence against their own members to ensure their loyalty. The outcome desired by the terrorists in this case is a prescribed pattern of behaviour: obedience to the state or to the cause, and full co-operation in identifying and rooting out infiltrators or enemies. The success of such terrorism again depends on the creation of an atmosphere of fear, reinforced by the seeming omnipresence of the internal security apparatus. As in other forms of terrorism, terrorism which is aimed at enforcing obedience contains elements of deliberate drama: defectors are abducted or mysteriously assassinated, dissidents are arrested at midnight, people disappear, and stories (often real) spread of dungeons, concentration camps, and torture. And, as in other forms of terrorism, the objective is the effect all this has on the target audience. However, enforcement terrorism seldom chooses victims at random and does not seek widespread publicity, especially at the international level.

Sixth, terrorism is frequently meant to punish. Terrorists often declare that the victim of their attack, whether person or object, is somehow guilty, or is the symbol of something the terrorists consider guilty. A person may be judged guilty because he has committed some`crime himself—actively opposed, disobeyed, or informed upon the terrorists—or because he has tacitly co-operated with a guilty party. 'Co-operated' is often interpreted rather broadly to mean that the individual worked for, tacitly supported, accepted a visa from, or travelled on the national carrier of an enemy government. Victims of terrorists also have been chosen because their success in business or their lifestyle represented a system despised by the terrorists. Objects or buildings have been destroyed because they were symbols of a despised government, institution, or system.

There is, in terrorism, a stronger connotation of guilt and punishment than in other forms of warfare or politics, and a narrower definition of 'innocent' bystanders. To terrorists, there are few innocent bystanders. Even the victims of the Lod Airport massacre in 1972, many of whom happened to be Christian pilgrims from Puerto Rico, were said by the organization responsible for the attack to be 'guilty' because they had arrived in Israel on Israeli visas and thereby had tacitly recognized the state that was the declared enemy of the Palestinians, and because by coming to Israel they had in effect entered a war zone. The Popular Front for the Liberation of Palestine, which was responsible for the attack, was not saying the victims were innocent bystanders unfortunately caught in a crossfire; neither was it saying that it would seek and kill all those holding visas from the State of Israel. The organization *was* saying that those who happened to get shot—simply because they happened to be there at the wrong moment—were nevertheless guilty or they would not have been shot. In other words, they did not become victims because they were enemies, but rather they became enemies because they happened to be victims.

It is through the assignment of guilt, and the often matching claim of the administration of justice that the terrorists not only rationalize their acts of violence but also seek to establish their moral superiority. Most political terrorists are imbued with a strong sense of moral outrage and an absolute conviction in the righteousness of their cause. By their acts, terrorists attempt to arouse the same sense of moral outrage which may be latent in the minds of the target audience, while at the same time reinforcing their own moral convictions.

INTERNATIONAL TERRORISM AND ITS EFFECTS

The simplest definition of international terrorism comprises terrorist acts with clear international consequences: in which terrorists go abroad

to strike their targets, select victims or targets because of their connections
to a foreign state (diplomats, local executives or officers of foreign corporations), attack airliners on international flights, or force airliners to fly to another country. International terrorism would not include the local activities of dissident groups when carried out against a local government or citizens in their own country if no foreign connection is involved.

International terrorism may also be defined as acts of violence or campaigns of violence waged outside the accepted rules and procedures of international diplomacy and war. Breaking the rules may include attacking diplomats and other internationally protected persons, attacking international travel and commerce, or exporting violence by various means to nations that normally would not, under the traditional rules, be considered participants in the local conflict.

International terrorism is a kind of warfare; as employed recently by revolutionary and other dissident groups, a new kind of warfare. It is warfare without territory, waged without armies as we know them. It is warfare that is not limited territorially; sporadic 'battles' may take place worldwide. It is warfare without neutrals, and with few or no civilian innocent bystanders.

The actual amount of violence caused by international terrorism has been greatly exaggerated. Compared with the world volume of violence or with national crime rates, the toll has been small. There were 507 incidents of international terrorism from January 1968 to April 1974.[1] These are incidents of *international* terrorism—that is where terrorists have attacked foreign officials, or have gone abroad to strike their targets, or have hijacked international airliners. The actions of the Irish Republican Army (IRA) in Northern Ireland or those of the National Liberation Movement (Tupamaros) in Uruguay are not counted in that figure. Those are local struggles. But the actions of the IRA in London are included in the above total, as are the occasions when Tupamaros kidnapped foreign diplomats. There are two other deliberate omissions: acts of terrorism associated with the war in Indochina and the numerous cross-border raids against kibbutzim or acts of terrorism in the Israeli-occupied territories, except for the major episodes, have not been included. These are still a part of local struggles and do not directly affect other nations. All truly international incidents of terrorism associated with the struggle in the Middle East are included, such as the killing of the Israeli athletes in Munich, the seizure of the Saudi Arabian embassies in Khartoum and Paris, and the killing of Palestinian leaders in Beirut and of suspected Arab terrorists in Europe by Israeli commando teams or agents. In all, since 1968, 520 people were killed, counting terrorists; 830 were wounded or injured.

This total is not large. It is less than the homicide rate of any major American city: there are more than 18,000 criminal homicides a year in the United States. It is small compared with the casualties of any war; and it is perhaps significant that during periods when there are wars (such as the most recent one in the Middle East), incidents of terrorism elsewhere are not reported. Perhaps only in times of relative peace in the world can world attention be attracted by lesser episodes of violence. Had any of these terrorist groups somehow acquired the means of conventional war fought within the internationally accepted rules of warfare, would the toll have been any less?

The effect produced by the small amount of actual terrorist violence is much greater. Headlines have been captured and valuable television time has been devoted to the terrorists. Terrorists have created disruption and alarm and have compelled governments to divert more of their resources to protection against terrorist attacks. Some governments have been willing to release captured terrorists if holding them is likely to make the country a target of further terrorist attacks.

The concept of using limited military means to generate international pressure was employed successfully during the anti-colonial struggles of the 1960s, when local insurgents attempted to attract international attention and embarrass the government of the colonial power. The same tactic had also been used earlier by those fighting to bring about the withdrawal of British forces and create a Jewish homeland in Israel. International attention was a prerequisite to international pressure, which could achieve what the local insurgents could not achieve militarily—induce the colonial power to withdraw. The difference between the anticolonial insurgents and today's terrorists is that during the colonial struggles the insurgents sought international attention by acts of violence in the colonies. Seldom was the metropole directly attacked. Now, terrorist violence may be exported anywhere in the world.

Recently terrorism has been used most successfully on an international scale by Palestinian guerrillas. That there is now pressure for an Israeli withdrawal and the creation of a Palestinian homeland, that the Palestinian Liberation Organization may be accorded international recognition as the government of a stateless people is owing, at least in part, to the success of Palestinian terrorists in bringing their cause violently and dramatically before the eyes of the world. Without endorsing terrorism, one must wonder what success they could have won had they operated within the established bounds of conventional warfare and polite diplomacy. At the same time, one must wonder what their success means for the future. Will it inspire groups with equal capacity for violence, but with far less claim to legitimacy, to try to extort concessions from the world merely in exchange for an end to their violence?

What has been demonstrated is that small groups with a limited capacity for violence can capture headlines, can cause alarm, and can compel governments temporarily to abandon their law enforcement function. To terrorists and to potential terrorists that makes terrorism a success.

Campaigns of terrorism or specific incidents of terrorism directed against targets in the foreign diplomatic or business community have no doubt embarrassed several governments, weakened some of them, and perhaps contributed to the downfall of a few. But where national governments did fall, were forced to step down, or grant greater authority to the military, as in Turkey, Argentina, and Uruguay, other factors were also present, such as grave economic problems, rampant inflation, widespread unemployment, or deep-rooted political struggles. No governments have fallen solely because of the activities of domestic or foreign terrorists.

Terrorism has exacerbated several local conflicts, expanding them beyond the locality involved, and has prolonged conflicts, making settlements more difficult. This is particularly true in the Middle East and Northern Ireland, but both conflicts are deep-rooted and would have been difficult to solve anyway.

In sum, terrorist violence has been greatly exaggerated, enabling the terrorists to gain publicity and some concessions. But, while raising some issues that still remain unresolved, terrorist violence cannot be said to have had as yet a major impact on the international order.

A FEEBLE RESPONSE

The international response to the threat posed by international terrorism thus far has been feeble. There has been only limited international co-operation against terrorists. Some nations directly or indirectly support with money, with weapons, and with training organizations that carry on terrorist activities. Nations continue to provide asylum to known perpetrators of terrorist acts, often giving them heroes' welcomes and even pensions. Many nations, which, while disapproving of terrorist tactics in principle, are unwilling to grant asylum themselves, are reluctant publicly to condemn acts of terrorism, or to condemn countries giving terrorists aid and asylum on grounds that such condemnations might offend other nations with which friendly relations are paramount. This is particularly true in the demonstrated reluctance of certain Western European nations to condemn Palestinian terrorists or their supporters.

There are many reasons to explain the lack of international co-operation. Few nations can agree on what international terrorism is; and, since for reasons of ideology or politics—not all nations are threatened equally by the current wave of international terrorism, defining it, outlawing it and carrying out countermeasures against terrorists tend to be matters of politics rather than issues of law. Furthermore, the overall effect of international terrorism, apart from the occasional publicity gained by terrorists, has been negligible. Most nations have more important problems to worry about than terrorists, especially someone else's terrorists. If lives can be saved and temporary tranquillity purchased by releasing a few prisoners, it does not seem unreasonable to do so, despite the offence thereby done to the law. Finally, it is difficult to enforce any sanctions against terrorist groups operating abroad and headquartered on foreign territory.

International law and the rules of warfare as they now exist are inadequate to cope with this new mode of conflict. The rules governing conflict were designed to deal with warfare between states. Conflict outside the 'system' poses a number of problems. First, the rules of war are consensual. The only means of enforcement are the moral force of international condemnation and the threat of retaliation in kind, a genuine constraint because the adversaries are normally roughly equal in vulnerability. Terrorist groups are not vulnerable as nations are. They have no security responsibilities to any civilian population, and therefore they are less vulnerable to retaliation. On the other hand, when a government decides to take direct military action against a terrorist group abroad it may be judged guilty of aggression, and it will bear the burden of any international condemnations or sanctions that result from the sanctions. The established system of diplomacy and the rules of war tend to be asymmetrical here. A state is at a disadvantage, not because it breaks the rules—so do the terrorists—but simply because it is a state.

Lacking international co-operation, nations have been compelled to deal with terrorism on their own. Some nations, such as the United States, have attempted to confront the challenge by increasing security against attacks by terrorists at home and abroad and urging greater international co-operation against terrorism. The latter effort has achieved only limited success. Other nations, while bolstering their security measures, have attempted to establish a live-and-let-live relationship with foreign terrorists operating on their territory, acceding to terrorist demands when necessary and avoiding crackdowns that could provoke retaliation. A few nations, notably Israel, have chosen direct action against the terrorists, retaliating for terrorist attacks with direct military action or the assassination of key terrorist leaders. If terrorism continues to be a problem and the international response continues to be feeble, we may see more of this type of response.

POSSIBLE TRENDS

What direction will terrorism take in the future? A number of terrorist groups share similar ideologies and are also willing to co-operate. Alliances have been concluded between terrorist groups, such as that between the Popular Front for the Liberation of Palestine and the United Red Army of Japan. It was Japanese terrorists from the Red Army who were brought in by the Palestinians to machine-gun passengers at the Lod Airport in Israel two years ago. It has also been reported that the Irish Republican Army has developed close relations with members of the Basque Homeland and Liberty Movement (ETA), a Basque separatist group in Spain. And recently four urban guerrilla groups in South America—the Revolutionary Left Movement (MIR) of Chile, the People's Revolutionary Army (ERP) of Argentina, the National Liberation Army (ELN) of Bolivia, and the Tupamaros of Uruguay—have created a 'junta for revolutionary co-ordination' in order to 'internationalize' their armed struggle. The better-trained, better-financed, and better-equipped guerrilla and terrorist groups are providing some military assistance and technical advice to less developed groups. Groups in one part of the world have shown themselves capable of recruiting confederates in other parts.

The growing links between terrorist groups are extremely important. They provide small terrorist organizations with the resources to undertake far more serious operations than they would be capable of otherwise. They make identification more difficult, since local citizens can be used to carry out attacks; and they could ultimately produce some kind of worldwide terrorist movement directed against some group of countries for vague ideological, political, or economic reasons, a concept that has been referred to by some terrorists as 'simultaneous revolution'.

A second possible trend is in the direction of more extravagant and destructive acts made possible by he creation of new vulnerabilities and new weapons, and made necessary as the public and governments become bored with what the terrorists do now. There are many new vulnerabilities. One that has received a great deal of public attention lately is nuclear power. The probable proliferation of nuclear power facilities in the next few decades, and the amount of traffic in fissionable material and radioactive waste material that will accompany this, raises a number of new possibilities for political extortion and mass hostage situations on a scale that we have not yet seen.

At the same time, technological advances are creating a new range of small, portable, cheap, relatively easy to operate, highly accurate, and highly destuctive weapons which, if produced on a large scale, will undoubtedly find their way into the hands of terrorists. Indeed, some of them already have—such as the Soviet-manufactured SA-7. The SA-7 and its American counterpart, *Redeye,* are already obsolete. Within the decade a new range of small, inexpensive weapons employing precision-guided munitions will be in mass production. What will be the consequences of these weapons? What will happen when the 'Saturday Night Special' is not a revolver but perhaps a hand-held, laser-guided missile? Such weapons will provide terrorists with new capabilities and suggest new targets.

On the other hand, terrorist violence may be self-limiting in the sense that terrorists depend to a degree on the support of some constituency or the toleration of at least some governments. Too much violence could provoke harsh reactions and greater international co-operation against the terrorists.

A third possible trend is that national governments will recognize the achievements of terrorist groups and begin to employ them or their tactics as a means of surrogate warfare against other nations. Modern conventional warfare is becoming increasingly impractical. It is too destructive. It is too expensive Few nations can afford it.

The alternative to modern conventional war is low-level protracted war, debilitating military contests in which staying power is more important than firepower, and military victory loses its traditional meaning as strategists debate whether not winning means losing or not losing means winning. These protracted wars seldom end, at least in any clear-cut fashion, though the level of fighting peaks and declines, often seasonally. War and postwar lose their traditional meanings. No nation or insurgent group can afford to mobilize all of its resources to fight for two generations.

Terrorists, whatever their origin or cause, have demonstrated the possibilities of a third alternative—that of 'surrogate warfare'. Terrorism, though now rejected as a legitimate mode of warfare by most conventional military establishments, could become an accepted form of warfare in the future. Terrorists could be employed to provoke international incidents, create alarm in an adversary's country, compel it to divert valuable resources to protect itself, destroy its morale, and carry out specific acts of sabotage. Governments could employ existing terrorist groups to attack their opponents, or they could create their own terrorists. Terrorism requires only a small investment, certainly far less than it costs to wage conventional war. It can be debilitating to the enemy. (Prior to the 1973 Yom Kippur war, a senior Israeli officer estimated that the total cost in men and money to Israel for all defensive and offensive measures against at most a few thousand Arab terrorists was 40 times that of the six-day war in 1967.) A secret backer of the terrorists can also deny sponsoring them. The concepts of subversion, sabotage, of lightning raids carried out by commandos, are not new, but the opportunities are.

How might terrorists be used in offensive surrogate warfare? Suppose a target nation has part of its strategic forces deployed overseas, including missile sites in another country. Perhaps there already has been some local opposition to the presence of these weapons. And perhaps also there are one or two extremist groups which have carried out relatvely minor acts of violence. The groups have some international links but they lack the resources for any major undertaking. It is conceivable that through their links with foreign power local terrorists could be provided with the intelligence and some of the equipment necessary to launch an attack on one of the sites. Shortly before a bilateral treaty allowing the use of the sites is to be renewed, the terrorists attack, but, of course, fail. They penetrate the perimeter, but little damage is done to the missiles. Local newspapers, however, receive an anonymous tip that some lethal radioactive material has been released as a result of the attack. Indeed, checks with primitive geiger counters show some presence of radioactivity. The country whose missiles they are claims that no radioactive material escaped, and that probably the terrorists themselves deliberately spread a small quantity of radioactive waste material to alarm the population; there is said to be no danger; the denial is not convincing. Meanwhile, the terrorists warn of further attacks. Demonstrations against renewal of the arrangement by which the weapons are there in the first place begin and grow, aided perhaps by the fact that, owing to tightened security, all locally hired employees of the country with the missiles have been temporarily laid off. The local government is shaken by the episode. There are further terrorist incidents. Relations between the two countries are strained. The owner of the missiles is finally asked to remove them.

We are reaching the point of industrialization and population growth when the technical interdependencies of modern society—food on fertilizer on energy on fuel on transportation on communications—are so great and the margins of surplus so slim that a minor disruption in any single area can have tremendous cascading effects on nearly everything else. As a result, the vulnerabilities to disruption have increased. And, as mentioned previously, so have the capacities for violence. Under such conditions, with a little help from their friends, any group of terrorists could ascend to the level of a genuine non-military threat to the national security of any advanced country.

The consequences of international terrorism may go far beyond anything yet accomplished or contemplated by the terrorists themselves, militarily or politically. The developments that have made international terrorism feasible could in the future have a profound effect on the world. We are approaching an age in which national governments may no longer monopolize the instruments of major destruction. The instruments of warfare once possessed only by armies will be available to gangs. It will not be possible to satisfy the real or imagined grievances of all the little groups that will be capable of large-scale disruption and destruction or to defend everyone against them. The few examples of international terrorism that have occurred thus far are the harbingers of this new era. How will the world be affected by this development? If the nature of warfare changes radically because of technical developments, then the concept of security, and of military power, and possibly the concept of government itself may also change.

NOTES & REFERENCES

[1] For a complete chronology of incidents of international terrorism, see Brian Jenkins and Janera Johnson, *International Terrorism: A Chronology 1968—1974.* R-1597-DOS/ARPA. Santa Monica: RAND Corporation, forthcoming.

Terrorist attacks carried out in Europe with stolen American M-26 grenades provide direct evidence of close cooperation between several terrorist groups. In the first article, Anable retraces the trail of stolen grenades to illustrate how this terrorist network functions. The second article examines the key role of several radical governments in the training, financing, and equipping of international terrorists.

Terrorism: Loose Net Links
Diverse Groups; No Central Plot

by DAVID ANABLE

Dec. 20, 1973. In the chilly predawn, agents of the DST, France's security service, burst into a villa in a suburb of Paris and arrest 10 members of the Turkish Peoples Liberation Army (TPLA). Among weapons found: American M-26 grenades.

Sept. 13, 1974. Three Japanese terrorists storm into the French Embassy in The Hague, seize 11 hostages, and demand that France release a Japanese Red Army (JRA) courier arrested at Paris's Orly Airport two months earlier. Four tense days later all four JRA members are flown 'to Damascus, Syria. They leave behind: M-26 grenades.

Sept. 15, 1974. An explosion tears through a crowd in "Le Drugstore," a Jewish-owned complex of shops on the Left Bank in Paris. Two people are killed, more than 30 injured. The weapon: an M-26 grenade.

June 17, 1975. Three DST officers with a Lebanese informer enter a Paris apartment on the Rue Toullier to arrest Venezuelan-born Ilich Ramírez Sánchez, better known today by his pseudonym, Carlos Martinez. But Carlos shoots his way out, killing the informer, two DST agents, and gravely wounding the third. Left behind by Carlos in Paris and London: M-26 grenades.

The trail of the M-26 grenades is only one of many indicators of a growing international web of terrorist cooperation. Western intelligence experts see it not so much as an all-embracing conspiracy with a single sinister figure or national lurking at its center. Rather, they view it as a series of interconnecting supply lines of funds, documents, and weapons that feed a great variety of terrorist or "liberation" causes. Perhaps most significant of all is a noticeable trend toward joint operations.

Such linkages provide an infusion of vital supplies, a boost for terrorist morale, and a greater ability to evade or penetrate purely national defenses. They are an ominously spreading part of what is becoming known as "transnational terrorism." In the words of a research study on terrorism drawn up last year by the United States Central Intelligence Agency (CIA):

> "The trend toward greater international contact and cooperation among terrorist groups that has already markedly enhanced the operational capabilities of some of the organizations involved seems likely to gain further momentum."

LOD AIRPORT RAID

An early example of such cooperation was the 1972 attack by three members of the Japanese Red Army on Israel's Lod Airport in which 26 people were killed. The Japanese fanatics had been trained at a camp in Lebanon run by one of the extreme groups that reject compromise with Israel—the Popular Front for the Liberation of Palestine (PFLP). They got Czechoslovak weapons in Rome, picked up false papers in Frankfurt, West Germany, and descended on Israel in a French plane in the guise of innocent Japanese tourists.

Since then, the inter-group links have become more pervasive. And, under the guidance of Carlos and his immediate boss, Waddieh Haddad, the PFLP has been the most skillful in forging and using these ties.

It was Carlos, for instance, who got hold of a batch of those M-26 grenades stolen by members of the Baader-Meinhof gang from a U.S. Army base in West Germany. He appears to have doled them out as occasion demanded to Turkish, Palestinian, and Japanese terrorists. At the same time, he was carefully assembling his own international network which continues to operate long after his narrow and violent escape from the Rue Toullier.

It was this Carlos-Haddad network that under Carlos's personal command kidnapped astounded oil ministers from the Vienna meeting of OPEC (Organization of Petroleum Exporting Countries) in December, 1975. The same network carried out the hijack of the Air France jetliner to Entebbe, Uganda, last year. Then, last August in retaliation for the Israeli rescue of the Entebbe hostages, members of the same group blew up a transit lounge in the Istambul airport, killing four people who were waiting for an El Al plane (including an aide to Sen. Jacob Javits (R) of New York).

Waddieh Haddad now is thought to be based in Baghdad, Iraq—reportedly seeking safety from a "contract" put out for his life by a more

WASHINGTON SEIZURES: NOT 'INTERNATIONAL TERRORISM'

The dramatic hostage seizures in Washington, D.C., March 9 [1977] rivetted international attention on the nation's capital. And the terrorists' surrender March 11 was helped by mediation of the Pakistani, Egyptian, and Iranian ambassadors.

But the incident was not an example of the international or transnational terrorism which has caused growing anxiety among Western security forces in recent years, because the Hanafi Muslims, who allegedly took 100 persons hostage in a 38-hour siege, were not linked to any other known terrorist group.

Transnational terrorism refers to operations across national borders by terrorist groups basically independent of any government. Such terrorists may have the backing of certain states, but for logistical or propaganda reasons they are taking their cause beyond the boundaries of their own country or hoped-for homeland.

A distinction also needs to be made between terrorism and guerrilla warfare.

Webster defines terrorism as "the systematic use of terror especially as a means of coercion." It is usually associated with extreme callousness and cruelty toward innocent victims, often using them for political blackmail. It is the staged violence of the weak designed to attract maximum attention to a cause.

Guerrilla warfare sometimes resorts to terrorism. But it is usually associated with more "legitimate" struggle against some form of repression.—D.A.

moderate guerrilla group. Carlos, together with his faithful retainer, Hans Joachim Klein, visited Haddad last fall. Carlos and Klein, a West German anarchist who was almost fatally wounded in the OPEC raid, traveled from Libya via Algiers and Belgrade to Baghdad, Both were back "at home" in Libya by year's end.

Such travels make Western security men edgy. They have to be constantly braced for new spectaculars. Nor do they lightly dismiss Carlos's boast that he controls some 40 seasoned professionals. "Violence," Carlos has said, "is the only language the Western democracies understand.

But the PFLP is far from being the only example of the terrorists' international skein. The linkages vary from innumerable shadowy gatherings of terrorist, leftist, rightist, and nationalist clans to a system of essential supplies that the CIA study describes as a "European-based terrorist 'service industy.' "

One Europe-wide meeting in 1974, for instance, brought together in Trieste a score of separatist and terrorist emissaries, a motley crew of militant Basques and Irish, Croats and Bretons, Welsh and Catalans, and many others.

On the other side of the Atlantic a gathering in Buenos Aires the same year saw four Latin-American underground groups from Chile, Bolivia, Uruguay, and Argentina set up a "junta for revolutionary coordination." A follow-up meeting in Lisbon a year later cemented the pact and brought in Paraguayans, Dominicans, Colombians, and Venezuelans.

Meanwhile, money has flowed between revolutionaries and terrorists in extraordinary volume. Argentina's groups, for instance, have collected well over $200 million over the past three years, mainly from ransoms for kidnapped local and foreign businessmen. Some of the cash has spilled from the overflowing coffers into other revolutionary groups. More than $2 million has been traced to Europe, spent by leftists who fled Chile after the fall of Salvador Allende Gossens in 1973.

LIBYA, IRAQ BACKING

The extreme Palestinian groups, including Carlos and the PFLP, have liberal backing from Libya and Iraq.

The factions of the Irish Republican Army have different arrangements. The Marxist "official" IRA reaches out to Eastern Europe. The supernationalist "provisionals" supplement their local sources of funds (bank robberies, rackets, and extortion) with dollar-raising in, and arms smuggling from, the U.S. And, on the other extreme, Northern Ireland's Protestant "loyalists" seek support and weaponry from Canada.

Training, too, has become international in scope. During the 1970s the Palestinians' camps in the Mideast have seen as disparate a bunch of trainees as can be imagined. Black Panthers and Weathermen from the U.S. once struggled over the assault courses. So have West Germans, Irishmen, Latin Americans, Scandinavians, Italians, Turks, Iranians, Eritreans, and many others.

When Lebanese Christians finally smashed their way into the Palestinians' Tel Zatar camp last July, among those surrendering was a member of the Japanese Red Army.

It is a moot point as to how many of these trainees have ended up as guerrilla fighters or terrorists. Certainly many have—from the three Japanese who seized the French Embassy in The Hague in 1974, to the two members of the Dutch "Red Help" group arrested last year while reconnoitering Tel Aviv and Bombay for a planned hijack of an Air France flight from Bombay to Israel to Paris.

TRAINING IN SOUTH YEMEN

These Japanese and Dutchmen were trained in the PFLP's camp in South Yemen. And it is the PFLP that the Iranian Government accuses of providing Iranian revolutionaries with training and arms.

The IRA provisionals, although one of the most active groups in the world (more than 5,000 bombings and 25,000 shooting incidents since 1969), have not set up a network like the PFLP's. But the "provos" have forged loose links with other groups, notably the Basque separatist "ETA." They are said to exchange tips with ETA members on obtaining and using weapons and explosives. In 1975 Belgian police cracked an arms-smuggling ring that had supplied guns and bomb materials to both the IRA and ETA as well as to the Palestinians.

One of the dangers of a spreading supply network is that dissident nationalists or terrorists could more easily be able to obtain sophisticated equipment. Rocket-launchers, for example, have been used on a number of occasions by the PFLP in attacks on airliners at Orly Airport (using American rockets stolen from U.S. bases in West Germany) and by the IRA against British military outposts (using Soviet equipment, probably a gift from Libya's Col. Muammar al-Qaddafi).

Still more ominous has been the appearance of the Soviet-built heat-seeking missile, the SA-7 or "Strela." This portable weapon is capable of hitting aircraft at ranges of up to several miles. In its first attempted use PFLP members were arrested in possession of Strelas near the Rome airport in 1973.

In January last year another Strela attempt was planned, this time on an El Al airliner coming in to land at Nairobi, Kenya. Three PFLP terrorists (two of whom had been involved in one of the Orly Airport rocket attacks a year earlier) were arrested at the Nairobi airport perimeter fence just as they prepared to fire the missiles.

Although the potential clearly exists for such weapons (and even more devastating ones) to circulate on a terrorist supply network, in both these cases they are thought to have come from Arab governments—probably via Libya and, in the Nairobi incident and thereafter, via Uganda's President Idi Amin.

But when it comes to phony documents there is ample evidence of a central supply system. Often during the '70s examination of captured terrorists' papers, such as passports, visas, and driving licenses, has indicated a single source. The Israelis refer to what they call a "sophisticated workshop" which they charge is run by the PFLP

Palestinians, West Germans, Japanese, and even Carlos all have traveled on these papers. The Japanese-Palestinian quartet that attacked a Shell Oil refinery in Singapore in 1974 carried a selection. So did the Japanese pair who were caught photographing embassy buildings in Stockholm shortly before six West German terrorists attacked their country's embassy there in 1975 and unsuccessfully demanded the release of Andreas Baader, Ulrike Meinhof, and 21 other West German anarchists.

Most recently, when the Baader-Meinhof gang's weapons specialist, Rolf Pohle, was arrested in Athens last July, he was using papers from the same nest of forgers. To complete the circle, it was probably Pohle who first organized the Baader-Meinhof raids on U.S. Army bases in West Germany that netted the much-spread-around consignment of M-26 grenades.

And it was the Greeks who were among the most edgy when Carlos suddenly turned up in neighboring Yugoslavia en route to Baghdad last September. They were anxious lest Carlos try to spring Pohle from his Greek cell. However, Carlos moved on; and Pohle was extradited back to jail in West Germany . . . 20 months after he and four companions had been released to South Yemen in exchange for kidnapped West Berlin politician Peter Lorenz.

Western officials tend to play down the extent of the terrorist network. "There is no central conspiracy, no central body of terrorists operating worldwide," says one American official. "Rather there is a loose-fitting collection of groups, coalescing, splintering, reforming in certain areas and at certain times."

Clearly, too, the terrorists themselves are keen to emphasize their links with each other so as to add propaganda impact to their violence. Hence it is necessary to avoid any exaggeration of their capabilities. Says one leading antiterrorist expert, Hans Josef Horchem, chief of the Office for the Protection of the Constitution in Hamburg:

> "Terrorism is overestimated in its threat to society, to democracy . . .
> More people are killed by dog bite in the world than by terrorism."

Such experts go on to point out that the number of terrorist incidents has declined over the past couple of years, perhaps partly because of the Palestinians' preoccupation with the Lebanese civil war. Also, they add, while most of these groups in the long run have little in common and frequently are split by raging internal feuds, the cooperation among Western security services has increased.

But it is equally clear that contacts, cooperation, and joint operations among terrorist groups are becoming more common, providing them with new opportunities to exploit the weaknesses of free societies. Meanwhile, say Western officials, reports are continuously coming in of new terrorist operations being planned. In the words of the CIA study:

> "All told, transnational terrorism promises to pose a continuing and potentially gravely unsettling problem for the world community until such time—possibly years hence—that the international system gets into new and generally accepted contours."

Terrorism: How a Handful of Radical States Keeps It in Business

A few miles along the coast from Libya's capital, Tripoli, a modest "hotel" looks out over the blue Mediterranean. It and other Libyan villas like it have seen a curious variety of nonpaying "guests."

Arch-terrorist Ilich Ramirez Sánchez, better known as Carlos Martinez or just plain "Carlos," has stretched out there luxuriously with his Palestinian friends. He probably is there right now. The five members of the Japanese Red Army (JRA) who attacked the American Consulate in Kuala Lumpur, Malaysia, in 1975 later did their jerky calisthenics on one of the villa's roofs—together with five JRA colleagues they had forced the Japanese Government to release.

West German anarchist Hans Joachim Klein, after treatment in a Libyan hospital for wounds received in December, 1975, during the Carlos-led kidnapping of the OPEC (Organization of Petroleum Exporting Countries) oil ministers from Vienna, convalesced along the same sunny coastline. Wilfred Base, another of Carlos's associates, knew it well before he was killed by Israeli commandos rescuing hostages he had helped hijack to Uganda.

The Abu Ali Iyad training camp spreads over several square miles of central Iraq. Equipped with its own small arms factory, the camp is filled with Palestinians and others puffing and panting through various stages of guerrilla and terrorist training under the expert guidance of al-Fatah defector Abu Nidal.

During the past six months terrorists have fanned out from there to attack targets in more moderate Arab states such as Jordan and Syria. They call their Iraqui-backed group "Black June"—in memory of Syria's massive thrust into Lebanon during that month last year.

Libya, Iraq, and a handful of other radical states fuel the flames of terrorism. They are the sanctuaries and supply bases, the training grounds and arsenals, the bankers and morale boosters of the terrorist cause. Without them the task of transnational terrorists such as Carlos would be far more difficult and dangerous.

SOVIETS IN BACKGROUND

But by far the largest of the world's "subversive centers," says Brian Crosier, director of the London-based Institute for the Study of Conflict, is the Soviet Union. The Russians, however, prefer to keep well in the background. They have no desire to have their carefully cultivated image of respectability tarnished by an association with terrorism. They are well aware, too, that they have a huge potential problem of their own with dissident nationalists.

In Mr. Crosier's analysis, outlined before the now-defunct Senate subcommittee on international security, there are two streams of Soviet subversion.

The first is through the training and indoctrination of orthodox Communists from around the world. They are processed, says Mr. Crosier, through the Lenin Institute in Moscow, where they are given, among other things, courses in guerrilla warfare, sabotage, explosives, and sharpshooting.

The second stream draws on national liberationists from the developing world. These are processed through the Patrice Lumumba Friendship University in Moscow, where students from around the globe are

A CHRONOLOGY

1970	September	Mideast: Popular Front for the Liberation of Palestine (PFLP) tries to hijack five airliners in one week: An attempt on El Al is foiled; Pan Am plane is flown to Cairo and blown up; Swissair, TWA, BOAC jets hijacked to Dawson's Field, Jordan, and blown up.
	September	Jordan: Army crushes Palestinian guerrillas.
1972	May	Three members of Japanese Red Army (JRA) kill 25 at Lod Airport.
	September	Munich: 11 Israeli athletes are killed when Black September Organization (BSO) attacks Olympic quarters. Weapons allegedly brought in by Libyan diplomatic pouch
	October	Munich: Lufthansa airliner hijacked, forcing release of three BSO survivors of Olympic attack; terrorists all flown to Libya.
1973	March	Khartoum: BSO seizes Saudi Embassy, executes a Belgian and two U.S. diplomats. Terrorists later reported moved to Libya.
	July	Amsterdam: JRA and four Palestinians hijack Japan Air Lines 747 to Libya, where it is blown up.
	August	Athens: Two Arabs attack passengers, killing three, wounding 55.
	September	Rome: Police arrest five Palestinians with Libyan-supplied SA-7 missiles near airport; three are later flown to Libya.
	September	Austria: Two Palestinians kidnap three Russian Jews, forcing Austrians to close Schonau Transit Camp; the Palestinians are later flown to Libya.
	October	Mideast: Arab-Israeli war.
	December	Rome: Libyan-sponsored group attacks U.S. and German planes, killing 32 people.
	December	London: PFLP (probably Carlos) nearly kills Joseph E. Sieff, leading British Zionist.
1974	January	Singapore: Two Japanese plus two PFLP attack Shell refinery, seize hostages.
	February	Kuwait: Five PFLP storm Japanese Embassy, seize hostages; Singapore and Kuwait terrorists flown to South Yemen.
	July	Paris: JRA courier arrested with forged documents.
	September	The Hague: Three JRA (with PFLP aid) seize French Embassy; all three, plus courier, flown to Syria.

enrolled in a wide variety of straightforward academic studies. But the tall monolith of a building is also the recruiting ground for potential guerrillas and terrorists who are extracted and trained in Tashkent and other parts of the Soviet Union.

For instance, in 1975 Dutch police arrested four armed Syrians shortly before they could attempt to carry out their plan to kidnap Russian Jews aboard a train traveling from Moscow through the Netherlands. Under questioning the four, thought to have been Lumumba University students, admitted they had been trained in weaponry, explosives, and propaganda at a small town near Moscow.

Carlos himself, son of a wealthy, life-long Venezuelan Communist,

	September	Paris: PFLP (probably Carlos) kills two, wounds 34, with hand grenade outside Le Drugstore.
1975	*January*	Paris: PFLP carries out two attacks on aircraft at Orly Airport; first group escapes, second seizes hostages and is flown to Iraq.
	February	West Berlin: Politician Peter Lorenz is kidnapped; five West German terrorists flown to South Yemen in exchange for his release.
	April	Stockholm: Six West Germans attack their embassy, which is blown up when demands denied.
	June	Paris: Carlos escapes French agents, killing two; three Cuban diplomats expelled.
	August	Kuala Lumpur: Five JRA trained in PFLP camps in Lebanon attack U.S. Consulate, force Japan to release five other JRA; all 10 flown to Libya.
	September	The Netherlands: Four Syrians planning to kidnap Russian Jews are arrested; they had trained in Soviet Union.
	December	Vienna: Carlos, PFLP gang kidnap OPEC ministers and end up in Libya.
1976	*January*	Nairobi: Three PFLP arrested with SA-7 missiles apparently from Libya via Uganda.
	June	Lebanon: Major Syrian intervention.
	June	Entebbe: Air France jumbo jet hijacked to Uganda by PFLP group; refuels in Libya; July 4 Israelis rescue hostages, killing seven terrorists.
	August	Istanbul: Two PFLP trained in Libya attack airport lounge; four are killed, including aide to Senator Javits.
	September	Belgrade: Carlos visits Yugoslavia en route to Iraq and back to Libya.
	September	Damascus: Semiramis Hotel attacked by "Black June" group trained in and backed by Iraq.
	October	Rome and Islamabad: Syrian embassies attacked by Iraqi-backed "Black June."
	November	Amman: Intercontinental Hotel attacked by "Black June."
	December	Damascus: Attempted assassination of Syrian Foreign Minister by "Black June."
1977	*January*	Paris: Abu Daoud, accused of planning 1972 Munich Olympic massacre, arrested, then allowed to fly to Algeria.

attended Patrice Lumumba. His later expulsion from the university in 1970 is assumed by many Western officials to have been merely a cover for his subsequent activities. Carlos's background and the connection of the Soviet Secret service, the KGB, with terrorism are detailed in a new book by Colin Smith entitled "Carlos, Portrait of a Terrorist" (Holt, Rinehart & Winston).

EAST GERMAN CAMP

As a rule of thumb, Western security services assume that the KGB works through and controls the secret services of most of its East European allies.

It is inconceivable, for instance, that the KGB would know nothing of Bulgaria's role in training guerrillas and terrorists of the Turkish People's Liberation Army, not to mention the dispatching of arms to them across the Black Sea. The East Germans run a sabotage training camp near Finsterwalde and are reported to have aided West German anarchists and other terrorists with funds and documents.

Again, it is difficult to believe that the KGB was unaware of the arms deal between the provisional Irish Republican Army (IRA), an American arms dealer, and the big Czech manufacturer Omnipol. This was uncovered in 1971 when four tons of weapons were seized by the Dutch police at Schipol Airport.

It is equally hard to believe that the Czechs, and hence the KGB, were altogether ignorant of the plans of the two Palestinians who in 1973 boarded a train in Czechoslovakia, kidnapped Russian Jewish émigrés aboard on arrival in Austria, and thereby succeeded in forcing the Austrian Government to close the emigration center for Russian Jews at Schonau Castle.

The KGB also is considered in the West to have been in complete control of Cuba's secret service, the Dirección General de Intelligencia or DGI, since the late 1960s. After Carlos narrowly and violently escaped arrest by French security agents in 1975, killing two of them and an informer, the French promptly expelled three Cuban diplomats. The three were accused to being members of the Cuban DGI. Top French officials dropped heavy hints about the well-known KGB-DGI connection.

Meanwhile, the number of radical countries ready to risk their own images by opening their doors to international terrorists has been declining. Algeria, for example, has pulled back noticeably in recent years.

RADICAL NATIONS

Left in the terrorist business are a hard core of radical states, nearly all of which have close ties with Moscow. Among them: North Korea, Cuba, Iraq, Somalia, South Yemen, and Libya. (Following Egyptian President Anwar al-Sadat's ouster of his country's Soviet advisers, Libya's anti-Arab-establishment Col. Muammur al-Qaddafi has gone out of his way to woo the Russians in spite of his personal anti-communism. Libya has become a huge arsenal of Soviet weaponry, from tanks and missiles to jet fighters and even warships.)

North Korea has long been a meeting place and training center for thousands of guerrillas, liberationists, and terrorists from Japan, the Middle East, and Europe. Some of its diplomats overseas, besides engaging in narcotics smuggling (for which they have been expelled from Scandinavia and elsewhere), are thought to have helped coordinate the activities of terrorists in Europe through an agent in East Germany.

Cuba has been a well-worn guerrilla-terrorist training ground for years. Carlos is among those who gained proficiency with guns and sabotage through Cuban courses. About 300 Palestinians even now are reported to be training there.

And Cuban instructors have long been active in the Mideast camps of the Popular Front for the Liberation of Palestine (PFLP), an extreme group which rejects compromise with Israel. Carlos is associated with this group.

South Yemen once was a favorite base of Waddieh Haddad, the PFLP's operations chief and Carlos's immediate boss. The Japanese Red Army raiders both of the Shell Oil refinery in Singapore and of the Japanese Embassy in Kuwait together sought refuge in South Yemen's sprawling port of Aden. So did the five members of the Baader-Meinhof gang, including weapons specialist Rolf Pohle, freed by West Germany in exchange for the life of kidnapped West Berlin politician Peter Lorenz. The PFLP's South Yemen training camp numbers among its many graduates the Japanese Red Army members who seized the French Embassy in The Hague in 1974.

African countries such as Somalia and Uganda also play a role. Somalia, where roughly 1,500 Cubans reportedly act as military advisers in this hitherto heavily Soviet-influenced country, was Waddieh Haddad's base during the PFLP's spectacular hijacking of Air France flight 139 to Entebbe, Uganda, in June-July, 1976.

HIJACKERS WELCOME

In Uganda, several hundred Palestinians reportedly fly that country's Russian MIG jets and act as bodyguards for President Idi Amin. As for Field Marshal Amin, he welcomed personally the hijackers of the Air France jumbo jet and allowed the hijackers to be reinforced by a local contingent of Palestinians plus Carlos's Ecuadorian pal Antonio Dages Bouvier. And it was apparently Uganda that supplied three Palestinian terrorists with heat-seeking SA-7, or Strela, missiles with which to attack an El Al airliner landing at neighboring Kenya's Nairobi airport last year; the men were arrested before they could fire.

Libya, however, with its huge oil revenues and its massive stockpiles of Soviet weaponry, remains the traditional haven, armorer, and bankroller of the international terrorists. Over the years Colonel Qaddafi's Muslim and nationalist fanaticism has prompted him to aid a multitude of dissident and rebel groups. Among those profiting are groups in Eritrea, Syria, Somalia, South Yemen, Chad, Morocco, Tunisia, Thailand, the Philippines, Panama, Sardinia, and Corsica.

Libyan aid to the "Black September" organization, which carried out the Munich massacre of Israeli athletes at the 1972 Olympic games, is reported by Western sources to have totaled many millions of dollars. And some intelligence sources claim that Carlos was rewarded with between $1 million and $2 million by Colonel Qaddafi for kidnapping the OPEC ministers. The wounded Hans Joachim Klein is said to have reaped a further $100,000.

Libya's backing for the provisional IRA came dramatically to light in 1973 with the Irish Navy's capture of the Cypriot coaster Claudia. The ship's holds were stuffed with arms obtained from the Libyans through a West German arms smuggler by Joe Cahill, Belfast boss of the "provos." Cahill, who was arrested on board, is the man to whom the New York-based Irish Northern Aid Committee has dispatched hundreds of thousands of dollars raised in the United States. INAC is being sued by the U.S. Government for violations of the Foreign Agents Registration Act.

Libya is considered almost certainly the source of Soviet rocket-launchers that the IRA provos have used against police and military outposts in North Ireland. It was the source, too, for the pair of Strela missiles found, fortunately before they could be used against air traffic, in the possession of Palestinians arrested in 1973 near Rome Airport. Three of the terrorists were later flown back to a warm reception in Tripoli.

One of the most dedicated "rejectionists" (rejecting compromise with Israel), Libya has used terrorism both to undermine more moderate Arab governments and to try to wreck peace moves.

It was a Libyan-sponsored group that killed 32 people in a bloody attack on Rome Airport in December, 1973. Members of the group questioned later in Kuwait said that the original aim had been to disrupt Arab-Israeli peace talks due to start that month by assassinating U.S. Secretary of State Henry A. Kissinger on his arrival in Beirut. When this was thwarted, the terrorist, supplied with weapons shipped through a Libyan diplomatic pouch and acting on the orders of a Libyan diplomat, switched their assault to Rome.

A more bizarre affair concerned Colonel Qaddafi's reported order in 1973 (when Libya and Egypt theoretically were federated) to an Egyptian submarine commander to torpedo Britain's liner Queen Elizabeth II as it cruised toward Israel filled with Jews celebrating Israel's 25th anniversary. Egyptian President Sadat is said to have promptly countermanded that order.

Although Libya remains perhaps the most overt sanctuary for terrorists, there are signs that Colonel Qaddafi is becoming concerned about his image. Recently he persuaded Chad's rebels (whom he has supported) to let long-captive anthropologist Françoise Claustre and her husband return to France; and he has been trying to mediate in the Philippines' Muslim insurrection (which he had earlier backed).

BACK-DOOR WARFARE

Meanwhile, Iraq (another vigorous "rejectionist") has taken a more active role on the terrorist scene. "Black June" terrorists operating out of Iraq appear to be responsible for a string of recent incidents: the attempted assassination of Syrian Foreign Minister Abdel Khaddam last December in Damascus; the attack on Amman's Intercontinental Hotel a month earlier; assaults on Syrian embassies in Rome and Islamabad in October; and the attack on Damascus' Semiramis Hotel in September.

It appears that Iraq is using "Black June" terrorists for a form of surrogate, back-door warfare against more moderate Arab states. The "Black September" organization started in much the same way, initially concentrating its fury against Jordan, which had routed the Palestinian guerrillas in September, 1970, and later broadening its scope internationally, with Libyan support. At the same time, Iraq now seems to have become one of the main bases for the extreme PFLP and its terrorist master-planner Waddieh Haddad as well as for Palestinian "rejectionists" fleeing Syrian-controlled Lebanon.

A curious sidelight in Iraq's role emerged in New York a couple of months ago. Agents of the U.S. Treasury's Alcohol, Tobacco, and Firearms (ATF) division discovered the purchase through a Greek middleman of 200 fully automatic submachine guns by the Iraqi mission to the United Nations. These "Mac-10s" are small, compact, 45-caliber weapons described by weapons experts as "ideal for terrorists."

When discovered, half of the order had been delivered to the Iraqi mission. But only 70 of the 100 weapons were handed over to ATF agents last Dec. 11. Some informed sources suspect that the 30 missing Mac-10s had been smuggled out of the country in the Iraqui diplomatic pouch. Since then, Iraqi mission diplomat Alaeddin M. al-Tayyar quietly has been declared unwelcome and recalled home.

Perhaps as the world settles into some new and more stable postcolonial, post-cold-war framework, the bitter rage of would-be terrorists will ebb. Meanwhile, the effort to strengthen national defenses, to build more effective international agreements, and to shift world public opinion against terrorism faces formidable obstacles—not least the overt or more subtle opposition of a handful of states.

Stiles considers contemporary terrorism particularly threatening because of the power relationship developing between terrorists and society, and the increasing operational flexibility available to terrorists as contrasted with the fixed patterns of the nation state. Clearly expecting the terrorist to become a greater threat, he asks, "Can the state as we know it control him?" This is a question which must be answered affirmatively.

This article is reprinted from *Air University Review*, Volume XXVII, Number 5, July-August 1976.

Sovereignty and the New Violence

by DENNIS W. STILES

A look to the future: The Western democracies have become audience societies, swaying to the rhythms of communication. Terrorism is theater; it is high drama. The actors are in the audience, improvising as they see new patterns, shifting tension from one corner to another, playing tricks with the lights. The audience is not sure who is in control, or who should be.

Because man is aggressive, political structure has always been related to the ability to envelop a social group with protection. Protection in turn has depended on technologies, on the ethos in which the political structure rests, and on the alien impingements to which it is subject. Thus, in the ninth and tenth centuries in Europe, Viking raids forced or accelerated the introduction of the manorial system, with the adoption of the heavy moldboard plow allowing economic surpluses which were translated into expensive cadres of heavily armed cavalrymen exploiting the new shock potential of the stirrup and lance.[1] This new form of political organization and protection, enforced by professional knights, gradually overpowered the raiders and pirates, who "soon lost their accustomed easy superiority. Their depredations consequently slackened and soon ceased."[2]

This manorial system lay the groundwork for secular forms of power which, in turn, undermined and eventually confronted the intellectual and social umbrella of the Holy Roman Empire. The manorial system fell victim of its own local wars, and social allegiance lent itself to the greater power which could impose the wider *pax,* the state monarchies, which adopted authoritarian organization with a supreme head from Rome and professional "enforcers" from the baronies. The shadow of the castle became the shadow of the king. The sovereignty of the state

> . . . is not an expression of anything universal or perennial in political experience or philosophy; it is a reflection of a particular phase of European history in which society escaped from an age of warring barons at the price of entering upon an age of warring States.[3]

This argument is oversimplified, but there is in history a visible pattern of political adjustment, shifts in governmental architecture and mood, in response to the ascendant form of violence. Such changes were slow, painful, and complex, fed by hundreds of tributary influences. The questions of protection and the power to protect, however often power was corrupted and turned back to gnaw on its own bowels, were central. Governments do change in character when threats to life and property are perceived as intolerable. Governments adjust to fill security gaps, or other forms of government are adopted. The changes previously noted were incremental, centuries in the making. The present potential for violence and the exposure of violence are accelerating rapidly, while the ability to implement institutional change in government is snagged (not trapped) in political folklore. Change when it does come may have to be sudden and vigorous. In this dynamic context, it is the potential of terrorism that disturbs me, not only for the havoc it can wreak in advanced forms but for the institutional disruption it can evoke.

The basic techniques of the contemporary terrorist are old. Hostages, random violence, and the murder of kings appeared as often in Greek literature as they have in twentieth century news. Russian history is laced with intrigue, subversive groups, bombs, knives, and poison. In the short period from 1894 to 1914 six Western heads of state were assassinated in the name of Anarchism.[4]

The American Navy was nurtured in the heat of anger and worry over extortion, looting, and the treatment of hostages by the Barbary pirates. Stories of cruelty, slavery in stone quarries, and a generally brutal life for American prisoners spurred both the payment of tribute and the construction of ships.[5] In a treaty signed in Algiers in 1795, the United States agreed to pay a lump sum of $642,500 to Algiers, along with an annual tribute in naval stores equal to $21,600, for release of the American captives held.[6] Such tribute, and similar arrangements negotiated with Tunis and Tripoli, continued until the United States could bring persuasive force to bear in the form of an effective fleet. The Barbary

States exploited the short range of American power until it was extended.

In a sense, such exploitation is an ideal, if miniature, expression of Liddell Hart's strategy of the indirect approach. In principle, Barbary piracy differed little from what terrorist groups do today: employ indirect or offset violence to attain a response from the government responsible for the protection of its citizens. The response can be political, economic, or a more subtle recognition of stature through publicity. Similar techniques have been used successfully on a lesser scale and in a different context for years by organized crime.

Given its historical roots, what makes contemporary terrorism more threatening than its antecedents? Two trends are critical. One is the power of the individual terrorist or terrorist squad relative to the vulnerability of industrial and postindustrial societies. The second is the growing anonymity, fluidity, and dispersal open to the terrorist relative to the fixed patterns and visible apparatus of the state.

Terrorist power is based on a potential for violence and on a perception of that potential. Among others, Brian Jenkins of the Rand Corporation has pointed out that terrorists have only begun to exploit their technological opportunities, and they have limited their arsenals to conventional small arms or homemade devices.[7] The potential for use of more exotic and powerful weapons is great. Recent attention has focused on the development of a nuclear device or the scattering of nuclear waste. These are difficult but possible terrorist resources with great emotional potential. More immediately probable, however, is the use of chemical poisons; bacteria; or the new, small hand-held surface-to-air and surface-to-surface missiles. The U.S. Redeye, for example, weighs less than 30 pounds, is only four feet long, and can be used against low-flying aircraft. The Russian SA-7 ("Strela" or NATO designation "Grail") is similar. The French/German "Milan" is a small antitank weapon with semiautomatic guidance. It can be operated easily by one man. West Germany alone plans to purchase 1200 launchers and 50,000 such missiles. A Belgian firm has developed a lightweight, silent mortar specifically designed for the destruction of utilities, communications, and light structures. "The full field unit, which weighs only 22 pounds, includes the firing tube plus seven rounds. All seven rounds can be put in the air before the first round hits."[8] Tiny submachine guns, new grenade launchers, small explosive mines, and miniature detonating devices are all available today. The point that Mr. Jenkins makes clear is that after years of steady evolution in large weapons, we are now seeing a sudden revolution in very small weapons, made possible by the new technology of miniaturization.

The modern urban complex, on the other hand, is an intricate system of flow patterns. Disruption of electric power, sewage disposal, or water supply can have a prompt and severe nuisance effect, with great publicity impact and minimal ethical revulsion. Trucks and trains carrying volatile substances follow schedules and routes. There are, moreover, hundreds of thousands of fleeting human congregations which form, pause, and disperse in predictable ways as people assemble for transportation, entertainment, and business. The modern environment, in short, is rife with easy targets.

These are trends with great momentum. By the year 1990 individual violence will be still more powerful and flexible than it is today, while the society will be more technologically dependent, more intricate, more fragile and delicately balanced, like a sprawling castle of toothpicks.

It is no surprise to anyone who has thought about terrorism that the major political impact of its violence depends on exposure to an audience and that the media serve as a kind of political catalyst in transforming a small drop of action into a wide stain of effect. The visual imagery of violence shocks and plants seeds of anxiety which can grow to influence political orientation. The communication of violence in nonvisual form (newspaper, radio) has a similar if less profound effect. The communications explosion has not exhausted its energy, particularly when viewed from a global perspective, and communications is still another area in which a simple projection of ongoing technological and cultural trends promises to facilitate terrorism as a political technique. Trauma can be sustained across great gaps in reality if the terrorist uses imagination in his timing, concentration of effort, and target selection. His dominant principle of war is always surprise.

Studies of terrorist activity often contend that denial of publicity to the terrorist amounts to cutting him off at the root. Such denial is a response option. It is also a very difficult response option, with obvious problems of basic freedoms as they are defined in American political mythology; problems of conflict with media interests; and, most significant, problems with the enormously powerful demand for information. People who are nervous about terrorism do not want to be cut off from information. They want to be informed for a variety of reasons: to prepare themselves, to entertain themselves, to relish their own good luck.

In an exchange of violence with terrorists, the problem of the state is far more difficult. It has to play a reactive role. It has to apply force which is certain, precise, and delicate. It can bring great resources to bear, but first it has to find the face in the crowd.

The second major trend advantage the terrorist holds over the status quo authorities is his anonymity versus their identity. The terrorist is fluid, ghostly, unpredictable. The government and its society are structured, scheduled, sprinkled with purposeful and persistent highlights. When faced with a targeting decision, the terrorist has an embarrassment of riches, the government an embarrassment of near-blindness. It has to grope before it can act, like Polyphemus in the cave. When the Barbary States harassed American ships, the government was able to develop appropriate forces and bring them to bear in a relatively straightforward way. It took time, but the situation was in focus in a crude geographic sense.

Today's terrorist groups can command their own profile. They are

mobile and dispersed. They can choose, claim, deny, and replace identities from day to day. They can achieve shock thresholds with varying
symbolic impact by targeting numbers (a full jumbo aircraft), celebrity
(presidents, ambassadors), or sentiment (children). Complex societies, on
the other hand, tend more and more to manage by exception. When
exception is purposeful but drifting, when it picks its own place and time,
the management process breaks down. The potential of terrorism, then,
threatens not only the political orientation of the democratic state but the
bureaucratic orientation as well.

The question of focus is further complicated by the international system, in which the executive machinery and legal vapors are shaped to
expedite the bilateral interface of governments. Terrorist groups are
multinational, or can be, in the sense that their centers of interest and
gravity move in a geographic plane which has only loose anchors in any
single state. Interaction or negotiation with terrorist groups has to pass
through state governments, sometimes a number of state governments.
While international agreement can facilitate both violent and nonviolent
approaches to terrorist groups, the problem for any single state is not
simple. Palestine Liberation Organization (PLO) elements in Lebanon are
the most obvious current example of a powerful and violent group in,
but not of, a friendly government. The challenge to the status quo powers
troubled by externally based terrorism is one of exorcism, driving out the
demon without battering the body.

As society grows more complex, it will be more dependent on planning, structured activity, and repetition. The computer is an appropriate
symbol for the modern state's administrative apparatus. In this matrix
of linear modes and memory circuits, the seeding of disruptive violence
will become simpler. At the same time, the individual pursuit of obscurity
will become simpler. The Patty Hearst case was a convincing demonstration.

I am not anxious to ring alarm bells, but I am interested in elevating
concern. Terrorism is lurid, and we tend to dwell on its individual cases,
its statistical curves, its motivation, and its logic rather than its long-term
institutional impact. The thought process behind the PLO's murder of
Olympic athletes in Munich concerns me less than an extrapolation of
technocratic trends and the role terrorism *could* play in, or against, future
Western societies.

This is usually considered a police rather than a military problem.
Perhaps it is. I can, however, foresee a threshold of violence at which
terrorism could become a national problem of such intensity that it would
obviate police and military lines of differentiation. The Air Force or National Guard, for example, with rapidly growing electronic sophistication,
flexible systems, and unique freedom of movement, could well become
a key player in both antiterrorist surveillance and still undefined methods
of terrorist suppression. In far-flung, unpredictable episodes of violence,
only aerial platforms and systems have the inherent potential to be persistently responsive, however the response is defined.

The world's economic future is troubling. American interests are already widespread and will spread further. Demographic pressures alone are likely to produce groups attracted to international terrorism by ideology or money. Extranational groups will continue to accrue money and money's power. Sources of violence hostile to the state will be more abundant and more threatening in the future. The dream of attack on order itself rather than on boundaries is an old one. Its moment has not arrived, but in the slow turn of the kaleidoscope I sense an imminent shift in which an old pattern of violence versus the established state will be both logical and radically dangerous in a new way.

Resistance to this violence may take controls and restrictions to privacy that are anathema to the freedoms Americans have come to relish most. There is today a great American re-emphaiss on traditional freedoms versus the eyes and fingers of the state. This is an appealing development, and I applaud it—but with a slightly sinking feeling at the end of the applause. Freedoms, sadly, can become too pure for their time, and I cannot help recalling the penetrating lines from Beckett's novel *Murphy*,

> Here there was nothing but commotion and the pure forms of commotion. Here he was not free, but a mote in the dark of absolute freedom. . . .[9]

Nothing so extreme is on any horizon, but when I look at the promise of the years ahead, I am forced to ask questions about the terrorist and his potential. Can the state as we know it control him? Can it continue to exercise true sovereignty as the individual microcosm gains power, turns ghostly? Will extranational allegiances introduce a kind of sovereignty without territory? Will extortion, traditionally one of the most personal of crimes, become a form of war with political rather than economic ends? I come back from these questions troubled.

If the citizenry of a state perceives itself as insecure at the basic physical level, some recourse will be in order. When society senses a slow clipping of the ordered threads that make up its fabric, how will it react? We may approach a form of sociogovernmental interface that could be called a Survival State, with a character that would belie the plural and polymorphous impulse we now enjoy and celebrate.

Terrorism, in other words, is a complex threat that has the potential to introduce a dangerous ebb and flow into the ethical, financial, and institutional support for the state. Too mild a concern now may demand later reactions and discipline that will be all the more traumatic. We live with a major external security threat focused on the Soviet Union. We have a new sense of economic threat focused on the Middle East. We should be equally concerned about a more subtle, diffuse threat, now best exemplified in Argentina, where violence, private protection, and martial law have been advancing hand in hand.

Terrorism is cheap. It amounts to affordable war, and it seems to work. If the future more-powerful and elusive terrorist can undermine the protective influence of the state at home and abroad and can infuse the ultimate relationship between government and the individual with growing tensions, what climax will result? What moods will rise and fall, and what institutions will be carried with them? Where will loyalties focus? What system will result?

In his excellent book *Swords and Symbols: The Technique of Sovereignty,* James Marshall asks:

> If the legal sanctions, the weapons, available to the sovereign are inadequate to enforce the law, then what becomes of the sovereign "supreme" or "absolute"? He either undertakes a losing fight or remains quiescently limited.[10]

Marshall goes on to cite the case of York in Shakespeare's *Richard II.* York went to Bolingbroke to protest the latter's rebellion against the realm, but seeing his enemy' strength and understanding his own weakness, York delivered these lines:

> . . . if I could, by him that gave me life, I would attach you all and make you stoop Unto the sovereign mercy of the King; But since I cannot, be it known to you I do remain as neuter.
>
> *Act II, scene iii.*

NOTES & REFERENCES

[1] William H. McNeill, *The Rise of the West: A History of the Human Community* (New York: New American Library, 1963), pp. 497–500.

[2] Ibid., p. 499.

[3] Arthur Larson, C. Wilfred Jenks, and others, *Sovereignty within the Law* (Dobbs Ferry, New York: Oceana Publications, 1965), p. 28.

[4] Barbara W. Tuchman, *The Proud Tower: A Portrait of the World before the War, 1890—1914* (New York: Bantam Books, 1966), p. 72. The heads of state assassinated were President Carnot of France in 1894, Premier Cánovas of Spain in 1897, Empress Elizabeth of Austria in 1898, King Humbert of Italy in 1900, President McKinley of the United States in 1901, and Premier Canalejas of Spain in 1912.

[5] Glenn Tucker, *Dawn Like Thunder: The Barbary Wars and the Birth of the U.S. Navy* (Indianapolis: Bobbs-Merrill Company, 1963), pp. 67–68.

[6] Ibid., p. 95.

[7] Brian Michael Jenkins, *High Technology Terrorism and Surrogate War: The Impact of New Technology on Low-Level Violence,* Project Rand Report # P-5339 (Santa Monica, The Rand Corporation, 1975). pp. 12–15. The summary of weapons' capabilities owes much to Mr. Jenkin's study, and the thrust of this article echoes some of his themes. For another excellent analysis of contemporary terrorism, see Brian Jenkins, "International Terrorism: A Balance Sheet," *Survival,* vol. XVII, no. 4, July/August 1975.

[8] Ibid, p. 14.

[9] Samuel Beckett, *Murphy* (New York: Grove Press, 1957), p. 112.

[10] James Marshall, *Swords and Symbols: The Technique of Sovereignty* (New York: Funk & Wagnalls, 1969), p. 7.

Cooper provides an in-depth examination of terrorist failures in 1976 with particular emphasis on Entebbe. He laments the rise of "official terrorism" and uses the Letelier assassination to illustrate his concern. Noting that terrorists may be running out of conventional techniques, he suggests that a maverick group might attempt to use high technology terrorism.

The following article is reprinted by permission from *Chitty's Law Journal*, Volume 25, Number 6, 1977, Toronto, Canada.

Whither Now?
Terrorism on the Brink

by H. H. A. COOPER

TERRORISM IS THE ETERNAL PARADOX

Political terrorism is curiously cyclical. These periodic eruptions of distinctively structured violence, though unpredictable in form and ferocity are, nevertheless, a consistent symptom of troubled times. The deep pools of hatred, discontent, frustration and animus, from which these spasms of desperate violence burst forth upon the community are ever with us, but at times their very stagnation and a deceptive surface calm belie the toiling and moiling in the depths. The political terrorist, when he emerges to disturb the social peace, is the unpleasant reminder of an insistent disquiet with the contemporary balance of power that some are unwilling to tolerate or forgive. Terrorism is a peculiarly ugly, unchivalrous manifestation of the struggle for political mastery. The Reign of Terror, epitomizing the resort to terror by the state and the Siege of Terror, symbolizing the resistance to authority by terroristic means are the dynamic indicators of the state of tension between the active protagonists in the struggle. Yet terrorism can never be more than a substitute for real authority. It is simply the employment of naked power in its crudest form, an embarrassing confession of weakness. Terrorism can be both a violent technique of social control, or a weapon for the overthrow of established authority, representing a belief in the inaptness of other more conciliatory means to achieve the goal of dominance. Terrorism is the eternal paradox. It is a striving for the efficacy and legitimacy of conceded authority by means essentially antithetical to the nature of the objective sought.

THE DOMESTIC SCENE

By any standard of measurement, 1976 can hardly be accounted a successful year for those seeking to challenge established authority by terroristic means. From the perspective of the protagonists of the Siege of Terror, the year will go down as one of fumbled enterprise and missed opportunity. It had opened in North America in a spirit of watchfulness and considerable apprehension.[1] Various "experts" had predicted dire happenings and spoilers of the radical left had threatened, boastfully, to "blow out the candles on Uncle Sam's birthday cake". To the north, Canada prepared apprehensively for the Montreal games in a worsening political climate with ever-sharpening racial antagonism. The shadow of the Munich tragedy four years earlier was oppressively present to those responsible for security and, while Israeli/Arab relations had in no way improved in the interval, other serious divergences of view were already emerging to engage the troubled minds of the Olympic Committee. Unemployment was rising to new highs throughout the United States, affecting, especially, minority group youth at a time when juvenile crime was increasing alarmingly. Many of the great urban centres were falling, irremediably, into further decay, and the vast sums of money spent on the control and containment of crime brought little relief and only a depressing resignation on the part of those entrusted with their disbursement. The ugly racism of Boston[2] and the busing issue generally indicated a considerable potential for mass violence, offering disturbing portents for another round of "long hot summers". On the West coast, the trial of Patricia Hearst was to focus upon one of the most significant events of recent history involving violence-prone radical groups in the United States. Many were concerned that it might provide not only a forum for a notable display of forensic skills but also a symbolic opportunity for the trial, both within the courtroom and without, of all that was claimed to be wrong with *Amerika*. The pathetic attempts on the life of President Ford in the fall of 1975 and the nature of the media attention paid to them, might not unreasonably have been expected to produce a rash of imitators, particularly in the year of a presidential election. The attack upon the United States intelligence capability, at federal, state and local levels continued unabated and the consequent weakening of this vital arm of defense against terrorism might have been expected to give the terrorist the edge in any new initiative.[3] The year witnessed, too, an unprecedented number of seminars and conferences devoted to various aspects of terrorism. This growing "terrorism industry" found no lack of subject matter for its debates, the tenor of which was invariably gloomy with respect to prospects, both short and long-term, for its control and containment. It would be uncharitable and, perhaps, mistaken to regard this concern as primarily self-serving.

The dire forebodings of the experts and others have, happily, not been fulfilled. Nothing untoward occurred to disturb the even tenor of the Bicentennial Celebrations. Indeed, the extraordinary, almost tangible spirit of amity abroad on July 4, 1976 will long remain a fond memory for those fortunate enough to have experienced it. Despite the unseemly wrangles that marred the opening of the Montreal games, no terrorist activity spoiled them in any way and, at their conclusion, a deeply moving ceremony united the nations that had participated in them. The summer came and went—with none of the contagious, mass violence anticipated in the cities. Whatever the discontent of the unemployed and the urban poor, it was clearly not yet ripe for extremist exploitation. The perpetual undercurrent of racism, sharpened by the busing issue, did not develop into a critical confrontation and, by summer's end, Police Commissioner Robert De Grazia, not a man to run away from a challenge, felt sufficiently confident to move to a more remunerative and less onerous situation in Montgomery County, Maryland.[4] The much ballyhooed trial of Patricia Hearst took place as expected, but apart from some unspecific, unexecuted threats and a somewhat amateurish bombing on the Hearst property, the opportunity to make a great, symbolic gesture against the hated representatives of capitalism was passed up by whatever radical groups might have been interested in the possibilities. Significantly, no new terrorist organization has risen phoenix-like from the ashes of the Symbionese Liberation Army. Despite the glare of publicity their actions received, Lynette Fromme and Sara Jane Moore found no imitators and the candidates in the long presidential campaign were not noticeably inhibited in their frequent, personal contacts with the American people throughout the length and breadth of the land. Despite the heavy blows it has suffered, the United States intelligence capabilities, at home and abroad on all levels, remain strong and there are encouraging signs that some of the ill-advised hysteria on civil libertarian matters has declined before a more reasonable approach to the whole intelligence question. Most pertinently, perhaps, the pronouncements of the experts at the many conferences that continue to take place on the subject of terrorism are beginning to take on a repetitious ring as though little new, for the moment, is to be said. An expectant hush is starting to take the place of the earlier, strident clamor.

THE SCENE ABROAD

If the year was a disappointing one for domestic terrorists in North America, it was even more so for domestic and transnational terrorists in other parts of the world. In the Federal Republic of Germany, the death in prison of the tragic ideologue of the RAF, Ulrike Meinhof, served to emphasize the impotence and isolation of the incarcerated members of the once powerful Baader-Meinhof group. Efforts to interfere with their trial proved fruitless and rescue attempts abortive. The militant wing of the IRA made no progress whatsoever in securing a political advantage from its continuing sporadic campaign of violence and its vicious intransigence substantially alienated the support of a large segment of its own natural constituency. A feeling of war-weariness descended upon the people of Northern Ireland, but terror on a level at which the IRA was prepared to engage was evidently quite ineffective for its prime, coercive purpose. What is very clear is that, for all practical purposes, the campaigns of terror and counter-terror had reached a plateau that was close to a stalemate. In Latin America, where the Siege of Terror had become almost endemic, terrorists continued their unremitting battle with the forces opposed to them. The results, from their perspective, were unimpressive. Gone were the days of terrorist spectaculars leading to the collection of huge ransoms such as those obtained in Argentina for the return of the Born brothers. As events showed, the life of the terrorist or even the suspected terrorist was all too likely to be Nastie, Brutish and Shorte. The elusive Carlos, like the Scarlet Pimpernel, was sought all over. Spotted here and rumored there, he kept security forces busily engaged in many countries. Neither directly nor indirectly, however, had he any exploit to his credit that might have justified the somewhat inflated image of him that was being created by the media. There is persuasive evidence that he is being very well watched and, accordingly, finding it increasingly difficult to operate.[5] Other dreaded transnational mercenaries, such as the Japanese groups also had a quiet, unspectacular year. The various Palestinian groups had an extremely difficult year. Driven out of Jordan in 1971, the Palestinian liberation movements had found haven in the Lebanon, but after appearing to be on the upsurge militarily and politically in that strifetorn country, their fortunes suffered a dramatic, and to the uninformed observer, surprising reversal through the military intervention of Syria. Duly attentive to the precept that terrorism is the weapon of the weak, the world waited with baited breath for the terroristic reaction to the systematic destruction of the safe havens of the Palestinian liberation movements. Terrorist reprisals when they came were so puny as to be derisory; a raid on the Syrian Embassy in Rome ended with the quick, ignominious surrender of the terrorists and an attack, shortly thereafter, upon a Damascus hotel was speedily and violently put down, the world being regaled with photographs of three captured terrorists swinging in the breeze from public gibbets. The year saw too a resurgence of skyjacking, starting in the Philippines and the first skyjacking in some years of a scheduled United States domestic flight.[6] All these skyjackings ended unsatisfactorily from the perpetrators' point of view, and when these incidents are examined in detail it will be seen that the anti-government terrorists have simply not been able to resolve some of the fundamental technical details involved in these operations.

From the terrorist perspective, the nadir was reached on July 4, 1976 with the successful rescue operation mounted by Israel at Entebbe Airport, Uganda. This was an event of unparalleled military and psychological significance from the point of view of transnational terrorism and governmental responses to it. The Siege of Terror is difficult if not impossible to sustain unless the beseigers have guaranteed safe havens to which they can retire securely following the completion of their operations. Safe bases, out of the enemy's reach, are a prerequisite for any successful terrorist campaign particularly where this extends itself into full-scale guerrilla warfare. All protracted terrorist campaigns of a classical nature have been facilitated by the terrorists gaining a secure foothold in a neutral or friendly country contiguous to that under attack. Elsewhere the terrorist, particularly the urban terrorist, has had to rely upon melting into the community after the completion of his operations in such a way as to escape apprehension and punishment. Skyjacking, because of the relative openness of the action and the direct confrontation with legitimate authority it necessarily provokes, poses logistical problems of a peculiar nature for the terrorist who engages in it. If the skyjacking is to be successful, in the sense of achieving the objectives for which it was undertaken—payment of ransom, release of imprisoned terrorists, broadcasts of propaganda, for example—and in permitting the skjackers themselves to escape the consequences of their actions, the cooperation of a friendly nation state willing to grant landing facilities and asylum is essential. With the increasing inflexibility of governments in negotiating with terrorists and terrorist groups, it has become necessary for them not only to have a prepared safe haven to which retreat might be made on conclusion of the entire operation, but preferably one which can be used in the course of the skyjacking itself, that is an airfield in a friendly country or one under terrorist control to which the seized aircraft can be flown and from which negotiations can be conducted. Fewer and fewer countries, with good reason, have shown themselves prepared to concede these facilities, however sympathetic they might feel, covertly, towards the skyjackers and their objectives. There is a large measure of self-interest in this that cuts across ideological considerations and even the boundaries of the Cold War and the Third World. No country with aviation interests of any kind can now afford to put its international relations in jeopardy or expose itself to reprisals by even appearing to give aid and comfort to skyjackers.[7]

ASSESSING ENTEBBE

The most important and novel lesson of the Entebbe rescue operation from the skyjackers' point of view is that the anti-terrorist forces have a very long reach indeed. No haven can now be considered so remote as to be safe from a military operation such as that mounted by the Israeli forces. This has necessitated a complete reappraisal of the viability of skyjackings of the Entebbe type. As a practical matter, the terrorist can no longer count upon the other side abiding by the "rules"; this has altered the whole concept of the game. Formerly, the sentiments underlying the well-known aphorism that one man's terrorist is another man's freedom fighter had greatly favored the transnational terrorist.[8] Now the lines were being more sharply drawn and the nation states themselves were having to stand up and be counted in a struggle that was beginning to turn against the terrorists. From the perspective of the transnational terrorist, sharp inroads had been made into the advantages that modern communications systems had bestowed upon him.[9] The pendulum had now swung hard in the opposite direction. These considerations have cast skyjacking in a totally different light. While it would be premature to opine that the skyjacking menace, so far as it was the product of true terrorist activity,[10] is now at an end, these latest developments certainly force a radical reappraisal of the value of skyjacking to organized, transnational terrorist groups. If skyjacking is to be once more a viable option for these groups, they will need to show greater care in the selection of their targets, which reduces, correspondingly, the bargaining value of the victims. They will also need to find a country relatively sympathetic to the skyjackers' cause which is yet sufficiently removed from the injured nation or nations to preclude the mounting of an Entebbe-style operation or alternatively a country which is strictly neutral in its attitude, eschews the violent response and is able to resist official, foreign incursions upon its territory even in the guise of international, mercy missions. Clearly, the range of options is now severely reduced and the Entebbe operation is some evidence for the efficacy of such actions as at least a short-term deterrent.

Additionally, the Entebbe rescue operation must be seen as having a marked psychological impact. What might be loosely termed the transnational terrorist movement has not only lost face, it has been seen manifestly to lose face. For too long the world was treated, often through a rape of the media,[11] to the monstrous gloating of those who had by their own fearful violence achieved a bargaining parity with even the mightiest of nation states. In consequence of the modern miracles of visual, electronic communication, the terrorist was quickly on the way to becoming larger than life. It would not have been surprising, therefore, had he become convinced of his own supremacy and of the inflated, near invincible image[12] he had sought to project. Entebbe represented an enormous psychological setback. For once, the glamor, the daring, the excitement of the event, that the media is all too ready to exploit and develop were with the anti-terrorist forces. The terrorist ego is a fragile thing and a loss of face is not easy to accept or endure. That the terrorists found themselves unable to strike back vengefully for the defeat inflicted upon them is some measure both of their unpreparedness for such a contingency and of the damage suffered to their confidence and self-esteem. The full implications of the Entebbe rescue operation remain to be studied with care, but it is certain that this forceful countermeasure has already led to a serious reconsideration of much that the modern transnational terrorist had come to take for granted. It would be fair to opine that, following Entebbe, transnational terrorism is down but certainly not out. The world is large and, despite this setback, it remains the terrorists' oyster. What has to be urgently considered by the forces of counter-terrorism is the new direction that the other side is likely to take following this retrench-

ment. The basic attractiveness of international civil aviation as a target
remains. The asset which can be put at risk is extremely valuable in human terms, in terms of property and in terms of international relations and communication. Private and governmental interests are inextricably intertwined. The diversity of the interests involved has great potential for confusion and conflict which inhibit effective response and lend themselves to exploitation by the terrorist. Most important of all, perhaps, civil aviation remains extremely vulnerable to attack in flight or on the ground. While terrorism directed against civil aviation has undoubtedly suffered a major setback, it is unlikely to go completely out of vogue and may well assume a new and more frightening dimension once the effects of the Entebbe incident have been fully digested.

ASCENDANT OFFICIAL TERRORISM

In striking contrast to the fallen fortunes of the transnational and domestic antigovernment terrorists, those of the purveyors of state or official terrorism seemed to be sharply in the ascendancy. Almost everywhere, the counter insurgency forces have registered telling blows, forcing an abatement of terroristic activity and, in many cases, virtually eliminating this threat to established authority. These successes have produced their own kind of reaction. The iron grip of repression has tightened with crushing effectiveness, but all too often it has squeezed out much of the good along with the bad. It has often been correctly, if somewhat incompletely, stressed that terrorism is the weapon of the weak. It is certainly a weapon of weakness and a confession of such by those who do not perceive themselves as strong enough to face the challenge without resort to these means. Recognition of this sometimes tends to obscure the fact that terror allied to the massive resources upon which the nation state can ordinarily draw makes for a peculiarly deadly combination, especially in a climate of uncritical or even approving public opinion. The chronicles of Amnesty International are tragically replete with an accounting of the growing, world-wide toll of this reactive, official terrorism. Resort to torture, often of a most horrifying and technologically sophisticated kind, is now endemic in many parts of the world. The impressive, terroristic violence of those who seek to overthrow established authority is surpassed in every department by the counter-insurgency forces pitted by government against them. In the modern world it seems, sadly, that terror and terrorism are inescapable. All that the ordinary citizen is offered is a choice of terrors, official or unofficial. In those countries where the light of democracy burns fitfully or has been summarily extinguished with some finality even that choice is substantially reduced.[14] Those concerned to avoid the mere substitution of one tyranny of violence for another, more permanent and effective one must view these developments with a high degree of anxiety. State or official terrorism is now becoming so widespread as to constitute an alternative form of government. State terror, as both Levin and Trotsky came to realize so long ago, is the only effective terror. The events of 1976 may well force upon the exponents of individual terror a reluctant acceptance of this. Yet the true terrorist is the fighter *par exellence* of the hopeless cause. For some, the realization will come slowly and bitterly if at all. It is this small, unyielding cadre that holds the future of individual or small group terrorism and, perhaps, the fate of the world in its hands.

It is certain that the victims of state terror are infinitely more numerous than those who suffer at the hands of small group or individual terrorists. The magnitude of official terror in this century alone is truly staggering. Even the most skeptical must recoil in horror at the evidence. Yet on a general rather than a particular view, the actions of the few are vastly more fear-producing than are the activities of those massive, state-supported instruments of terror. In part, no doubt, this is due to the influence of the mass media, but there is also a subtle, scarcely articulated bias in favor of submission to authority.[15] In those totalitarian countries where the Reign of Terror pervades like a dull, chronic ache, the populace has become mainly habituated to the pain; like so many in Nazi Germany they merely avert their eyes lest they, too, be touched by the fire. This is understandable, yet it has led to a depressing acquiescence in much that is truly terrifying. Those who are fortunate enough to live under a more benevolent yoke generally shrink even from inquiry. This studied indifference and general apathy towards the condition of such a large segment of humanity does much to encourage these ugly practices and is strikingly in contrast to the reactions and overreactions produced by the terrorism of the few. This observation should in no way be taken to justify the latter but rather as an expression of surprise that, if concern for one's neighbor is the hallmark of a civilized society, so little regard is currently paid to a scale of official terror that can scarcely be ignored.[16]

A large-scale dehumanizing process seems to have taken place so as to give renewed vibrancy to Stalin's chilling remark that one death is a tragedy but millions of deaths are only statistics. In our own times, the resultant attitudes seem to be productive of strange consequences. The violent assassination of Orlando Letelier, former Chilean ambassador to the United States, a political exile at the time of his death, produced the immediate cynical reaction that his demise had been engineered by official agents of the present Chilean government, the dreaded DINA.[17] The reaction to that reaction was to insist that the killing had been too crude to be the work of experts, which comment speaks volumes for the held and fostered beliefs as to the respective efficacy of state as against "private" terrorism. The hunting down and execution of feared enemies on foreign soil and under foreign protection is nothing new. What is somewhat strange is the lack of outrage displayed by the American public at the brutal killing, in the nation's capital of a friendly, cultured exile in circumstances which, had the killing been less "professional", might well have taken many more American lives than that of his unfortunate companion. It is interesting to reflect back on the killing of Leon Trotsky. Of that assassination it has been written:[18]

President Cardenas and his government were outraged by the fact that Trotsky had been killed while under the protection of the state as a political refugee. The fact that a foreigner had come to Mexico to kill an internationally known revolutionary who enjoyed the right of asylum seemed to the Mexican public particularly reprehensible.

The seeming impotence of the United States law enforcement machinery either to give protection to the victim or to apprehend his killers also appears to have produced less disquiet than might, under the circumstances, have been expected. Whatever the truth of the matter, the impressions left by it are extremely unfortunate.

A careful analysis of the events of 1976 suggests that, for the moment, the balance of advantages has swung sharply against small group terrorism whatever its political complexion, affiliations or goals. There is presently an uneasy hiatus recalling the comparatively quiescent months of the "Phony War" of 1939/40. Experienced campaigners and students of history are unlikely to take more than momentary comfort from the respite. As a new year begins, many will be looking to an uncertain future with a growing concern, for the terrorist options are dwindling. The sharpening differential of success between official and non-governmental terrorism has further emphasized the impotence of the ordinary individual. Those who saw in the earlier successes of modern, small group or individual terrorism a renascence of heroism, the triumph of the "little man" against the titanic, dehumanizing power of the state must have been sadly disappointed in the extent and duration of the victory. The nation-state may have been battered and a trifle bruised by these efforts, but its mastery remains unchallenged. It is the idealists who have been fatally damaged in the struggle, for it becomes more and more evident that behind even small group terrorism of the more successful kind there lies the somber shadow of the nation-state.[19] Such surrogate terrorism is clearly no precursor to the Millenium; it is simply the erratic, mechanical jerking of the marionette. It is interesting to speculate what might have brought about this latter change. Certainly there is now money in abundance for the financing of terroristic operations; to adapt the MacMillan election slogan, which echoed through the United Kingdom in 1959, the terrorists have probably never had it so good. There is comparatively little need for the better organized groups and their affiliates to engage in hazardous criminal enterprises, such as bank robbery, in order to finance their operations. It is still true, however, that he who pays the piper calls the tune, and the onset of affluence has undoubtedly had its price for the small group terrorist in a loss of operational independence and a noticeable subordination to the grand designs of the paymaster. While control of the pursestrings has undoubtedly had its effect in imposing some external standards upon terrorists' operations, the accompanying governmental penetration and oversight has also altered both operations and perspectives. Those groups that aspire to legitimacy and political recognition have had to establish contacts with the appropriate power blocs. In return for a patina of respectability, moderation—so antithetical to the terrorist creed—has been demanded, and generally secured. The easy assimilation of the erstwhile terrorist to the ranks of the conventional power structure is a further blow to the idealists and ideologues who had thought, rather, in terms of wholesale destruction of existing institutions. The effects of this inevitable disillusionment have yet to make themselves felt.

IMPENDING DOOM?

It is not unreasonable to take the view that the present uneasy lull presages the inevitable storm to come. The intermission ought to be put to good use. It has been well observed in another, similar context:[20]

> For all the horrors of the past, man has never before shown such an interest in intra-specific aggression. It is a very reasonable interest, as he may never get the opportunity to reflect on it again.

Whatever the short-term advantages of the Entebbe operation, and, on even the most jaundiced view, they are considerable, it is likely that these events have carried the world a good stride closer to a terrorist Armageddon. The one lesson that comes over all too strongly from the Entebbe experience, particularly when it is evaluated in the light of the other forms of state and official violence to which reference has been made, is that such violence seems to do the job. No matter that it is launched on account of a "righteous" cause; to the confirmed terrorist his own cause is righteous and it is those who oppose him that stand in the wrong. It is, rather, the very success of these "state" enterprises that seems to confirm him, more than ever, in his folly.

The terrorist is ever conscious of his own material as opposed to moral inferiority in the struggle in which he is engaged. Indeed, it is this acknowledged weakness that leads to the resort to terror. There is no moral lesson of worth in the measures taken to repress terrorism, at least not one which the terrorist would care to learn. Rather, there is the practical demonstration, repeated and underlined from the time of Lenin onward, that massive terror, ruthlessly applied, is a most effective means of social control. The state has what small terrorist groups do not ordinarily possess, namely the means by which massive terror can be effectively applied. It cannot be too long, in an age which prides itself on its technological miracles, before the frustrated, individual terrorist seeks redress of this strategic imbalance of resort to the only means open to him for the purpose, namely high technology terrorism. This is no new fear; the basement atomic bomb has been on the minds of many for long enough. The threat of the nuclear device has tended, indeed, to overshadow all else in this field. The possibilities have been thoroughly canvassed by the theorists.[21] To some the threat looms exceedingly large while to others it seems to be of little practical consequence. The threat has certainly passed out of the realm of science fiction and must be taken into proper account in

any calculation regarding future terrorist scenarios. High technology ter-
rorism is, however, by no means confined to the development and use of "pocket" nuclear, explosive devices. Once more, official "experimentation" may serve as an unforeseen stimulus to individual or small group initiation. The American public has now been informed, officially, of disturbing experiments of which the more knowledgeable had long been aware and others had darkly suspected. Not only were diabolical tests carried out on unsuspecting individuals, but governmental curiosity as to the consequences of some of the more dreaded agents available for employment in unconventional warfare has led to secret experiments on whole communities. Such revelations constitute to the terrorist mind not only a demonstration of the feasibility of such acts of aggression against innocent and defenseless victims, but also a release from whatever moral constraints that might have existed in the matter; "if it's all right for them, it's all right for us". Countless agents of mass destruction, toxins, organic and inorganic, lasers, bacteria and viruses are now available to the destructively inclined, while many have been officially trained in their development and use. There is no lack of sophisticated weaponry for those who would seek this route to set the pendulum upon its swing in the other direction.

Having thus established opportunity and motive, it might usefully be enquired who, at this time might set the world upon a disaster course of this kind? It may be said with a fair degree of confidence that it is no more in the interests of nation states, even the least responsible ones giving clandestine support to terrorist groups or using them for surrogate warfare, to encourage a foray into the field of high technology terrorism than it would be to engage, overtly, in nuclear or germ warfare. For this reason it may be expected that those groups operating under some sort of patronage by "official" paymasters will be restrained in the use of even the most deadly "toys" with which they are supplied by their sponsors.[22] To argue from history is sometimes unsound and often unwise,[23] but past experience does seem to suggest that it is the tight rein of the master rather than any benevolent impulses towards the potential victim that has kept modern terrorism within its present bounds. Highly sophisticated weaponry has been around for a long time and government "operatives" on special assignments have made use of exceedingly advanced technology for essentially terroristic purposes. Yet terrorists generally and particularly those who might be regarded as the "out" groups are still content with relatively primitive, limited means of wreaking destruction. In the age of the nuclear weapon, laser technology and the deadliest of germ warfare, the "average" terrorist remains in the dynamite and black powder stage. The conventional pattern, it is proper to speculate, is most likely to be broken by a maverick group with access to the technology that official sources might clandestinely provide, yet which somehow eludes the controls imposed upon its use or some group or individual from outside the "magic circle" for whom the ordinary inhibitors do not work.

A thoughtful scholar, Nicholas Kittrie, has likened the terrorist to the psychopath.[24] However controverted the whole category of psychopathy may be, there is generally agreement that an outstanding characteristic of the psychopath is that he cleaves to a set of values of his own markedly at variance with those of society as a whole. That which might inhibit the average law-abiding member of the community is, therefore, often no restraint at all for the psychopath. The lone psychopath with a modicum of knowledge and access to modern technology might wreak unbelievable havoc on society. Psychopaths generally do not make good terrorist material, and few "responsible" terrorist organizations would purposefully recruit them to their ranks. The dangers of their employment, even under the closest of controls are graphically depicted in the recent novel Black Sunday.[25] Their constitutional peculiarities nevertheless may be perceived to have value under certain circumstances and their employment, inadvertently or by design, should not be discounted. The lone psychopath is a more fearsome prospect. Individual and organizational inhibitors are absent or ineffective, but perhaps of greater importance is such an individual's likelihood of having escaped notice by those responsible for preventive or strategic intelligence. He has no colleagues who might betray him and no organization that might be penetrated by counter-terrorist forces. In former times, his individuality would have constituted a major weakness and a natural limitation upon the extent of his destructiveness. Nowadays, the benefits of high technology might make him, under certain circumstances, the equal, momentarily, of the most powerful nation on earth. This is heady stuff for the loner who stalks malevolently, in our midst.[26] It is very true that:[27]

> The bigger and stronger we get, the more vulnerable we become to lone and fugitive assault. We can hold empires at bay with megaton weapons but cannot make the corner drugstore safe.

Were our problems confined to the corner drugstore in this regard, they would be serious enough as those taken hostage by quasiterrorists in frustrated robberies would all too willingly testify. One of Tony Parker's psychopaths says.[28]

> Hatred, violence, I'm full of it. I think if I had the chance I'd destroy the whole world.

Such wistful or wishful thinking is now frighteningly close to reality and realization. Some future Gary Gilmore, blinded by some inner rage and coldly indifferent to the meaning of life for others,[29] may well turn his hand not against two innocent victims but 200,000. The means are there for those who would take the dread step towards them.

We are ill-prepared to face such a possibility. All our defense endeavors against high technology weaponry are postulated upon its employment by duly authorized agents of the conventional nation-state. The proliferation of armaments and, in particular, nuclear devices, has alarmed many, but the situation has not been beyond containment for the international regulators, based as they are upon subtle but well understood distributions of power, are sufficient for keeping the employment of such weaponry within acceptable bounds. The "lunatic fringe" of the terrorist world is clearly outside such a scheme of regulation. Protective measures are much needed but the miniaturization of devices[30] makes their obtaining, concealment and use by a single person increasingly likely. The first effect of this is to give the threat a much higher degree of credibility than it has hitherto enjoyed. Threats to employ weapons of mass destruction must now be taken very seriously indeed, and a new technique and criteria for evaluating them must be urgently developed.

If whole cities are soon to be taken hostage[31] and held for ransoms that would once have seemed absurd we must rapidly adjust to the possibility and create an effective defense system against it. We cannot hope to cope with real situations of this kind by the hasty development of *ad hoc* measures once the scenario is in full bloom. The disruption caused by the credible threat of this nature is awesome to contemplate. The result of ignoring it is even worse. It is to be expected that terrorists will concentrate more and more upon the massive disruption of society and its everyday business in the hope of alienating the governed from those who govern. A sharpening of the division between those who engage in what might be called purely destructive terrorism and those whose aims and activities are more realistically compatible with the eventual attainment of legitimacy is to be expected. Thus bombing, conventional and escalated can be expected to take on an even more ugly character, prior warnings will become fewer and the toll in terms of human life and limb higher. "Stand-off" or confrontation type terrorism may decrease, but it may be predicted that any diminution will be compensated by a rise in non-confrontation type situations where destruction often of an indiscriminate kind is the primary objective and the creation of a bargaining situation of comparatively little importance. That nations already perceive the change and the possibilities is evident from the recent release of Abu Daoud.[32] Patterns of terrorist response will change to an even more nihilistic stance because the terrorist has been thrown back on to the defensive and his inherent weakness critically exposed.

ALTERED TERRORIST AIMS

Modern terrorism is rapidly losing its bargaining power; all that is left is the road to frustration and consequent destructiveness, for which the possibilities are endless. It is no longer easy to skyjack aircraft with a meaningful political strategy in mind. It is still frighteningly easy to destroy them, individually, in the air or on the ground so as to create terror and chaos among the world's air communications systems. If pure destruction is all that is in contemplation, the destruction of a key air traffic control center would certainly serve the terrorists' ends. The world's energy resources, particularly oil, are frighteningly at the terrorists' mercy. Attacks on tankers and oil refineries and storage tanks may well become the new target for the "weak". We must attune ourselves, psychologically as well as practically, to these altered terroristic aims and strategies. International accord is woefully thin and it cannot be expected that it will improve, noticeably, in the present climate of world affairs. We can expect more individual state repression and a spilling of innocent blood in lands foreign to the real matter in contention. In a world where the rule of law is not only weak but manifestly seen to be weak, Abu Daoud can only expect the eventual fate of Orlando Letelier. This ultimate irony is perhaps the most fearful reflection of all.

NOTES & REFERENCES

[1]*See,* among many similar examples, The Washington Post, February 10, 1976: *Bombings Increase Sharply; Bicentennial Wave Feared.* Mr. Richard W. Velde, Administrator of the United States Law Enforcement Assistance Administration stated in 1974 before the House of Representatives Committee on Internal Security, Terrorism, Part 4, Washington, D.C.: U.S. Government Printing Office, 1974, page 4137:

International terrorism may also be expected to target on the United States as our country prepares to commemorate the 1976 Bicentennial of its founding. The possibility of such terrorist activity will require even more diligent activity from already taxed police personnel. LEAA plans to commit $1 million for planning support for the Bicentennial celebration, and could serve as a means to avoid possible violence and terrorist activity.

[2]One of the saddest pictures of the Bicentennial year, and one which dramatically emphasizes the racial polarization of the United States in crucial areas was that published on the front page of The Washington Post of April 6, 1976. The photograph showed a white demonstrator charging viciously at a black bystander with an American flag held lance-like. The incident occurred outside Boston City Hall.

[3]Mr. Brooks McClure of the U.S.I.A., a very sound and knowledgeable commentator on these matters has said (Terroristic Activity, Hostage Defense Measures, Hearings before the Subcommittee to Investigate the administration of the Internal Security Act and other internal security laws of the Committee on the Judiciary. United States Senate, Washington, D.C.: U.S. Government Printing Office, 1975, page 293):

Looking at the situation in the United States, there has been a tendency in recent years to clean up old police intelligence files and criminal files—to eliminate vast numbers of them. In New York early this

year, the Puerto Rico Liberation Army (FALN) blew up the Fraunces Tavern, killing four people and wounding more than 50. The police were unable to get any kind of a lead on this group, because 2 years earlier they had destroyed the entire file on Puerto Rican suspects.

See, too, the publication of the same Committee (1975) entitled, The Nationwide Drive Against Law Enforcement Intelligence Operations.

[4]*See* II Law Enforcement News, No. 10, October 5, 1976.

[5]His "nuisance" value, apart from his operational performance is considerable. In late 1976 he managed to cause serious embarrassment to United States/Yugoslavian relations through his presumed emergence in Yugoslavia and a seeming unwillingness of the Yugoslavian authorities to assist in his apprehension.

[6]This represented an evident, material setback to those who, on slight and unscientific demonstration had claimed that the measures taken by the United States against skyjacking represented a "success story". (Irving Slott, LEAA, Georgia Journal Constitution, Atlanta, March 21, 1976). The fact is that these skyjacking measures have never been effectively evaluated and it is misleading to draw "cause and effect" conclusions from them. There is much evidence to suggest that, in operational terms, these measures are quite ineffective in preventing the introduction onto aircraft of dangerous materials, and we ought not to be lulled into a false sense of security on this account. A determined terrorist, skilled in weapon concealment techniques would have little difficulty in getting whatever he required past the majority of security checks as they are presently operated.

[7]In a very real sense, the West has reaped what it had sown for it did nothing to discourage the disaffected from using any means at their disposal to escape from be-

hind the iron curtain. To complain when the tables were turned was unrealistic to say the least. It is evident that a much more realistic attitude now prevails in international circles and those who would applaud such violence have now learned to do so relatively discreetly.

[8]These sentiments remain strong for they constitute a serious barrier to international accord even on the definition of terrorism. What seems to be eroded by the current term of events is the erection of these sentiments into a positive source of support for transnational terrorists on other than a very selective basis.

[9]However else the modern terrorist may be regarded, he is certainly a man (or woman) with a message, albeit a violent and shocking one. Essential to the carriage of that message to its intended audience is the modern, communications media and, in particular, television. Even the slightest shift in focus of the television camera can convey a message quite different from that which the terrorist desires and the media is a fickle mistress at times.

[10]It would be a great mistake to overlook the complex psychological factors in any skyjacking however ostensibly "political" at first sight. See David G. Hubbard, The Skyjacker, New York: Collier Books, (1973); pages 180/181.

[11]For an examination of the aptness of the expression "rape" in this context see H.H.A. Cooper, Terrorism And The Media, (9-1976) 24 Chitty's L. J. 226-39.

[12]This is something deserving of further study. André Malraux, noted for his utter recklessness in action and disregard for personal danger is said to have believed himself "aided by feelings of irrational invulnerability".

[13]As evidenced by the spate of films dealing with the Entebbe raid rushed onto an eager market. There is no doubt about the identity of the "heroes" in these presentations.

[14]Yet even the Soviet Union has not managed wholly to crush all possibility of individual acts of terrorism against the government. See, for example, Terrorism Hits Soviet Georgia, The Washington Star, May 3, 1976, at A-12.

[15]It is worth recalling Milgram's illustrative experiments involving the conditioning of quite ordinary people to inflict pain upon others in obedience to authority. Conditioning Of Obedience And Disobedience To Authority, International Journal of Psychiatry, (1968), page 259.

[16]This phenomenon is worthy of close attention. It has been said (W. Lindesay Neustatter, Psychological Disorder And Crime,

New York: Philosophical Library (1957). page 227):

> The Nazi regime was an outstandingly dreadful example of the danger which can arise in a society where official sanction is given to the hidden forces of sadism and brutality which it is the aim of civilization to hold in check.

[17]See, for example, Jeffrey Stein, Assassination In The Streets Of Washington, Washington Newsworks, September 30 - October 7, 1976, at 7.

[18]Isaac Don Levine, The Mind Of An Assassin, New York: Farrar, Straus and Cudahy, (1959), page 150.

[19]On this, see the detailed information provided by Brian Crozier, Director of the Institute for the Study of Conflict, London, to the Committee on the Judiciary of the United States Senate, Terroristic Activity: International Terrorism, Washington, D.C.; U.S. Government Printing Office, pages 183/188.

[20]John Gunn, Violence, New York: Praeger Publishers, (1973), page 42.

[21]For a very good survey and extensive bibliography, see Analysis Of The Threat To The Commercial Nuclear Industry, Vienna, Virginia: The BDM Corporation, (1975).

[22]How else can one reasonably explain the forbearance of those groups equipped with Russian heat-seeking missiles that might make short work of a commercial airliner from a relatively safe vantage point?

[23]An excellent example of the dangers and fallacies is given by Edward Hodnett in The Art Of Problem Solving, New York: Harper and Row (1955), page 146.

[24]Cited by Jeffrey A. Tannenbaum, The Terrorists, The Wall Street Journal, Tuesday, January 4, 1977.

[25]This is but one of a number of recent books dealing with theme of the lonely, disordered killer seeking a large congregation of persons, such as the spectators at a sporting event, upon whom to inflict massive, cathartic violence.

[26]Much speculation surrounds the deaths of the 29 American Legion Conventioneers who attended the Annual Convention in Philadelphia in July, 1976. See, for example the secret report quoted by the usually reliable Jack Anderson and Les Whitten in The Washington Post, October 28, 1976 under the title: Paranoid Suspected In Legion Deaths.

[27]Douglas Davis in Newsweek, June 14, 1976, at 11.

[28]The Frying Pan, New York: Basic Books (1970), page 86.

[29]See the chilling, impersonal attitude of Gilmore towards his victims and their symbolic or representational character for him

as evidenced by his letters published in the National Enquirer, January 11, 1977, at 33.

[30]This is particularly so in the case of computers. Devices that once required huge facilities and power supplies have now been supplanted by relatively inexpensive artifacts that can be comfortably housed in the coverage living room without detracting from its other uses. No longer is it necessary for radical students to enrol in graduate classes to gain access to a computer for revolutionary activities. It is far from certain that these developments have been properly appreciated by some of our "Generals" who are in danger of fighting the next war with the tactics and equipment of the last.

[31]This possibility was projected by William E. Nelson, Deputy Director of Operations for the CIA as reported in the New York Post, March 8, 1976.

[32]The man suspected of having masterminded the operation against the Israeli athletes at the Munich Olympic Games in 1972 was apprehended in January, 1977 by the French authorities after having entered France illegally with falsified papers. Despite the existence of grounds for extradition both to West Germany and Israel he was released by France to Algeria where he was given a hero's welcome. It seems that France was prepared to incur the somewhat stylized, diplomatic wrath of Israel rather than possible terrorist reprisal for acting according to law. It is by no means certain that any other European country would have acted differently.

Laqueur considers the threat of international terrorism to be overestimated. He explains that this is caused by myths created by terrorists which distort the strength of terrorism and exaggerate the weaknesses of the societies attacked. Laqueur encourages a stronger response to the threat through greater international cooperation. However, his conclusion that terrorism is futile has not been accepted either by active terrorist organizations or by the majority of analysts coping with the problem.

The Futility of Terrorism

by WALTER LAQUEUR

A few days before Christmas [1975] a group of terrorists broke in to the OPEC building in Vienna; the rest of the story is still fresh in the memory and need not be retold. Coming so soon after the attacks of the South Moluccan separatists in the Netherlands, the incident occasioned great hand-wringing and tooth-grinding among editorialists all over the globe with dire comments about the power concentrated in the hands of a few determined individuals and harrowing predictions as to what all this could mean for the future. Because the significance of terrorism is not yet widely understood, such a nine days' wonder could be regarded as an action of world-shaking political consequence. Yet, when the shooting was over, when the terrorists had vanished from the headlines and the small screen, it appeared that they were by no means nearer to their aims. It was not even clear what they had wanted. Their operation in Vienna had been meticulously prepared, but they seemed to have only the haziest notion of what they intended to achieve. They broadcast a document which, dealing with an obscure subject and written in left-wing sectarian language, might just as well have been broadcast in Chinese as far as the average Austrian listener was concerned.

The Vienna terrorists claimed to be acting on behalf of the Palestinian revolution, but only some of them were Arabs and it is not certain that there was a single Palestinian among them. Their leader was the notorious

"Carlos," a Venezuelan trained in Moscow and supported by Cuban intelligence in Paris—a branch of the Soviet KGB. Yet the operation, according to the Egyptian press, was paid for by Colonel Qaddafi. The working of modern transnational terrorism with its ties to Moscow and Havana, its connections with Libya and Algeria, resemble those of a multinational corporation; whenever multinational corporations sponsor patriotic causes, the greatest of caution is called for.

Similar caution is required if one is to avoid exaggerating the importance of terrorism today. It is true that no modern state can guarantee the life and safety of all of its citizens all of the time, but it is not true that terrorists somehow acquire "enormous power" (to quote our editorialists) if they kidnap a few dozen citizens, as in Holland, or even a dozen oil ministers, as in Vienna. If a mass murder had happened in Vienna on that Sunday before Christmas, long obituaries of Sheik Yamani and his colleagues would have been published—and within twenty-four hours, ambitious and competent men in Tehran and Caracas, in Baghdad and in Kuwait, would have replaced them. Terrorists and newspapermen share the naive assumption that those whose names make the headlines have power, that getting one's name on the front page is a major political achievement. This assumption typifies the prevailing muddled thinking on the subject of terrorism.

In recent years urban terrorism has superseded guerrilla warfare in various parts of the world. As decolonization came to an end there was a general decline in guerrilla activity. Furthermore, rural guerrillas learned by bitter experience that the "encirclement of the city by the countryside" (the universal remedy advocated by the Chinese ten years ago) was of doubtful value if four-fifths (or more) of the population are city dwellers, as happens to be the case in most Western industrialized countries—and quite a few Latin-American countries too. With the transfer of operations from the countryside to the cities, the age of the "urban guerrilla" dawned. But the very term "urban guerrilla" is problematical. There have been revolutions, civil wars, insurrections, and coups d'etat in the cities, but hardly ever guerrilla warfare. That occurs in towns only if public order has completely collapsed, and if armed bands roam freely. Such a state of affairs is rare, and it never lasts longer than a few hours, at most a few days. Either the insurgents overthrow the government in a frontal assault, or they are defeated. The title "urban guerrilla" is in fact a public-relations term for terrorism; terrorists usually dislike being called terrorists, preferring the more romantic guerrilla image.

There are basic differences between the rural guerrilla and the urban terrorist: mobility and hiding are the essence of guerrilla warfare, and this is impossible in towns. It is not true that the slums (and the rich quarters) of the big cities provide equally good sanctuaries. Rural guerrillas operate in large units and gradually transform themselves into battalions, regiments, and even divisions. They carry out political and social reforms in "liberated zones," openly propagandize, and build up their organizational network. In towns, where this cannot be done, urban terrorists operate in units of three, four, or five; the whole "movement" consists of a few hundred, often only a few dozen, members. This is the source of their operational strength and their political weakness. For while it is difficult to detect small groups, and while they can cause a great deal of damage, politically they are impotent. A year or two ago anxious newspaper readers in the Western world were led to believe that the German Baader-Meinhof group, the Japanese Red Army, the Symbionese Liberation Army, and the British Angry Brigade were mass movements that ought to be taken very seriously indeed. Their "communiqués" were published in the mass media; there were earnest sociological and psychological studies on the background of their members; their "ideology" was analyzed in tedious detail. Yet these were groups of between five and fifty members. Their only victories were in the area of publicity.

TERRORIST MYTHS

The current terrorist epidemic has mystified a great many people, and various explanations have been offered—most of them quite wrong. Only a few will be mentioned here:

Political terror is a new and unprecedented phenomenon. It is as old as the hills, only the manifestations of terror have changed. The present epidemic is mild compared with previous outbreaks. There were more assassinations of leading statesmen in the 1890s in both America and Europe, when terrorism had more supporters, than at the present time. Nor is terrorist doctrine a novelty. In 1884 Johannes Most, a German Social Democrat turned anarchist, published in New York a manual, *Revolutionary (Urban) Warfare,* with the subtitle "A Handbook of Instruction Regarding the Use and Manufacture of Nytroglycerine, Dynamite, Guncotton, Fulminating Mercury, Bombs, Arson, Poisons, etc." Most pioneered the idea of the letter bomb and argued that the liquidation of "pigs" was not murder because murder was the willful killing of a human being, whereas policemen did not belong in this category.

It is sometimes argued that guerrilla and terrorist movements in past ages were sporadic and essentially apolitical. But this is not so; the Russian anarchists of the last century were as well organized as any contemporary movement, and their ideological and political sophistication was, if anything, higher. The same goes for the guerrilla wars of the nineteenth century. The guerrilla literature published in Europe in the 1830s and 1840s is truly modern in almost every respect. It refers to "bases," "liberated areas," "protracted war" as well as the gradual transformation of guerrilla units into a regular army. The basic ideas of Mao and Castro all appeared at least a hundred years ago.

Terrorism is left-wing and revolutionary in character. Terrorists do not believe in liberty or egality or fraternity. Historically, they are elitists, contemptuous of the masses, believing in the historical mission of a tiny minority. It was said about the Tupamaros that one had to be a Ph.D. to be a member. This was an exaggeration but not by very much. Their manifestos may be phrased in left-wing language, but previous generations of terrorists proclaimed Fascist ideas. Nineteenth-century European partisans and guerrillas fighting Napoleon were certainly right-wing. The Spanish guerrilleros wanted to reintroduce the Inquisition, the Italian burned the houses of all citizens suspected of left-wing ideas. Closer to our own period, the IRA and the Macedonian IMRO at various times in their history had connections with Fascism and Communism. The ideology of terrorist movements such as the Stern gang and the Popular Front for the Liberation of Palestine encompasses elements of the extreme Left and Right. Slogans change with intellectual fashions and should not be taken too seriously. The real inspiration underlying terrorism is a free-floating activism that can with equal ease turn right or left. It is the action that counts.

Terrorism appears whenever people have genuine, legitimate grievances. Remove the grievance and terror will cease. The prescription seems plausible enough, but experience does not bear it out. On the level of abstract reasoning it is, of course, true that there would be no violence if no one had a grievance or felt frustration. But in practice there will always be disaffected, alienated, and highly aggressive people claiming that the present state of affairs is intolerable and that only violence will bring a change. Some of their causes may even be real and legitimate— but unfulfillable. This applies to the separatist demands of minorities, which, if acceded to, would result in the emergence of nonviable states and the crippling of society. It is always the fashion to blame the state or the "system" for every existing injustice. But some of the problems may simply be insoluble, at least in the short run. No state or social system can be better than the individuals constituting it.

It is ultimately the perception of grievance that matters, not the grievance itself. At one time a major grievance may be fatalistically accepted, whereas at another time (or elsewhere) a minor grievance may produce the most violent reaction. A comparison of terrorist activities over the last century shows, beyond any shadow of doubt, that violent protest movements do not appear where despotism is worst but, on the contrary, in permissive democratic societies or ineffective authoritarian regimes. There were no terrorist movements in Nazi Germany, nor in Fascist Italy, nor in any of the Communist countries. The Kurdish insurgents were defeated by the Iraqi government in early 1975 with the greatest of ease, whereas terrorism in Ulster continues for many years now and the end is not in sight. The Iraqis succeeded not because they satisfied the grievances of the Kurds but simply because they could not care less about public opinion abroad.

Terror is highly effective. Terror is noisy, it catches the headlines. Its melodrama inspires horror and fascination. But seen in historical perspective, it has hardly ever had a lasting effect, Guerrilla wars have been successful only against colonial rule, and the age of colonialism in over. Terrorism did have a limited effect at a time of general war, but only in one instance (Cuba) has a guerrilla movement prevailed in peacetime. But the constellation in Cuba was unique and, contrary to Castro's expectations, there were no repeat performances elsewhere in Latin America. The Vietnam war in its decisive phase was no longer guerrilla in character. There is no known case in modern history of a terrorist movement seizing political power, although terror has been used on the tactical level by radical political parties. Society will tolerate terrorism as long as it is no more than a nuisance. Once insecurity spreads and terror becomes a real danger, the authorities are no longer blamed for disregarding human rights in their struggle against it. On the contrary, the cry goes up for more repressive measures, irrespective of the price that has to be paid in human rights. The state is always so much stronger than the terrorists, whose only hope for success is to prevent the authorities from using their full powers. If the terrorist is the fish—following Mao Tse-tung's parable—the permissiveness and the inefficiency of liberal society is the water. As Regis Debray, apostle of the Latin-American guerrillas, wrote about the Tupamaros: "By digging the grave of liberal Uruguay, they dug their own grave."

The importance of terrorism will grow enormously in the years to come as the destructive power of its weapons increases. This danger does indeed exist, with the increasing availability of missiles, nuclear material, and highly effective poisons But it is part of a wider problem, that of individuals blackmailing society. To engage in nuclear ransom, a "terrorist movement" is not needed; a small group of madmen or criminals, or just one person, could be equally effective—perhaps even more so. The smaller the group, the more difficult it would be to identify and combat.

Political terrorists are more intelligent and less cruel than "ordinary" criminals. Most political terrorists in modern times have been of middle- or upper-class origin, and many of them have had a higher education. Nevertheless, they have rarely shown intelligence, let alone political sophistication. Larger issues and future perspectives are of little interest to them, and they are quite easily manipulated by foreign intelligence services. As for cruelty, the "ordinary" criminal, unlike the terrorist, does not believe in indiscriminate killing. He may torture a victim, but this will be the exception, not the rule, for he is motivated by material gain and not by fanaticism. The motivation of the political terrorist is altogether different. Since, in his eyes, everyone but himself is guilty, restraints do not exist.

Political terror therefore tends to be less humane than the variety practiced by "ordinary" criminals. The Palestinian terrorists have specialized in killing children, while the Provisional IRA has concentrated its attacks against Protestant workers, and this despite their professions of "proletarian internationalism." It is the terrorists' aim not just to kill their opponents but to spread confusion and fear. It is part of the terrorist indoctrination to kill the humanity of the terrorist—all this, of course, for a more humane and just world order.

Terrorists are poor, hungry, and desperate human beings. Terrorist groups without powerful protectors are indeed poor. But modern transnational terrorism is, more often than not, big business. According to a spokesman of the Palestine "Rejection Front" in an interview with the Madrid newspaper *Platforma,* the income of the PLO is as great as that of certain Arab countries, such as Jordan, with payments by the oil countries on the order of $150 million to $200 million. Officials of the organizations are paid $5,000 a month and more, and everyone gets a car as a matter of course; they have acquired chalets and bank accounts in Switzerland. But the "Rejection Front," financed by Iraq, Libya, and Algeria is not kept on a starvation diet either. The Argentine ERP and the Montoneros have amassed many millions of dollars through bank robberies and extortion. Various Middle Eastern and East European governments give millions to terrorist movements from Ulster to the Philippines. This abundance of funds makes it possible to engage in all kinds of costly operations, to bribe officials, and to purchase sophisticated weapons. At the same time, the surfeit of money breeds corruption. The terrorists are no longer lean and hungry after prolonged exposure to life in Hilton hotels. They are still capable of carrying out gangster-style operations of short duration, but they become useless for long campaigns involving hardship and privation.

All this is not to say that political terror is always reprehensible or could never be effective. The assassination of Hitler or Stalin in the 1920s or 1930s would not only have changed the course of history, it would have saved the lives of millions of people. Terrorism is morally justified whenever there is no other remedy for an intolerable situation. Yet it seldom occurs, and virtually never succeeds, where tyranny is harshest.

THE TERRORIST'S FRIENDS

Events in recent years offer certain obvious lessons to terrorists. These lessons run against the terrorist grain, and have not yet been generally accepted. For example, terror is always far more popular against foreigners than against one's own countrymen. The only terrorists in our time who have had any success at all are those identifying themselves with a religious or national minority. It is sectarian-chauvinist support that counts, not drab, quasirevolutionary phraseology; Irish, Basques, Arabs, and the rest have found this out by trail and error. The media are a terrorist's best friend. The terrorist's act by itself is nothing. Publicity is all. Castro was the great master of the public-relations technique, from whom all terrorists should learn; with less than 300 men he created the impression of having a force of overwhelming strength at his disposal. But the media are a fickle friend, constantly in need of diversity and new angles. Terrorists will always have to be innovative; they are the super-entertainers of our time. Seen in this light the abduction of the OPEC ministers rates high marks.

The timing of the operation is also of paramount importance, for if it clashes with other important events, such as a major sports events or a natural disaster, the impact will be greatly reduced. Whenever terrorists blackmail governments, it is of great importance to press realistic demands. Democratic authorities will instinctively give in to blackmail—but only up to a point. The demand for money or the release of a few terrorist prisoners is a realistic demand, but there are limits beyond which no government can go, as various terrorist groups have found out to their detriment.

Psychiatrists, social workers, and clergymen are the terrorist's next-best friends. They are eager to advise, to assuage, and to mediate, and their offer to help should always be accepted by the terrorist. These men and women of goodwill think they know more than others about the mysteries of the human soul and that they have the compassion required for understanding the feelings of "desperate men." But a detailed study of the human psyche is hardly needed to understand the terrorist phenomenon; its basic techniques have been known to every self-respecting gangster throughout history. It is the former terrorist, the renegade, who has traditionally been the terrorist's most dangerous opponent. Once again, the terrorist should never forget that he exists only because the authorities are prevented by public opinion at home and abroad from exercising their full power against him. If a terrorist wishes to survive, he should not create the impression that he could be a real menace, unless, of course, he has sanctuaries in a foreign country and strong support from a neighboring power. In this case political terrorism turns into surrogate warfare and changes its character, and then there is always the danger that it may lead to real, full-scale war.

Recent terrorist experience offers some lessons to governments too. If governments did not give in to terrorist demands, there would be no terror, or it would be very much reduced in scale. The attitude of Chancellor Bruno Kreisky and his Minister of the Interior, who virtually shook the terrorists' hands, is not only aesthetically displeasing, it is also counterproductive. It may save a few human lives in the short run, but it is an invitation to further such acts and greater bloodshed. However, it would be unrealistic to expect determined action from democratic governments in present conditions. In wartime these governments will sacrifice whole armies without a moment's hesitation. In peace they will argue that one should not be generous with other people's lives. Western politicians and editorialists still proclaim that terrorism is condemned "by the whole civilized world," forgetting that the "civilized world" covers no more than about one-fifth of the population of the globe. Many countries train, equip, and finance terrorists, and a few sympathetic governments will always provide sanctuary. Western security services may occasionally arrest and sentence foreign terrorists, but only with the greatest reluctance, for they know that sooner or later one of their aircraft will be hijacked or one of their politicians abducted. Ilyich Ramirez Sánchez ("Carlos"), the Venezuelan terrorist, is wanted in Britain for attempted murder, yet Scotland Yard decided last December not to press for his extradition from Algiers. For, in the words of the London *Daily Telegraph*, "the trial of an international terrorist could lead to political repercussions and acts of terrorist reprisals." A good case could be made for not arresting foreign terrorists in the first place but simply deporting then. The European governments on a West German initiative have had some urgent deliberations in recent weeks as to how to collaborate in combating terror. But, according to past experience, it is doubtful whether international cooperation will be of much help unless it is worldwide.

These observations do not, of course, refer to the South Moluccans, the Kurds, and other such groups in the world of terrorism. They fight only for national independence; they are on their own because they fulfill no useful political function as far as the Russians and the Cubans are concerned. The Libyans and Algerians will not support them because they belong to the wrong religion or ethnic group, and even South Yemen will not give them shelter. They are the proletariat of the terrorist world.

Terrorism is, of course, a danger, but magnifying its importance is even more dangerous. Modern society may be vulnerable to attack, but it is also exceedingly resilient. A plane is hijacked, but all others continue to fly. A bank is robbed, but the rest continue to function. All oil ministers are abducted, and yet not a single barrel of oil is lost.

Describing the military exploits of his Bedouin warriors, Lawrence of Arabia once noted that they were on the whole good soldiers, but for their unfortunate belief that a weapon was dangerous in proportion to the noise it created. Present-day attitudes towards terrorism in the Western world are strikingly similar. Terrorism creates tremendous noise. It wll continue to cause destruction and the loss of human life. It will always attract much publicity but, politically, it tends to be ineffective. Compared with other dangers threatening mankind, it is almost irrelevant.

CONCLUSION:
Terrorism Today and Tomorrow — Prognosis and Treatment

by BROOKS McCLURE

If, as Senator Moynihan declares in these pages, "terrorism is a disease," then the disease is cancer. There are hundreds of theories for treating it, but nobody knows the cure. Sometimes radical therapy alleviates the condition—for reasons not always fully understood. But the cost can be high; often as much healthy as malignant social tissue is destroyed by the treatment.

The widely varying analyses in this volume describe the current state of the art of dealing with terrorism, and they inevitably take different perspectives on the nature of the threat and how to combat it. Anthony Cooper, for example, talks of "the inevitable storm to come," and half a dozen writers stress the danger of high-technology terrorism and the possible use of mass-destruction weapons. But Walter Laqueur cites the traditional weakness of terrorists, the enormous magnification of their power through modern communications, and the success-through-default they have enjoyed because of weak official response to their extortions. The difference here is not irreconcilable, but it illustrates the range of views to be found among specialists in this complex field.

When it comes to the crux of the issue—how to deal with the demands of political hostage-takers—opinions differ sharply. Laqueur and John Wolf support a no-concessions policy, while Andrew Pierre suggests the policy is not credible and should be reconsidered. Edward Mickolus reviews both sides of the argument in detail and then concludes that "the answer may lie somewhere between a stated 'no ransom' position and a pragmatic view of on-the-scene bargaining."

Thus the doctors are at odds about the treatment, and this may have something to do with different conceptions of the disease itself. Like cancer in humans, this particular social virulence has a score or more of forms, and they may require as many distinct antidotes to be cured.

Meantime, however, one must cope with this mysterious malady with the inadequate tools at hand. Terrorist kidnap-extortions continue—in Italy they have achieved a new level of sophistication and impact—and the question is what can be done *now*. The answer is: Amputate. It is crude; it is tragic; but those who are making the hard decisions these days say it is necessary, to keep the disease of terrorism from spreading.

This response runs counter to some of the basic instincts and imperatives of a democratic society. As Robert Bell points out, "a democratic government must compromise when faced with the imminent murder of the victims." Or as I. M. H. Smart puts it: "The immediate value of the individual life outweighs the ulterior interest of the group." The decision to "amputate"—to risk sacrificing human lives so as to avoid making concessions—is indeed a departure from the accepted norm.

As this is written, former Italian Premier Aldo Moro has been held by the Red Brigades for a month and a half. One deadline for his "execution" has passed, and his letters indicate he is undergoing almost intolerable stress and may even be near a breakdown. The government so far refuses to yield to the kidnappers' demands for release of their comrades in Italian prisons.

This is one of the most dramatic tests of a nation's will in the history of modern terrorism. For Aldo Moro is no ordinary individual: he is the country's most prominent senior statesman, political architect of the present government, five times prime minister and putative next president of the Republic; an intimate friend of Pope Paul VI for 35 years, the mentor and sponsor of Prime Minister Giulio Andreotti, and president of the Christian Democratic Party, Italy's largest. Moro is the pre-eminent symbol of Italy's political system, hence the ideal hostage for the *Brigatisti* determined to destroy that system.

Why should this distinguished public figure not be saved by the simple expedient of meeting the terrorist demands? That might have been possible, even likely, five years earlier. But these are different times. What occurred meantime is not the development of a sterile crisis-management doctrine for dealing with terrorism, but a series of painful experiences which have dictated a pragmatic, hard line against political kidnappers.

Paradoxically Moro, because of his importance, had less chance of being "negotiated" to freedom than would have some hapless average Italian seized in a barricade-hostage situation.

The Italian government's decision rests on precedents in other countries which are difficult to ignore. In February 1975, the mayoral candidate of the Christian Democratic Union in Berlin, Peter Lorenz, was kidnapped just before the election by the Second of June Movement. Five members of the Baader-Meinhof gang were released and Lorenz was recovered. Two months later, the terrorists struck again, seizing the German Embassy in Stockholm. The demand this time was for release of 26 prisoners—including all the Baader-Meinhof leaders in custody—and the German government refused. Two members of the embassy staff were killed during the action which brought that incident to an end.

The German government had hardened its position rather than face what promised to be a continuous escalation of extortionate demands. This posture then was put to test with the kidnapping, in October 1977, of Hanns Martin Schleyer, chairman of the German industrialists' association, in Cologne. His kidnappers, members of the Red Army Faction, made political ransom demands worthy of their captive and supported them with psychological-warfare techniques—among them issuance of a photo of the hostage and letters written in his hand—which were later to be used by Moro's captors. The government refused to make concessions, and Schleyer was murdered.

This pattern of resistance to terrorist demands has lately been followed in The Netherlands, where in the past the government had released prisoners and paid ransom to free hostages. It has held firmly to the hard line through three South Moluccan terrorist incidents since 1975, on one occasion resisting steadfastly although more than a hundred children were being held hostage.

This body of international precedent has been reinforced by two other noteworthy cases. In 1975—in what has proved to be a landmark example of "no concessions"—the London police laid siege to an apartment house in Balcombe Street where two IRA gunmen held an elderly couple hostage, and they made the terrorists surrender without conditions. Only weeks earlier, the Irish Republic police had forced a well-known IRA activist, Eddie Gallagher, and an accomplice to give up after they had held a Dutch factory manager prisoner for five weeks.

These incidents were particularly significant because there was a "soft" alternative to holding out for unconditional surrender. It would have been possible in either case for the authorities to grant safe passage to the terrorists—a concession which would have been considered irresistible a year or two earlier—and win release of the victims. Instead the hostages were kept waiting, in conditions of stress and danger, so their captors could be denied any claim of victory.

There has been a parallel development of effective defense in aircraft hijackings, although it may be too early to call it a trend. The Entebbe rescue of 1976, a brilliant operation born of desperation, was considered by many to be a one-time spectacular not likely to be imitated. But then came the 1977 successful assault by a German special counterterror force (GSG-9) against a parked Lufthansa aircraft in Mogadishu, Somalia—another "first" in counterterrorist tactics. This feat showed new possibilities and added one more success for the defense. It was followed by the disastrous attack by Egyptian commandos on a Palestinian-held plane in Larnaca, Cyprus in 1978, but that did nothing to discredit the principle of aircraft assault. No hostages were lost and the Palestine terrorists promptly surrendered; the rest was essentially an ambush of the Egyptians by Cypriot and perhaps Palestinian forces.

One minus on the air-terrorism scene was the successful extortion-hijacking by the Japanese Red Army (JRA) of a Japan Air Lines plane which landed in Bangladesh just as a coup was being hatched. This incident, almost coinciding with the Mogadishu operation, can be excused partly on technical grounds (Bangladesh wanted no rescue attempts and the plane flew off to Algeria) although Japan was not ready then for any counterterrorist operations abroad.

What has emerged over the past several years, then, is a pattern of hard-line resistance by democratic countries to terrorist demands. Each new case fortifies the position, making it easier—and at the same time perhaps more necessary—for elected authorities everywhere to resist terrorist extortion. The Moro case fits into this mosaic and will either strengthen or diminish the no-concessions doctrine, depending on its outcome.

This is not to dismiss Pierre's hypothetical case of the jumbo jet with 350 hostages about to be blown up—or any other such quite conceivable scenario. What would we do? That perhaps depends, as the military say, on the circumstances and terrain, and also on the actors. But there remains the example of the hundred Dutch school children—the most pathetic hostages of all. Who would have thought the Dutch government could resist that extortion, and capture the culprits in the bargain? Almost no one five years ago.

Part of the answer in certain situations may lie in the immaterial, or non-material, concession—one which can help end the incident without advancing the terrorist cause. In the triple-faceted Hanafi Muslim incident in Washington in 1977, for example, the authorities made three concessions: paying the leader (a religious extremist rather than political terrorist) $750 to reimburse him for earlier legal expenses; stopping (for a day) the showing in New York of a film he considered sacreligious; and, permitting him to return to his home after arraignment (where he was watched closely until properly jailed). These were controversial concessions which some critics considered a serious compromise of principle. But the Hanafi group was then tried, convicted, and imprisoned with dispatch. Was there any *material* loss in the arrangement by which more than a hundred hostages were rescued? This point might be disputed, but the principle seems to fit Miklous's "pragmatic view of on-the-scene bargaining."

When considering big-league political terrorism, however, it is dangerous to ask easy questions and fantasize neat answers. Half a dozen JRA fanatics holding 350 persons on a 747 jet are not going to be bought off with non-material concessions. Furthermore, they will ask for a ransom commensurate with what they consider to be the value to us of those 350 lives. This is a worst-case scenario, but it has been played out before, successfully for the terrorists in most cases, and may well be re-run one fine day.

This is the problem which the Germans faced in Mogadishu, when the lives of more than 90 passengers and crew on the *Landshut* had to be put at risk. bit is also the problem confronting the Italian government as it refused to meet the Red Brigades' demands; Moro's life hung in the balance. What these incidents show is that there is a limit—that a human life cannot be spared "at all costs," for that can lead to a miserable existence in perpetual fear for everyone. Kidnapping must not become the unanswerable weapon by which a society's whole quality of life and very freedom is jeopardized. Somewhere short of its destruction—which is the goal of the terrorists—society has to draw the line. Some countries have done just that.

Those countries in the vanguard of the fight against terrorism have, through test and daring, redefined the realm of the possible. No longer is an assault on a hijacked jet assumed to mean death for everyone aboard, although the danger remains substantial. Nor need the prolonged imprisonment of a hostage mean that he must succumb. More options are now open; there is no necessity to be stampeded into an immediate settlement on the terrorists' terms.

As Cooper notes, "the terrorists can no longer count upon the other side abiding by the 'rules.' " It is a tighter, tougher game, with the defense gaining and the terrorists' opportunities being narrowed. It is hard on the nerves, but the public as well as the policy makers have adjusted to a new reality—one more favorable to the forces of social order.

So much for treating the symptoms of the cancer called terrorism. The procedure, for the most part, has been surgery—a hurried attempt to remove malignant tissue when it is recognized. But the underlying disease remains a puzzle. Until we know more about the root causes, the basic pathology of terrorism, we will be severely hampered in dealing with it.

In keeping with the purpose of this text, the bibliography has been annotated to alert readers to the general contents of selected books which would serve well for further research. Selections have been deliberately arranged in this order to enable the reader to expand his understanding of terrorism by building upon basic concepts in a logical fashion.

ANNOTATED BIBLIOGRAPHY

Robert Moss. *The War for the Cities.* New York: Coward, McCann and Geohegan, Inc., 1972. 288 pp. $6.95.

Moss' account is by far the best of the early attempts to warn the public of the potential of urban guerrilla warfare. He reports on the origins of this political-military technique by reviewing case studies of all major urban guerrilla movements of the early seventies in order to assess the seriousness of this contemporary threat to organized societies.

A.S. Cohan. *Theories of Revolution: An Introduction.* New York: John Wiley and Sons. 1976. 228 pp. $9.95.

Cohan, after explaining what theories and models are supposed to accomplish, discusses Marxist theories of revolution and compares these with two contrasting schools of thought: *functionalism* (primarily as developed by Chalmers Johnson) and *mass society theory* (viewed from the work of Arendt and Kornhauser). His analysis concludes with psychological explanations of revolution which center around Gurr's theory of relative deprivation.

Barbara Salert. *Revolutions and Revolutionaries.* New York: Elsevier, 1976. 161 pp. $12.95.

> Salert concentrates on four theories: Olson's rational choice theory, Johnson's structural-functionalism, Gurr's psychological research on political violence, and Marxism. Unlike Cohan, Salert employs a quantitatively based argument to present an analytical view of these theories.

Paul Wilkinson. *Political Terrorism.* New York: John Wiley and Sons, 1974. 160 pp. $11.95.

> Wilkinson considers three major areas of study in his analysis of political terrorism: motivations and objectives of terrorists stemming from the variety of societal conditions that cause and sustain terrorism; the political and socioeconomic measures which might preclude the development of the terrorist personality; and short-term countermeasures which could be taken by nations already under attack. Wilkinson counsels a hard-line approach and approves the integrated European response that is slowly making headway.

Gerald McKnight. *The Terrorist Mind: Why They Hijack, Kidnap, Bomb and Kill.* London: Michael Joseph, Ltd, 1975. 182 pp. $6.95.

> McKnight aims to fill a gap that has long been a source of concern. Extensive interviews are included which represent a wide range of global revolutionary leadership giving readers a thorough view of the terrorist mind. McKnight's commentary on the terrorist rationale for violent activities as related to the deaths of innocent victims provides a particularly interesting focal point.

Walter Laqueur, *Guerrilla: A Historical and Critical Study.* Boston: Little, Brown and Company, 1976. 462 pp. $17.50.
       Terrorism. Boston: Little Brown and Company, 1977. 277 pp. $15.00.

> These two books express Laqueur's critical interpretation of both guerrilla and terrorist theory and practice throughout history. His general conclusion that terrorism is politically ineffective challenges the alert reader's interest and the preconceptions of many analysts.

Albert Parry. *Terrorism: From Robespierre to Arafat.* New York: Vanguard Press, Inc., 1976, 624 pp. $17.50.

> This encyclopedic study of terrorism describes patterns of change during modern times. Parry analyzes the nature of terrorism using ex-

tensive case studies to support his contention that terrorists do not
moderate their vicious tactics after assuming power.

Richard Clutterback. *Living With Terrorism*. New York: Arlington House
Publishers. 1976. 160 pp. $7.95.

Clutterback believes we can live with terrorism only if we make substantial efforts to understand and protect ourselves against the terrorist threat. He uses short case studies of the IRA, SLA, PLO, and
other contemporary terrorist organizations to illustrate terrorist tactics, techniques, and weapons in addition to examining their motivation and goals.

Francis M. Watson. *Political Terrorism: The Threat and the Response.* Washington, D.C.: Robert B. Luce, Inc., 1976. 238 pp. $10.00.

In the *threat* section, Watson defines terrorism and emphasizes the
persuasive characteristics of its propaganda dimension to set the
boundaries of conflict for contemporary terrorism. Using case studies
characterized by the Tupamaros and the Palestinians, he explains how
terrorism works, who does it, who supports it, and why. In the *response*
section he considers where terrorism is headed and how society can
best respond to the threat it presents.

Yonah Alexander (ed). *International Terrorism: National, Regional, and
Global Perspectives.* New York: Praeger Publishers, 1976. 390 pp. $23.50.

The editor has organized the book to deal with terrorism from national, regional, and local perspectives. That task is accomplished by
establishing an information base using historical precedents. Country-
based explanations then describe contemporary terrorist activities by
addressing three questions: what acts constitute terrorism, what are
terrorism's underlying causes, and how should society deal with terrorism.

Ernst Halperin. *Terrorism in Latin America.* Beverly Hills, California: Sage
Publications, 1976. 92 pp. $3.00.

Analysis of the causes leading to terrorism forms the salient features
of this book. Searching for these among the roots of the population,
Halperin emphasizes the role of student activists in Latin American
universities. His conclusions regarding students' key role in generating pressure for political and social change are reinforced by terrorism's origins in Uruguay, Brazil, and Argentina.

J. Bowyer Bell. *Transnational Terror*. Washington, D.C.: American Enterprise Institute, 1975. 89 pp. $3.00.

Bell examines the intentions of several well known terrorist organizations to argue his point that their use of terror has been part of a planned, comprehensive strategy. Unlike many other analysts, he does not believe that an inflexible, harsh response provides a suitable counter to the terrorist threat. His analysis of the threat facing the United States and critique of actions taken thus far are given greater import when one reviews his thoughtful suggestions on developing a United States counter strategy with international possibilities.

Brian Jenkins. *International Terrorism: A New Mode of Conflict*. Los Angeles, California: Crescent Publications, 1975, 51 pp. $2.25.

Jenkins broadens the analytic scope of terrorism by considering new targets and new capabilities which it may have in the future. Growing links between terrorist groups and the increasing vulnerability of industrialized society to more terrifying weapons are given new emphasis by analyzing the possibilities of nuclear theft and the possible introduction of mass hostage situations.

Anthony Burton. *Urban Terrorism: Theory, Practice and Response*. New York: The Free Press, 1976. 259 pp. $12.95.

Burton conducts a detailed examination of several well known contemporary terrorist organizations to explain their motivations. Helpful information is provided on terrorist theoreticians such as Marighella, Debray, and Guevara to demonstrate how contemporary terrorists have utilized and adapted their teachings. Most troubling is his critique on the available response of threatened governments to cope with this problem.

Yeshayahu Ben-Porat, Eitan Haber and Zeev Schiff. *Entebbe Rescue*. New York: Delacorte Press, 1977. 346 pp. $10.00.

Entebbe's basic story is well known as a result of extensive news media coverage and several Hollywood film productions. But this account is particularly important because it may be considered to be an "official" report. Details of the skyjacking, the hostage negotiations, and the raid are exhaustively explained to fill gaps in the reader's knowledge and to correct errors that may have been created by other accounts.

Christopher Dobson and Ronald Payne. *The Carlos Complex: A Study in* 303
Terror. New York: G. P. Putnam's Sons, 1977. 254 pp. $8.95.

A major contribution is provided by these two journalists' assessment of Carlos role in the complicated network of international terrorism. Others have alluded to the basic linkages which these authors describe between Carlos and other terrorists. Not so well known, however, is the growing evidence of involvement on the part of the Soviet KGB that is highlighted in this text.

ABOUT THE AUTHORS

DAVID ANABLE *is a Staff Correspondent of the* Christian Science Monitor based in New York City.

MAJOR MARSHALL D. BEALL *is the Executive Officer of the Directorate of Combat Developments, United States Army Military Police School, Fort McClellan, Alabama.*

ROBERT G. BELL *is an Analyst in National Defense for the Congressional Research Service of the Library of Congress in Washington, D.C.*

H. H. A. COOPER *is Director of European and Middle Eastern Studies, Aberrant Behavior Center in Dallas, Texas.*

MAJOR JOHN D. ELLIOTT *is a Political-Military Officer at the United States Army Concepts Analysis Agency in Bethesda, Maryland.*

DAVID FROMKIN *is a practicing attorney-at-law in New York City.*

LESLIE KNIGHT GIBSON *is Project Manager of the Clandestine Tactics and Technology data service of the International Association of Chiefs of Police.*

BRIAN MICHAEL JENKINS *is Associate Head of the Social Science Department and the Director of Research on Guerrilla Warfare and International Terrorism for the Rand Corporation in Santa Monica, California.*

WALTER LAQUEUR *is Chairman of the Research Council of the Center for Strategic and International Studies in Washington, D.C.*

JAY MALLIN *is Director of the Institute for Study of Change in Miami, Florida.*

BROOKS McCLURE *is Program Coordinator of the United States Department of Commerce Working Group on Terrorism providing threat assessment for United States businesses operating abroad.*

EDWARD F. MICKOLUS *is an Intelligence Analyst for the United States Central Intelligence Agency in Washington, D.C.*

DAVID L. MILBANK *is an Intelligence Analyst for the United States Central Intelligence Agency in Washington, D.C.*

BOWMAN H. MILLER *is a Counterintelligence and Terrorism Research Analyst, Acquisitions and Analysis Division, Directorate of Counterintelligence, Headquarters Air Force Office of Special Investigations in Washington, D.C.*

DANIEL P. MOYNIHAN *is a United States Senator representing the State of New York.*

LLOYD NORMAN *is a Pentagon Correspondent for* Newsweek *magazine based in Washington, D.C.*

ANDREW J. PIERRE *is a Senior Research Fellow, Council on Foreign Relations in New York City.*

DAVID M. ROSENBAUM *is a Consultant to the Comptroller General of the United States General Accounting Office in Washington, D.C.*

CHARLES A. RUSSELL *is the Chief, Acquisitions and Analysis Division, Directorate of Counterintelligence, Headquarters Air Force Office of Special Investigations in Washington, D.C.*

DENNIS W. STILES *is an Analyst assigned to the Concepts and Objectives Division, Headquarters, United States Air Force in Washington, D.C.*

JOHN B. WOLF *is Chairman, Department of Criminal Justice, Union College in Cranford, New Jersey.*

This book was designed by E. S. Qualls. Production assistance was furnished by Gerry Hylla. The text type is Baskerville, a classic eighteenth-century type chosen for its grace and legibility; display type is set in Korinna. The book was set in type by Compositors, Inc., Lanham, Maryland. It was printed by Publication Press, Baltimore, Maryland, on basis 55 antique finish paper. It was bound in Holliston Mills' Sail Cloth, by GAFCO, Baltimore, Maryland.